JANET HEIMLICH

BREAKING THEIR WILL

SHEDDING LIGHT ON
RELIGIOUS CHILD
MALTREATMENT

Prometheus Books

59 John Glenn Drive
Amherst, New York 14228–2119

Published 2011 by Prometheus Books

Cover image © 2011, Media Bakery, Inc.
Cover design by Grace M. Conti-Zilsberger

Inquiries should be addressed to
Prometheus Books
59 John Glenn Drive
Amherst, New York 14228–2119
VOICE: 716–691–0133
FAX: 716–691–0137
WWW.PROMETHEUSBOOKS.COM

15   5 4 3 2

Library of Congress Cataloging-in-Publication Data

Heimlich, Janet, 1962–
    Breaking their will : shedding light on religious child maltreatment / by Janet Heimlich.
        p. cm.
    Includes bibliographical references.
    ISBN 978–1–61614–405–0 (pbk : alk. paper)
    ISBN 978–1–61614–406–7 (e-book)
    1. United States—Religious life and customs. 2. Child abuse—Religious aspects. 3. Child abuse—United States. I. Title.

BL2525.H445 2011
201'.762760973—dc22

                                                                                    2011004989

Printed in the United States of America on acid-free paper

to children who have been denied the right to question

CONTENTS

PART 2: HARM WITHOUT HITTING—RELIGIOUS CHILD EMOTIONAL ABUSE

PART 3: VIOLATING A SACRED TRUST—RELIGIOUS CHILD SEXUAL ABUSE

PART 4: SIN OF DENIAL—RELIGIOUS CHILD MEDICAL NEGLECT

12 CONTENTS

ACKNOWLEDGMENTS

Bringing this book to fruition required the help of many extraordinary people. I first want to express my thanks to experts in various fields, all of whom have made a significant impact in helping to improve the lives of children. These individuals were kind enough to speak with me about the child maltreatment problems that exist in America's faith communities, and some shared with me their own painful childhood experiences. They include Salma Abugideiri, Wisconsin State Rep. Terese Berceau, William H. Bowen, Barbara Dorris, Rev. Dr. Marie M. Fortune, Philip Greven, Marci A. Hamilton, David Jensen, Flora Jessop, Tim Kosnoff, Dr. Asher Lipner, Patricia Merkley, Bonnie J. Miller-McLemore, Dr. Anne Owens, Phil E. Quinn, Kathryn Goering Reid, Rev. Dr. Sarah M. Rieth, Daniel Shea, Rabbi Ze'ev Smason, Rita Swan, Keith Wright, and David Yoder.

My deeply heartfelt appreciation goes out to the dozens of individuals who agreed to be interviewed for the purpose of talking about their own histories of abuse and neglect. While I will not list their names here to protect their identities, I cannot express how grateful I am for their honesty and trust. I also admire these individuals for finding the strength to face their hurtful pasts and build successful lives as strong and compassionate adults.

I thank Prometheus Books for publishing this work, a testament to the company's continued efforts to educate the public about problems that exist in religious settings. Everyone there has been courteous, supportive, and professional. I especially appreciate the work of copyeditor Jacqueline May Parkison, who gave my manuscript the polishing it so needed.

This was a research-heavy project, and it could not have been turned around in a timely way without the help of research assistants Heather Young, Meghan Hall, Gordon Wilkins, Allyson Whipple, and, above all, Chris Bennett, who stuck with the project until the end. I also extend a warm note of thanks to my local editor, Kathleen Magor.

Along the way, several close friends gave me unflagging moral support; some even took time to read parts of the book and provide helpful feedback. I also thank my parents, who never tired of encouraging me, listening to my complaints, and believing in the project. Finally, a special note of appreciation goes to my young daughter, who put up with me spending many hours on my laptop instead of doing fun activities with her such as playing chase, making lanyards, and going to Chuck E. Cheese's.

To all who have helped toward the completion of this text, I will always be grateful.

AUTHOR'S NOTES

W hen it comes to discussions about religion, people have all kinds of ways of defining the same terms and viewing the same concepts. Therefore, I feel it's important to explain my particular literary choices.

For starters, this book looks solely at what I call *religious child maltreatment* in the United States. (For the purposes of this book, a child is anyone under the age of eighteen.) The book addresses all three Abrahamic faiths: Christianity, Judaism, and Islam. That said, readers will likely notice that there are many more pages devoted to Christian-based problems than Jewish or Muslim. This is not to assert that Christianity is a more worrisome faith (all faiths have doctrines that can be used to hurt children) but is simply because most of this country's worshippers are Christian. I should also add that problems can occur in any belief system, including Eastern and New Age religions.

Why the United States? Certainly, serious problems are occurring all over the globe. However, I felt it best to limit the focus to this country for a number of reasons. In part, I simply had to keep content to a manageable size, but, more important, I feel more attention needs to be paid to religious child maltreatment in America. While Americans seem able to recognize problems when they happen in other countries—especially those involving religions with which they are not very familiar—many in this country seem blinded to what goes on here.

Many biblical passages appear throughout this book, and almost all come from the New King James Version. I realize that many see newer translations as more authentic; however, my purpose is not to reveal religious "truths" but to explain how and why certain believers religiously justify abuse and neglect, and these perpetrators often adhere to the King James text. (I chose the newer version to save readers the headache of plowing through archaic language.)

I use the terms *religion, faith,* and *spirituality* interchangeably, although I usually avoid the use of the word *cult*. It has such negative connotations that I fear readers will discount information presented about these small, newly formed (and often unconventional) religious groups. In fact, I believe many Americans—even mainstream believers—can learn a great deal from problems that arise in cults. After all, the harmful aspects of some cults can manifest themselves in any faith, small or large. University of Illinois at Chicago psychology professor Bette L. Bottoms—one of only a few researchers to empirically examine the issue of religious child maltreatment—raises this point in one study. She notes that the public is quick to condemn cults that, for example, use excessive "Godly discipline" on children. Bottoms writes that these cases are "immediately highlighted in the news media, and criticized and rejected by society with much self-righteousness. Yet 'cult' beliefs and practices may differ only in degree from those of mainstream religious groups such as Methodists, Baptists, and Catholics."[1]

I interviewed many people for this book who shared with me their personal histories. Some subjects are identified by first name only or by a fictitious first name. While I encouraged everyone to be identified with both first and last names, I ultimately allowed interviewees to decide how they would be identified. Many who wanted anonymity explained that, while they had left their childhood faiths, they continued to have relationships with people still in those faiths. These individuals felt revealing their identities would jeopardize those relationships.

Many people have asked about my upbringing, often assuming I had a terrible religious experience as a child. As I describe in the first chapter, I was raised with next to no religion. Both my parents are Jewish; however, religion was almost entirely absent from the household in which I grew up. As I describe in more detail later, I became interested in the subject of religious child maltreatment much the same way I have become interested in other subjects I have covered as a journalist. I learned that child abuse and neglect motivated by religious belief is a serious problem and one that needed more indepth scrutiny.

Another disclosure: My book discusses problems of medical neglect in the Christian Science Church. Without fully realizing it, I used to indirectly work for the church. In the late 1990s, I was hired as a freelance reporter by Monitor Radio, a radio network that was owned by the church before being closed down in 1997. At the time, I knew next to nothing about the religion and generally enjoyed working on the handful of stories I reported for the network.

Finally, I want to include a few notes about the many tragic stories that are discussed in *Breaking Their Will*. First, I realize that a person's accusation against another does not in and of itself constitute guilt. However, I only included cases in which I wholeheartedly believed the allegations rang true. For example, in criminal cases, just about all the perpetrators I discuss were convicted by a judge or jury at trial, and many received long sentences. Also, I scrutinized interviewees who alleged that someone had harmed them.

Uncovering raw brutality, as many of these cases do, comes with a cost. I realize it will prevent some people from picking up the book; many will probably find my associating religion with these incidents to be sacrilegious. However, I feel it is important to expose these horrific acts. Shedding light on religious child maltreatment, including its egregious manifestations, is essential to raising awareness of a subject that has gone little noticed for a very long time. I concur with Ephesians 5:8–11, which urges us to face even the ugliest of truths: "Walk as children of light (for the fruit of the Spirit is in all goodness, righteousness, and truth). . . . And have no fellowship with the unfruitful works of darkness, but rather expose them."

INTRODUCTION

The term *religious child maltreatment* did not exist before I began writing this book. At least, Google had never heard of it. I found its absence indicative of just how little has been said about religion's potential to harm children. Very few books look at this problem in a comprehensive way. I have learned, too, that the topic makes many people uncomfortable, even defensive.

It's not news that religion in the wrong hands can be dangerous. Religious wars continue to be waged around the globe. Yet many have a hard time believing that religious faith can also lead to child abuse and neglect. In fact, the worst perpetrators tend to be those who aim to be perfectly pious. Other factors might come into play, such as mental illness or a need to overpower the vulnerable. Still, most who commit the abuses addressed in this book appear to sincerely believe their actions are religiously righteous.

And yet, *Breaking Their Will* is not a diatribe against all faith or any particular religion. Rather, it stands to deliver a warning about certain religious cultures in America (specifically, those that are authoritarian). Thus, the book is not structured according to various religions or types of religious organizations. Rather, it is structured according to four commonly accepted forms of child maltreatment—physical abuse, emotional abuse, sexual abuse, and (medical) neglect—and explains how each is manifested in a religious context. In addition, there are two chapters that discuss two forms of religious child maltreatment I feel deserve special attention: child ritual abuse and male and female circumcision.

To begin, chapter 1 provides important background. Specifically, it defines *religious child maltreatment,* describes different ways that it manifests itself, and explains that this kind of abuse and neglect is a serious and pervasive problem. The chapter also describes how I became interested in covering this topic.

Chapter 2 looks at America's general unwillingness to see religion as something that can harm infants, children, and teenagers. This country is one of the most religious in the world, and so it is not surprising that many Americans tend to see faith as only a force for good. In addition, many faith communities are in denial about the fact that their own worshippers abuse and neglect children, despite much evidence that the pious are just as culpable of such crimes as nonbelievers.

Chapter 3 answers the question of what the difference is between healthy faith and dangerous faith, where children are concerned. Based on my research, I conclude that it comes down to whether children are living in a religious authoritarian environment, due to the way such cultures affect parents. In more tolerant climates, parents are allowed the necessary autonomy to make their own decisions about child rearing, whereas in religious authoritarian cultures, mothers and fathers tend to follow prescribed norms that are often not designed to meet children's individual needs.

Chapter 4 scrutinizes the most popular religious text of all time: the Bible. While the book has some wonderful things to say about children, it could say a lot more about them. What's more, the Bible contains many passages that depict children as victims of violence—violence that is sometimes ordered, or perpetrated, by God. We should question how such passages might affect worshippers' views of children, particularly worshippers who interpret the Bible to be literally true.

The next four chapters (chapters 5 through 8) make up part 1, which covers religious child physical abuse. Because most physical abuse entails corporal punishment gone awry, this section looks at various scriptural passages and religious teachings and ideologies that encourage the use of corporal punishment and have even been used to justify physical abuse. The section covers such religious concepts as an obsession with child obedience and a view of children as inherently sinful. In addition, part 1 looks at the potential harm caused by religious conservatives who heavily promote the physical punishment of children.

Part 2's four chapters (chapters 9 through 12) look at the significant ways that religion psychologically and emotionally harms children. While religious belief has usually been shown to have a salutary effect on the mind, there are many ways in which a faith-filled upbringing can be detrimental. This section examines how four types of emotional maltreatment—spurning, terrorizing, isolating, and exploiting—manifest themselves in a religious context.

The four chapters of part 3 (chapters 13 through 16) look at religious child sexual abuse, which occurs when perpetrators are religious authorities. Remarkably, some religious groups have sanctified sexual relations between adults and minors. But, even as most faith organizations openly condemn child sexual abuse, there have been problems. Namely, the power bestowed upon religious leaders allows child sexual abuse to occur and sometimes to continue for years. In addition, faith communities, including congregants and high-ranking religious officials, often fail to meet victims' needs when sexual abuse is alleged or discovered.

Part 4's three chapters (chapters 17 through 20) examine a particular form of religiously motivated child neglect: the withholding of needed medical care. Many sick children are denied this care due to their caretakers' unwavering beliefs that faith healing is superior to the care that is provided by doctors and hospitals. As a result, untold numbers of children have suffered with, and died from, illnesses that would be treatable with standard medical care.

Chapter 20 looks at a highly misunderstood phenomenon, child ritual abuse. Part of the problem dates back to a time during the 1980s and early 1990s known as the satanic panic, when many Americans believed children were being horrifically abused by devil worshippers. Eventually, many realized that their fears were for naught, as most of those abuses never took place. However, this realization created a problem: Today, many Americans believe child ritual abuse never happens, and that is not the case. Many children are ritually abused through exorcisms as adults attempt to "cast out" evil forces from their bodies.

Chapter 21 discusses male and female circumcision (genital cutting), which is motivated by both cultural and religious beliefs. Americans consider female circumcision to be abusive, and so it is illegal in this country, yet many girls from immigrant families are at risk of being taken to their homeland to be genitally cut. In contrast, male circumcision is common in the United States, although many Americans are not aware that the procedure is associated with many of the same risks as female circumcision, including death. The chapter also exposes another little-known fact: For decades in the nineteenth and twentieth centuries, girls in this country were circumcised, and Christian religious beliefs about the "sin" of children masturbating played a key role in causing these abuses.

Chapter 22 examines what is being done to reduce religious child maltreatment and what more should be done. The chapter discusses legislative solutions, such as requiring clergy to report actual or suspected cases of child maltreatment, getting rid of faith healing–related "religious exemptions," and extending or eliminating child sexual abuse statutes of limitations. In addition, the chapter suggests that governmental agencies become more familiar with religious groups that allegedly maintain harmful child-rearing practices; it encourages parents to raise children in nonauthoritarian religious environments; and it urges faith communities to be more open to discussing problems related to child abuse and neglect.

Finally, chapter 23 looks at the importance of acknowledging the rights of children. The failure to recognize and grant children's rights is a significant underlying cause of all child maltreatment, including that which is religiously motivated. Unfortunately, some religious institutions and faith groups have resisted granting children rights, such as religious conservatives' opposition to the United States ratifying the international treaty, the United Nations Convention on the Rights of the Child (CRC).

As mentioned earlier, the main message of *Breaking Their Will* is not to turn people against all faith. Rather, this book aims to expose child abuse and neglect enabled by certain kinds of religious belief. By raising awareness of this issue, the book aims to initiate a discussion about religious child maltreatment in hopes of someday eradicating it.

As psychology researcher Bette L. Bottoms notes in a University of Illinois at Chicago study, "If religion-related child abuse is not acknowledged now as a problem by our society, it will be our legacy to the future."[1]

Chapter 1
WHAT IS RELIGIOUS CHILD MALTREATMENT?

A religious upbringing can be a wonderful experience for a child. I have spoken to many people who are very happy that they were raised with faith. For example, a friend of mine named Mary Ann, who grew up Catholic, told me that as a child, she felt at peace in church and loved the rituals. Even as an adult, she said, hearing a hymn can bring her to tears. I also spoke to a young woman named Devora, who grew up in an Orthodox Jewish home. Devora told me how important it was that her family observed the Sabbath. When telephones were turned off and no one drove vehicles, her family had lots of uninterrupted time to visit with relatives and friends.

A missionary with the Church of Jesus Christ of Latter-day Saints, who asked to be referred to as Elder Budge, said he loved going to church when he was young, describing the environment as "a place of refuge." He added that the feeling of safety stayed with him later in life; for example, he said he felt God's spirit while he was traveling on mission. Sam, a former member of the Fundamentalist Church of Jesus Christ of Latter-day Saints (FLDS), talked about appreciating the sense of community while growing up in the polygamous sect. When he was a child, he said, "I could pretty much walk into any of my neighbors' houses, and they would treat me like I was one of their own kids."

Religion can offer comfort to children in distress or crisis. Joanne suffered bouts of rheumatic fever throughout her childhood; each time, she was confined to her bed for months. To escape the boredom and loneliness, she turned to the Bible and read its "uplifting and promising" passages. David suffered horrendous abuse at the hands of his father. One night, when David was in his room, he believed he saw Jesus standing at the foot of his bed. The vision brought David peace. "I had a sense that somebody loved me. I knew I was going to survive after that," he told me.

More often than not, religion is good for children. In an essay in *Handbook of Parenting: Theory and Research for Practice*, psychosocial professor Stephen Frosh of Birkbeck College at University of London chronicles numerous studies that show how religious activities are good for families: "There is some evidence that religious parents are more likely to have harmonious family relationships rather than the converse, and less likely to use physical punishment against their children."[1] Similarly, an article in the medical journal *Pediatrics* states that children's sense of spirituality or engagement in a religious community "may provide a structure for positive coping strategies," such as when children are faced with difficult experiences like illness, psychological problems, substance abuse, disability, or the death of a loved one.[2] The article goes on to say that religious involvement can help children withstand emotional trauma caused by sexual abuse, racism, and isolation from their homeland. In addition, write the authors, religious activities have been associated with health-promoting behavior, better adolescent decision making, less delinquency and violence, increased academic and social competence, less stress, lower suicidal ideation, and reduced sexual aggression among male teens. Conversely, low religiosity tends to be related to higher rates of smoking, drinking, drug use, and adolescent pregnancy.[3]

Considering all this, it seems ludicrous—perhaps even blasphemous—to conclude that religion can be harmful for children. But the fact is, faith can both help and hurt.

RELIGION AS HARMFUL

There is, indeed, a dark side to religious belief—one that many people would rather not examine. For as long as humans have worshipped deities, we have been abusing and neglecting children in the name of faith. In ancient times, young ones were sacrificed to pagan gods, and there is evidence of children having been sacrificed in pre-Columbian cultures. For centuries, worshippers have believed that the severe physical punishment of children was necessary to please gods or expel evil spirits. Children with epilepsy were once beaten to drive out the devil, since the convulsions were believed to have been caused by demonic possession. Until the seventeenth century, children in Europe were whipped on Innocents' Day to remind them of Herod's ordered execution of all young male children in Bethlehem.[4] Even with the advance of medicine, parents have continued to refuse their sick children medical care, believing instead that prayer will cure them. Religious authorities the world over, enabled by beliefs that they could do no wrong, have sexually abused children.

While most believers praise religious texts for their ability to inspire, others see that scriptures can also be a tool for victimizing children. In an e-mail sent to me on October 4, 2010, Episcopal priest and pastoral psychotherapist Sarah M. Rieth explains that a religious text can be a source of hope, consolation, and joy for children who have suffered trauma, including abuse. But, Rieth adds, depending on how religious texts are interpreted,

> scripture can also be a source of sorrow, confusion, oppression, and re-traumatization. Abusers sometimes distort scripture and use it as a rationale for abuse, as if God is on the side of abuse and the abuser but not, as scripture promises, in solidarity with the brokenhearted and oppressed. Abusers sometimes use scripture to heap shame and guilt upon an already-traumatized child in order to maintain control over the child and strengthen the trauma bond.

Rather than honoring children as important members of society, theology has largely given children short shrift. As Marcia J. Bunge writes in *The Child in Christian Thought*,

> Until very recently, issues related to children have tended to be marginal in almost every area of contemporary theology. For example, systematic theologians and Christian ethicists have said little about children, and they have not regarded serious reflection on children as a high priority. . . . Theologians have not offered sustained reflection on the nature of children or on the obligations that parents, the state, and the church have to nurture children.[5]

Similarly, in *Let the Children Come: Reimagining Childhood from a Christian Perspective*, Bonnie J. Miller-McLemore states, "Mainstream congregations have not seemed too interested in current child-rearing dilemmas. Meanwhile, contemporary theologians mostly neglect the subject." Like many critics, Miller-McLemore points out that many conservative Christians proclaim themselves as parenting experts and, through Internet sites as well as for-sale books and DVDs, advise parents about child rearing. However, much of this advice leans toward promoting authoritarian parenting and the use of corporal punishment.[6]

Just as many adults have discussed with me how much they adored their religious upbringings, many others have contrasting stories. For example, one man who wanted to go by the name Matt explained how his Catholic mother regularly physically abused him in her attempt to "beat the devil" out of her son. When Russell was ten, he was placed in a Church of Christ orphanage after his alcoholic mother was no longer fit to take care of him. The orphanage staff seemed more invested in indoctrinating Russell than in offering emotional support; Russell said he was made to kneel in prayer, even though he did not believe in the faith's dogma, and was baptized against his will.

Rose spent much of elementary school hiding in the bathroom and suffering from stomachaches. A shy child, she was terrified at the prospect of carrying out her Pentecostal Christian parents' stern wishes that she "save the souls" of her classmates and teachers. Her failure to convince others to "give their lives over to Jesus" led Rose to develop fears that God would be angry at her and that demons would possess her. Cheryl was molested by her Seventh-Day Adventist minister when she was a teenager. As most sexual abusers do, the man began psychologically manipulating Cheryl to first gain her trust. After that, he sexually abused her until she was twenty-five. Kelly was betrayed by Jehovah's Witness elders, who, though aware that Kelly's stepfather was physically abusing her and her sister and emotionally abusing them and their mother, refused to report him or excommunicate him from the church. Instead, they "disfellowshipped" Kelly's mother (a form of shunning that can precede excommunication) for drinking too much and talking about having an affair.

After Joel's family confronted his former yeshiva (Orthodox Jewish school) about the principal having allegedly molested Joel when he was eight, school officials said they would investigate and probably fire the man, a rabbi. But that didn't happen. Once Joel turned twenty-three—at which time the statute of limitations on prosecuting child sexual abuse in the state had run out—the school claimed that the rabbi had done nothing wrong and kept him on the payroll.

These anecdotes represent only a small sampling of stories told to me by abuse survivors. There are many, many more that have been documented by researchers. For example, the authors of the aforementioned *Pediatrics* article point out that religious or spiritual traditions can emphasize guilt and thus cause low self-esteem in children. Other potential negative effects, note the authors, include the promotion of religiously sanctioned prejudice, hatred, and violence, including homophobia. Furthermore, the authors write,

> children may be susceptible to abuse resulting from parental religious beliefs about discipline and corporal punishment, or from some religious therapies. Adolescents who come out as gay or lesbian may encounter their religious communities' censure, and/or violence from peers who have been taught that homosexuality is a sin. Adolescents may also suffer psychological and emotional harm resulting from involvement in a group that proves to be a cult.[7]

Most tragically, some children have died from religious child maltreatment, such as from the type of corporal punishment just mentioned. In addition, children have suffered long-term health problems and died from religiously inspired medical neglect, which is often committed by parents who believe that divine intervention through faith healing is more likely to cure their sick children than modern medicine. Children are also denied vaccinations for religious reasons, which has led to disease outbreaks.

Empirical studies on the subject of religiously motivated child maltreatment are lacking, but the little research that has been done reveals potentially serious problems:

- A 1984 study reviewing the "health status" of children in religious cults shows that these groups have unusually high incidences of physical abuse, sleep deprivation, and medical neglect.[8] Another 1984 study on cults details appalling abuses, leading researchers to conclude that "there is a primacy of ideology over biology" in that "childcare may be seen as a disposable superfluity."[9]
- A 1984 survey of Quaker families reveals that Quaker fathers reported more acts of violence toward their children than did fathers nationally, and Quaker sibling violence was significantly higher than sibling violence rates reported nationally.[10]
- A 1995 study examined surveys sent to mental health professionals asking about patients' allegations of childhood abuse involving ritualistic, ceremonial, supernatural, religious, or mystical practices. In the findings, abuses largely fell into three categories: torturing or killing a child to rid him or her of evil, withholding needed medical care for religious reasons, and abusing a child under the cover of a religious role.[11]
- A 1998 study that looked at 172 child deaths occurring in church groups that strongly promote faith healing found that most of the victims would likely have survived had they received timely medical care.[12]
- A 1999 study shows that Christian fundamentalist parents hinder their children's efforts to go to college if those children do not subscribe to fundamentalist beliefs.[13]
- A 1999 study shows that individuals who are extrinsically religious are at greater risk for being perpetrators of child physical abuse than those who are intrinsically religious.[14]
- A 2002 report detailing physical and sexual abuses that took place in a missionary boarding school in Africa—a school overseen by an American religious institution—notes that the long-term psychological effects of those abuses were "of staggering proportions."[15]

- A 2003 study shows that adults who experienced "religion-related" abuse (defined in the study as abuse by religious authorities, denial of medical care on religious grounds, and beatings to rid children of evil) in childhood suffered from more serious psychological problems than those who experienced abuse that was not "religion-related."[16]
- A 2008 paper published in the *Southern Medical Journal* concludes that conservative Protestants, particularly those who believe in biblical literalism or inerrancy, spank and/or physically abuse their children more than other Christian denominations.[17]
- Most of the approximately twenty states that have laws permitting corporal punishment in schools are located in the southern United States, an area commonly called the Bible Belt.[18]

CHILD MALTREATMENT

To understand how these tragedies take place, let us define some terms. For starters, what is *child maltreatment*? According to the federal Keeping Children and Families Safe Act of 2003, it encompasses abuse and neglect, which is defined as "any recent act or failure to act on the part of a parent or caretaker which results in death, serious physical or emotional harm, sexual abuse or exploitation; or an act or failure to act which presents an imminent risk of serious harm." In crafting child abuse laws, most states break down child maltreatment into at least four categories: physical abuse, psychological (emotional) maltreatment, sexual abuse, and neglect.[19]

Child maltreatment is a big problem in America. In 2009, the last year statistics were available, child protective service agencies received more than three million reports of alleged abuse or neglect. Of those reports, more than 60 percent warranted investigations,[20] involving nearly 700,000 children.[21] That same year, an estimated 1,770 children died from abuse or neglect,[22] a figure that represents an average of nearly five children dying every day.

The negative effects of child maltreatment are staggering. In addition to physical trauma, abuse and neglect can interfere with brain development and lead to serious mental health problems, such as depression, anxiety disorders, psychotic experiences,[23] and posttraumatic stress disorder.[24] Psychological trauma stays with an abuse victim "long after the external bruises have healed," reports the American Academy of Child and Adolescent Psychiatry. "Often the severe emotional damage to abused children does not surface until adolescence or even later, when many abused children become abusing parents."[25]

In his memoir detailing his own abuse as a child, *Spare the Rod: Breaking the Cycle of Child Abuse*, Phil E. Quinn states, "Child abuse does more than cause hurts. It damages. It leaves scars that never go away, damage that never heals. It is permanent. Severe and prolonged child abuse usually results in perpetual physical, mental, spiritual, or emotional limps in an already troubled and desperate life."[26]

The societal harm caused by child maltreatment is illustrated by the fact that a high percentage of criminals are themselves former victims of abuse.[27] Child maltreatment also presents an enormous economic burden. A 2007 economic impact study estimates the yearly cost associated with abused and neglected children to be nearly $104 billion.[28]

RELIGIOUS CHILD MALTREATMENT

A subset of this larger phenomenon, *religious child maltreatment* is child abuse or neglect that is largely caused by religious beliefs held or propagated by perpetrators or a surrounding community. Religious child maltreatment manifests itself in many ways, including

- justifying abusive physical punishment with religious texts or doctrine;
- having children engage in dangerous religious rituals;
- taking advantage of religious authority to abuse children and procure their silence;
- failing to provide children needed medical care due to a belief in divine intervention;
- terrifying children with religious concepts, such as an angry and punitive god, eternal damnation, or possession by the devil or by demons;
- making children feel guilty and shameful by telling them they are sinful;
- neglecting children's safety by allowing them to spend time with religious authorities without scrutinizing the authorities' backgrounds;
- inculcating children with religious ideas; and
- failing to acknowledge or report child abuse or neglect to protect the image of a religion or a religious group.

Religious child maltreatment happens for a host of reasons, some of which mirror general child maltreatment. For example, perpetrators may be responding to a desire to dominate and overpower victims. Mental illness can also be a factor. However, this book focuses on cases involving adults who are convinced that their acts are righteous expressions of piety.

Phil Quinn gets across this point in *Spare the Rod*: "Too many parents are willing to do just about anything to their children if they believe . . . that it is God's will. . . . They most often appeal to a higher principle, such as religious duty or love of their child. . . . My adoptive parents told me hundreds of times, during the endless beatings, that they loved me. If that was their way to love, they very nearly loved me to death!"[29]

HOW PREVALENT?

How often is religious belief a factor in cases of child abuse and neglect? This is impossible to say. There are no national statistics that track this phenomenon. But we do know that religion plays a significant role in the way children are raised. Parents' theological beliefs guide many aspects of child rearing. For example, parents' religious views affect how they discipline children. One study that examines why conservative Protestants spank their children more than other Christian believers concludes that two aspects of evangelical theology are associated with the approval of corporal punishment: a belief in a hierarchical God and a belief in hell.[30]

"Spiritual and religious worldviews can shape parents' approaches to all aspects of having and raising children, including family planning, pregnancy, childbearing, postpartum experience, the feeding and care of an infant, child-rearing, and images of fatherhood and motherhood," note the writers of the *Pediatrics* article. They add that caregivers even assess their religious and spiritual worldviews to make sense of children's illnesses or disabilities, at which times "parents may see themselves as being tested or even punished."[31]

Religious child maltreatment appears to be quite common, as criminal cases involving defendants who are accused of harming children in this way routinely pop up in the news. There is a myriad of memoirs on the market written by people who grew up in harmful religious environments. The Internet is abuzz with websites that provide support to survivors of religious child maltreatment.

"Our current methods of measurement cannot accurately quantify the extent to which children are abused or neglected within a particular religious context. Yet child welfare officials, therapists, medical providers, law enforcement officers, and court professionals confront such issues," writes Karel Kurst-Swanger, public justice professor at the State University of New York at Oswego, in *Worship and Sin: An Exploration of Religion-Related Crime in the United States*.[32]

Atheistic philosopher Christopher Hitchens asks in *God Is Not Great: How Religion Poisons Everything*, "How can we ever know how many children had their psychological and physical lives irreparably maimed by the compulsory inculcation of faith?"[33]

Religious child maltreatment is so common that I am no longer surprised when I talk to strangers or acquaintances, tell them about this book and my blog, and hear them say, "You should interview *me*."

A PSYCHOLOGICAL AND SPIRITUAL COST

As with all child maltreatment, those who are abused or neglected for reasons tied to faith suffer not only physically but also emotionally. A 2003 study calls particular attention to this problem. It looked at two groups of adults. Both had been abused as children, but one group's abuse was categorized as "religion-related" (defined in the study as abuse by religious authorities, denial of medical care on religious grounds, and beatings to rid children of evil); the other group's abuse, however, had no religious component. The study's lead researcher, University of Illinois at Chicago psychology professor Bette L. Bottoms, one of the few to empirically examine the issue, conducted psychological tests on the subjects and found that the group who experienced religion-related abuse more severely suffered from such psychological problems as depression, anxiety, hostility, and psychotic personality disorders.[34]*

In that study, Bottoms opines as to why abuse involving religion might be more traumatic than abuse in which religion is not a factor:

> Religious contexts and justifications may add an additional layer of complexity and harm to the experience of child physical abuse. . . . We speculate that there is an additional sense of betrayal involved and much internal cognitive dissonance and perhaps guilt as victims deal, not only with the physically abusive actions, but also with the confusing relation of the actions to religion, which they are taught to believe and follow.[35]

Bottoms adds that young victims may come to believe through religious teachings that the abuse is "supernaturally sanctioned" or "a punishment for their own sins." More than one-quarter of the religion-related victims in the study had come to believe their abuses were religiously justified.[36]

Victims of religious child maltreatment often suffer a spiritual loss. For example, experts say children may feel angry at, or terrified of, a deity if their abuser is active in the victim's place of worship. Many victims are unable to pray and can reject their faith altogether.[37] In a 1995 study by Bottoms, she notes that a significant number of alleged victims of childhood religion-related abuse changed their faith or became atheists.[38] Retired Princeton Theological Seminary pastoral psychology professor Donald Capps states in *The Child's*

Song: The Religious Abuse of Children, "The abuse of children in the name of religion may well be the most significant reason for why they leave the faith."[39]

In a booklet that aims to educate the public about child maltreatment in Amish communities, one woman writes about the beatings she received as a girl: "Where was God when those awful beatings occurred? Did He care? How would I know? God is Our Father, the Bible says, but is He also like my earthly father—ready to strike me down and call me 'worthless' when I fail. How could I trust God? . . . Many times I've tried to persuade God to just let me die."[40]

Many grown victims I interviewed talked about being spiritually confused or resentful of religion. Take, for example, sixty-two-year-old Barbara Dorris, the national outreach director for the Survivors Network of those Abused by Priests (SNAP), who says she was ritually, physically, and sexually abused by a group of Catholic priests when she was young. When I asked Dorris on March 12, 2009, about her current spiritual beliefs, she responded, "I certainly believe in God, and I certainly believe that you have to lead a Christian life." But, she added, "I don't have any faith anymore in any religion. I'm done with religions. I've seen too much and hurt too much. I try and honor, in many ways, what I was taught as a child, but I don't go to church."

On August 26, 2010, I spoke with Kathryn Goering Reid, the former general secretary of the Church of the Brethren, who now runs the Family Abuse Center, a domestic violence shelter in Waco, Texas. Reid is particularly concerned about how abuses connected to faith rob victims of their spirituality. "I'm convinced that any kind of abuse that has any kind of religious context raises long-term spiritual questions for people. You can meet thirty- and forty-year-old women who still have very serious questions about the nature of God," says Reid. Speaking from the women's viewpoint, she asks, "How can a loving God allow what happened to them as children?"

MY STORY

I myself have never been religious, largely because of how I was raised. Both my parents are Jewish, but they raised me with a very watered-down version of Judaism. The reasons for their lack of devotion stemmed partly from anti-Semitism. Before I was born, my mother's parents, who were in entertainment, knew they had to downplay their Jewishness to be welcomed by a mainstream American audience. Therefore, my mother was not raised with any religion, and after my father married my mother, he did not push the issue. Growing up, family friends sometimes took my sister and me to synagogue, but we hardly ever spoke about God in our household. Each December, a

Christmas tree adorned our living room, and the only copies of the Old Testament I came across were in hotel rooms.

I did not become interested in religion's impact on children until I became a mother at the age of forty-one. When my daughter began attending a Montessori school in 2006, I was fascinated by the respectful way the teachers communicated to the children. Like most American children raised in the 1960s, I was rarely addressed with this kind of compassion and understanding. In fact, few adults expressed an interest in what I thought or felt. If I did something that really angered my father, there was no discussion—just a stiff belt across my bottom.

As I became more attuned to compassionate methods of child rearing, I began talking to friends and colleagues about their upbringings and was surprised to learn that not only had many people been raised with a lot of religion, their experiences were, for the most part, negative. The treatment of these individuals may not have always risen to a level of abuse, but there was certainly a great deal of emotional neglect and other problems. An example is my friend Tim, who was expected to go to church every week, even though the services were drawn-out, dull, and meaningless to a child. Tim told me he so hated going to church that he got headaches every Sunday. As an adult, Tim learned that his father regularly used to beat his brother after church because the boy fidgeted in the pew.

High-profile news stories began to catch my attention. In fact, in 2008, two significant events occurred in the same week. One was the pope's visit to the United States, during which the pope tried to console the untold numbers of people who had been molested by Roman Catholic priests as children. The other was the removal of hundreds of children from a west Texas polygamous sect known as the Fundamentalist Church of Jesus Christ of Latter-day Saints. State officials raided the group after it was alleged that adult members were sexually abusing girls by entering into "spiritual" marriages with minors.

Still, I was not yet convinced that religious child maltreatment was a serious problem. My feelings changed, however, on March 14, 2008, when I read a brief and shocking article in the *New York Times*. The news item explained that four members of a Baltimore cult had been charged in the starvation death of a toddler because he did not say "amen" after meals. Even more incredible, one of the alleged perpetrators was the victim's mother. I realized then that religious child maltreatment was serious enough to cause death. Later, I would learn that the child victim from Baltimore was just one of many children who have died at the hands of pious Americans practicing their own brand of twisted, often self-serving, faith.

I agree with Bette Bottoms when she states in one study that maltreatment that is tied up in religious belief should be considered "distinct from other forms of child abuse."[41]

CRITICS SPEAK OUT

Critical voices have tried to bring attention to the subject of religious child maltreatment, even if they have not employed that term.

"Horrible things . . . have been done to children beneath the cloak of religion in the United States," writes Marci A. Hamilton in *God vs. the Gavel: Religion and the Rule of Law*. "Children have been raped, beaten, and permitted to die excruciating deaths."[42]

When Donald Capps gave the presidential address to the Society for the Scientific Study of Religion in 1991, he called his talk "Religion and Child Abuse: Perfect Together." During the controversial speech, Capps said that he considered children "a group whose desire to love and be loved has been betrayed, exploited, and abused in the name of religion."[43]

In an article that appeared in the *Huffington Post*, Frank Schaeffer—who was raised in conservative Christian circles only to later become a critic of the religious Right—states, "Thousands of children in this country are raised in everything from polygamous child-abusing religious communes to homes where medical care is denied because of 'religious freedom.' Tens of thousands more are beaten according to the teachings of . . . pro–corporal punishment child-intimidation manuals. Where is the law?"[44]

In 1997, the International Humanist and Ethical Union Board declared in its board resolution, "There still exists one form of enduring and pervasive child abuse that has gone on for centuries but has been ignored and deliberately neglected: child abuse perpetuated in the name of religion." Furthermore, the board resolved that "countries that are tackling issues of child protection must seriously examine the issue of all abuse of children, including in particular in the name of religion and God."[45]

FIRST STEPS

Can religion be bad for kids? The answer to this question is a resounding yes. So where do we start to try to do something about it? The first step is to acknowledge the fact that religious child maltreatment exists and to learn how to recognize it. Of course, getting even that far means coming to grips with the fact that religion can be a force for both good and bad.

This duality was made especially clear to me after interviewing two women, my friend Mary Ann and Cheryl, the woman who was molested by her minister as a teenager. Like Mary Ann, Cheryl told me that she, too, cries when she hears religious hymns. However, her emotions come from a very different place. Whereas Mary Ann's reaction is one of overwhelming joy, Cheryl's tears are of sadness and loss.

Presbyterian minister Keith Wright explains this dichotomy well in *Religious Abuse: A Pastor Explores the Many Ways Religion Can Hurt as Well as Heal*:

> We need to give up the idea that religion is perfect—that the church of which we are a part is perfect or infallible. Religion, like our parents, has the capacity to bless us and to wound us and it inevitably does both at different times. . . . Only when we are aware of the capacity of religion to abuse can we guard against that abuse and take steps to curb it where it exists.[46]

As I made clear in the introduction, this book is not a diatribe against all religion. It does not intend to praise one faith over another or to talk anyone into abandoning his or her beliefs. In the words of British actor and writer Stephen Fry, "It would be impertinent and wrong of me to express any antagonism towards any individual who wishes to find salvation in whatever form they wish to express it."[47] Americans have the right to practice the religion of their choice, and parents should be allowed to teach their children whatever faith gives their own lives meaning. Many children are raised in loving homes by responsible religious parents, and children certainly suffer abuse and neglect in nonreligious homes and communities.

But there are times when the teaching and practice of religion crosses a line that should not be crossed—a line that the United States Supreme Court drew back in 1944. In *Prince v. Massachusetts*, the Court states, "The right to practice religion freely does not include the liberty to expose the community or child . . . to ill health or death."[48]

With a renewed, realistic, and balanced understanding of faith's capabilities, we can begin a discussion on how to raise children in a safe and healthy religious environment. Recognizing the connection between faith and child abuse and neglect is the first step to reducing the impact of religious child maltreatment and ensuring that a religious upbringing is a positive experience for all children.

Chapter 2
A COUNTRY IN DENIAL

As has been explained, religion is not always child friendly. But many people have a hard time believing this. It's an understandable viewpoint. After all, no religion out-and-out condones harm to children.

"All religions have at the core of their teaching a central ethic of love and harmony," writes Keith Wright in *Religious Abuse*.[1] In fact, all three Abrahamic faiths—Christianity, Judaism, and Islam—have tenets that urge people to protect society's most vulnerable, giving special regard to orphans as well as widows.

Many people of faith believe that since God created man in his image, we then see the image of God in every human being. Therefore, as one rabbi put it, "harming one child is like harming all of humanity."[2]

The Torah explicitly prohibits child sacrifice, a ritual that was practiced to some degree among the ancient Hebrews, and the early Christians rejected infanticide, as did the early Muslims. Both Jewish and Islamic law set limits on the corporal punishment of children. Baba Batra 21a in the Talmud states, if one were to strike a child, one should do so "only with a shoelace"; and Book Two, Number 0495 of the Hadith tells parents to wait until a child is ten years of age before spanking him or her for not praying. In Matthew 18:6, Jesus sternly warns followers, "Whoever causes one of these little ones which believe in me to sin, it would be better for him if a millstone were hung around his neck, and he were drowned in the depth of the sea." Psalm 127:3–6 proclaims that children are "a heritage from the LORD" and states, "The fruit of the womb is a reward."

In Islam, stories about the faith's leader, Muhammad, exemplify him as a role model for parents and all adults who interact with children. Such stories depict Muhammad delighting in the company of children and being affectionate with them.[3] The religious leader, who was himself an orphan, also spoke to adults about the need to care for children, provide them a good education, and respect their emotional needs.

Therefore, it is no surprise that many in this country might find it preposterous as well as sacrilegious to think that religion would have anything to do with something as heinous as child abuse. Still, anyone who thinks faith is only good for children is wearing spiritual blinders. One reason has to do with the fact that Americans are a very religious people.

A RELIGIOUS AMERICA

If recent surveys are any indication, Americans are some of the most religious people in the world. Consider these statistics:

- More than 80 percent of Americans belong to one religion or another;[4] more than half of Americans say religion is "very important" in their lives;[5] and more than a quarter of Americans say they attend church at least once a week.[6]
- Eighty-six percent of Americans believe in God, a "universal spirit," or a higher power; more than 80 percent believe in heaven; nearly 70 percent believe in hell; and 70 percent believe in the devil.[7]
- Americans are more likely to believe in the devil, hell, and angels than in Darwin's theory of evolution,[8] and a higher percentage of Americans "firmly reject" the concept of evolution than do those living in any of thirty-two European countries and Japan.[9]
- More than three-fourths of Americans believe God sometimes intervenes to cure people who have a serious illness.[10]
- More than 40 percent of Americans believe Jesus will return to Earth within the next forty years.[11]
- More than one-third of Americans believe the Bible is the "Word of God."[12]

So it stands to reason that many of the country's devout would object to even the insinuation that religious belief could enable someone to abuse or neglect a child. When I talk to people of faith about this book, many insist religious belief is not a factor in crimes of abuse. Rather, they say, those who harm children in ways that involve religion are motivated not by theological beliefs but by other things, such as mental illness or sadism. Very often, I am told that perpetrators of such abuse who claim they are driven by faith are not *truly* religious, because those abusers are misinterpreting religious tenets or twisting them to fulfill their own needs for power.

This viewpoint is illustrated in the third edition of *Child Maltreatment: A Clinical Guide and Reference*. In the book's well-intentioned chapter on abuse and neglect in religious communities, Kibbie S. Ruth states, "All major world religions esteem children; however, some of the original guiding principles and faith tenets have been distorted over the centuries to harm rather than protect youth. Such toxic theology is used to justify the abuse of children and suggests that abuse is supported by the power of the divine."[13]

Apologists commonly proclaim that—even when evidence points to widespread abuse within a faith institution—neither the religion nor the system on which that institution is built is to blame. Instead, these naysayers insist that the blame lies solely on fly-in-the-ointment individuals. As an example, on April 23, 2010, I received an e-mail from a devout Catholic woman with whom I had been corresponding about her views on motherhood and how her belief in God guided her parenting decisions. When I asked her what she thought of the way the pope had been handling the child sexual abuse scandal, she sent me this carefully worded response: "I feel like when people do not value a belief in God, they take the failings of individuals and associate them with the religion at large. Since the church is made up of a community of people, it will not be perfect."

I do not dispute most of these claims. Certainly, there are times when perpetrators abuse children and commit that abuse by contorting religious messages, as Ruth points out. For example, a member of the clergy might tell a child that she must do what he wants because God orders it. Mental illness can also play a role, especially in egregious cases. But it is too easy to simply write off all these crimes as the result of a damaged mind. In most criminal cases of religious child maltreatment I have reviewed, defendants rarely qualify as being incompetent or plead insanity. And very often, perpetrators act in tandem with other adults. Sometimes a church's entire congregation joins in. Clearly, not all these people can be mentally ill or sadistic.

It is likely that, at their origins, all major faiths honored children and that religions' core values have been hijacked over time by the unscrupulous, as Ruth asserts. But what is religion, after all, but a set of beliefs that help people define their relationship with a supreme being? Doctrine and scripture that emanate from those belief systems are, for better or worse, created by human beings, with all their decency and shortcomings. I take issue with Ruth's assumption that all major faiths esteem children. In my view, religion is, and has always been, only as good as those who promote it and subscribe to it.

Even in cases where mental illness is a dominant factor leading to child maltreatment, religious belief still can play an influential role. Take, for example, the case of Andrea Yates. In 2001, the Houston housewife killed her five young children by drowning them in the bathtub. Yates said she did this to save them from going to hell.[14] Yates, who had been suffering with mental illness for years, was ultimately found not guilty by reason of insanity and ordered to live in a state-run, high-security mental health facility. There is no question that Yates's psychosis greatly contributed to the murders. However, the devout Christian had also been under the influence of a fanatical fire-and-brimstone preacher named Michael Woroniecki, who, perhaps unintentionally, made Yates feel responsible for raising children who would never be spiritually saved.[15]

What about the criticism that perpetrators of religious child maltreatment should be discounted because they are not "real" believers, that they are misguided as to what faith is truly about? In response, I question whether anyone is qualified to ascertain just what constitutes a righteous individual. I know that I am not in a position to know what makes someone a "good" Christian, a "real" Jew, or a perfectly devout Muslim. I do know, however, that in case after case of religious child maltreatment I have studied, the perpetrators believed without a doubt that they were the real deal.

As for the Catholic mother's claim that the whole problem rests with the "failings of individuals" and her implication that those who "do not value a belief in God" are blowing the child sexual abuse scandal out of proportion—a scandal Catholic officials themselves have called "a crisis without precedent in our times"[16]—this position is nothing short of denial. In *God vs. the Gavel*, Marci Hamilton, a lawyer who has written extensively about the Catholic child sexual abuse scandal and others, contradicts those who, like my Catholic correspondent, sees the problem confined to sinners within the faith community:

> To those who would argue that these are just the bad apples, that is simply not the case. These are only a very small number of the many, many instances of religious entities putting children's interests second, or even worse. But even if these are only the bad apples, these bad apples are precisely whom the law is intended to deter and punish. Even one child's life sacrificed for an adult's religious beliefs is one too many, and to be sure, there are far more than one.[17]

Breaking Their Will shows that in many instances, there are serious problems with "religion at large," a point highlighted by retired Princeton Seminary professor Donald Capps in his 1991 presidential address to the Society for the Scientific Study of Religion: "I suggest that many religious ideas which children are taught cause them emotional torment and are therefore inherently abusive."[18]

All child maltreatment is a complicated problem with a multitude of risk factors, including poverty, mental illness, stress and anger management issues, and child behavior issues. Many perpetrators simply repeat violent patterns of behavior they grew up with. My main point is that we should also throw into the mix one more risk factor: religious belief. As this book will show, people throughout the country have harmed children, convinced that they are following a religious mandate. We may disagree with their particular interpretations of scripture or doctrine, but the fact remains that these individuals *are* religious, and they are acting according to their own set of beliefs.

But there is another form of denial among the pious that presents yet another challenge—the refusal to believe that religious people are capable of any kind of child maltreatment.

NOT IN MY PLACE OF WORSHIP

All religions have their heroes. One who is not nearly appreciated enough is Etta Wheeler, a Methodist mission worker of New York City. In 1874, Wheeler went to a tenement house to check on a child she had heard was being harmed. When she arrived at the given address on a bitterly cold day, she found in the apartment a thinly dressed, barefoot girl by the name of Mary Ellen. The child's parents were both dead, and she was living with a woman named Mary Connelly who had been given custody by the Department of Charities. As Wheeler wrote in a case report, "She was a tiny mite, the size of five years, though, as afterward appeared, she was then nine." Wheeler also noted that the girl was washing dishes, "struggling with a frying pan about as heavy as herself. Across the table lay a brutal whip of twisted leather strands and the child's meager arms and legs bore many marks of its use. . . . I went away determined, with the help of a kind Providence, to rescue her from her miserable life."[19]

Wheeler was unable to find an organization or governmental agency that would help Mary Ellen. Finally, she persuaded the president of the American Society for the Prevention of Cruelty to Animals, who, acting as a private citizen, arranged for Mary Ellen to be removed from the home. Soon after that, Mary Ellen appeared before a judge. Dressed in ragged clothing, bruised all over her body, and with a gash on her face where Connolly had struck her with a pair of scissors, the child spoke in harrowing detail of the severe abuses she had experienced over the years at the hands of Connolly: "I have no recollection of ever having been kissed by any one—have never been kissed by mamma. I have never been taken on my mamma's lap and caressed or petted. I never dared to speak to anybody, because if I did I would get whipped." A court ultimately permitted Wheeler's family to take charge of the girl. Her story gained widespread media attention and led to the 1874 creation of the New York Society for the Prevention of Cruelty to Children, the first organization of its kind.[20]

You would think that many people of faith would find it important to follow in Etta Wheeler's footsteps and reach out to child victims of abuse, and some do. But it happens far too little. In fact, critics—including those who come from within faith communities—maintain that America's religious have largely failed these young people, often by turning a blind eye and even ignoring their pleas for help.

Such neglect is painfully pointed out in Phil Quinn's memoir, *Cry Out! Inside the Terrifying World of an Abused Child*:

> As an adult survivor of six years of severe child abuse—both physical and emotional—I often wonder why the church did nothing to help me, my brothers, and my parents. Was it that they could not see the bruises, the cuts, scratches, and abrasions covering my body? Could they not see the desperation out of which my parents lived? . . . Surely as I attended church school classes someone must have noticed the pain and terror in my eyes, the hopelessness with which I moved, my withdrawal into isolation, or, at least, the swelling in my hands and feet. . . . The priest was often in our home socially, as were other members of the church. Relatives were also there frequently. Could they not see what was happening to me? . . . For six years I was ignored by everyone who came into contact with me. I would have given anything during that time if my prayers to God for help had been answered. But God was silent, his people were silent, and I suffered in silence.[21]

Episcopal priest and pastoral psychotherapist Sarah Rieth says churches historically have ignored children's needs and revictimized those who have sought help after having been abused. As Rieth explained in our October 4, 2010, interview, instead of providing victims counseling and holding perpetrators of abuse accountable, cases get swept under the carpet. Rieth points to a historical "mandate" to "forgive seventy times seven" (as Jesus commands in Matthew 18:21–22), which she believes has allowed abuse to continue "because forgiveness has been confused with accountability."

Kathryn Goering Reid, who runs a domestic violence shelter in Waco, Texas, and often speaks to church leaders about domestic violence, says, "I have yet to come across a faith community that thinks they have a problem. No matter where they stand, whether they're liberal, conservative, Catholic, Mennonite, Protestant, Presbyterian, Lutheran, there's always somebody else who has the problem, not them. I've had pastors say to me, 'I've been here for thirty years. I don't know any child that's ever been maltreated.' Those kinds of broad, sweeping statements I just find everywhere I go."

In *Religious Abuse*, Presbyterian pastor Keith Wright writes, "If one reads or watches television, and if one thinks at all, it is almost impossible to ignore the magnitude of the problem of child abuse in society at large, yet many people still believe that their own faith community will be immune to this problem."[22]

While there are no meaningful statistics that compare abuse in religious settings versus abuse in secular settings, studies and investigations into child maltreatment occurring in faith communities indicate that they are no more immune to the problem than anyone else:

- A 1984 report released by the United Methodist Church reveals that one in every nineteen church members reported having been physically abused as a child, and one in fourteen claimed to have been a victim of incest.[23]
- A 1989 survey among members of the Christian Reformed Church shows that nearly 30 percent had been victims or perpetrators of physical, sexual, or emotional abuse. In addition, most victims reported that the abuse began before they reached their teens.[24]
- A 2002 report on child sexual abuse in the Catholic Church shows that 4 percent of priests nationwide—nearly 4,400—had been accused of sexually abusing minors.[25]
- A 2007 study that looked at sexual abuse among married Sabbath-observant Jewish women reveals that 16 percent of respondents reported having been sexually abused by the age of thirteen and that the rate of reported abuse was higher among "ultra-Orthodox Jews" than "modern-Orthodox Jews."[26]

Even when faced with egregious cases, some believers refuse to acknowledge that a member of their flock is a lawbreaker. I am reminded of a 1990 case in which a woman in an Orthodox Jewish community in New York was charged with beating her eight-year-old son to death. When interviewed by the *New York Times* about the alleged crime, a rabbi from the mother's community would not admit that abuse had occurred. While he acknowledged that the family had problems, he would only speak kindly about the woman who stood accused of killing an innocent child: "She is a family person. She has good children. She is a good mother."[27]

Or take the more recent case of five-year-old Brandon Williams. On September 18, 2008, Diane Marsh of Tucson, Arizona, was sentenced to ten years in prison for torturing Brandon, who was autistic. That torture, which involved tying him down, scalding his legs, and medicating him with sleeping pills, had been going on for months. Marsh's attorney pled for leniency for Marsh, who suffered from depression, pointing out that she had "enormous" support from her community and that Marsh's pastor had said she was "a model of motherly love." The judge, however, was not moved to sympathy: "You may be a good person to [fellow church members], but you were a horrible person to Brandon."[28]

TOO FAITHFUL TO FAITH

But America's love affair with religion extends beyond places of worship, and this can prove costly to child victims of abuse. This problem is most apparent in the legal system.

"The United States has a romantic attitude toward religious individuals and institutions, as though they are always doing what is right," writes Marci Hamilton in *God vs. the Gavel*. "The unrealistic belief that religion is always for the good . . . is a hazardous myth."[29]

To see how this "romantic attitude" can play out, consider the famous kidnapping case of Elizabeth Smart, the fourteen-year-old who was taken from her Salt Lake City home and repeatedly sexually assaulted by Brian David Mitchell over a period of nine months in 2002. When the case came to trial in 2010, Smart testified that Mitchell disguised her when they went out in public by making her wear a robe that fully covered her. On one occasion, a police detective became suspicious that the robed figure was Smart and asked her to remove the veil that hid her face. When Mitchell stated that their religion did not allow anyone but the female's husband to see her face, the detective pressed the issue once and then walked away. "I felt terrible that the detective hadn't pushed harder," said Smart.[30]

Powerful religious organizations facing allegations of child sexual abuse have coasted on America's reverence of faith. For example, courts have given special treatment to religious organizations by allowing them to keep employee records sealed—despite the fact that those records might very well provide evidence of child sexual abuse.[31] On the April 11, 2008, airing of his HBO comedy television program, *Real Time with Bill Maher*, the show's host exposed the preferential treatment that religious organizations enjoy with his depiction of the Catholic Church's child sexual abuse scandal: "If the pope was, instead of a religious figure, merely the CEO of a nationwide chain of daycare centers where thousands of employees had been caught molesting kids and then covering it up, he'd be arrested faster than you can say, 'Who wants to touch Mr. Wiggle?'"

When cases do come to trial, perpetrators of child maltreatment receive relatively lenient treatment if they claim their actions were religiously motivated. As will be explained in more detail later, many state child abuse laws have exemptions for parents who deny their children medical care if that denial is based on the parents' beliefs in faith healing, even in the case of a death. These exemptions essentially state that the life of a child who is the victim of religious maltreatment is worth less than the life of a child whose abuse was not connected to faith.

Even when laws do not explicitly talk to religiously motivated crimes, courts have given perpetrators of religious maltreatment a pass. One example is an astounding case that came to trial in Georgia in 2009. Sandra Alfred stood accused of conducting a three-day-long exorcism on her fifteen-year-old son. According to a law enforcement official, the ritual included the boy being handcuffed for hours at a time and going without food and water for twelve consecutive hours. Despite this treatment—and the fact that doctors believed the boy had the onset of schizophrenia—the judge dismissed the charges because he said the evidence did not show a crime had been committed. In explaining one reason why he ruled the way he did, the judge apparently found Alfred's claim that she needed to cast out the devil from her son's body to be reasonable: "I'm going to have a hard time believing you're going to get anybody to say in Gwinnett County, Georgia, that Satan doesn't exist."[32]

What is at the root of these failures? America's inability to see religion as a force for doing harm. What's more, this denial makes religious child maltreatment all that more insidious. In *Train Up the Child,* Louise Anne Owens writes that "abuse-by-religion" is particularly harmful because society often fails to acknowledge its presence. According to Owens, it is "hidden and protected by icons as sacred as Mom and apple pie."[33]

Owens notes that Americans tend not to connect abuse with religion, a fallacy that often makes its way into American households and places of worship:

Parents have a fundamental notion that teaching children about god is being a good parent. I submit that god as presented by religious doctrines and leaders is not always good for children. Sometimes in churches, instead of moral values, children learn a crippling fear that leads them to hate instead of love their neighbor. . . . It should not surprise anyone that they are harmed in ways that affect them for the rest of their lives.[34]

It's time for people of all faiths—and of none at all—to come to grips with a couple realizations. The first is that religious belief can be harmful to children. The second is that people of faith are just as capable as anyone else of abusing or neglecting a child. As long as Americans remain enamored with religion, they will be complicit in allowing child maltreatment to continue. Just like fire, cars, and guns, religion can be used to our benefit, but it can also turn the lives of children into a living hell.

Chapter 3
WHEN RELIGION BECOMES HARMFUL

A s was said in chapter 1, many children benefit from being raised with religion. For these fortunate ones, faith provides an enriching experience devoid of maltreatment. Given that a religious upbringing can be both positive and negative, it makes sense to ask: Is there a difference between healthy and unhealthy faith? Are some religions, perhaps, safer than others? At what point does religion go from being a nurturing and uplifting experience for a child to a frightening and dangerous one?

My research tells me that there is indeed a difference, and that difference has little to do with whether children are raised in Christian, Jewish, or Muslim families; whether they pray to a deity they call God, Jehovah, or Allah; or whether they read from the New Testament, the Torah, or the Qur'an. Instead, it's necessary to look at a child's religious environment and ask: Is it *authoritarian*?

An important scientific discovery illustrates this point.

In the 1990s, archeologists in Peru found the frozen bodies of four children: two fifteen-year-old girls, one six-year-old girl, and one seven-year-old boy. The children had apparently been sacrificed by the Inca around 1500 CE, probably to propitiate weather gods. Because the bodies were so well preserved, much could be determined about the children's last days. For instance, according to a report on the findings, researchers figured out that the children were drugged with coca leaves. Scientists also surmised how the children suffered. While it was not obvious exactly how each child was killed, one girl did receive a blow to the head. Vomit and diarrhea covered the clothes of the seven-year-old boy, write the authors of the report, indicating "a state of terror. . . . His death was likely caused by suffocation, his body apparently having been crushed by his textile wrapping having been drawn so tight that his ribs were crushed and his pelvis dislocated."[1]

Yet scientists were left scratching their heads on one point. The bodies were found in shrines located some 20,000 feet above sea level. Trying to reach such an altitude put the children at risk for "acute mountain sickness, high-altitude pulmonary edema, and high-altitude cerebral edema," according to the report. The children had probably already been part of extended rituals in the city center of Cuzco closer to sea level.[2] So why go to the trouble of scaling the treacherous mountains to conduct the ceremonial killings, a hike that put everyone's lives in danger?

The answer seems to be wrapped up in the Inca's need to show off their power. As the scientists point out in their report, the Inca were rapidly expanding their empire at the time the children were sacrificed. Wrote the authors, "The logistical effort involved in the ritualized killings of children at high peaks was unprecedented and presumably designed to inspire awe and instill fear."[3] This need to "inspire awe and instill fear" illustrates an important characteristic of the Incan civilization—that it was highly authoritarian. The Incan government was a tightly run, hierarchical theocracy, headed by an emperor believed to be a descendant of the sun god. In fact, the emperor had such control over his people that prisons were largely unnecessary; Incan subjects knew that anyone who dared to disobey the emperor would be swiftly punished by being hurled off a cliff.[4]

Even though people no longer sacrifice children to gods, the authoritarian nature of the Inca is significant toward understanding the root causes of religious child maltreatment. After interviewing many victims and perpetrators, as well as examining dozens of court cases and empirical studies, I conclude that virtually all cases of religious child maltreatment have a common characteristic: The victims had been living in religious authoritarian environments.

AUTHORITARIANISM AND RELIGION

What is *authoritarianism*? Usually this term refers to an oppressive form of government where leaders have great control over their subjects. Dictionary.com describes authoritarianism as "favoring complete obedience or subjection to authority as opposed to individual freedom."

Nori J. Muster, who grew up in the International Society for Krishna Consciousness (ISKCON), a religious group also known as the Hare

Krishnas, writes in *Cultic Studies Review*, "In an authoritarian system, everyone obeys someone else in a chain of command. People near the top have more power over others, while a large segment at the bottom has no power in the system whatsoever."[5]

In his online book, *The Authoritarians*, psychology professor Robert Altemeyer, who recently retired from his teaching post at the University of Manitoba in Winnipeg, Canada—and who is considered by many in his field to be the go-to guy on the subject of authoritarianism—describes this form of governance as a two-way street and one that can stir up terror among subjects. According to Altemeyer, authoritarianism is "something authoritarian followers and authoritarian leaders cook up between themselves. It happens when the followers submit too much to the leaders, trust them too much, and give them too much leeway to do whatever they want—which often is something undemocratic, tyrannical and brutal."[6]

A hallmark of such cultures is that they subscribe to a particular ideology, such as one of nationalism or religion. Religion is particularly common because it can help drive home beliefs about obedience.

It's no secret that religion itself is steeped in authoritarianism.

"God has established a hierarchy with God at the top, followed by men, then women, then children, and, finally, the rest of creation," is how Keith Wright describes traditional Christian theology in *Religious Abuse*. Wright believes that such a model "has taught that those at the top of this chain of command have the right and obligation to force their will upon those who are beneath them, because they are inferior and must be dominated and controlled for their own good." Wright adds that the church's "unquestioned power structure" brings about "terrible and destructive forms of abuse."[7]

The King James Bible is, itself, a product of authoritarianism. In 1611, King James ordered that a new Bible be written after he became infuriated by notes included in the existing Protestant version, the Geneva Bible—notes that undermined the belief that kings have divine rights.[8]

As Wright indicates, God is portrayed in the Bible, particularly in the Old Testament, as an all-powerful, angry, and unpredictable male force. He is capable of extreme violence, including genocide. While the deity is, at times, loving, his love is often conditional. That is, it is only awarded to those who offer God complete and unquestioning devotion. Mortals are also supposed to fear God. In fact, just speaking against God can bring serious penalties, including excommunication, as ordered by Numbers 15:30, or stoning, as in Leviticus 24:34.

Humans, on the other hand, are often described in theological circles—especially Christian circles—as being lowly, flawed creatures, or, as John Calvin described himself, "so miserable a sinner."[9] Much of religion strongly promotes the need for mortals to obey God, no matter what. In the Bible, Abraham and Moses set an example of unquestioned obedience, as they unblinkingly carry out God's orders, even when those orders call for brutal violence.

In some faith settings, religious authorities have great power, and this power is all the more accentuated when those authorities are perceived to have divine power, such as in many Christian denominations. For example, a religious leader may be believed to enjoy the privilege of being able to talk directly to God. The result is that believers do not simply respect these leaders, they *worship* them.

Fear and authoritarianism often go hand in hand, as religious leaders can use terror tactics to maintain order and control. The Bible illustrates this point with the previously mentioned passages in Numbers and Leviticus that recommend excommunication and stoning. And according to Deuteronomy 13, people should kill family members or friends who as much as suggest worshipping gods other than the Almighty. Commenting on this passage, About.com's atheist blogger Austin Cline remarks, "The penalty is designed to create fear among the rest of the population in order to keep everyone else in line."[10]

Theologians and religious leaders have long taken advantage of fear-filled religious concepts to scare the living daylights out of worshippers. One of the great masters of such fear-mongering was the eighteenth-century preacher and theologian Jonathan Edwards, who, in his famous sermon, "Sinners in the Hands of an Angry God," warned congregants that God "holds you over the pit of hell, much as one holds a spider, or some loathsome insect over the fire, abhors you, and is dreadfully provoked."[11]

Most religious authorities today do not make things seem so dire, yet many still depict the God-human relationship in authoritarian terms. This teaching is exemplified on the conservative Christian website GotQuestions.org as it answers the question, "What does it mean to have the fear of God?" The site states, "Fearing God means having such reverence for Him that it has a great impact on the way we live our lives. The fear of God is respecting Him, obeying Him, submitting to His discipline, and worshipping Him in awe."[12]

RELIGIOUS AUTHORITARIAN CULTURES

Does religious authoritarianism exist in America today? Fortunately, most people of faith want nothing to do with the power grabbing, fear mongering, self-righteousness, and blind obedience that go along with that style of worship. David Jensen, the interim dean at Austin Presbyterian Theological Seminary and author of *Graced Vulnerability: A Theology of Childhood* asserts that authoritarianism in religious communities actually "belies a presence of faith." As he told me on September 13, 2010, authoritarian-style believers often are geared toward establishing certainty and "imposing something upon someone else." Whereas faith, Jensen says, is about seeking "openness and trust in God's presence in the world. So many times authoritarianism or certainty gets substituted for faith, and I think they're antithetical to faith in the end."

In the New Testament, Jesus seems to notice that people were beleaguered from the rule of one oppressive regime after the other and promises not to do the same. In Matthew 11:29–30, he tries to assure the people that he is "gentle and lowly in heart [humble]," offering an "easy" yoke. "My burden is light," the religious leader adds.

Yet we are never in short supply of individuals who wish to control other people, as well as those who wish to be controlled. And so religious authoritarian cultures exist throughout the United States and elsewhere. In these environments, the culture is largely identified by its religious ideology; faith becomes the glue that holds the culture together. Such cultures come in all sizes, such as a community, sect, place of worship, or home, and aspects of religious authoritarianism appear in all large, mainstream institutions.

Religious authoritarian cultures maintain a number of characteristics: They tend to be ultraconservative, so members are apt to seize onto literalistic and legalistic interpretations of scriptures and doctrine; they are narcissistic, often convinced that they possess the one "true" faith and all other worshippers are wrong, misguided, or evil; they are collectivist, so the needs of the overall culture take precedence over the needs of individuals; obedience to authority is paramount, and, as in the case of the Inca, such a society maintains a strict social hierarchy; they have many rules, and those who break them can be subject to stiff punishment; and, finally, fear is a big component, as members believe that spiritual or real-life negative consequences await those who do not meet the expectations of the culture.

Not surprisingly, religious authoritarian cultures do not prize individualism. "Religious orthodoxy is not democratic. One cannot vote on religious practices," notes religious scholar Stephen Frosh in *Handbook of Parenting*. "This is particularly true with fundamentalist versions of religion, where the task is the maintenance of traditional authority structures and beliefs, which are seen as more important than the welfare of individuals." Frosh adds, "Faced with the choice between authority and humane insight, the fundamentalist chooses authority every time."[13]

Boiling it down, however, I find that there are three key aspects that create a "perfect storm" situation in which religious authoritarianism develops:

1. *The culture adheres to a strict, authoritarian social structure.*

Religious leaders, as well as men, generally possess great power, while women and children have few rights, if any. The social hierarchy is clear-cut, as everyone knows who possesses the most power, who is second in command, and so on.

2. *The culture is fearful.*

Fear abounds in religious authoritarian cultures, as members understand that they will pay a price if they do not behave or believe correctly. For example, they might believe that harboring religious doubts jeopardizes their chances to be "saved" in the next life. If members do not abide by certain social norms, they can be formally or informally ostracized.

3. *The culture is separatist.*

As a way to maintain the culture's purity, members live apart from general society. This separation can be simply social, in which members are discouraged from forming close relationships with outsiders, but sometimes, members create a physical distance by locating themselves in remote areas.

RELIGIOUS AUTHORITARIANISM AND CHILDREN

We don't know a whole lot about how religious authoritarianism affects children. While many criticize oppressive churches and cults for promulgating "toxic faith" and committing "religious abuse," most critics talk about only the negative effects on adults, not children. Some books that are critical of religion, such as Keith Wright's *Religious Abuse*, include a chapter on children, but this is a rarity.

So, when I was researching this topic, I had little to go on. But then a friend advised me, "If you want to understand how religion harms children, you have to look at cults." Initially, I had resisted this idea because I had wanted my book to focus only on mainstream faiths. But then I learned that not only do the worst problems concerning children occur in such totalistic religious communities, the same harmful aspects of cults can be seen in even large religious institutions.

In fact, reading what experts have to say about child maltreatment in cults provided a key to unlocking this puzzle. According to these researchers, children are harmed in those oppressive groups largely because of how the groups affect children's most important caretakers: their parents.

"In cults, parents do not function as they do in the regular world," Margaret Thaler Singer writes in *Cults in Our Midst: The Continuing Fight against Their Hidden Menace.* "They are more like middle-management personnel in a business: the cult leader dictates how children are to be reared, and the parents simply implement these orders." Singer adds that cult children "are total victims—even the parents on whom they should be able to depend are controlled by the cult leader, and thus the children's fate is in his hands."[14]

What Singer is saying is that parents in religious authoritarian cultures are denied autonomy. Instead of making their own decisions according to their own instincts, mothers and fathers largely do what is expected of them. For example, they might make child-rearing decisions based on what a preacher said in church or according to the norms of the culture. Most often, parents are urged to adopt authoritarian methods of child rearing that fail to meet children's individual needs. Many mothers and fathers resort to using corporal punishment to keep children in line.

Does this mean that these cultures don't care about children? Quite the contrary. In fact, they care a great deal about children. But in these cultures that prioritize obedience over individualism, the focus on children is usually couched not in terms of children being amazing individuals, but of them being the next generation offering hope for the future. This hope can be achieved only if parents relinquish autonomy in how they raise their children and become, as Singer says, "middle managers." To be blunt, the leadership controls children *through* their parents.

After all, parents are the most influential people in children's lives. According to studies, the way parents interact with their children helps define how young ones conceptualize God.[15] In *A Parents' Guide: Religion for Little Children,* the late, esteemed Catholic educator Christiane Brusselmans notes, "Through parent-child relationships and interaction, an individual's religious values and attitudes are developed in early years. The child identifies with his or her parents by adopting their attitudes, their values and their vision of life— both explicitly stated and implicitly contained in their approach to life."[16]

No parent is perfect, and many mothers and fathers need guidance, but most parents, left to their own devices, intuitively know how to raise their offspring so they feel loved and safe. As psychologist Benzion Sorotzkin writes on his website, "The love that parents feel for children is a natural instinct."[17]

The problem with religious authoritarian cultures, however, is that parents can be subject to great pressure to comply with certain social norms, including norms that dictate how children should be raised. To varying degrees, these pressures interfere with parental instincts and simultaneously weaken the parent-child bond. Despite talk about the importance of family cohesion, family bonds in authoritarian cultures—especially the parent-child bond—threaten those collectivist cultures' overall goals.

This phenomenon is discussed in the Bible. In Matthew 10:34–47, which appears in a section entitled, "Christ Brings Division," the religious leader tries to turn sons and daughters against their parents so that those children will worship him. Striking a highly unusual authoritarian tone, Jesus states,

> Do not think that I came to bring peace on earth. I did not come to bring peace but a sword. For I have come to set a man against his father, a daughter against her mother, and a daughter-in-law against her mother-in-law; and a man's enemies will be those of his own household. He who loves father or mother more than Me is not worthy of Me. And he who loves son or daughter more than Me is not worthy of Me.

The middle-management dynamic was expressed well by Carolyn Jessop in a press interview, when she described what it was like to be a parent in the Fundamentalist Church of Latter-day Saints, which was tightly controlled by its leader, Warren Jeffs. "Everything you did was monitored and controlled and everybody reported on everyone else," said Jessop. "It was a police state. You were not allowed to make decisions in your life. I had no power over my life or the lives of my children. It was a terrible way to live."[18]

The middle-management phenomenon also happens in so-called mainstream faiths. On November 23, 2010, I received an e-mail from a woman in her forties who was a direct descendant from Brigham Young. As such, Kathleen Phair Jones grew up in the Church of Jesus Christ of Latter-day Saints in Utah and raised her own children in the faith. She is no longer a member after finding the church to be too controlling of families. Jones spoke to the middle-management aspect of parents in the faith. In fact, she describes the relationship between church leaders and parents as "extremely codependent." Jones states in her e-mail,

> Adults are never real grown-ups. They are not encouraged to make normal adult choices on their own. Often, members ask their Bishop if they should take a new job or move or buy a new house, let alone a host of other life choices that would be normal adult decisions. There's talk about free agency and "personal revelation," but if your answer isn't the same as the church's (or your church leader), you simply didn't pray hard enough, or you weren't worthy to get the correct answer. Grown adults will often, if not usually, obey church leaders' advice over their own personal guidance they receive through prayer, because their leaders are supposed to be speaking for God.

In *Religion for Little Children*, Christiane Brusselmans seems to reject religious authoritarianism as she implicitly condemns the Catholic Church's traditional dominance in Catholic education: "Religious education should be returned to where it belongs, to the family. It is from the family that it will extend and expand. From this strong base, as the world of the child extends to the Christian community, to school, parish, neighborhood, and nation, our children will be able to mature into adult Christians." Brusselmans states that parochial schools and Confraternity of Christian Doctrine programs have a role in teaching children about religion, but their role is "complementary to the role of the family; their influence is secondary."[19]

RIGHT-WING AUTHORITARIANS

There is something else that should be pointed out about authoritarian cultures. While many people might not appreciate being under the thumb of the powerful, plenty of followers in that position feel as though they are in their element. In other words, they gravitate to the idea of submitting to authority. Perhaps this is what the biblical passage Jeremiah 5:31 is getting at when it warns against false prophets who "rule by their own power" and then adds, "And my people love to have it so."

As it turns out, it takes more than just oppressive leaders to make an authoritarian system hum—you also need willing followers. That is what retired psychology professor Robert Altemeyer means when he states that authoritarianism is something authoritarian leaders *and* followers "cook up between themselves." In fact, Altemeyer has a specific name for these followers: *right-wing authoritarians* (RWAs). Altemeyer concludes that RWAs possess three main characteristics: They are submissive, conventional, and aggressive.[20]

Altemeyer also discovered that RWAs tend to be religious fundamentalists.* And vice versa. In an earlier writing, Altemeyer and a coauthor explain that about two-thirds of people who score highly on psychological tests that measure RWA-ness also score highly in exhibiting religious fundamentalist attributes. The authors state, "Some authoritarians are not fundamentalists, but most are. And some fundamentalists are not right-wing authoritarians, but most are."[21]

There is no reliable, empirical data that proves that religious fundamentalists—be they Christian, Mormon, Jewish, Muslim, or of any other faith—are more abusive to children than anyone else. Still, it would be interesting to try to figure out if there is a link between child maltreatment and intense degrees of religiosity. Altemeyer says RWAs have an aggressive side—for instance, when defending an authority figure, they express their aggression "in dark and cowardly ways." He adds, "Women, children, and others unable to defend themselves are typical victims. Even more striking, the attackers typically feel morally superior to the people they are assaulting in an unfair fight."[22] Could RWAs' aggressive characteristics come out against their own children?

Here's another question: Given the tendencies of authoritarian followers and their similarity to religious fundamentalists, would they be more likely than liberal believers to follow along with abusive child-rearing methods advocated by or perceivably condoned by a source of authority? In one extreme example, followers did just that, and hundreds of children died as a result.

REMEMBERING JONESTOWN

The most horrifying example in living memory of religious authoritarianism harming children happened in Guyana on November 18, 1978. That was when 918 people, most of them members of the People's Temple religious community (also known as Jonestown), died. Nearly all had drunk, or had been forced to drink, Flavor Aid that had been laced with the poison potassium cyanide.[23]

When the story of the deaths first broke, the media commonly referred to the event as a "mass suicide." Later, the public learned how many children were among the dead and were forced to take the poisoned drink. Nearly two-thirds of those who died—276 individuals—were minors.[24] Still later, it would be discovered that this was not a tragedy that brewed overnight. It began years before, as the group's leader, Jim Jones, began to develop a psychological hold on the group. At the time of the killings, Jones had men pointing rifles at the members. Still, many believed in following Jones's orders to kill themselves and even their own offspring.

Jones began his rise to authoritarian power when the People's Temple was still meeting in California. As Jones grew more maniacal, he held public beatings of disobedient members.[25] Once it was time to leave for Jonestown, it was evident he sought to control children and usurp parental autonomy. For instance, the children were told to call Jones "Dad,"[26] and boys and girls were rewarded for spying on their parents and reporting disobedient behavior.[27] Mothers and fathers spent a great deal of time working for the commune, and so children were largely supervised by surrogates.

Jones also decided how children should be punished. As Kenneth Wooden writes in *The Children of Jonestown*, "Belts were used at first, then were replaced by elm switches, which in turn were replaced by the 'board of education,' a long, hard piece of wood, swung by 250-pound [People's Temple member] Ruby Carroll." Wooden adds, "Jones rarely hit anyone himself. As a rule, he simply sat and laughed hysterically as big Ruby Carroll's 'board of education' delivered between one and two hundred strokes to children and adults." Also, children considered to have misbehaved were hung in a well at night, blindfolded, and told that monsters lived inside.[28]

On the day of the killings, some members protested against taking the poisoned drink, but then Jones announced that Congressman Leo Ryan was dead. Ryan had been visiting the group with a small entourage after hearing about alleged abuses, and he had just left with two dozen defectors and gone to the island's airstrip. As Ryan and the others attempted to board their plane, some of Jones's men opened fire on the group. Jones also told members that one of the defectors had been killed, and he led them to believe that Ryan and the defector had been killed by US government troops. This piece of news helped bolster Jones's deceitful argument that the government was planning to annihilate the group, and people began to consume the poison more willingly.

Journalist Tim Reiterman, who was part of Ryan's group and sustained injuries during the shooting, chronicles in his book, *Raven: The Untold Story of the Rev. Jim Jones and His People*, how Jones engineered the group's final event so masterfully that parents ultimately fed their children the poisoned drink: "The sequence of death would be children, young adults, adults, the elderly. Such a clever way to make sure all died: What would the adults have to live for after they watched the next generation die?"[29]

The entire episode leading up to the killings was recorded on audiotape, presumably by Jones. Again in *Raven*, Reiterman chronicles how the children of Jonestown suffered that day:

Youngsters were bawling and screaming. Some were fighting, pulling away from their elders. Some had the potion shot to the back of their throats with syringes, where the swallowing reflex would bring it home. Parents and grandparents cried hysterically as their children died—not quickly and not painlessly. The doomed convulsed and gagged as the poison took effect. For several minutes, they vomited and screamed, they bled.[30]

On the recording, Jones is heard pleading with a woman who undoubtedly is refusing to kill her child: "Mother, mother, mother, mother, mother, mother! Please, mother, please, please, please, don't do this! Lay down your life with your child, but don't do this." Apparently, the woman then gives in, for Jones can be heard yelling, "Free at last!"[31]

PARENTS AS "MIDDLE MANAGERS"

Hopefully, there will never be another Jonestown. Still, some religious authorities have never stopped bullying, manipulating, and cajoling parents into raising their children the way those leaders see fit. A classic example is the 1970s parenting book *How to Rear Children*, written by the late Baptist megachurch pastor Jack Hyles. In addition to extolling the virtues of physical punishment, the book provides list after list of rules for parents to follow "to rear clean, chaste, and moral young people." Those rules include never allowing children to see their parents naked, preventing little boys from playing with little girls, prohibiting children from being "alone unclothed or scantily clothed," and making sure that girls do "girl's work" and boys do "boy's work."[32]

Many religious leaders are not above using fear to get parents to raise church-worthy children. For instance, the website for Joyce Meyer Ministries, a worldwide fundamentalist Christian organization, gives this alert: "Satan will look for your child's weakest area and attack at that point. He will attempt to fill your child with worry, reasoning, fear, depression and discouraging negative thoughts. Negative, hopeless thinking and depression have become a serious problem for many young people today. In order for this to change, we need to teach our kids how to line up their thinking with God's Word."[33]

With these kinds of pressures, parents become somewhat powerless, and harm can result. Take the case of an African missionary school run by the Florida-based New Tribes Mission (NTM)—one of a number of similar schools that have seen egregious abuses of children. In a report detailing those abuses, which took place during the 1980s and 1990s, it was revealed that NTM officials guilt-tripped parents into leaving their children so those mothers and fathers could work as traveling missionaries for the organization: "Parents were often reminded that if God sacrificed His only Son, missionaries should be willing and prepared to do the same." Unfortunately, such a sacrifice resulted in the probable abuse of "almost the total school population," according to the report.[34]

But parents are not only rendered powerless by religious authorities. As Robert Altemeyer indicates, many followers go along with the system, and these members can also pressure parents to comply with religious and social norms, even if they do not bode well for children. An illustration of this phenomenon appears in the educational film *Tahara*, written, produced, and directed by Sara Rashad. In this drama, which takes place in Los Angeles, a Muslim woman named Amina struggles with whether to have her young daughter circumcised. We learn that Amina had the procedure done in her unidentified homeland when she was a girl and was left physically and psychologically scarred as a result. In one scene, Amina's mother, Zeinab, is adamant that the girl should be circumcised:

> ZEINAB: It's time.
> AMINA: Again, Mom.
> ZEINAB: This is the right time—before she grows up.
> AMINA: Suha is too young.
> ZEINAB: The girl must be cleansed!

The process of disempowering parents and weakening family bonds happens in many ways. And it is frequently subtle, occurring in religious authoritairan cultures generation after generation.

BIG DEMANDS

Very often, parents find themselves in situations where they feel obligated to fulfill the demands and expectations of religious leaders and the culture, which can pull families apart. For example, mothers and fathers can be called upon to spend an inordinate amount of time engaged in religious activities, such as attending church services and Bible study classes, doing community service on behalf of their faith, and fundraising. Many parents are expected—if not outright told—to raise big families and give a portion of their income to a religious institution, which can lead to stress and make child rearing especially challenging.

Critics say this happens in the Quiverfull movement, an evangelical Christian trend in which parents adopt traditional roles and aim to have many children. In *Quiverfull: Inside the Christian Patriarchy Movement*, Kathryn Joyce describes a female former member who talks about the difficulties of running a single-income household that is bursting with children. The woman said that families struggle to feed, clothe, homeschool, and otherwise care for their children and that many families live in poverty. All the while, says the woman, mothers "are in a constant cycle, often, of pregnancy, breastfeeding, and the care of toddlers."[35]

Such demands make it difficult for parents to develop healthy bonds with their children. In an article written by Doni Whitsett and Stephen A. Kent, the authors discuss how cults "assault" parent-child bonds as "members must spend almost every waking hour doing chores for the group." The end result is that "parents have little if any time or energy left for their children. Moreover, the parents likely make substantial financial contributions to the leaders and their projects, so that they have diminished resources to devote to persons in their care."[36]

Even in less oppressive religious environments, parents are expected to give a great deal to their faiths, and children can feel the effects. On March 22, 2009, Susan, aged fifty-six, described the demands placed on her family in their Jehovah's Witness community in Florida:

> On a regular basis there would be a minimum of three meetings, Tuesday night, Thursday night, and Sunday morning, in addition to meetings before field service [door-to-door proselytizing]. . . . It could be Thursday night . . . the kids were sleepy, their bedtime could be eight thirty, but it could be the meeting wasn't over until nine. Most of the time the kids were falling asleep. Just dragging them through that their whole life, I regret that. Making them go door-to-door. I really regret that.

Other parents I interviewed spoke of the same pressures. When former Mormon Kathleen Phair Jones was growing up, she had to care for her many younger brothers and sisters because her parents were so busy working for the church. As she wrote in her e-mail, the responsibilities became only more intense when she became a parent:

> All of us are taught, our entire lives, that our only goal in life is to become Mothers and Fathers in Zion, and we are taught that we must raise our children to be with us in the Celestial Kingdom, the highest level in "Heaven," and if your children stray, you're a failure as a parent, let alone your Eternal Family circle is broken. It is entirely YOUR fault if your children stray. Therefore, there is not any reason to raise your children with any sort of critical thinking skills. Obedience, is the only answer to stay together forever. There is no other goal in life than to make it into the Celestial Kingdom, and only there, will we be with our families for Eternity.

UNQUESTIONED OBEDIENCE TO AUTHORITY

In religious authoritarian cultures, a middle-manager parent is often too willing to hand over his or her children to others who are in charge. We are now familiar with countless stories of parents expressing shock after they find out the clergy members they thought were trustworthy had molested their children. In March 2011, evidence came to light that FLDS families in Canada allegedly sent across the United States border as many as thirty-one underage girls, some as young as twelve, to be "celestially married" to American men in the sect.[37] Similar abuses also take place when children are sent to missionary boarding schools, faith-based rehabilitation programs, and other facilities.

On September 19, 2010, twenty-five-year-old Joel Engelman described to me how common it was for parents in his Orthodox Jewish community in Brooklyn to allow rabbis in yeshivas to physically punish their children:

> We were beaten on a regular basis by everyone, by our teachers, by the principal. Any adult, basically, in the school system had the right to beat us up. Physical punishment was delivered to me from a very young age as soon as I entered the school system. They would smack us in the face. They would beat us with belts, and every teacher had what they called the *shteken*, which means "the stick," which he hand-chose and was to his liking, and he used that kind of stick on the class.

Parents in religious authoritarian cultures tend to look to scriptures and religious doctrines as sources of authority and fail to question their reasonableness. One man who suffered because of this unquestioned obedience was David Yoder, who grew up in the conservative Schwartzentruber Amish clan in Ohio. On October 24, 2009, the fifty-three-year-old Yoder explained that, like many Amish people, his father strictly obeyed their church's *ordnung*, a set of rules that dictate all aspects of Amish life. In fact, some Amish believe that failure to obey the *ordnung* is tantamount to being sent to hell. Obedience was also expected in the home, and so Yoder's father frequently and severely beat his son for supposed bad behavior. But to Yoder's father, he was abiding by Amish law. Yoder remembers sitting on his father's lap as a child and hearing his father justify the violence he inflicted: "Son, if I don't whip you, I will burn in hell forever and ever. You don't want that, do you, son?" Yoder says he replied, "No, Daddy, I don't want to see you burn in hell for what I did wrong."

PATRIARCHY AND WEAKENED MOTHERS

Patriarchy is rife in all major religions, as women have long struggled to gain positions of prestige in faith institutions. Episcopal priest and pastoral psychotherapist Sarah Rieth explained to me on October 4, 2010, that male supremacy and the objectification of women are rooted in Christian theology. Furthermore, she explains, this inequality also jeopardizes children's rights, since patriarchal theology promotes the idea that "a child is a man's property." Religious patriarchal concepts are dangerous, as they can easily be used to justify violence.

Kelly, aged thirty-three, who grew up in a Jehovah's Witness community in Texas, was emotionally and physically abused by her stepfather for many years. As Kelly told me on April 17, 2009,

When [her stepfather] was being abusive, he would talk about the scripture, saying things like "Spare the rod, spoil the child." He would quote some passage from the Bible about the father being the head of the household and "what I say, goes." He did that a lot, essentially asserting and reasserting his authority over us with that scripture, and whenever there was a talk at the kingdom hall regarding the hierarchy of the family, he would say, "See? See?"

In religious authoritarian cultures, even when mothers might appear to have a great deal of power in the household, the extent of their power is largely determined by their husbands. This dynamic can severely weaken maternal autonomy. The more a mother's autonomy is weakened, the less able she is to protect her children from abuse, particularly if the abuser is her dominant husband.

"The suppression of children increases in direct proportion to the degree of patriarchy and misogyny," writes psychologist Robin Grille in *Parenting for a Peaceful World*. "When a mother is crushed underfoot, and when she lives under threat of violence, how can she be the kind of mother she wants to be, the mother her children need her to be? Children are the ultimate victims when their mothers live in bondage."[38]

No doubt Morrow C. Graham, the mother of famed evangelist Billy Graham, never considered herself a woman "living in bondage," yet Graham admits in her autobiography that she remained silent when her husband harshly and physically punished young Billy:

Billy was always full of pranks; sometimes he carried things a bit too far, and off came his father's belt. Mr. Graham never punished in anger or desperation, but when he did see the necessity for correction, I winced. At such times I had to remind myself of another Proverb: "Withhold not correction from the child: for if thou beatest him with the rod, he shall not die" (Proverbs 23:13). More than once I wiped tears from my eyes and turned my head so the children wouldn't see, but I always stood behind my husband when he administered discipline. I knew he was doing what was biblically correct. And the children didn't die![39]

Writing in the newsletter *Freethought Today*, a young woman named Sarah Braasch describes her painful past growing up as a Jehovah's Witness with "a subservient and submissive mother and a domineering father." In fact, she writes, her father was abusive and believed that it was "within his God-given authority" to beat her. Braasch says she "knew the pain of loving a mother who will not protect you, because she believes that God will condemn her for doing so."[40]

In writing about child sexual abuse, Thaeda Franz of Liberty University says in an online article that a mother may remain silent in such a case "not because she doesn't want to protect her children, but because the church tells her that her opinion comes second to that of her husband."[41]

A tragic example of such child suffering is illustrated in the 2007 documentary *Damned to Heaven*, which examines problems of incest and other forms of child sexual abuse in the FLDS. Flora Jessop, who left the sect when she was a teenager, describes what happened to her sister Ruby, who was married to her stepbrother Haven at the age of fourteen and nearly died after he brutally raped her:

> She hemorrhaged out for three days. They couldn't stop the bleeding. And this happened just down the hall from my mother's bedroom. And my mother didn't have the right to go in and help her because she now belonged to Haven and he was allowed to do what he wanted with her. You know, I made excuses for why Mom didn't protect me from the sexual abuse when I was growing up. You know, it was always she had younger babies to protect. . . . But Ruby *was* her baby, and that I can't understand. Because who was she trying to protect then?[42]

SEPARATISM

As mentioned earlier, religious authoritarian cultures tend to not mingle much with the outside world. This choice is largely motivated by fear. For example, members prefer not to be noticed too much by outsiders for fear the community will be persecuted for their beliefs. (These fears are only heightened in communities that have been persecuted in the past.) Some Christian sects often refer to 1 John 2:15, which says, "Do not love the world or the things in the world. If anyone loves the world, the love of the Father is not in him." Some sects see "the world" as evil and controlled by Satan.

Separatist religious cultures are not just unconventional groups that seal themselves off in rural areas. Sometimes the separatist nature only manifests itself socially. For example, on December 15, 2009, fifty-seven-year-old Mary Casey described how she was raised in the Pentecostal Assembly of God Church in New Mexico, whose members were terribly frightened by outside influences: "That's why we didn't have a TV in the house. We didn't have radio. As a teenager, I couldn't go to the movies. I couldn't go to dances because all of that was evil, and the devil was out there and could use a movie or anything to draw me away from Jesus and draw me into evilness."

A closed community is not all bad for children, for it can keep children safe from negative societal influences, such as drugs and violence. But too much separation from the outside world can also be detrimental for a host of reasons. For one, separatist teachings commonly instill fear in members, including the young.

"Mom reminded us often that we were to be separate," writes Hillary McFarland in *Quivering Daughters: Hope and Healing for the Daughters of Patriarchy*. McFarland, who grew up in the Quiverfull movement, in which families typically are not geographically isolated yet still remain socially separate from nonmembers, explains that she was taught to see her community as "peculiar," a term from the Bible that means special. "It was us against the System. That's what we called modern convenience, government, the way of the world. How 'normal' people lived," writes McFarland.[43]

Separation also keeps many parents ignorant of how to properly care for children. Some adults do not even know what abuse is, or at least how larger society defines it. In *Damned to Heaven*, Flora Jessop says about people living in the FLDS, "If you ask them if they were beaten and bruises were left on their bodies, most of them will tell you, 'Well, yeah, isn't everybody?'" After the FLDS made headlines and women in the group were being interviewed by the media, they denied that abuse happens more in their community than on the outside, which initially infuriated Jessop. But later, she realized, "They *are* telling the truth. They are telling the truth as they know it. . . . They don't know that every home in America doesn't have that abuse in it."[44]

Another serious problem is a failure to seek outside help, even when children are suffering abuse or neglect. This book provides many examples where abused children in such communities suffer in silence because no one will call the police or child protective services. Children can also be denied medical and mental healthcare. For instance, in December 2010, the *Huffington Post* reported that many young Orthodox Jewish women were suffering from eating disorders. In fact, a doctor who studied the problem in 1996 found that the rate of eating disorders among that population was about 50 percent higher than the general US population. As it turns out, families are so reluctant to acknowledge the illness, they tend to seek help only when a girl's condition requires hospitalization. Experts say this reluctance is due to Orthodox Jews placing great importance on arranged marriages and the need for brides to appear "as flawless as possible," as one prominent rabbi put it. A mental illness, such as an eating disorder, said the rabbi, "would be a terrible, terrible blemish and people will go to unbelievable lengths to hide it."[45]

Finally, separatist cultures often fail to hold perpetrators accountable, which essentially gives abusers carte blanche to do harm. This partly explains why some of the worst cases of child maltreatment I have come across have occurred in Amish communities. While the Amish have recently begun to address problems of domestic violence, children have paid a dear price for the long-held separatist tradition. David Yoder told me about an egregious case in which a bishop in his church beat his teenage son to death for disobeying him. The bishop confessed to what he had done and repented to the congregation, and so the matter was, to all intents and purposes, forgotten. Yoder says church members simply referred to the incident as "a beating gone bad."

Seattle attorney Tim Kosnoff, who represents victims in child sexual abuse cases against religious institutions, told me on June 3, 2010, that he believes more children are victimized in religious environments than in secular ones, which have "mechanisms that ensure greater transparency about what goes on." He adds,

> For example, sexual abuse of students by teachers is a problem, but I would assume that it is not nearly as bad a problem as it is in the Catholic Church or the Mormon Church or the Jehovah's Witnesses, in part because these are democratically run institutions. There is oversight. There is a school superintendent. They can fire people. There is a school board that is elected that is accountable to the public. So, in a larger society, there is a greater opportunity to shine a light into some of these places and to expose sexual abuse.

For the same reason, Episcopal priest and pastoral psychotherapist Sarah Rieth believes that small, insular, single-denominational churches may be at even higher risk for having problems of child maltreatment than churches belonging to large institutions. "They don't have a larger body to whom they are accountable," says Rieth. "They have their own infrastructure that is dominated by the pastor, and often those pastors are charismatic. Many of them are very, very faithful pastors, so I'm not trying to indict that kind of congregation by any means, but it's also a perfect environment for someone who is not up to good with children."

PARENTS' REGRETS

No one understands the negative effects of the usurping of parental autonomy in religious authoritarian cultures more than mothers and fathers who have left those environments and regret how they treated their children. Writing for a website designed for women who have left the Quiverfull movement, a woman named Daisy explains that she was a "near-perfect" member and a well-meaning mother:

I adored my children, poured my life out for them, and simply could not imagine that my best and most sincere efforts at applying what was, after all, God's methodology might be harming them in any way.

But it was.

While I thought I was training my children for godliness, they thought I was denying them the right to exist as independent and valuable entities. I thought I was shielding them from evil; they felt I was controlling their every breath. Although I knew I loved them more than my own life, they believed that they were to be sacrificed to a domineering God they already knew for certain they would not choose to serve.

Daisy now says that patriarchal Christianity and Quiverfull fundamentalism even "at their best, can be destructive of children's souls. I would give anything if I could go back and undo the damage . . . I inflicted on my children."[46]

Then there is the case of Russ Briggs. The former member of the Oregon-based Followers of Christ, a sect that shuns medical care in lieu of prayer, watched his two sons die at birth, as no medical professionals were called in to assist when complications arose. "I could have saved them, but I let them die," Briggs told *Time* magazine in 1998. "If there had been an incubator, or modern medicine, I know they would have made it." Briggs questioned the blind faith that ultimately led to such an enormous loss: "It's only when you no longer have that belief that all the sudden it comes to you: How could I ever have done that?"[47]

In another egregious case, a mother named Karen Robidoux allowed her baby to starve to death. Robidoux was a member of a one-family, Massachusetts-based Christian cult called The Body. By 1999, her baby Samuel was eating solid food, but after a member of the group said God wanted Samuel to be breastfed only, Robidoux did as she was told. But Robidoux was pregnant at the time, and so she stopped lactating. After having been denied food for more than fifty days, Samuel died from starvation three days short of his first birthday.[48] In 2004, a jury decided that Robidoux had been psychologically manipulated to commit the heinous act and acquitted her of murder. Robidoux told the media, "I'm not a crazy woman. I'm not a hardcore, cold mother." She added, "If I had the control, there's no way this would have been allowed at all. There's just no way."[49]

Susan, the woman whose family had to spend many hours in church, recalls her own feelings of regret for having raised her children as Jehovah's Witnesses. "When you're a parent, your number one responsibility—the most foundational thing about being a parent—is that you will protect your child against harm. But when your mind has been manipulated by cult thinking or whatever other kind of extreme thinking, you're no longer protecting your child."

Chapter 4
CHILD MALTREATMENT AND THE BIBLE

T here is no book that has affected the lives of Americans as the Bible has. While other religious texts have been in wide use in this country, including the Qur'an and the Book of Mormon, the Bible is by far the most read, with sales estimated to be in the billions. Countless individuals—the religious and the nonreligious—look to the text for spiritual inspiration and moral guidance. Biblical passages have made their way into books, movies, and colloquial speech. Both presidents Ronald Reagan and George H. W. Bush approved proclamations glorifying the Bible as the most "fundamental and enduring"[1] of influences that have shaped the United States and a book that has been "prized above all others by generations of men and women around the world."[2]

Many Christians believe the Bible is divinely inspired and interpret its passages to be literally true. Actually, more than one-third of Americans believe the Bible is the "Word of God," and nearly 25 percent of Americans believe the same of the Torah,[3] the central Jewish text consisting of the first five books of the Old Testament. Evangelical Christians, who tend to believe in a literal interpretation of the Bible, make up more than one-quarter of the country's population.[4]

"Far more than anyone realizes, all of Western life has been deeply shaped by the fact that the content of this Bible has washed over our civilization for more than two thousand years. Biblical concepts are so deeply written into our individual and corporate psyches that even nonbelievers accept them as both inevitable and simply a part of the way life is," writes retired Episcopal bishop and theologian John Shelby Spong in *The Sins of Scripture: Exposing the Bible's Texts of Hate to Reveal the God of Love.*[5]

Therefore, given the Bible's influence, it makes sense to ask: What does the Bible say about children?

THE GOOD NEWS

Without doubt, there are biblical passages that glorify children, both in the Old and New Testaments. For example, Psalms 27:10 provides comfort to those whose fathers and mothers have abandoned them, for then "the LORD will take care of me." Psalms 68:5 portrays God as a father to orphans. In Psalms 127:3–6, children are described as "a heritage from the Lord" and states that men who have many children will be happy. "The fruit of the womb is a reward," reads the text.

Some parenting advice in the Bible seems respectful of children. For instance, Proverbs 22:6 urges adults to "train up a child in the way he should go," which some interpret to mean that we should not try to control children by parenting with a one-size-fits-all approach but recognize children's individualism.[6] Isaiah 11:6 imagines what a peaceful society would look like, and the vision positions children in a significant role:

> The wolf also shall dwell with the lamb,
> The leopard shall lie down with the young goat,
> The calf and the young lion and the fatling together;
> And a little child shall lead them.

The New Testament has some of the most talked-about passages concerning children. For example, Matthew 18:1–6 begins with Jesus' disciples asking him, "Who then is greatest in the kingdom of heaven?" Jesus shocks his audience by calling over a small child and saying that, to enter the kingdom of heaven, people must be "converted and become as little children. . . . Therefore whoever humbles himself as this little child is the greatest in the kingdom of heaven." Then Jesus famously warns, "Whoever causes one of these little ones who believe in Me to sin, it would be better for him if a millstone were hung around his neck, and he were drowned in the depth of the sea."

Mark 10:13–16 encourages people to reach out to children with compassion and model their humility. As Jesus gets annoyed because some of his followers ridicule a person who has brought forth a child to stand before him, the religious leader says, "Let the little children come to Me, and do not forbid them; for of such is the kingdom of God." Jesus goes on to say,

"Whoever does not receive the kingdom of God as a little child will by no means enter it."

And Jesus is not the only biblical character to speak up for children.

In Genesis 33:13–14, as Esau and Jacob were to travel back to Israel together, Jacob says he will take the journey at a slower pace because it would be better for his young children. In Genesis 37:20–22, Reuben talks his brothers out of killing their other brother, seventeen-year-old Joseph. In 2 Samuel 26–30, Absalom avenges the rape of his sister Tamar by killing her attacker, their brother Amnon.

Finally, something should be said about Samuel, a child who is revered in all three Abrahamic faiths for his devotion to God. In 1 Samuel 3, God talks to the boy, asking him to deliver a message to his father, Eli. It is notable that the deity chooses to deliver the message to a child instead of speaking directly to the adult for whom the message is intended.

All these passages are inspiring. They say that children *matter*. If only there were more like them.

WHERE ARE THE CHILDREN?

The Bible was written a very long time ago, when children had few rights, if any. They were largely viewed as the property of their fathers, who could give them away or sell them.[7] The sacred text reflects this outlook, not just in what it says about children but in what it *doesn't* say.

Take, for example, the Ten Commandments, laws that purportedly were handed down by God. The regulations mention the word *children* only once, and not in a loving way. Both Exodus 20:5 and Deuteronomy 5:9 state that, because God is a jealous deity, he will punish "the children to the third and the fourth generations of those who hate Me." In other words, this unfair injunction says the children, grandchildren, and great-grandchildren of those who refuse to worship the deity must suffer, even though those later generations had nothing to do with the choices made by their forebears. Nothing in these laws tells people to respect children, nor do the laws instruct adults on how to enrich children's lives.

While the New Testament is often hailed as promoting the value of children, it has also been criticized for failing to discuss parenting and parent-child relations. In the international journal *Transformation*, British researcher Adrian Thatcher points out that Luke 20:35 discourages marriage and childbearing by declaring that those who are "counted worthy" should never marry. He also notes that, while 1 Peter 3:1–7 discusses the duties of wives and husbands, the passage does not mention children at all.[8]

CHILDREN AS VICTIMS OF VIOLENCE

When the Bible does speak of children, it often depicts them as victims of abuse and neglect. (Admittedly, *children* does not necessarily mean minors but offspring who could be adults. Still, it's worth examining what was said about this younger generation as well, as they are often forced to pay a penalty for acts committed by others.) The book is riddled with threats, and actual acts, of violence against children, including murder, animal attack, rape, incest, and cannibalism. This violence is often carried out by humans, but in a number of instances, they do so on God's orders. And God himself commits some of the acts.

For instance, in Isaiah 13:16, God says the children of sinners "will be dashed to pieces before their eyes." In Hosea 13:16, God states that women who are infidels, too, will see their infants "dashed in pieces" and those who are pregnant "will be ripped open." In Numbers 31:17, Moses, who has just led the Israelites to defeat the Midianites, tells his soldiers to "kill every male among the little ones." Psalm 137:8–9 talks about how joyous the people of Babylon will be when they overpower the despised people of Edom: "Happy the one who takes and dashes your little ones against the rock!"

Sometimes this talk of violence against young people goes beyond simple threats. On the contrary, the Bible contains many instances of genocide, in which children are unmentioned, yet assumed, collateral damage. Take, for example, the Great Flood, which God engineers to destroy all life except Noah's family and the animals on the ark. Genesis 7:23 explains that, in carrying out this purge, God regrets having created humankind, whom he finds wicked and evil, although there is no mention of why children deserve to be among those who perish.

Children are victimized in many other biblical incidents. For example, in Numbers 16:31–33, God is unhappy with Korah, Dathan, and Abiram because they challenge his authority, and so the deity buries them alive along with their families. In 2 Kings 2:23–24, two bears rip apart forty-two children for making fun of the prophet Elisha's bald head. In Genesis 37:20–22, after Reuben succeeds in preventing his brothers from killing Joseph, Reuben leaves the scene only to return and discover that his brothers have sold Joseph into slavery.

Young women are sexually assaulted in the Bible. (These victims were probably minors, since they are commonly depicted as unmarried virgins, and most young women were considered marriageable at the time of puberty.)[9] As mentioned before, while Absalom avenges the rape of Tamar in 2 Samuel 26–30, the Bible describes in detail how Amnon gains his sister's sympathy by feigning illness, forces himself upon her, and then sends her away in disgust. The Bible indicates that incest is wrong when Absalom avenges his sister; however, the text seems to condone other forms of rape. Take, for example, the aforementioned story of Moses helping the Israelites to wage war on the Midianites. In addition to arranging for boys to be killed, Moses also tells soldiers to "keep alive for yourselves all the young girls who have not known a man intimately."

Another example is Genesis 19:8, when Lot offers his virgin daughters to men in Sodom as compensation for the men not attacking an angel who is in Lot's house. Later, in Genesis 19:32–35, Lot's daughters decide that they will get their father drunk and have sex with him to get pregnant. The story of Lot leaves readers with two disturbing messages. One, girls can be given away by their fathers to be raped by strangers. And two, victims of incest instigate sexual activity, an all-too-common and damaging misconception.

Biblical passages about cannibalizing children are particularly gruesome. In Leviticus 26:22 and 29, for instance, God warns the Israelites that if they turn against him, he will not only "send wild beasts among you, which shall rob you of your children" but members of the race will be so hungry they will have to "eat the flesh" of their sons and daughters. In another instance, Deuteronomy 28:53 says parents will "eat the fruit of your own body, the flesh of your sons and your daughters whom the LORD your God has given you." In 2 Kings 6:28–29, a woman describes how she arranged with another woman to devour their own offspring. "So we boiled my son, and ate him," she says.

Most Christians believe that the New Testament does not portray children in a negative light and that Jesus only spoke of love for children. That is simply not the case. In Matthew 2:16, Herod gets so mad at having been deceived by a group of wise men that, following his orders, his men kill all male children aged two and under in Bethlehem and the surrounding area. The preceding chapter of this book discusses Matthew 10:34–37, in which Jesus threatens to break up families. Then there is the little-known Matthew 15:26–28. In this bizarre series of passages, Jesus and a mother rationalize why it's acceptable to throw food meant for children to dogs.

SACRIFICING SONS AND DAUGHTERS

The Bible also discusses the most horrific form of religious child maltreatment: the sacrifice of one's own offspring. In 2 Kings 3:26–27, for example, King Moab sees that he is about to lose the battle against the Israelites, and so he "took his eldest son who would have reigned in his place, and offered him as a burnt offering."

Religious apologists are quick to point out that the God of the Bible repudiates the practice of sacrificing sons and daughters. For instance, in Jeremiah 7:31, the deity is livid that people living in and around Jerusalem would "burn their sons and their daughters in the fire" in a place called the Tophet. And in Jeremiah 7:20, the deity is so angry about such acts that he threatens to pour his anger "on man, and on beast, on the trees of the field, and on the fruit of the ground; and it will burn and will not be quenched."

However, it appears that God is driven more by jealousy than ethics. After all, the deity does not oppose *all* child sacrifice, only that which involves offering up sons and daughters for gods other than himself. In Judges 11:30, when Jephthah regretfully decides that he must sacrifice his virgin daughter to God, the deity is silent. And, of course, the centerpiece of Christianity is God's decision to sacrifice his own son, Jesus, so that believers can enjoy "everlasting life," according to John 3:16. Never mind that this "gift," the crucifixion of Jesus, causes him unimaginable suffering.

And yet, there remains another disturbing Bible story about child sacrifice that is the most well known. In Genesis 22:1–13, God tells Abraham to make a "burnt offering" of his son without giving a reason, and Abraham agrees. He takes Isaac to the sacrificial site, at which point the young man asks about the whereabouts of the lamb to be sacrificed. In response, Abraham misleads him, saying that God will provide the lamb. Fortunately, Abraham does not go through with the task, as "the angel of the LORD" arrives and says he does not have to sacrifice Isaac after all, since he fears God.

This story is eerie on many levels. In its attempt to focus on Abraham's unwavering obedience to God, it completely disregards Isaac's rights as a human being. Not only is he not allowed the ability to decide his fate, he is lied to about it. And, even as the young man likely figures out what is in store—Abraham ties up his son, lays him on top of a wood pile on the altar, and stretches out his hand holding the knife—Isaac does not protest. It is worth noting that in Rembrandt's haunting painting, *Abraham and Isaac*, Abraham's enormous hand firmly covers his son's face. Meanwhile, the mute Isaac lies barely clothed on a pile of wood, his back arched in fear.

The fact that the Bible fails to address what Isaac is going through bothers many, including some Christians. In our interview, David Jensen, professor of constructive theology at Austin Presbyterian Theological Seminary, pointed out that people have only interpreted the story from Abraham's vantage point, not Isaac's. He says that a full understanding of the story has to include Isaac's perspective, which, says Jensen, "is horrific."

A NEED FOR SCRUTINY

What to make of all this biblical talk about violence against young people? Certainly, we have to accept it as a necessary reflection of the times, when children's rights were not paramount. We cannot negate the fact, for instance, that child sacrifice was a reality in ancient times.

"The Gospels were written in a particular historical context that may or may not speak to today," says Episcopal minister Sarah Rieth.

Of course, I do not suggest that we rewrite the Bible so that it is full of happy endings. But shouldn't we at least consider what effect the Bible's depiction of children has on the faithful, especially those who interpret the book to be literally true and inerrant? To those worshippers, nothing between the book's covers is obsolete. In other words, the potential problem is not simply the fact that the Bible contains stories about violence against children but believers' unflinching *glorification* of the text. How might this reverence influence those adults' views or treatment of children?

It is no secret that pious adults justify child maltreatment by quoting religious texts, and this book provides numerous examples of this. In addition, it is common for devout worshippers to uphold biblical passages even when they include abusive acts. The story of Abraham and Isaac is a perfect example. You would be hard-pressed to find a person of faith who concedes that the story sends a bad message. Instead, believers tend to tie themselves in theological knots trying to extract meaning from the story. For example, at one point, the conservative Christian website GotQuestions.org called Abraham's decision to sacrifice his son his "highest and finest hour." A later version of the site says Abraham's "unquestioning obedience to God's confusing command gave God the glory He deserves and is an example to us of how to glorify God."[10] Another Christian website goes so far to exclaim, "What a joyful return trip that must have been for Abraham and Isaac. I wonder what they talked about as they made their way home."[11] The idea that this tale and many others warrant criticism seems unfathomable to many worshippers.

It is also concerning that some of the Bible's violent tales are shared with young readers. I was shocked at a popular bookstore to find a number of children's Bible story books that showed—complete with color illustrations—Solomon suggesting that a baby be cut in half, Cain killing Abel, Abraham about to sacrifice Isaac, Jephthah telling his daughter that he must sacrifice her, John the Baptist's head being served on a platter at the request of a girl, Judas hanging himself, Exodus's killing of Egyptians' firstborn, and Jesus being crucified. One wonders if publishers and parents would find such stories appropriate for children had they not originally come from the Bible.

Obviously, there is not a big danger of readers duplicating the violent acts that are portrayed in the Bible. However, later chapters will discuss how some parents have physically abused and even killed their children based on their following parenting advice in the Bible. And there are isolated cases where parents, mostly those with mental illnesses, have harmed children just as they were described in the Bible. One particularly disturbing case has been linked to the Abraham and Isaac story.

On January 6, 1990, Cristos Valenti stabbed to death his youngest child, an infant, after he believed that God told him to sacrifice the child. Carol Delaney writes about the crime in her book *Abraham on Trial: The Social Legacy of Biblical Myth*. Delaney, an associate professor of cultural and social anthropology at Stanford University, sat in on Valenti's trial and notes that Valenti had been a loving father who was never violent or showed signs of long-term problems with mental illness. In the months that led up to the killing, however, Valenti had been drinking too much and hearing voices.[12] A jury convicted Valenti of first-degree murder but then found that he was insane on the day of the killing, and he was assigned to live in a mental hospital.[13]

Delaney concludes that the way Christians, Jews, and Muslims glorify the biblical story of Abraham and Isaac played a part in the murder. "This story, at the foundation of the three monotheistic religions, has shaped the social, cultural, and moral climates of the societies animated by them," writes Delaney.[14] According to the author, Abraham has become "the model of faith" at the foundation of those religions for "his willingness to obey God's command. . . . His story has been inscribed on the hearts and minds of billions of people for millennia. . . . With that cultural model readily available, it is not so surprising that Cristos Valenti felt he must obey God's command."[15] Delaney points out that Valenti did not believe he was insane. Rather, he saw himself as a devoted Catholic. "You don't say no to God," he told Delaney.[16]

We should not discount the Bible as a whole simply because some of its content is disturbing. Many passages hold timeless, compassionate words of wisdom. Some stories are thrilling, suspenseful, and downright entertaining. But the book deserves more in-depth scrutiny than it has been given. If more people of faith are willing to admit that certain biblical passages, such as those describing Abraham's near sacrifice of his son, are not worth glorifying and, instead, simply reflect a time when populations cared little about children's rights, we might have a better chance of leaving acts of religious child maltreatment where they belong: in the past.

Part 1
THE PAIN OF CHASTISEMENT
Religious Child Physical Abuse

INTRODUCTION

O n April 6, 2009, I interviewed a sixty-year-old man named Matt who talked about how his mother physically punished him when he was a boy:

> She would take me into the utility room, her domain, and pull this big belt off of the wall which she had hung in the closet. I think it was my uncle's Marine belt—one of those big wide leather belts with the big brass buckle on it—and she'd whale on me, on my bottom and the backs of my thighs. Every once in a while she would ask me to pull down my pants and do it on my bare skin. I do remember a couple of times that she was hitting me so hard and flailing so hard that she lost control of the belt, and the buckle hit me a couple of times and made these gashes in my skin. Generally, I'd start crying and yelling, and then she'd say "OK, go to your room." And I'd go to my room, and not only would I close the door to my room, but I'd go in my closet, and I'd close the door to my closet so I had double protection. And then I would cry, and I would say things like, "Nobody loves me," and "I hate my mom."

Matt's mother likely had a problem controlling her anger, yet there was another force at play: her religious beliefs. The woman was a devout Catholic and was petrified of the devil.

"I remember my mom saying something like, 'I'm going to have to beat the devil out of you,'" remembers Matt. "And that is certainly what we were taught in school, that there was a dark side and there was a light side. There were legions of angels led by Lucifer that had split away from the other ones."

75

I asked Matt if his mother really believed that her whippings could chase Satan from his body, to which he replied, "I believe that she did believe that. It wasn't just a metaphor for her. My mom was very much surrounded by this supernaturalism, so the devil was a large figure in the play of life."

Because Matt's mother's abuse was strongly linked to her religious beliefs, he was a victim of *religious child physical abuse.*

Matt is not alone. The religious aspect aside, most physical abuse is committed by mothers and fathers trying to "correct" the behavior of children, or, as one study puts it, to "teach them a lesson."[1]

"From the earliest days of research on the dynamics of child physical maltreatment, studies have revealed that most physical abuse incidents were the result of parents attempting to punish their children," writes University of Michigan at Ann Arbor professor Elizabeth T. Gershoff in a 2008 report on corporal punishment in America.[2] Gershoff is one of the country's leading researchers in the field of corporal punishment and an opponent of its practice.

Matt's case is common from another standpoint as well. One study shows that mothers who spank frequently or use an object to spank, such as a switch or paddle—or, in the case of Matt's mother, a belt—are much more likely to injure their children than mothers who do not spank with an object or who only occasionally spank.[3]

CHILD PHYSICAL ABUSE

Before addressing the religious component of this form of maltreatment, let's answer the question of what constitutes physical abuse. According to Child Welfare Information Gateway (CWIG), a governmental agency that disseminates information about child maltreatment based on states' child abuse laws, child physical abuse is a type of maltreatment that "refers to physical acts that caused or could have caused physical injury to a child. For example, bruising."[4] Abusive acts can include punching; beating; kicking; biting; shaking; throwing; stabbing; choking; hitting with a hand, stick, strap, or other object; or burning.[5]

Physically abusive acts are not accidental; however, they can happen without perpetrators meaning to cause harm, such as with spanking. As CWIG states, "The injury may have resulted from severe discipline, including injurious spanking, or physical punishment that is inappropriate to the child's age or condition. The injury may be the result of a single episode or of repeated episodes and can range in severity from minor marks and bruising to death."[6] Most states have determined that corporal punishment is not abusive as long as it is "reasonable and causes no bodily injury to the child."[7] (While controversial, this definition of abusive spanking is important to heed. Contrary to what many assume, corporal punishment does not have to be so severe as to cause serious injury to be considered physically abusive. If spanking leaves so much as a minor mark, it has gone too far.)

The number of children who are physically abused each year is disturbing. During 2009, more than 18 percent of children who suffered maltreatment—more than 123,000 children—were physically abused,[8] although experts warn that many cases do not get reported. What's more, physical abuse was the cause of nearly one-quarter of all child maltreatment deaths.[9] The physical harm due to such abuse is obvious. However, as was explained in chapter 1, in addition to the scratches, bruises, bleeding, welts, bone fractures, and internal injuries physical abuse causes, it also produces serious short- and long-term psychological effects.

THE CORPORAL PUNISHMENT CONTROVERSY

There remains a huge debate over whether corporal punishment is good or bad for children. It's safe to say that no other child-rearing issue ignites passions as does the subject of corporal punishment, or, as some call it, *physical punishment*, *physical discipline*, or *spanking*.

What is corporal or physical punishment? Simply put, it is the attempt to alter a person's behavior by inflicting pain upon the body or causing physical discomfort.* In addition to hitting with a hand or object, corporal punishment can also entail putting something unpleasant in the mouth, such as hot sauce or soap, or forcing a child to sit or stand in a painful position for a long period of time.[10] I add to the list the denial of food, as in the case of a child being sent to bed without supper.

The corporal punishment of children in the United States has been losing popularity over the years. A 2010 poll of parents shows that most parents prefer alternative disciplinary methods, such as explaining or reasoning with a child, taking away privileges, and using timeouts or grounding. Still, the survey also shows that one in five parents believe they would spank in some scenarios.[11] Unlike many countries that have outlawed corporal punishment in schools, approximately twenty American states still permit kids in public school to receive "swats."[12] As noted earlier, most of those states lie in an area known as the Bible Belt. In fact, during the 2002–2003 school year, 70 percent of the more than 300,000 American schoolchildren who were physically punished were in the southern United States.[13]

Spanking proponents say it provides parents a quick and effective way to improve children's behavior. They attest that there is a big difference between properly administered corporal punishment and that which is excessive, and if spanking is done right, children are not physically or psychologically harmed. One University of California at Berkeley study finds that occasional spanking does not damage a child's social or emotional development.[14] Proponents of corporal punishment state that precautions can be taken so that parents do not spank abusively. For example, one way is to have a "cooling down" period after a child misbehaves so that hitting is not done out of anger. Some believe children are unlikely to be emotionally harmed by spanking if the practice is widely accepted within their culture.[15]

Opponents, on the other hand, disagree with the federal government's conclusion that there is ever a "reasonable" use of physical discipline. They believe that spanking is often demeaning and dangerous, and they point out that America is among a minority of Western countries supporting the practice. In fact, at least one hundred countries have prohibited corporal punishment in schools, and more than two dozen countries have banned it in the home.[16] Empirical data has consistently shown that children who are physically punished are at greater risk for injury and physical abuse.[17]

Contrary to what many proponents say, spanking has not been shown to be very effective at improving children's behavior. According to studies, spanking produces only limited short-term effectiveness. In fact, research shows that children who are spanked tend to grow defiant and aggressive.[18] Spanked children tend to suffer mental health problems,[19] and there is concern that corporal punishment interferes with parent-child relationships.[20] In addition, children who are spanked are more likely to have sexual problems as teens or adults[21] and lower intelligence levels than those who are not spanked.[22] Spanking opponents remark that there is a greater negative societal effect to take into account as well, that spanking sends a message that problems should be solved through violence.[23]

In full disclosure, I would never physically punish my child. Philosophically speaking, I do not believe that I, even as a parent, have the right to inflict pain on anyone, young or old, except in self-defense. I have yet to speak to an individual who was spanked in childhood who, during the treatment, did not find it demeaning and humiliating. In *For Your Own Good: Hidden Cruelty in Child-Rearing and the Roots of Violence*, Alice Miller writes that corporal punishment is "*always* degrading, because the child not only is unable to defend him- or herself but is also supposed to show gratitude and respect to the parents in return."[24]

But regardless of which side of the fence one is on in regard to the corporal punishment debate, no one questions that such treatment can get out of hand. This section examines how various religious beliefs contribute to corporal punishment, including that which injures, and even kills, children. It also reveals how the pious who have abused children—including cases in which victims have died—justify their actions with religious texts or doctrine. A good place to start is with the Bible.

Chapter 5
"THE ROD OF CORRECTION"

I f you ask a conservative Christian whether the Bible condones the spanking of children, he or she will undoubtedly tell you that it does.

"Parents are urged by the Bible to spank their offspring when they misbehave," writes the website Conservapedia, the conservative Christian answer to Wikipedia.[1] In *Spanking: A Loving Discipline: Helpful and Practical Answers for Today's Parents*, minister and Bible teacher Roy Lessin opines that spanking is an essential part of child rearing because "God instructs parents to do so in His Word."[2] James G. Dwyer, assistant professor of law at the College of William and Mary, writes in *Religious Schools v. Children's Rights* that fundamentalist Christian educators "claim biblical authority" in uniformly supporting corporal punishment.[3]

Comments like these lead many to conclude that scripture is highly influential in getting parents to physically punish their kids. "The most enduring and influential source for the widespread practice of physical punishment, both in this country and abroad, has been the Bible," writes Rutgers professor emeritus Philip Greven in *Spare the Child: The Religious Roots of Punishment and the Psychological Impact of Physical Abuse*.[4]

Just what does the Bible say about physical punishment? Plenty, especially if you turn to the book of Proverbs in the Old Testament, in which a number of passages refer to something called *the rod*:

10:13: "Wisdom is found on the lips of him who has understanding,
But a rod is for the back of him who is devoid of understanding."

13:24: "He that spares his rod hates his son,
But he who loves him disciplines him promptly."

22:15: "Foolishness is bound up in the heart of a child;
The rod of correction will drive it far from him."

23:13–14: "Do not withhold correction from a child,
For if you beat him with a rod, he will not die.
You shall beat him with the rod,
And deliver his soul from hell."

Just what is *the rod*? The term is well known in both religious and secular communities. Many assume the common expression "Spare the rod and spoil the child" comes from the Bible.

But the fact is, there is great debate—and some might say misunderstanding—over what *the rod* actually means. First of all, "Spare the rod and spoil the child" does not appear in the Bible, but rather, comes from a 1662 satirical polemic about the English Civil War by Samuel Butler called *Hudibras*. (The reference has nothing to do with the physical punishment of children.)

Many disagree that *the rod* in the Bible means corporal punishment. The Hebrew word for *the rod* is *shebet,* which can mean many things, such as a shepherd's crook, a scepter, or a tribe of people. In fact, in some instances, the Bible's use of *the rod* is clearly meant to symbolize guidance and care. Take, for example, Psalm 23:4, "Your rod and Your staff, they comfort me." And Ezekiel 20:37, "I will cause you to pass under the rod." In both usages, *rod* is an analogy for a shepherd's crook, not a device to cause the disobedient pain.

Rabbi Larry Kaplan of Temple Israel in Pennsylvania says Proverbs is about properly educating children and that *the rod* is meant "to point out right from wrong, not to beat our children into submission." Kaplan adds that the Talmud, the central religious text of mainstream Judaism, says that if an adult must strike a child, "do so only with a shoelace."[5] Samuel Martin, who has written an online book about the meaning of *the rod*, notes that traditional Jewish family law did allow corporal punishment but "only under the strictest of circumstances."[6] Martin adds that *the rod* is to be understood "in a broad sense. It includes many things, such as a frown and pretended disappointment."[7]

Yet the meaning of *the rod* is subjective and often depends on whether the interpreter is for or against corporal punishment. Conservative Christians, often state that *the rod* means corporal punishment, pure and simple, and link it not with guidance but with authority.

"The Bible teaches that physical discipline is appropriate, beneficial, and necessary," says the conservative Christian website GotQuestions.org. Citing

Proverbs 23:13–14, the site continues, "Don't fail to correct your children. They won't die if you spank them."[8] In *What the Bible Says about . . . Child Training*, J. Richard Fugate stresses to parents that they "chastise" their children using physical punishment. "God's Word says to use a rod. God has specifically established the rod as the symbol of human authority," Fugate writes.[9]

The Watchtower Bible and Tract Society (WTS), the legal organization that oversees Jehovah's Witnesses, has stated that *the rod* of the Bible often is used symbolically to represent authority.[10] Furthermore, its parenting literature frequently cites Proverbs and other biblical passages in giving the green light to parents to use corporal punishment. A parenting book sold on the Watchtower Society's website notes that, for children who do not obey when spoken to, "the occasional punishment administered for disobedience may be lifesaving."[11]

Lisa Whelchel, a born-again Christian known for her role as Blair on the 1980s television show *The Facts of Life*, is now a mother and author of Christian-based parenting literature. In her book *Creative Correction: Extraordinary Ideas for Everyday Discipline*, Whelchel defends spanking by asserting, "God's Word frequently addresses the subject of raising children. Corporal punishment is no exception," and she provides a "rod" passage as proof. Whelchel adds that she quotes Proverbs to her children in justifying to them why she must spank them.[12]

Some religious conservatives even see *the rod* as a literal device for whipping children. For example, in *What the Bible Says about . . . Child Training*, Fugate defines *the rod* as both a symbol of human authority and as "a narrow flexible stick used on a rebellious child by his parents."[13] In *Spanking: A Loving Discipline*, Roy Lessin defines a rod as a "flexible twig or stick," and he tells parents that "God has instructed parents to use a 'rod' not the hand when they need to lovingly correct their children with a spanking."[14]

A number of companies sell spanking instruments, claiming they are Bible-approved rods. Some quote "rod" passages from Proverbs to encourage buyers. In marketing its rod, a company in Bakersfield, California, stated in a flyer, "Fulfilling the purpose and function of the biblical rod, yet designed with today's parents in mind, our chastening instrument is perfectly suited for the loving correction of your children."[15]

SOMETIMES IT IS ABOUT CORPORAL PUNISHMENT

Some of these literal interpretations might border on the ridiculous, but there is no denying that at least some mentions of *the rod* in Proverbs or other parts of the Bible, do, in fact, mean corporal punishment. Take, for example, 2 Samuel 7:14, which states, "I will be his Father, and he shall be My son. If he commits iniquity, I will chasten him with the rod of men and with the blows of the sons of men."

In ancient times, Jews commonly practiced a punishment for adults known as "beating with rods," which is mentioned in 2 Corinthians 11. According to *Unger's Bible Dictionary*, a person who was to undergo such punishment "was extended upon the ground, and blows, not exceeding forty, were applied to his back in the presence of a judge."[16]

"A preponderance of biblical proverbs clearly imply that the rod was used for beating,"[17] writes Randall J. Heskett in *Interpretation* magazine.

Consider the likely author of Proverbs. Many believe that many of the book's passages were written by, or at least in honor of, King Solomon, the son of David and the third ruler of Israel.[18] This attribution is made clear in Proverbs 1:1, which mentions "the proverbs of Solomon." Many people of faith favorably look upon Solomon. The Qur'an describes him as a prophet, while many Christians view him as a wise and powerful ruler. But just what kind of a father might Solomon have been? Since the Bible does not speak of his personal life, we don't have much to go on, but some suspect he was quite the authoritarian father, based on how he ruled his people.[19] 1 Kings 12:14 notes that Solomon taxed his people heavily and physically punished them. Interestingly, this last point is made by Solomon's son, Rehoboam, who proclaims that he will emulate his father's harsh governing style: "My father made your yoke heavy, and I will add to your yoke: my father also chastised you with whips, but I will chastise you with scorpions."

Frankly, I don't think Solomon liked children very much. What kind of a lover of children would suggest, as Solomon does in 1 Kings 3:16–28, to cut a baby in half to settle a dispute, even if he never intended to go through with the act? Mark Twain was also not a fan of the ruler. In *The Adventures of Huckleberry Finn*, Jim objects to Huck calling Solomon wise in threatening to sever the infant. "De man dat think he kin settle a 'spute 'bout a whole chile wid a half a chile doan' know enough to come in out'n de rain," says Jim.[20]

Yet even if *the rod* in Proverbs does mean corporal punishment, that's no reason to follow such a dictum, say child advocates. Rabbi Joshua Waxman writes on *Beliefnet*, "Just because Jewish law permits certain forms of corporal punishment doesn't mean that they're right."[21]

Many Christians urge parents to pay more attention to what is said about children in the New Testament than in Proverbs. Spanking opponents, like Philip Greven, are confounded why so many Christians insist on physically disciplining their children since Jesus never laid a hand on youngsters. As Greven states in *Spare the Child*,

When a Christian parent tells a child who is about to be punished that "Jesus teaches that you must receive the rod," he cannot justify this with any text from the Gospels. Jesus never advocated such punishment. Nowhere in the New Testament does Jesus approve of the infliction of pain upon children by the rod or any other such implement, nor is he ever reported to have recommended any kind of physical discipline of children to any parent.[22]

THE ROD AND PHYSICAL ABUSE

Critics worry that adults adhering to "rod" passages in the Bible or others that condone physical punishment will motivate adults to not only spank, but spank too harshly.[23] Kibbie Ruth writes in her chapter in *Child Maltreatment*, "'Spare the rod, spoil the child' is often used to rationalize excessive physical discipline of children."[24] In *The Sins of Scripture*, John Shelby Spong states that Proverbs passages "suggesting that physical discipline of children is appropriate have played a major role in the history of child rearing and, I would argue, in the history of child abuse."[25]

One real-life example of alleged rod-related abuse sprang up in the news in March 2011. The pastor and seven members of the Aleitheia Bible Church in a small town in Wisconsin were charged with using wooden rods to spank a dozen infants and children for being "emotional, [being] grumpy, or cying," according to authorities. All church members pleaded innocent. The sheriff's office said that the pastor "expressed his belief that the Bible dictates the use of a rod over a hand to punish children. He stated that children only a few months old are 'worthy' of the rod and that by 'one and half months,' a child is old enough to be spanked." According to the sheriff's office's report, children were hit with twelve- to eighteen-inch-long rods whose diameters measured about the size of a quarter. Parents told detectives that "redness and bruisings" commonly resulted from the spankings.[26]

But we can attribute to scripture only so much blame for the promotion of corporal punishment. Religious ideologies and doctrines are even more powerful motivators.

Chapter 6
AN OBSESSION WITH CHILD OBEDIENCE

On December 6, 2009, forty-one-year-old Jennifer Gordon told me that her life greatly changed when she was about eleven years old. That was when her parents became born-again Christians and joined a charismatic, nondenominational, fundamentalist church in their Oklahoma town. Prior to their conversion, Gordon says they were permissive. They didn't spank her, and at times were even negligent, leaving her unsupervised for hours.

But once they got "saved," Gordon says, "all the rules in our household changed. They cut off the phone line. They burned the rock-and-roll records. Any books in the house, if they were secular, they did these kind of demonic purges to them." Gordon says she went from being "completely invisible, getting away with murder" to her parents "watching my every move, searching all my belongings, taking away all my stuff. It was intense."

Gordon says she was not a bad kid, yet she seemed to keep getting into trouble. To correct her behavior, Gordon's parents, believing that demons were the cause, conducted exorcisms on her. They also used corporal punishment. Gordon describes one beating which involved "making me strip from the waist down while my dad chased me around the room and beat me with a belt while my mom watched."

To be sure, it's important to set limits for children. Setting appropriate, consistent limits on children's behavior helps reduce the chances that young people will be delinquent, abuse drugs, and be aggressive, according to Craig H. Hart, chair of the Marriage, Family, and Human Development Program in the School of Family Life of Brigham Young University. Hart says children who are given this guidance, compared to those who are not, "are better at thinking through the consequences of actions and are more willing to abide by laws. They also tend to be more capable of moral reasoning and are more self-controlled."[1]

But sometimes adults set too many limits on children. Some mothers and fathers adopt an authoritarian style of parenting, placing high demands on sons and daughters while offering little emotional support. Experts believe that authoritarian parenting, which often includes corporal punishment, is largely ineffective and potentially harmful. "While coercion often leads to immediate conformance by the child, research indicates it rarely results in a long-term solution and often leads to the child's being more defiant, depressed, aggressive or withdrawn, and manipulative in the home and with peers," writes Hart. Instead, he and other experts advocate for an *authoritative* stance, a parenting style that is marked by both firmness and compassion. Hart describes authoritative parenting as "consistently connecting with children in a loving way, setting reasonable limits, and allowing children an appropriate measure of autonomy."[2]

Psychologist Benzion Sorotzkin rejects authoritarianism in the home. As he writes on his website, "By and large, parents who act responsibly—by being sensitive and responsive to their children's emotional needs—will not suffer from rebellious children."[3]

Parents' strictness is influenced by cultural factors, but authoritarian parenting also has theological roots. For example, the Bible is clear on the importance of child obedience. "Honor your father and your mother, that your days may be long upon the land which the LORD your God is giving you," read Exodus 20:12 and Deuteronomy 5:16, arguably the most repeated of the Ten Commandments. Ephesians 6:1 reads, "Children, obey your parents in the Lord, for this is right." And Colossians 3:20 goes so far as to say, "Children, obey your parents in all things, for this is well pleasing to the Lord." This passage is closely followed by similar instruction given to bond servants who also must obey their masters "in all things," giving credence to the idea that in biblical times, children were considered to be, like bond servants, property.

In addition, scriptural stories promote child obedience by depicting sons and daughters as astonishingly compliant. For instance, as has been discussed, Isaac fails to cry out in protest even as he realizes his father plans to sacrifice him to God. In another tale of sacrifice, Jephthah's daughter expresses not a shred of anger or bitterness upon learning that her father has promised God that she must be sacrificed. In fact, she fully accepts the news and only asks that she head to the countryside to "bewail my virginity" to friends.

Many faiths emphasize the need for children to obey their parents. Speaking about Christianity, Robin Grille writes in *Parenting for a Peaceful World* that, up until the late eighteenth century, Christian pedagogy about child rearing was about one thing: obedience. "Obedience was the be-all and end-all—parenting relations were based on authority and control, rather than affection," states Grille. "Few violent means were spared in extracting obedience from the 'little devils.'"[4]

A 1732 letter written by Susanna Wesley, the mother of John and Charles Wesley, who founded Methodism in England, shows how this ideology is put into practice. The woman clearly wasted no time in establishing authoritarian rule in the home. For instance, when John and Charles were no more than one year old, she writes, "They were taught to fear the rod and to cry softly, by which means they escaped abundance of correction which they might otherwise have had: and that most odious noise of the crying of children was rarely heard in the house." Wesley adds, "No sinful action, as lying, pilfering at church or on the Lord's Day, disobedience, quarrelling, etc. should ever pass unpunished."[5]

JUMPING ON THE BANDWAGON

Many adults like the idea of controlling children, and that includes adults of faith. Therefore, it is no surprise that they seize on biblical passages and religious ideologies that demand that children honor and obey their parents "in all things."

"The Bible states that obedience must be complete. . . . Children are not to obey their parents only when and if they feel like it. God wants them to respond to their parents' authority and to learn to obey them in every area," writes Roy Lessin in *Spanking: A Loving Discipline*.[6]

Along the same vein, *The Secret of Family Happiness*, a book published by the Watchtower and Tract Society, tells Jehovah's Witness parents that children need discipline "constantly."[7] Also, an article in the Witness magazine *Awake!* states that "permissiveness is hateful."[8]

Meanwhile, others also state that parents should rule their homes with a commanding presence. "God has established the institution of the parent as one of His ruling authorities on earth," writes J. Richard Fugate in *What the Bible Says about . . . Child Training*. "To this position has been delegated both the right to rule children and all the power necessary to succeed in training children according to God's plan."[9] To drive this point home, he quotes Deuteronomy 21:18–21, which states that parents of a rebellious and drunken son should have him publicly stoned to death. "As you can see," Fugate writes, "God is very serious about children being obedient."[10]

Kelly, who was introduced earlier as having been abused by her Jehovah's Witness stepfather, remembers how leaders in her church community often harped on child obedience when she was growing up. As she explained in our interview, "When we heard talks about child raising, it was always that children were subservient to the parents. It was always that children must be obedient to their parents. That was required to be loyal to Jehovah." Kelly says parents were instructed to be loving to their children and not to abuse them. However, if parents were abusive, children were expected to obey their parents anyway. "Even if you are in a difficult situation, you must show proper respect to your parents because they gave you life," says Kelly.

Certain controversial religious groups have been criticized for their use of corporal punishment. An example is Twelve Tribes, which is based in the northeastern United States. The group, which has been investigated for physically abusing children in years past,[11] is up-front about its favored use of corporal punishment to make children obedient. On its website, Twelve Tribes denies that it abuses children but makes clear, "When children are disobedient or intentionally hurtful to others we spank them with a small reedlike rod, which only inflicts pain and not damage. . . . We know that some people consider this aspect of our life controversial, but we have seen from experience that discipline keeps a child from becoming mean-spirited and disrespectful of authority."[12]

Some religious leaders use the pulpit to emphasize the need for unquestioning child obedience. One who has become a lightning rod for such teachings is fundamentalist Christian minister Gwen Shamblin of the Tennessee-based Remnant Fellowship. According to its website, the church webcasts services to members in more than one hundred cities worldwide.[13] In an audiotaped presentation for parents on child discipline (a copy of which was e-mailed to the author by a source who asked not to be identified), Shamblin stresses that children, when commanded, must learn to obey "on the first time." In summarizing her child disciplinary teachings for the media, Shamblin said, "I would have to snap my finger and they would want to obey."[14]

Shamblin seems to be succeeding with her teachings. As she proudly notes on the recorded presentation, children sit through church services that are two and a half hours long "with a great attitude." She explains how she has taught young children sitting in the pews how to draw and turn pages in a journal so that "there is no sound coming out of that child. . . . They sit there and are happy to do it."

In 2001, one fundamentalist Christian group called the Church of God in Ontario, Canada, was investigated for its child "disciplinary" practices. Due to allegations of physical abuse, authorities removed children from the custody of members and placed them in foster care. The church's pastor, Rev.

Henry Hildebrandt, defended the group's beliefs and expressed his alarm that parents' losing the right to use corporal punishment on their children was akin to "giving our children up to becoming wayward." In speaking to the media, the pastor stated, "It takes more than a slap on the butt to obey. There has to be pain. There will be pain."[15]

SPANKING TOO MUCH AND TOO HARD

Children who are raised by pious parents obsessed with child obedience not only are likely to be physically punished but also are at risk for being spanked too much. I have heard many stories from people who said they were regularly beaten, and for the most minor infractions. An example is thirty-six-year-old Alex Byrd, who grew up in a fundamentalist Pentecostal household in the southeast part of the country. As Byrd told me on November 23, 2009, he was spanked just about any time he was seen as being "bad."

"And by 'bad,'" says Byrd, "I mean pretty much anything from laughing at specific words during mandatory family Bible reading to wrestling with my sister in a way that the parents did not approve of to not going to bed at a specific time or going outside of the yard or talking to people my mom did not want me talking with." These tough standards meant Alex was sometimes spanked four or five times a day. "I would be made to pull a switch off of a tree, be whipped with it, basically be told in some cases that I had sinned against God because I had disobeyed my parents, and would pretty much be made to pray and essentially repent to God."

According to Irwin A. Hyman, author of *Reading, Writing, and the Hickory Stick: The Appalling Story of Physical and Psychological Abuse in American Schools,* Catholic schools have a long history of using physical punishment for just about every perceived act of defiance on the part of students. Speaking about disciplinary methods that were widespread decades ago, Hyman notes, "No restraint was considered prudent in the vigorous application of the yardstick on open hands, across knuckles, and to derrieres in an effort to save the souls of errant youth." Hyman says that viewpoint has since softened—most dioceses forbid the use of corporal punishment today—yet "children in conservative Christian schools are still at risk."[16]

Jason Wilkinson remembers that kind of treatment when he was in school. On July 22, 2008, the thirty-one-year-old explained how he attended a small Christian school in central Texas, where administrators used corporal punishment "every chance they could."

> It was very liberally used for the most minuscule things. If kids talked too much in class or talked back to the teacher, they were sent to the principal for corporal punishment. I remember getting "swats," as they called it, if they were referring to middle school, or "spankings" if they were referring to a younger child. I even heard of some high schoolers getting hit with a paddle. . . . There were times where I heard about where the principal had hit other kids so hard he broke it and had to go buy new ones. There were times I was hit only once. There were times I was hit maybe fifteen, twenty times. Sometimes the principal would insist on dropping pants.

Orthodox Jewish schools, too, have been criticized for their excessive use of corporal punishment. The blog *Seraphic Secret* includes a slew of posts by former students of yeshivas who describe how their former teachers and administrators were quick to use abusive corporal punishment. A number of posts point to one notorious principal, a man named Joel Braverman, after whom the Yeshivah of Flatbush Joel Braverman High School is named. The blog proprietor writes of one incident in which a teacher reported to Braverman that she was "very disappointed" in the boy's school performance. After that, the principal took the student out in the hall, and, without asking questions, "grabbed me by the ears, twisted hard, then slammed my head against the wall. My skull actually bounced and made a hollow cracking sound."[17]

Twenty-year-old James Chatham says corporal punishment was common in the Remnant Fellowship Church, which he attended with his mother when he was a boy. As he explained on December 12, 2009, many children were not "happy" to sit through long church services, as Gwen Shamblin claimed in her presentation to parents. In fact, Chatham says it was "completely absurd" to expect children to sit quietly through church services that could last as long as three hours. Furthermore, children who got restless, shifted too much, made too much noise, or "did anything except sat there and stared" were punished. "It was hell, and most of the kids hated it," says Chatham. "It was not what church was meant to be."

Like Jennifer Gordon's parents, who intensified their disciplinary practices when they became born again, William Coburn's mother dramatically changed her parenting style when she became a Jehovah's Witness. In his memoir, *The Spanking Room*, Coburn describes how his family went from being "the archetypal middle-class American family. Textbook. Norman Rockwell," to a life filled with "emotional, mental, and physical suffering."[18] According to Coburn, church literature and the kingdom hall his mother attended frequently promoted the corporal punishment of children, which his mother called "blessings from Jehovah."[19] He remembers receiving his first "blessing" when he was four and his family was in church. As Coburn tells it, his mother was passed a microphone so she could ask an elder a question, at which time little William uttered the words, "Bye, microphone." He continues:

> My voice came back softly through the loudspeakers sounding so BIG. Neat-o. . . . There was a collective gasp as the entire congregation reacted to my apparently shocking and wicked behavior. The next thing I knew I was airborne—Mom yanked me straight out of my seat by my hair. It hurt. A lot. I grabbed her wrist with both hands, trying to keep my hair from being torn out by the roots and stop the pain, but she held tight and dragged me all the way to the women's bathroom. . . . Once we were in the women's room, my mom proceeded to beat the devil out of me for committing such a heinous crime. She made certain I understood that I had not only embarrassed her, but I had shown disrespect to Jehovah-God. I was a *terrible* child—an "awful, rotten child," to use her favorite catchphrase. She punctuated each and every word of her litany with a blow to make darn sure I understood. . . . When my tears had all run out, we returned to the hall where my brother Joe stared at us as if his eyes were going to bug out of his head. . . . The other adults, meanwhile, looked on with obvious approval. Later some of them yelled at me too, for disrupting their meeting—all because of the innocent mistake of saying good-bye to the microphone.[20]

Religious environments in which the pious are obsessed with child obedience constitute an unfair world for children. Not only are they spanked for behaving in ways that are normal for their age, they are often presumed to be guilty once accused of wrongdoing. Take for example, what occurred in Texas, where a pastor was found guilty of battery in March 2009 after he administered weekly beatings of a twelve-year-old girl.[21] According to the girl's court testimony, Rev. Daryl Bujak based the number of blows on reports given by the girl's mother as to how the girl had been behaving. Fifteen blows was "a good week," the girl testified. She also said that the beatings left welts on her backside. What initiated the beatings was the daughter handing her mother a note describing sexual abuse by a man. The mother took the girl to Bujak for "counseling" because she believed her daughter was lying.[22]

Earlier, we were introduced to a formerly Amish man named David Yoder. Yoder remembers an incident that took place when he was eleven. Some forty years later, he still has trouble telling what happened. Yoder says that he and a friend got into a minor squabble at school after which a teacher sent a note home with each boy, saying they had been fighting. Yoder remembers his friend and his friend's father coming to Yoder's house just before dinnertime that night. After some discussion, the two fathers decided they would punish the boys in concert.

"I was immediately taken away from the supper table and out to the wash-house, where I met the other father and the boy," remembers Yoder. At that point, the men began whipping the boys with straps and continued for such a long time, they got tired and had to stop. After a break, the men changed places and each whipped the other's son. After growing exhausted once more, the men again paused and then changed places "to give each of us one more whipping." Yoder says he does not know how long it went on: "It seemed like forever."

Once it was over, Yoder could barely stand. As he made his way back to the house, he saw his friend, barely able to climb into the family's buggy. It is an image that haunts Yoder to this day. Meanwhile, Yoder was ordered to return to the dinner table.

> I couldn't see straight. I had a hard time walking to the table, but I got there. When I got there I had a tougher time to sit down. I was told to eat. I'm telling you I don't know how I managed to get that first bite. My mouth wouldn't hold still. I was told, if I didn't eat now I would be taken back out and he [his father] would finish what he started. So with that I prayed to the only person I knew and that was God. I said, "You've got to help me, Lord, because I can't take no more." And somehow I got it down. I was still shivering when I went to bed. I don't know how I made it.

THE FEAR FACTOR

When people talk about the dangers of corporal punishment, they frequently focus on the physical harm. But, as any recipient of the treatment will say, the emotional toll is often the most detrimental. That's because fear usually accompanies physical punishment, intentionally or unintentionally. The late evangelist Billy Graham knew such fear. In his autobiography, *Just as I Am*, Graham explains how his fervently religious parents were very strict with their children and "never hesitated when necessary to administer physical discipline to us." Graham adds, "I learned to obey without questioning."[23]

In the introduction to his book *Spare the Child*, Philip Greven, who grew up in a Protestant Christian household, describes a personal incident that occurred when he was eight years old. The boy had been outside playing when he got a water hose hopelessly stuck in the sand. His mother told him that he should wait for his father to come home to deal with what apparently seemed to be naughty behavior. "I waited, seemingly forever—time can be an eternity to an eight-year-old expecting punishment," writes Greven. He then goes on to explain that his father came home, freed the hose, and spanked Greven.

Many years later, my father reminded me of that incident, acknowledging how angry he had been at the time and recollecting that he had given me one of the hardest spankings of my life. When a man who weighs over two hundred pounds, stands six feet, and has huge hands spanks a small boy hard, it surely must hurt. Yet to this day, I have no conscious memory of the actual pain that he inflicted and I felt. I only can remember the events that led up to the punishment itself.[24]

Pro–corporal punishment religious authorities sometimes state that fear is a necessary component in correcting a child's behavior. It is a point made clear by Lutheran minister Larry Christenson in *The Christian Family*: "If the punishment is of the right kind, it not only takes effect physically but through physical terror and pain. It awakens and sharpens the consciousness that there is a moral power over us, a righteous judge, and a law which cannot be broken."[25]

The fear of corporal punishment hangs over children who live under authoritarian rule in many pious homes and places of worship. On December 31, 2009, forty-one-year-old Bethany Fenimore told me how terrifying it was to try to sit through long, tedious sermons in her family's fundamentalist Christian church in southern California as a young child, because she knew that moving too much would warrant a spanking:

I would sit there and my butt would get so numb, and I would think, "Well, if I move a little bit, I wonder if that's too much?" and I would be daydreaming and starting to fall asleep, and I would be scared when I'd wake myself up 'cause that might have been an offense. I remember once when my mother had just had it with us. Why couldn't we sit still in church? And she took us into my brother's bedroom and she had each of us take turns. We were completely naked from the waist down, and she had us take turns holding onto the dresser while she whipped us.

Remnant Fellowship pastor Gwen Shamblin, too, believes in instilling fear in disobedient children. On an audio recording obtained by a television news station, Shamblin tells her followers that, when it comes to disciplining children, "If they're not scared of a spanking, you haven't spanked them. If you haven't really spanked them, you don't love them. You love yourself."[26] In the audiotaped presentation on child discipline, Shamblin directly addresses children and threatens the disobedient with eternal damnation:

Children, you've all got to learn that God is the one you answer to, but the way that you show God that you are answering to Him is through obeying your mother and your father for the first time, and if you obey the second and the third time or if you are slow to obey, you are being your own god, and nobody playing around like that can ever go to heaven. You will only live a few years on Earth and then you will have a horrible afterlife, and the people that obey God and obey their parents are going to live forever.

A DEADLY DICTUM

There are times when adults' attempts to control children's behavior through corporal punishment result in death, and sometimes religious belief plays a part. An example is one of the worst cases of child abuse ever investigated by the Chicago Police Department. On November 11, 2001, Larry Slack, a devout Jehovah's Witness, whipped his twelve-year-old daughter, Laree, to death with electrical cords. Slack engaged the help of his wife and also Laree's siblings. When questioned by police, Slack and his wife said Laree had been "uncooperative" in finding a credit card as instructed, so the couple decided to mete out the biblical punishment of "forty lashes minus one, three times."[27] The Slacks were said to be very religious and strict with their six children. All children showed indications of having been physically abused. At the Slacks' trial, Laree's older brother testified that his father routinely beat him and his siblings with electrical cords, both on their backs and on their chests. The boy described the force of the beatings as "hammering a nail into wood."[28]

I stated in the first chapter that one case that helped motivate me to write this book involved the death of a toddler in Baltimore. In that case, too, adults' obsession with child obedience led to deadly corporal punishment. The public learned about it in 2008, when police found the decomposed body of Javon Thompson hidden in a suitcase. It was later revealed that the child had been starved to death by a small religious group in Baltimore called One Mind Ministries, led by a woman who went by the name of Queen Antoinette. According to court testimony, the woman ordered the group, which included the child's mother, not to give Javon food or water, since he did not say "amen" at mealtimes. Queen Antoinette reportedly called for the punishment to cure what she called Javon's "spirit of rebellion."[29]

An obsession with child obedience also creeps into Muslim communities, sometimes with deadly consequences. On October 9, 2010, I spoke with Salma Abugideiri, psychotherapist and codirector of the Peaceful Families Project, which helps Muslim communities overcome problems of domestic violence. Abugideiri says Muslim immigrants come from countries that adhere to strict theological and cultural codes about female purity and honoring the family, and they bring those beliefs with them. So, for example, if a teenage girl has acted out sexually or taken up with a boyfriend—especially a non-Muslim boyfriend—the family might see to it that she pays a steep penalty. "Their range of punitive action could be anything from restricting her from going out to beating her, and, unfortunately, in some cases, you hear about the honor killings," says Abugideiri.

Honor killings are murderous acts against someone who has brought disgrace upon a Muslim family. While honor killing is largely believed to be a cultural practice—it does not appear in the Qur'an—some Muslims believe it is religiously mandated.[30] Often, the victims are teenage girls and women whose "crimes" can include not keeping one's head covered, talking to a man who is not one's husband, having an affair, and even being raped. Commonly, perpetrators of honor killings are male relatives of the victim. Abugideiri says that, while honor killings in this country are rare, they are still cause for concern. She remembers counseling an Arab man who had become incensed that his daughter had been acting out sexually: "He said, 'If I were back home, I would've killed her or had her killed.'" Fortunately, and surprisingly, the man ended up being very cooperative in treatment and reestablishing a good relationship with his daughter, says Abugideiri.

But things did not turn out that way for Sarah and Amina Said of Dallas. On January 1, 2008, the two teenagers—Sarah was seventeen and Amina was eighteen—were found shot dead in their father's car. As of October 2010, the victims' father, Yaser Abdel Said, remained a fugitive. Friends of the victims told the media that the Muslim Egyptian immigrant was very strict with his daughters and critical of popular American lifestyles, and that Said tried to control the girls, dictating what they wore and with whom they socialized.[31] The victims' great-aunt told the media that Said had been abusing his daughters for two years and ended their lives as honor killings. The woman said the father had felt that Sarah and Amina brought shame upon their family by dating non-Muslim boys and acting Western.[32]

While it's difficult to understand how an adult could abuse a child, it is inconceivable how such a perpetrator could justify abusive acts, particularly in cases where children have been killed. However, those who buy into the idea that child obedience is religiously condoned or mandated tend to do just that. What's more, they commonly attract supporters.

In *Abraham on Trial*, Carol Delaney writes about her work in the 1980s counseling people accused of child abuse. "The most noticeable characteristic of my clients' stories was the stress they placed on the *obedience* of children and the religious justifications for it," she explains. "To my clients, punishment was justified because the parents felt that obedience was their due. Citing sermons from their preachers or the Bible, these people expected that children should be brought up to obey their parents and that they, as parents, could demand obedience. They were acting in place of God and they construed their actions as in the best interests of the child."[33]

This same self-righteousness was evident in a 2003 criminal trial in Kansas City, Kansas, that involved the death of a child and the severe abuse of three other children. As the trial was under way, two dozen members of the God's Creation Outreach Ministry showed up to support the accused, who included the church's leaders, Neil and Christy Edgar, and a handful of other church members.[34]

"The Bible teaches us to bring up our children," said one supporter. "We are to teach children the principles and the standards of righteousness." Another member added, "We don't believe in the abuse of not only children, but anyone." Supporters apparently were not swayed by prosecutors' allegations that the children in question had been frequent victims of abuse that involved being bound and gagged before bedtime. Nor did churchgoers seem concerned that, in examining the dead boy's body, a coroner said that there were signs he had been bound around the chest, had something like a sock stuffed in his mouth, and had his mouth taped shut.[35]

Later, trial testimony would reveal that the children had been hogtied with extension cords, belts, and plastic ties and had had duct tape placed over their mouths, punishment for disrespecting adults and not paying attention in church.[36] It was clear that the Edgar children had been well indoctrinated in a belief system that emphasized obedience. During court proceedings, their twelve-year-old daughter testified, "We were really, really bad," and recited some Bible verses. "To learn, you must love discipline," she added.[37]

NO COMFORT FOR ABUSE VICTIMS

Beliefs about unquestioned child obedience also get in the way of helping abuse victims. Salma Abugideiri of the Peaceful Families Project says the idea of honoring one's parents is important in Islam, and sometimes it can work against abuse victims. If a child in a Muslim community tells someone that a parent has been mistreating him or her, says Abugideiri, that child might get help from that person—for example, the child might be allowed to live with another relative. However, she notes, the child could also be told, "These are your parents. You have to obey your parents, no matter what."

Domestic violence expert Kathryn Goering Reid, who used to train clergy on child sexual abuse prevention, says that religious leaders she encountered were all in agreement that it is wrong to sexually abuse children and that steps should be taken to prevent it. But, she says, her audience was far less willing to go along with the idea that children should be taught to say no to their abusers. "When you start to teach the child that they have a right to say 'no,' that they have a right to question authority, that became the sticking point in the curriculum," says Reid.

Critics call attention to the fact that the Bible's insistence on honoring parents provides no loophole for children of abusive mothers and fathers. A friend of mine, Kevin Archer, grew up in the Church of Christ and was a victim of abuse at the hands of his parents. Eventually, Archer and his entire family abandoned the faith, and his parents grew to regret having followed their church's strict disciplinary guidelines. Archer believes that the Bible's dictum for sons and daughters is unjust. "Children are told to obey their parents and honor them, but what if they're not 'honorable'?" Archer told me on March 9, 2009. "It's a trap, because if you don't honor parents, it is displeasing to God, so you're stuck. There's no escape for the abused child."

Must we insist that children honor and obey adults "in all things"? There are plenty of people, past and present, religious and nonreligious, who balk at this concept. That includes nineteenth-century congregational clergyman and theologian Horace Bushnell, who recognized the potential dangers of parents assuming too much power in the family. In his book *Christian Nurture*, published in 1861, Bushnell advocates for a "strong and decided government in families," but he also remarks that there are "many who talk of the rod as the orthodox symbol of parental duty, but who might really as well be heathens as Christians; who only storm about their house with heathenish ferocity, who lecture, and threaten, and castigate, and bruise, and call this family government." Bushnell adds:

> So much easier is it to be violent than to be holy, that they substitute force for goodness and grace, and are wholly unconscious of the imposture. It is frightful to think how they batter and bruise the delicate, tender souls of their children, extinguishing in them what they ought to cultivate, crushing that sensibility which is the hope of their being, and all in the sacred name of Christ Jesus. . . . You are not to be a savage to them, but a father and a Christian.[38]

In *The Body Never Lies: The Lingering Effects of Cruel Parenting*, Alice Miller argues that the biblical commandment to "honor" one's parents is "a kind of life insurance for old people, which was perhaps necessary in biblical times but is certainly no longer required in this form." She adds, "It is highly significant, perplexing to say the least, that we have been bound for thousands of years to a commandment that hardly anyone has questioned, simply because it underscores the physical reality that all children, whether abused or not, always love their parents."[39]

While there is nothing wrong with encouraging children to honor their parents, scriptures and religious concepts that promote child obedience offer an unbalanced and unhealthy parent-child relationship model. That is, while theology says plenty about what children must do for parents, it is largely silent on what *parents owe children*. Expecting children to honor and obey "in all things" promotes the use of corporal punishment, fear, and, sometimes, physical abuse.

Chapter 7
CHILD SINFULNESS—A CHRISTIAN PROBLEM

The way adults treat children has a lot to do with how they view children. Therefore, it's important to examine how religious people in America look upon children. Which brings us to the doctrine of original sin.

If you're a Christian—and more than three-quarters of Americans are[1]—chances are you believe in the doctrine of original sin. This doctrine states that all humans are born sinful due to "the fall" of Adam and Eve and that Jesus Christ suffered for the sins of humankind to allow them to atone for their sins. The belief in original sin affects how many Christians look at the world, themselves, and their children.

Not all Christians subscribe to this doctrine. More left-leaning believers are convinced it does not exist, pointing out that the term *original sin* does not appear in the Bible. Mormons do not believe in original sin, nor do Jews or Muslims. Still, for many Christians, particularly conservative believers, original sin remains a cornerstone of their faith.

As far as children are concerned, viewing all humankind as inherently sinful is one of the worst ideas to come along since Abraham and Isaac set off for Mount Moriah. Children, even newborns, are not excluded from this doctrine, as they are believed to share the same depraved nature as everyone else. This disturbing viewpoint was made clear to me by an evangelical Christian man, who stated in no uncertain terms, "When the baby comes out of the womb, it wants what it wants, and it wants it *now*. And if it doesn't get it, it's going to start crying. That's nothing but sin."

BEHOLD THE CHILD SINNER

Christians have followed a centuries-old path of viewing children in a loathsome light—a path paved with ideas about sinfulness. According to psychologist Robin Grille in *Parenting for a Peaceful World,* Saint Augustine set this idea in motion with his negative depictions of children and the expressed need to control them. For example, Augustine warned against allowing a child to do what he wants because "there is no crime he will not plunge into." Grille notes that the theologian even asked, "Is it not a sin to lust after the breast and wail?"[2] Eighteenth-century Calvinist Jonathan Edwards referred to children who are "out of Christ" as "young vipers" who are "infinitely more hateful than vipers, and are in a most miserable condition."[3]

The vast majority of Christians have softened their views of "child sinners" since Edwards's time, yet conservative believers have not strayed very far from the theologian's thinking. As Michael Lienesch notes in *Redeeming America: Piety and Politics in the New Christian Right*: "Theologically, religious conservatives see the character of children as being dominated by sin. In contrast to most mainline Christians, and even to some other evangelicals, they tend to say little about the idea of original innocence. Instead, they look on their children skeptically, almost fearfully, as inheritors of original sin."[4]

Conservative Christian parenting books written from the 1970s until recently portray children just as Lienesch describes.

"A child need not be taught how to lie, to be selfish, or to do wrong; these things come naturally," writes J. Richard Fugate in *What the Bible Says about . . . Child Training.* "Every sweet, innocent, cuddly baby possesses within his flesh the constant temptation to fulfill the strong desire of sin. Under the control of sin, the child is totally self-centered; he wants what he wants when he wants it. A child wants to be fed what and when he wishes, to have the total attention of others, to play always, and generally to have his every desire fulfilled without regard for anyone else."[5]

In full agreement, syndicated conservative Christian parenting columnist John Rosemond writes in his popular *Parenting by the Book: Biblical Wisdom for Raising Your Child,* "Grandma knew that every child came into the world bearing a nature that was already corrupt, depraved; that each and every child was a natural-born criminal; and that to steer the little criminal in a prosocial direction required a combination of powerful love and powerful discipline."[6] Rosemond goes on to refer to a crying and demanding child as "the Spawn of Satan" and "the demon-child."[7] In defining the "Adam and Eve Principle," Rosemond warns parents: "No matter how good a parent you are, your child is still capable on any given day of doing something despicable, disgusting, or depraved."[8]

In *Understanding Your Child's Temperament*, evangelical Christian activist Beverly LaHaye warns parents that children have a "sin nature," and that children have a desire for both good and evil. Quoting Psalm 51:5, which says, "in sin my mother conceived me," LaHaye concludes that all mothers are "born with sin, and therefore I was born with a sinful nature also."[9]

James Dobson, who founded the evangelical Christian organization Focus on the Family, offers a milder approach. In *The New Strong-Willed Child: Birth through Adolescence*, Dobson does not question children's "preciousness as creations of God," yet he still maintains that children are "naturally inclined toward rebellion, selfishness, dishonesty, aggression, exploitation, and greed. They don't have to be taught these behaviors. They are natural expressions of their humanness."[10] Meanwhile, the Focus on the Family website rebukes mothers and fathers who heed the advice of "secular parenting gurus who preach that children are brimming with innate goodness and should be allowed to create their own values. Such humanistic advice denies the fact that all of us are inclined toward selfishness and self-deception."[11]

"Your child was born a sinner because he has inherited the sin of Adam," writes Ginger Plowman in *"Don't Make Me Count to Three!": A Mom's Look at Heart-Oriented Discipline*. Plowman explains, "This is called original sin. This explains why a roomful of toddlers do not have to be taught how to fight over a toy. They just know."[12]

One bizarre illustration of this negative portrayal is a quote that has been passed around the Internet often by conservative Christian websites:

> Every baby starts life as a little savage. He is completely selfish and self-centered. He wants what he wants when he wants it: his bottle, his mother's attention, his playmate's toys, his uncle's watch, or whatever. Deny him these and he seethes with rage and aggressiveness which would be murderous were he not so helpless. He's dirty, he has no morals, no knowledge, no developed skills. This means that all children, not just certain children but all children, are born delinquent. If permitted to continue in their self-centered world of infancy, given free rein to their impulsive actions to satisfy each want, every child would grow up a criminal, a thief, a killer, a rapist.

Many attribute the quote as having appeared in a report published by the Minnesota Crime Commission in 1926. (The Minnesota Crime Commission never published such a passage in 1926 or any other year, according to documents obtained by the Minnesota Legislative Reference Library.) J. Richard Fugate is one such author, writing in *What the Bible Says about . . . Child Training*, "It's virtually impossible to imagine any government agency saying anything similar today. But that excerpt accurately reflects what the Bible says about original sin and the responsibility of parents and society to love, teach and discipline."[13]

The view of children as sinful creatures is also maintained by conservative Christian schools. In *Religious Schools v. Children's Rights*, James G. Dwyer explains that fundamentalist Christian schools adhere to "a puritanical belief in the corruptness of the body and the utter depravity of human nature." Dwyer quotes the director of Christian Schools International, the largest Christian school association in the United States: "If you believe that your students came into this world with human nature that is morally good, your view is in direct contradiction to the teachings of God's Word, which says, 'The heart is deceitful above all things, and desperately wicked.'"[14]

CHILD SINFULNESS AND ABUSE

Does viewing children as sinful, evil, wicked, and depraved necessarily lead to child abuse? No, but it could be a risk factor for abuse. Consider the fact that parents who *do* abuse their children often have negative perceptions of their victims. For example, studies show that abusive parents tend to view children in a negative light and demonstrate bias against them.[15] In writing about counseling parents who were accused of abusing their children, Carol Delaney remarks in *Abraham on Trial* that parents "seemed to have an idea" that their child was "born bad."[16]

This link between abuse and negative perceptions of children crystallizes more fully when one considers abuse rates among children with disabilities. As it turns out, children with disabilities are more than three times as likely to be abused and neglected as children who do not have disabilities.[17] Researchers cite many reasons for this, but one of them happens to be that abusers hold negative perceptions of their children with disabilities.[18]

"Our attitudes about the good and/or evil of children are vitally important," writes Janet Pais in *Suffer the Children: A Theology of Liberation by a Victim of Child Abuse*. "If we believe that there is evil in children, this belief may seem to justify authoritarian forms of relationship with them, punishment for their aggression, and efforts to train them to be good." Furthermore, adds Pais, "Belief that there is evil in children may serve as a rationalization, in short, for abuse."[19]

PURIFYING CHILDREN

In addition to encouraging negative perceptions of children, the belief in child sinfulness also gives adults a specific reason to spank them: to subdue or wash away sin and evil. University of San Antonio sociology professor Christopher G. Ellison, who has done extensive research on corporal punishment trends among Christians, states in a study he cowrote for the *Journal of Family Issues* that a key reason conservative Protestants spank is to "correct" children's sinfulness.[20]

Again, this idea goes back to Saint Augustine's time, as Robin Grille points out in *Parenting for a Peaceful World*. Grille notes that back then, children were believed to have been born evil, "and the purpose of parenting was thought to be the correction of that evil."[21] Grille goes on to say that this pedagogical concept led to a parenting style that "emphasised the need to beat children, often severely, and mould their behaviour."[22]

A number of self-proclaimed parenting experts who are also conservative Christian believers have encouraged parents to spank disobedient children by quoting from Proverbs 20:30, which states, "Blows that hurt cleanse away evil, as do stripes the inner depths of the heart." In *How to Rear Children*, Jack Hyles concludes that, based on this passage, "The parent who disciplines cleanses the child from evil character and inward sin."[23] What's more, states Hyles, "Sometimes spanking should leave stripes on the child."[24]

Roy Lessin continues with this theme in *Spanking: Why, When, How?*: "It is better for children to carry a few temporary marks on the outside than to carry within them areas of disobedience and wrong attitudes that can leave permanent marks on their character."[25] (Lessin removed this controversial language in his later book, *Spanking: A Loving Discipline*.)

In his first edition of *Dare to Discipline: A Psychologist Offers Urgent Advice to Parents and Teachers*, Focus on the Family founder James Dobson calls the pain used to punish a rebellious child a "marvelous purifier."[26]

For a very long time, Christians have associated demons and the devil with sinfulness. In the late 1500s, each of the seven deadly sins was paired with a demon. Many Christians speak of sin as what separates believers from God—a separation that makes a person vulnerable to being possessed by Satan or demons. Therefore, some Christians believe that when a child misbehaves—thereby exposing his or her sinfulness—a proper remedy is to drive out the evil forces that might have taken over the child's soul. Such was the case with Matt's mother, who tried to "beat the devil" out of her son. In fact, one study shows that some adults who have been accused of physical abuse were making an attempt to "rid a child of evil."[27]

In his memoir, *The Spanking Room*, William Coburn describes how people in his Jehovah's Witness community justified corporal punishment as a way to cast out evil spirits. He describes how, one day, his mother confides to a friend that she sometimes "feels so bad about beating Billy," to which the friend replies: "Don't think of it as beating Billy. Think of it as beating the evil system of things out of him. That will help you hit him harder. Just keep that in mind—you're really only beating him because of the evil system of things." Coburn continues:

> Yes indeed. That's the whole theory behind the "spare the rod" philosophy. The Jehovah's Witnesses' belief is that when a child disturbs a [kingdom hall] meeting, it's actually not the child causing the problem. It's a demon attack— an attempt on the part of Satan to distract the members of the congregation from learning about their religion. If you think "discipline" in the kingdom hall is, shall we say, draconian, or harsh, or cruel, you simply don't understand that it takes a lot to beat a demon out of a small child.[28]

Alex Byrd remembers the same mantra from his Pentecostal childhood. "My church was very much into 'Spare the rod and spoil the child.' Pretty much their opinion was that if you didn't knock the hell out of your kid, it was actually an act of *cruelty*, because you were basically going to be sending them into perdition in that it would risk the child being essentially infested with demons. If you didn't whack your kid regularly, Satan would beam a strong hold into the child and potentially possess the kid."

Before Jason Wilkinson attended the Christian school that frequently paddled the students for misbehaving, he went to a Church of the Nazarene school, where he experienced corporal punishment of a different sort. Wilkinson says that when he was in the first grade, his teacher repeatedly hit him with a ruler for writing with his left hand.

> She would tell me that "No child of mine in my classroom is going to write with the devil's left hand, and if you are going to write in here, you are going to write with the right hand of God." And so, about the second or third time she hit me with the ruler, I yanked the ruler out of her hand and broke it in two and tossed it on her desk and said, "You are not going to hit me anymore. I am going to write with my left hand, and that's how it's going to be." And she didn't like that, and I would get sent to the principal's office, and we would go through this on a weekly basis.

Wilkinson is one of many children who have suffered this treatment in Christian schools. According to Irwin Hyman, author of *Reading, Writing, and the Hickory Stick*, "Conservative Catholic and Protestant educators are often obsessed with the concept of original sin and its relation to teaching. Their preoccupation with saving children from the devil results in sanctimonious adherence to a 'spare the rod' mandate."[29]

In one tragic 1997 case in California, a five-year-old girl was paddled to death and the killing was blamed on satanic possession. Three women took part in the beating, including the victim's mother. Testifying in court, Deborah Reynolds, the mother of Breeann Spickard, stated that the beating was an effort to rid the child of the devil.[30]

The researcher who conducted the aforementioned study that revealed the belief that spanking can rid a child of evil, Bette Bottoms, explains in that study that sin is not only the "vehicle to hell" but one that is "inspired by a literal Satan—ergo both sin and Satan must be stopped."[31]

SAVING SOULS

The ultimate goal of cleansing children of sin and evil through physical punishment is to prevent them from going to hell. In explaining this mind-set, Bottoms notes in her study, "It is better that children experience a temporary hell inflicted by loving parents than that they burn in an eternal hell."[32] Echoing this idea, sociology professor Christopher Ellison notes in the previously mentioned study that another key reason conservative Protestants spank is to save children from eternal damnation. Ellison points out that the threat of hell is very real to this population: "Conservative Protestants tend to believe in a literal hell, to which the souls of all unsaved persons will be consigned."[33]

Considering conservative Christians' literal and frightening interpretation of hell, it is understandable that those parents will do what is necessary to prevent their children from ending up there. This brings us back to Proverbs—specifically, Proverbs 23:13–14: "Do not withhold correction from a child, for if you beat him with a rod, he will not die. You shall beat him with the rod, And deliver his soul from hell."

Independent researcher Samuel Martin remarks in his book, *Thy Rod and Thy Staff They Comfort Me: Christians and the Spanking Controversy*, "There is no doubt that on the basis, primarily, of this one verse, many thousands of Christian parents have lived lives of supreme pain and immense suffering over their wayward children and the thought that their children will be assigned a place in eternal torment."[34]

This conclusion rings true in a number of contemporary parenting books by conservative Protestants. For example, Jack Hyles, referencing Proverbs 23, states plainly in *How to Rear Children*, "The parent who spanks the child keeps him from going to hell." Hyles goes on to assert that saving a child's soul is accomplished by "teaching him truths that can be learned only by discipline and the use of the rod."[35]

This teaching also emerges in literature published for Jehovah's Witnesses. An article in *Awake!* magazine concludes, "Discipline may need to take the form of more than verbal correction. . . . The very life of the child is at stake! If he is allowed to pursue a wrong course, it will lead to his own unhappiness and eventual death outside God's favor. . . . Yes, it shows real love on the part of a parent to do whatever he can to correct his child, including administering a good spanking."[36]

In *"Don't Make Me Count to Three!"* Ginger Plowman asserts that while parents are "working on the buttocks, God is honoring our obedience and working on the heart. Therefore, if you are going to rescue your child from death . . . you must use the rod."[37] And in *Parenting by the Book*, John Rosemond makes the plea that a lack of discipline "contributes to death—in the everlasting sense . . . . Parents! Give the gift of hope to your children!"[38]

With such a fear of eternal damnation looming over the heads of parents, it is little wonder that some mothers and fathers take corporal punishment to abusive levels. Such was the case of a small Christian church in Michigan. In the early 1980s, police looked into the House of Judah after it was discovered that a boy in the group had been beaten to death. State authorities removed dozens of children from their homes after their investigation turned up stocks, a switch, and a broom handle that members had used for disciplinary purposes. After the children were taken, parents expressed alarm because they feared refraining from physically punishing their children might lead to the eternal damnation of their souls.[39]

Around that time, the Tennessee sect then known as the Northeast Kingdom Community Church—now called Twelve Tribes—also faced allegations of child abuse following a large-scale police raid. The group's leader was quoted saying, "The infliction of pain upon a child's rear end with the use of a reedlike rod is not child abuse but rather their salvation." A former member amplified these sentiments when he summed up the group's beliefs about corporal punishment: "Better that you should beat a child within an inch of his life than that he would be cast into the Lake of Fire for all eternity."[40]

There is yet another religiously inspired motivation of corporal punishment, one that is tied to beliefs of sinfulness and eternal salvation—the breaking of children's wills.

BREAKING WILLS

Back in 1831, an article appeared in *American Baptist Magazine* entitled "A Case of Conviction." The article, whose byline only reads, "A Plain Man," provides a vivid description of a Christian man's relentless and abusive attempts to gain his toddler son's affections. The point of the story, writes the author, is to "illustrate religious truths."[41]

The father begins by explaining that his fifteen-month-old son was "more than usually self-willed," and so the man was convinced "of the necessity of subduing his temper." One morning, the child began to "cry violently." He was very hungry, but when the father offered him some bread, the boy threw it away. At that point, the father put the boy in a room by himself and told others not to speak to him or give him any food or drink. The father occasionally visited the boy "and spoke to him in the kindest tones, offering him the bread and putting out my arms to take him." But the boy refused to go to the man or take the bread, although he "greedily" drank a cup of water that the man held. When his father dropped a crumb on the floor, the boy picked it up and ate it but would not take it directly from the man's hand. Since the boy refused to come to his father—he turned away and cried instead—the father left him by himself in the room overnight. The boy "went to bed supperless. It was now twenty-four hours since he had eaten anything." The forced fasting went on for another twelve hours until the boy's eyes were "wan and sunken. His breath hot and feverish, and his voice feeble and wailing." At one point, the boy took from his father a piece of bread and a cup of milk but still would not hug his father, so he was kept in isolation longer. The next day, the father writes, "the tones of his voice in weeping were graver and less passionate, and had more the appearance of one bemoaning himself." Finally, that afternoon, the boy came to his father, who observes, "He was completely subdued" and "repeatedly kissed me, and would do so whenever I commanded." The author concludes, "I could not avoid looking upon the whole of this little incident, as illustrative of the several steps in the ordinary progress of a sinner's conversion. . . . *God* can offer a sinner *no other terms than repentance.* To yield to the sinner's will, and save him without the unconditional surrender of his will, would be to make the sinner's will the centre of the moral universe."[42]

The article was later discovered to have been written by Reverend Francis Wayland, a Baptist educator who served as president of Brown University from 1827 to 1855. (Brown University's website describes the starvation incident but makes no comment about Wayland's actions being abusive.)[43] Wayland's story exemplifies a long-held practice of evangelical and fundamentalist Christians—the breaking of children's wills. In *Spare the Child*, Philip Greven explains this phenomenon, which is closely tied to beliefs about child sinfulness:

> Breaking the child's will has been the central task given parents by successive generations of preachers, whose biblically based rationales for discipline have reflected the belief that self-will is evil and sinful. From the seventeenth century to the present, evangelical and fundamentalist Protestants have persistently advocated the crushing of the will even before a child can remember the painful encounters with punishment that are always necessary to accomplish such goals.[44]

Greven has traced back the phrase *breaking the child's will* to two British eighteenth-century evangelicals: John Wesley, who helped found the Methodist movement, and itinerant minister George Whitefield. According to these men's writings, which Greven quotes in *The Protestant Temperament*, "breaking the will" is believed to save children from hell, and the earlier it is done, the better. "With remarkable consistency and persistence," writes Greven, "evangelicals through the centuries insisted that parents must control and break the emerging will of children in the first few years of life." Greven notes that, for these believers, "The autonomous will and self-assertiveness of the child must be reduced to impotency . . . or the child ultimately would be damned for eternity."[45]

When I spoke to Philip Greven on November 3, 2009, he told me when he was researching this idea, he expected to see the phrase *breaking the child's will* appear only in centuries-old tomes on Protestant child rearing. But, in fact, he found numerous mentions in Christian parenting books from the 1960s and 1970s. For example, in instructing parents on how to spank children, Jack Hyles writes in *How to Rear Children*, "*The spanking should be administered firmly. It should be painful and it should last until the child's will is broken. It should last until the child is crying, not tears of anger but tears of a broken will. As long as he is stiff, grits his teeth, holds on to his own will, the spanking should continue.*"[46]

In my research, I have come across the concept—if not the actual term— of breaking children's wills time and time again. I spoke to one man who grew up in a small Mennonite community in Indiana in the 1950s and 1960s who described a church sermon from his youth in which a minister compared teenage boys to colts that had not yet been broken:

> [The minister said] a farmer would not be doing his duty . . . if he just let a colt run wild and [in] the same way, a father would not be doing his job to just let his teenage boys run wild. "You have to break their will" was the phrase that was used. . . . You had to break the will of that child so that that child becomes obedient. . . . I was probably in about fifth or sixth grade, and the reason I remember it so well is because I had a distinct feeling in myself, "That's wrong. What that person is saying is not right. That cannot be the truth." It felt to me like someone had just spoken a lie over the pulpit, even though they had the Bible verses and everything else to back it up.

Carolyn Jessop, a former member of the FLDS, has tried to call attention to the "breaking in" method of babies through the use of water torture. "They spank the baby and when it cries, they hold the baby face up under the tap with running water. When they stop crying, they spank it again and the cycle is repeated until they are exhausted," Jessop said in a media interview.[47]

The importance of breaking a child's will appears on numerous conservative Christian websites. One article entitled "Breaking Their Will and Gaining Their Heart," written by Matthew Chapman, advocates for the "full surrender" of the will in disciplining and "chastening" children.[48]

Similarly, in the previously mentioned recorded presentation on parenting, Remnant Fellowship pastor Gwen Shamblin warns that mothers and fathers "have a window of time to get these kids straight." Shamblin adds that parents might have to "go through some tears," in disciplining children, but, Shamblin says, it's necessary. "You are really going to have to break those kids."

A common theme emerges from the writings of John Wesley, Francis Wayland, Jack Hyles, and other conservative Christians who describe the concept of will breaking. That is, they depict it as a high-stakes battle, a call to action in which parents must do whatever it takes to defeat the formidable enemy of child willfulness, no matter how long it takes.

"The will [of the child] to dominate is amazing in its strength, profound in its dedication and consistency, and evil in its disregard for the needs of others," says the website for the Tennessee-based No Greater Joy Ministries, owned by evangelical Christian minister Michael Pearl.[49]

Even as the phrase *breaking the child's will* is no longer commonplace, the concept has by no means gone away. In his online magazine, Michael Pearl writes a personal story that is eerily familiar to Francis Wayland's. In Pearl's article, "Child Training Marathon," a family asks Pearl and his wife to visit for a week and critique their parenting methods. Late one night, when the family is driving, the family's toddler son, whom Pearl calls a "brat," wants to sit on his mother's lap and begins to cry when this request is refused. Pearl then instructs the father to stop the car and spank the child, which he does, but this only leads to the child crying more. The next twenty minutes are then spent with the father telling the boy to stop crying, and, when this fails, the father stops the car and spanks the child. No one seems to heed the mother's concerns that the boy is hungry, sleepy, and cold. Pearl then writes:

> I told the father to command the boy to stop crying immediately or he would again be spanked. The boy ignored him until Father took his foot off the gas, preparatory to stopping. In the midst of his crying, he understood the issues well enough to understand that the slowing of the car was a response to his crying. The family was relieved to have him stop and the father started to resume his drive. I said "No, you told him he was to stop crying immediately or you would spank him; he waited until you began stopping. He has not obeyed; he is just beginning to show confidence in your resolve. Spank him again and tell him that you will continue to stop and continue to spank until you get instant compliance." He did. . . . This time, after the spanking, when Daddy gave his command, the boy dried it up like a paper towel. The parents had won, and the boy was the beneficiary.[50]

The idea that children's wills must be broken through corporal punishment has been taken to injurious, and even deadly, extremes by people of faith. On October 5, 1982, Joseph Green, aged twenty-three months, was paddled to death by his parents, Stuart and Leslie Green. The Greens belonged to a fundamentalist Christian sect in West Virginia whose culture so emphasized corporal punishment that parents walked around openly carrying monogrammed paddles. According to court documents, the Greens took turns paddling Joseph and would not stop because he refused their command that he apologize for hitting another toddler.[51]

Stuart Green pleaded guilty to involuntary manslaughter, and a jury found his wife guilty of the same charge.[52] In addition, the group's leader, Dorothy McClellan, was also found guilty, even though she was not present during the beating. The judge who sentenced McClellan said that she was even more culpable than the Greens because through her religious teachings, "she instituted therein a policy of child discipline which ultimately encouraged the acts which brought about Joey Green's death."[53]

In writing about this case in *Religious Abuse*, Keith Wright expresses dismay that the judge failed to see that McClellan was not introducing a new or bizarre brand of religious disciplinary teaching. McClellan was "simply pushing to the limit what generations of Christians have advocated for centuries," notes Wright, which is the "church's advocacy of corporal punishment in breaking the child's will and in bringing the child into submission to the parent, who represents God."[54]

I interviewed people who have fallen victim to this concept. For instance, Alex Byrd says his Pentecostal parents beat him and his siblings until they cried: "If you did not whip the child until they cried, it was not seen as being effective. My sister learned to cry on command. I pretty much took more the Rambo approach. According to family legend, I reportedly turned to my folks when I was four years old during one of these spanking sessions and told them that they could whip me until their arms fell off, but I was not going to cry for their pleasure."

Bethany Fenimore, the woman who was described earlier as having been forced to sit still in church or else be spanked, says her father spanked her and her siblings for what seemed like a very long time. "The idea was you spanked a child for as long as they were rebelling. What you wanted to hear was 'a broken cry.' A cry of 'I give myself over to you and I am now really sorry for what I did.' That was the kind of spirit that God wanted because that was the kind of spirit that could be malleable in the ways of God."

Chapter 8

THE PERILS OF MIXING FAITH AND CORPORAL PUNISHMENT

A re conservative Protestants, whom studies show are more likely to spank children than other Christian believers, also more likely to abuse their children? University of Texas at San Antonio sociology professor Christopher Ellison sees little reason to be concerned. In his study that appeared in the *Journal of Family Issues*, Ellison notes that evangelical Christians who advocate for corporal punishment go to "considerable lengths" to distinguish between mild and moderate use of corporal punishment and abusive behavior. Also, Ellison points to studies that indicate that conservative Protestant parents may express more warmth and affection than parents from other backgrounds. Based on these findings, Ellison states that the effects of spanking in conservative Protestant homes are "less harmful, or perhaps not harmful at all."[1]

Yet there is clearly a need for more research in this area. Ellison bases his latest findings on literature written by these spanking proponents—not data collected on abuse statistics and religious beliefs. Several studies leave questions about abuse rates among America's most conservative believers. For example, a 1979 study shows that fundamentalist Christian parents possess attitudes that are similar to those of abusive parents.[2] A 1995 study shows that, of physical abuse cases where perpetrators were attempting to rid children of evil, most were fundamentalist or Protestant.[3]* A 2005 study shows that conservative Protestants have a slightly higher propensity toward abuse than other Christians and those who are religiously unaffiliated.[4] These studies are limited,** but they suggest a need for further study before society can be assured that conservative Christian homes are not more abusive than other homes.

Ellison himself admits there is still a great deal more to be learned about this subject. As he notes in his *Journal of Family Issues* study, we know little about how children are affected when raised in homes in which corporal punishment is religiously supported.[5] Ellison acknowledges that no one knows to what extent parents actually adhere to guidelines offered by spanking advocates that aim to prevent abuse, such as not spanking in anger. What's more, Ellison points out, some of these advocates' guidelines "vary significantly across evangelical authors."[6] For instance, some say to spank with the hand; others, with an object. Some say to administer punishment immediately after a child has misbehaved; others suggest taking time for parents to cool their emotions.

In addition, while all can agree that parents should be affectionate with their children, as many conservative Protestants seem to be, one wonders if children in these families would do even better if they received that affection and were *not* spanked. Some worry about the potentially damaging psychological effects of children being made to endure pain inflicted by parents with whom they share a loving relationship.

"If you are both very affectionate with your children and you're physically punitive with them, that's a very mixed message, and I think it has long-term consequences," Philip Greven told me in our interview.

Questions have also been raised about parents who spank—even if they do not abuse—fixating on the methodology of spanking and its purported benefits rather than being tuned in to what recipients of spanking are going through. As Phil Quinn states in *Spare the Rod*, many adults abuse children while believing their actions are "for their own good." Quinn stresses that children need parents to be empathetic rather than focused on their own ideologies: "Without empathy, parents are likely to inflict far more [pain] upon their children than was their original intention."[7]

In fact, the aforementioned 2005 study finds that conservative Protestants "anticipate feeling little guilt if they use corporal punishment because of their religion-supported belief in the necessity and effectiveness of corporal punishment." Also, the authors warn, "The relatively frequent use of corporal punishment by some of the parents in this study, as often as three or more times per week, may put children at particular risk for the behavioral, psychological, and relationship problems that are associated with corporal punishment."[8]

But of even greater concern is just what effect *advocacy* for corporal punishment has on America's faithful.

POISONOUS PREACHING

Christians in America frequently hear about the benefits of using corporal punishment. The virtues are discussed in churches and on religious radio and television programs. Worshippers read about why and how they should spank in church literature and on Christian parenting websites. Evangelical and fundamentalist Christian organizations sell books and videos on the subject. An example is Focus on the Family, which was founded by James Dobson, a licensed psychologist whose parenting books have sold in the millions. According to the organization's website, Dobson's radio broadcasts are heard around the globe by 220 million people every day.[9] Dobson does not talk only about corporal punishment. In fact, his most recent books say nothing about it. But he has promoted spanking in his most popular books and on his website.

Many Christians who give parenting advice and advocate for corporal punishment are looked upon as religious authorities. In fact, many are church leaders. That said, with the exception of James Dobson and a few others, these individuals usually have no credentials in child psychology, pediatrics, and other child-related fields. To support pro-spanking positions, they commonly quote scripture instead of empirical data. All the while, though, these advocates are sure that God wants parents to physically punish their kids.

Spanking "is God's idea," writes Roy Lessin in *Spanking: A Loving Discipline*. "He is the one who has commanded parents to use this type of discipline as an expression of love. . . . Do we love God enough to obey him? Do we love our children enough to bring correction into their lives when it is needed?"[10] Even more frightening, Larry Christenson states in *The Christian Family* that parents' failure to physically punish children will incur God's wrath.[11]

Michael Pearl of No Greater Joy Ministries tells parents on his website that, by spanking their children, they are "representing all authority to the child, including the authority of God."[12] And in his book *To Train Up a Child*, Pearl asserts that refraining from employing "the rod in training up their children . . . is an indictment against God himself."[13]

Similarly, Lisa Whelchel asserts in *Creative Correction* that a correctly handled spanking can be "a gift from God."[14]

Given all this, it is likely that many Christian audiences take the words of these "experts" as gospel, which increases the likelihood that they might spank children too harshly or too often. Ironically, James Dobson raises this concern himself in the first edition of his bestselling *Dare to Discipline*: "One of my greatest concerns in recommending corporal punishment (spanking) is that some parents might apply the thrashings too frequently or too severely."[15]

As Ellison points out, many of these advocates urge parents to use caution when punishing. For example, on his ministry's website, Michael Pearl explains in no uncertain terms:

> You are abusing the child when it [corporal punishment] starts doing harm to the child. Listen to your friends—especially to those friends that share your philosophy. Ask the opinion of people you respect. If they think you are abusive, get counsel in a hurry. Ask the opinion of your older children. If your child is broken in spirit, cowed and subdued, you have a problem.[16]

But this kind of counsel with its specific instructions is a rarity among conservative Christians. On the contrary, much of the pro–corporal punishment parenting literature fails to define child physical abuse, if it mentions it at all. Instead, abuse is often discussed as a problem that happens to "other people," or it is brought up as one reason that some parents do not spank (implying that it is an unnecessary fear). Rarely do these advocates remind parents that child abuse is against the law and should be reported to authorities.

University of San Antonio researcher Christopher Ellison was kind enough to sit down with me on January 28, 2009, and communicate via e-mail afterward to talk about his work. When I raised concerns about the widespread promotion of corporal punishment among conservative Christians, Ellison let me know that he was not particularly concerned with evangelicals who largely administer "garden-variety" corporal punishment. Rather, Ellison worries about some religious parents who do not take seriously the need for, as he wrote in an e-mail, "restraint, clear explanation, loving reconciliation, or other practices that are recommended by many evangelical authors and pastors." These individuals, says Ellison, might use severe and abusive corporal punishment upon hearing about the virtues of physical disciplinary practices from religious conservatives.

"I think it's a big risk," says Ellison, "and it worries me the most. We need a lot more research on the effects on kids. Not just the mean patterns but also the outliers in the extreme cases. I see the potential danger. There is no question about it."

A SPANKING ADVOCATE'S DANGEROUS ADVICE

What led me to get in touch with Bethany Fenimore, the woman who was frequently spanked by her father, was something she wrote on an antispanking website. On September 7, 2005, Fenimore posted "An Open Letter to Roy Lessin." As it turns out, her fundamentalist Christian parents not only read Lessin's book, they knew him personally; Fenimore's family and Lessin attended the same church. Fenimore's letter describes how she paid a dear price for her parents' adherence to Roy Lessin's first book, *Spanking: Why, When, How?*

> Dear Roy,
>   After 19 years I have found the courage to write you this letter declaring how your choice to teach and write about spanking has affected me. My purpose in writing you this open letter is to share with you and others that the spanking approach you recommend is harmful. . . . Should just one parent spare their child the kind of pain that I endured at the hands of my parents implementing your spanking recommendations, my pain will have more meaning than it does now.[17]

Given the close relationship that Fenimore's parents had with Lessin, one would think they would not have misconstrued Lessin's advice about spanking and would have taken seriously his precautions to minimize abuse. And yet, as Fenimore tells it, her "Roy Lessin spankings" left her traumatized. In the letter, Fenimore explains that her mother spanked her before bedtime when she was only six months old:

> She had to spank me repeatedly to teach me to not cry when she put me down. I know about this incident because my mother used to tell all new mothers about how young I was when she started spanking me. My last spanking occurred when I was thirteen years old. The Roy Lessin spankings that I remember most vividly took place between the ages of three and seven, because I hardly went a few days without a spanking at that time.[18]

Fenimore writes that anticipating a spanking made her physically ill. Most of the spankings were delivered by her father, who would spank her on her bare bottom. "Trying to pull away and defend myself would only mean that the spanking would be longer, or I'd get a back-to-back spanking." She says she was struck with different implements, including a paddle inscribed with scriptural verses. Afterward, while Fenimore was in great pain, she had to sit on her father's lap while he "would wrap his arms around me and comfort me." Fenimore believes that the spankings caused her long-term psychological and sexual problems. Finally, she concludes, "I hope that by this point you begin to see how your simple, sweet words about raising children are actually harmful."[19]

In fairness to Roy Lessin, *Spanking: Why, When, How?* does not advocate spanking babies or a child's bare skin. In fact, he warns parents not to "force something upon children that they are not prepared to handle because of age."[20] However, he does not caution *against* these actions and stresses that "good contact is important" for a spanking to be effective.[21] (In the later *Spanking: A Loving Discipline*, Lessin encourages parents to spank on a child's "lightly-clothed bottom.")

One wonders what Lessin thinks about Fenimore's letter. According to an e-mail Fenimore sent me on November 24, 2009, she sent him a copy but received no response. I asked Lessin via e-mail if he would speak to me about the letter, but he sent an e-mail back, declining.[22] Regardless, Fenimore's story illustrates the problem of mixing faith with advice on corporal punishment. It appears as though her parents were well intentioned, trying to follow what they believed to be good advice. Fenimore writes in her letter that her father "thought he was doing the right thing" because he believed in Lessin, who was a leader in their church and a friend.[23]

NO GREATER JOY MINISTRIES

Two children have died at the hands of adults who followed the child-rearing advice of Michael Pearl, the fundamentalist Christian minister from Tennessee, who, with his wife, Debi, runs No Greater Joy Ministries. The couple gives parenting advice on the website and sells books and videos on the subject. The Pearls have been highly criticized for their heavy promotion of corporal punishment and controlling methods of child rearing. But the Pearls' methods were thrust into the spotlight when it was discovered that a woman who killed her child was one of the Pearls' many followers.

On June 12, 2008, Lynn Paddock of South Carolina was convicted of first-degree murder and sentenced to life in prison for the death of her four-year-old adopted son, Sean. Sean died from suffocation after Paddock wrapped Sean tightly in blankets, a technique witnesses said she used to keep children from getting out of bed.[24]

Michael Pearl does not advocate that parents wrap children in blankets. However, he does suggest that parents spank children with quarter-inch plumber's supply line. As his website states, the pipes "will fit in your purse or hang around your neck. You can buy them for under $1.00 at Home Depot or any hardware store. They come cheaper by the dozen and can be widely distributed in every room and vehicle. Just the high profile of their accessibility keeps the kids in line."[25]

At Paddock's trial, six surviving adopted children revealed that Paddock beat them almost daily with flexible plastic rods and other objects, among other abuses.[26] What's more, investigators found two-foot lengths of plumbing supply line in several rooms of Paddock's home. Paddock's attorney said that she read a great deal of the Pearls' literature and chatted with other mothers in her church about their child discipline tips.[27] Her stepsister told the media that Paddock "really believed this stuff [the Pearls' writings]" and was "wrapped up" in it.[28]

Then, on February 5, 2010, seven-year-old Lydia Schatz was allegedly killed by her adoptive parents, Kevin and Elizabeth Schatz of Paradise, California. In what came to be known as the "biblical chastisement" case, authorities said Lydia was beaten for several hours with quarter-inch plumbing supply line as her parents took turns holding her down. Lydia's eleven-year-old biological sister, who was also adopted by the Schatzes, reportedly received a similar treatment by the couple the night before and had to be hospitalized. According to authorities, Lydia, who is from Liberia, may have been punished for mispronouncing a word during a homeschooling lesson.[29] As of February 2011, the Schatzes faced charges of murder, torture involving great bodily injury, and misdemeanor child abuse for their alleged abuse of Lydia's sister. The couple pleaded not guilty.[30]

Like Lynn Paddock, the Schatzes were apparently big believers in the Pearls' child-rearing methods. A prosecutor told *Salon.com* that the Schatzes had explicitly described to police how they adhered to the teachings of Michael and Debi Pearl.[31] What's more, prosecutors say the Schatzes had in their home both the quarter-inch plumbing line that the Pearls advocate for the use of disciplining children and one of their child-rearing books.[32]

Michael Pearl denied culpability in both the Paddock and the Schatz case. In response to the latter, Pearl states on his website,

> It is regretful that our teachings were not able to turn them from their predisposition to abusive habits. Those of us who deal with substance abuse, psychological impairment, and family issues try to make positive changes in every person, but sometimes our best efforts are too little or too late. But for the sake of our precious children, we must double our efforts and move forward.[33]

While Michael and Debi Pearl are not directly responsible for the deaths of Sean and Lydia and the injuries sustained by their siblings, many worry that their teachings legitimize the harsh punishment of children. Their book, *To Train Up a Child*, has sold more than five hundred thousand copies since it was published in 1994, and many more read the literature posted on NoGreaterJoy.com. Michael Pearl has estimated that one-sixth of the nation's probable three million homeschooling families use their training methods.[34]

Critics from around the world urge people to ignore what the Pearls preach, but many find the couple's promises that their methods will bring about complacent children difficult to refuse. One former follower of the

Pearls told the media that she was "sucked in" by the words of Michael Pearl: "He makes you think he has the ear of God." But the mother later gave up using his methods. "You have to suppress your natural instincts and natural mothering to be able to do this."[35]

THE REMNANT FELLOWSHIP CHURCH

On March 27, 2007, Joseph and Sonia Smith from Atlanta were sentenced to life plus thirty years in prison for killing their eight-year-old son, Josef. The Smiths maintained they were innocent, that Josef died from a bacterial infection. But jurors voted to convict the parents after seeing photographs of what appeared to be bruises on Josef's head, shoulders, torso, and legs. Also, Josef's brother testified that Josef died after being shut up in a wooden box. Two medical examiners ruled the death a homicide. Josef's parents reportedly admitted to repeatedly spanking their son according to their beliefs about what the Bible says about raising children.[36] They were also members of Gwen Shamblin's Remnant Fellowship Church. Shamblin has maintained that she leaves child discipline to parents and believes that corporal punishment should be used as a last resort.[37]

But former Remnant Fellowship members tell a different story. They admit that Shamblin has never advocated abusing children outright but say her disciplinary teachings encourage parents to administer excessive corporal punishment. "Two or three spankings would not be enough. It could be ten spankings," a former member told the media.[38] In the aforementioned recorded presentation to parents, a church leader gleefully describes how he and his wife, after having been "blessed" with Shamblin's advice, brought under control their two-and-a-half-year-old daughter one evening:

> We had a real showdown with her, and her will was just ruling, and enough was enough, and we had a leg spanking over and over and over and over and over and over again. . . . And we stayed on top of it for a couple, three weeks, and that has been a different child in this last year because of that, and now, I can say I feel *real* confident that we are training up that child in the way that she should go and she won't depart from it.

Josef's father reportedly admitted to spanking his son with a glue stick, the kind that is used in large hot glue guns.[39] Former church members say others were also using glue sticks to hit their children, although Shamblin has stated that the idea came from outside the church. In the wake of Josef Smith's death, former members said they feared for the safety of other children in the Remnant

Fellowship because some members believe Shamblin is a prophet. As one former Remnant Fellowship member told the media, "If Gwen speaks about parenting, you can bet people are going to listen. They are going to take her advice and follow it."[40]

Authorities investigated the church but could not find a link between the church's teachings about punishing children and Josef's death. Years after the Smiths were convicted, Shamblin maintained that they were innocent.[41] But a conversation between Shamblin and Sonia Smith, Josef's mother, seemed to foreshadow the tragedy. The discussion took place during another recorded teleconference presentation Shamblin made to church members. (The recording was sent to this author by a source who did not want to be identified.) At one point, Sonia Smith speaks up to heartily thank Shamblin for parenting advice she received from a Remnant Fellowship leader. Smith tells Shamblin that her seven-year-old son, presumably Josef, had been "very destructive," that he had tried to strangle her baby and set the house on fire. Smith says that she was at the end of her rope and did not know what to do. "He was not even crying during a paddling," says Smith. But now, "It's like looking at a different child."

Smith explains that things changed after she did "exactly" what the church leader told her to do. That is, "to spank him on the back of his thighs, take everything out of his room—and that was like a two-hour job but we got everything out of there—and locked him in there from that Friday until Monday and only left him in the room with his Bible, and I just praise God for you guys." Now, Smith says, her son comes to her regularly, asking, "Mom, is there anything I can do for you? Can I help you? What do you need done, Mom?"

In response, Shamblin does not question the advice that Smith received from the church leader. Nor does she suggest that Smith see a specialist about her son's alarming behavior. Instead, Shamblin replies, "That's a miracle. You've got a child that's going from just bizarre down to in-control, so I praise God."

CONCLUSION

Americans, including those of faith, have been moving away from using corporal punishment on children, yet there still exists a strong advocacy for the practice, especially in conservative Christian communities. In the words of Rev. Marie M. Fortune, the executive director of the FaithTrust Institute,

> The Christian community must . . . determine why circumstances of severe child abuse are occurring in Christian contexts. We must challenge the teachings (that children need corporal punishment) which have been adhered to so

long that they have come to be associated with orthodox Christian belief. This mistaken belief leads, in too many cases, to child abuse.[42]

Of course, everyone has a right to believe in any religious doctrine, no matter how controversial. But there is a point where the practice of religion infringes on a child's right to feel safe. As Philip Greven writes in *Spare the Child*,

> So much pain has been inflicted on so many children for so many centuries in the name of Jesus Christ! So many tears shed, so much suffering experienced, so much anger and hatred generated, so much aggression and violence summoned forth, so much destruction and death brought about—all because of the oft-repeated but misguided belief that physical discipline is indispensable to "Christian" child-rearing and soul-saving and salvation.[43]

Some theological ideas are dangerous. While those that justify authoritarian parenting and using corporal punishment might appeal to adults who relish the idea of gaining control over children, there are more compassionate, healthy ways to raise boys and girls so that they grow up to be happy, strong, and responsible grown-ups. As long as the faithful require of children unquestioning obedience, see them as inherently sinful, and believe that adults must break children's wills to help them earn eternal salvation, children will continue to suffer injury and die violent deaths.

Part 2
HARM WITHOUT HITTING
Religious Child Emotional Abuse

INTRODUCTION

Whe I asked forty-year-old Rose on July 28, 2009, to tell me about her childhood growing up in Redwood City, California, she did not talk about going on fun family trips, playing with friends, or enjoying math class. Instead, she talked about the many hours she spent in the girls' bathroom of her elementary school. It started in kindergarten. Rose was a shy child, and her fervent Pentecostal Christian parents had big expectations of her.

"I was to be saving souls, witnessing to my classmates and my teachers," says Rose. "That pressure was almost unbearable. I had intense, intense anxiety. I had a lot of stomachaches, headaches." But Rose's religious education began even earlier than kindergarten.

"My earliest childhood memory is of accepting Jesus as my Lord and Savior," says Rose. "I am about two and a half years old. I remember the circumstances, the room, and my mother explaining this to me. Another important concept I was told early on was that sin is a sin no matter what, and any little thing I did could send me to hell for eternity."

So, terrified of the task of "saving" souls—and disappointing Jesus by committing an error that could send her to hell—Rose hid in the school bathroom. Not knowing what to do with her, teachers escorted her to the principal's office. "Back then, there were no counselors. There was no special ed. There was no one to help a child like myself. I just could barely function because it was so scary. It was so painful, and I was so afraid of everybody."

Such feelings of fear are common among children who are the victims of *religious emotional or psychological abuse and neglect*. To understand how children are harmed this way, it's important to first understand emotional maltreatment that is not necessarily committed in a religious context.

CHILD EMOTIONAL OR PSYCHOLOGICAL MALTREATMENT

Emotional or psychological abuse or neglect is commonly described as "a repeated pattern of caregiver behavior or extreme incident(s) that convey to children that they are worthless, flawed, unloved, unwanted, endangered, or only of value in meeting another's needs."[1] (The words *emotional* and *psychological* are commonly used interchangeably when experts describe this form of maltreatment.)

Unlike physical abuse and neglect, psychological maltreatment usually does not produce obvious effects. So how to identify it? According to experts, emotional maltreatment is not identified by its *effects* but by perpetrators' actions[2]—actions that fall under one or more of six categories:

1. *Spurning*: verbal or nonverbal acts that reject and degrade the child
2. *Terrorizing*: behavior that threatens or is likely to physically hurt, kill, abandon, or place the child or the child's loved ones or objects in recognizably dangerous situations
3. *Isolating*: acts that consistently deny the child opportunities to meet needs for interacting or communicating with peers or adults inside or outside the home
4. *Exploiting or corrupting*: acts that encourage the child to develop inappropriate behaviors
5. *Denying emotional responsiveness*: acts that ignore the child's attempts and needs to interact; showing no emotion in interactions with the child
6. *Neglecting mental health, medical, and educational needs*: unwarranted acts that ignore, refuse to allow, or fail to provide necessary treatment for mental health, medical, and educational problems of the child[3]

How prevalent is emotional maltreatment? A recent study estimates that this form of abuse and neglect has a significant presence in the childhood histories of more than one-third of American adults, while approximately 10 to 15 percent of the country's population has experienced especially severe and chronic forms of this type of abuse and neglect.[4] However, experts say we are far from understanding just how pervasive emotional maltreatment really is. According to the second edition of *The APSAC* [American Professional

Society on the Abuse of Children] *Handbook on Child Maltreatment*, studies that have looked at this problem have not been consistent in defining and measuring it, and many cases most likely do not get reported.[5]

"Emotional abuse is harder to spot and easier to deny [than other forms of abuse]," writes Gregory L. Jantz in *Healing the Scars of Emotional Abuse*. "Emotional abuse always accompanies physical or sexual abuse but stands fully on its own as damaging and destructive to an individual."[6]

It's also difficult to assess the effects of this form of abuse. One, resulting problems can take a long time to manifest. According to the APSAC handbook, much emotional maltreatment is not episodic but chronic, often occurring as neglectful acts that "slowly and persistently [eat] away at children's spirits, until they have little will to connect with others or explore the world."[7] Two, it's hard to know whether negative effects, which can include lags in development, learning problems, and speech disorders, are caused by abuse or other factors.[8]

Compounding the problem further, psychologically abusive acts are commonly accepted as normal by those in the victim's presence. No doubt, Rose's mother believed the religious teachings that proved so stressful for Rose were good for her daughter. Often, people who are or were targets of emotional abuse or neglect as children do not see themselves as victims; instead, they tend to accept the maltreatment as a normal part of life.[9] One physician writes that the emotional abuse of children "can be subtle and hidden, buried in discipline," and, what's more, nearly impossible to prove in a court of law.[10]

HARM TO VICTIMS

While it might be tricky to identify emotional maltreatment, the damage—which manifests as both psychological and physical problems—is often undeniable. During childhood, victims may fail to thrive or their developmental progress may be halted, while teenage victims find it difficult to trust others and form healthy interpersonal relationships. Emotionally abused children have a tendency to develop such lifelong psychopathologic problems as depression, estrangement, anxiety, low self-esteem, inappropriate or troubled relationships, or a lack of empathy. When victims of emotional abuse eventually have children of their own, they may have trouble recognizing and appreciating the needs and feelings of their own children and often emotionally abuse them as well.[11]

Other negative effects can include poor appetite, lying and stealing, incompetence or underachievement, inability to become independent, emotional withdrawal, suicide, homicide,[12] acting out sexually, loneliness, perfectionism, unrealistic guilt, unresolved anger and resentments, addictions, allergies, asthma, digestive disturbances, hypochondria, chronic fatigue syndrome, difficulty sleeping, migraine headaches, panic attacks, phobias, unexplained skin rashes, and unexplained physical pain.[13]

As harmful as other forms of abuse and neglect can be, emotional maltreatment is often the most damaging. As one psychologist put it, when various forms of abuse are present, children are most affected by the perpetrator's "psychological stance."[14] Write the authors of the APSAC handbook, "Empirical research suggests that the most common and lasting effects of physical abuse, sexual abuse, and neglect tend to be related to associated and embedded psychological experiences."[15]

Indeed, victims who have suffered various forms of abuse commonly say that the emotional abuse had the most detrimental impact on their lives. An anecdotal example appears in Richard Dawkins's *The God Delusion*. In describing a letter written by an American in her forties who was brought up Roman Catholic, Dawkins explains that the woman discusses two events that took place when she was seven. The first was having been sexually abused by her parish priest, while the second was the death of a school friend who had been raised Protestant. Of the two traumatic events, the woman said that the second was worse, because, while having been molested was "yucky," her belief that her friend was burning forever in hell left her with "cold, immeasurable fear." She writes, "I spent many a night being terrified that the people I loved would go to hell. It gave me nightmares."[16]

In describing the physical, sexual, and emotional abuse of her father in *Train Up the Child*, Louise Anne Owens writes, "More than the physical or sexual trauma, the fear of hell that my father implanted in me with his self-righteous brainwashing had the most far-reaching effects."[17] Nate Phelps, the son of the ultra-conservative and highly controversial Baptist preacher Fred Phelps, expressed a similar reaction in a speech he gave to the American Atheists Convention in 2009. In the speech, the younger Phelps described having been physically abused by his father when he was young. But, Phelps noted, "As extreme and violent as his physical assaults were, his verbal attacks were far more destructive."[18]

Kelly, the woman who grew up a Jehovah's Witness and suffered at the hands of her physically and emotionally abusive stepfather, says that as bad as it was to get a surprise smack or to be beaten and thrown against walls, the emotional torment was worse:

> I can tell you right now, the physical abuse, I would take that over the verbal any day, because the bruises heal. The words, specific words, stay in my head

and they are like little termites. They don't leave my head. They are still there doing whatever kind of damage that they do. Pretty much on a daily basis, we were "stupid," "lazy," and "fat." And he said it over and over and over again. It was funny because I wasn't a fat kid. It wasn't even like he was making fun of the pudgy kid, which would be cruel. He was saying it because he knew that that was where my self-esteem was lowest—how I felt about myself. So he pretty much targeted whatever you felt worst about yourself and would say it as though it were true.

Chapter 9
IS RELIGION GOOD OR BAD FOR A CHILD'S PSYCHE?

Is worshipping a supreme being, carrying out religious rituals, and learning about faith good or bad for mental health? To put things in context, being taught or maintaining religious beliefs is far more likely to help than to harm a person's mental state. "Most research suggests religiosity has a positive association with well-being and mental health," write the authors of one study. They point out that research shows that religion provides people with a "potent coping strategy" that helps them deal with stress. Religion helps lower symptoms of depression among the elderly, and religiously active college women appear to be less prone to anxiety.[1]

The fourth edition of *The Psychology of Religion*, by Ralph W. Hood Jr., Peter C. Hill, and Bernard Spilka, describes many significant benefits of religious belief. For example, belief may foster positive psychological states, such as joy or hope; buffer stress; protect against such negative feelings as fear, sadness, and anger; and enhance a sense of control. Religious belief, conclude the authors, "can be of a particular benefit for people dealing with a chronic illness or death of a loved one," while involvement in a religious group "may provide a greater social support network."[2] The content of religious belief "facilitates in the experience of powerful emotions";[3] spirituality can lower boredom and give people a sense of purpose;[4] and believing in a supreme being, attending religious services, and praying can lead to high self-esteem and well-being. Furthermore, conversion to a particular faith and performing rituals can have beneficial and therapeutic effects on the believer.[5] One study shows that fundamentalists are significantly more optimistic than moderate believers, who are themselves more optimistic than liberals.[6]

128

The authors of *The Handbook of Religion and Health*, Harold G. Koenig, Michael E. McCullough, and David B. Larson, note that emotional and physical healing play a vital role in the belief systems of Judeo-Christian traditions as well as in those of Hindus, Buddhists, Muslims, and Jews. Many patients who suffer with mental illness "may turn to religion as a source of comfort and strength to help them cope with their trials," write the authors.[7] They also point out that clergy throughout the United States serve as counselors and that "the field of pastoral care has grown into a recognized and respectable discipline."[8]

According to *Psychology Today* blogger Clay Routledge, an assistant professor of psychology at North Dakota State University, "To the extent that religion serves to bolster feelings of hope, optimism, self-esteem, belongingness, and meaning, it may be an important psychological resource for many people."[9]

Even skeptics of religion are convinced of its benefits. While Eli S. Chesen disagrees with those who claim that religion is necessary for a healthy mental state in *Religion May Be Hazardous to Your Health*, he believes that faith "is very often a supportive and even enriching force that can facilitate mental well-being and general happiness."[10]

NEGATIVE EFFECTS

But while religion can be kind to the human psyche, it also has the potential to cause harm. *The Psychology of Religion* points to a large-scale analysis of psychological studies relating indices of religion to psychopathology up through 1983. The analysis finds that fourteen studies showed a favorable relationship between religion and mental health; however, seven indicated that religion is positively associated with pathology, and nine revealed no association. "It is an overgeneralization to say that religion is necessarily good or bad for one's health," write the authors.[11] "Just as religion can strengthen moral commitments, enhance optimism, and stimulate ego development, it may also activate disordered thinking and behavior."[12] Studies show that people's self-esteem is tied up with how they view God. This can bode well if someone views God as merciful, kind, forgiving, and understanding, but seeing God as distant, uninterested, punishing, or vindictive has less salutary health effects.[13]

Places of worship can hinder emotional and spiritual growth by instilling fear in believers. Religious leaders often use guilt to manipulate worshippers—refusing to discuss members' feelings of doubt or enforcing rigid "thou shalt not" rules, for instance.[14] Critics talk about oppressive religious communities proliferating "toxic faith" and committing "spiritual abuse." Untold numbers of websites are set up by and for former members of religions and faith groups who need support after suffering psychological harm. People sometimes become suicidal after leaving strict religious communities.

The American psychologist Albert Ellis believed that "devout, orthodox, or dogmatic religion" is "significantly correlated with emotional disturbance." Ellis came to this conclusion based on the idea that "people largely disturb themselves by believing strongly in absolutistic shoulds, oughts, and musts, and most people who dogmatically believe in some religion believe in these health-sabotaging absolutes."[15]

An earlier chapter discussed the harm caused by religious authoritarian cultures. The most oppressive and totalistic societies are known as "high-demand" groups or cults and have been shown to be exceedingly psychologically harmful. Experts conclude that such groups foster an unhealthy form of submission and obedience to religious leaders. In cults, the leadership sets up a demanding and confusing set of rewards and punishments, leaving members in a state of "anxious dependency" as they constantly try to measure up, thereby intensifying the leadership's control of members.[16] In some instances, this control has proved dangerous, as cult members have murdered members of the public and those belonging to the group, such as the killings in Jonestown and the Manson murders.

While religion can serve as a coping mechanism for those with mental illness, some professional mental health providers believe that certain religious teachings can have a deleterious effect on patients. Such mental illnesses as schizophrenia, acute mania, or psychotic depression can be accompanied by bizarre religious delusions and obsessive ritualizing, although it is unclear whether religious beliefs and practices in these cases cause, or are the result of, mental illness.[17]

Critics point to biblical passages that warn against self-love and feeling confident, which can lower self-esteem. For example, in 2 Timothy 3:2–5, Paul tells people to reject all those who are "lovers of themselves." Isaiah 64:6 declares that humans are "all like an unclean thing, and all our righteousnesses are like filthy rags" whose "iniquities, like the wind, have taken us away."

Religion can be a source of pathological perfectionism,[18] as well as an obsessive-compulsive disorder known as *scrupulosity*, in which sufferers repeatedly perform religious rituals or are mired in fear about feeling sinful.[19] Sometimes religious communities demand that individuals conform, to those individuals' detriment. The authors of *The Handbook of Religion and Health* write, "Individuals who deviate from accepted standards may be judged negatively and consequently be marginalized."[20]

Many see Christianity's doctrine of original sin as a source of mental distress. According to *The Psychology of Religion*, the concept of sinfulness can be "a constructive control on behavior" but also "an arouser of guilt, depression, and distress." Furthermore, note the authors,

Obsession with sin and guilt seems to be a correlate of religious frameworks that stress moral perfection. . . . Such an emphasis can incite feelings of low self-esteem and worthlessness, which have the potential of contributing to mental disorders. We also find the presence of sin and associated guilt in the motivation for mysticism, conversion, prayer, scrupulosity, confession, bizarre rituals, self-denial, and self-mutilation.[21]

"Increasingly, psychologists are finding stronger links between serious emotional problems and religious upbringing," writes reporter Virginia Culver in the *Denver Post*. "Instead of inner peace and happiness, for some people, religion evokes feelings of despair and self-doubt."[22]

Studies conducted on particular sects and mainstream believers reveal potentially inordinately negative impacts on mental health:

- Studies that examined two Anabaptist sects, the Amish and the Hutterites, show that members suffered significant psychological problems, including stress, anxiety, guilt, and depression.[23]
- One study that looked at Christian fundamentalists who engaged in faith healing shows that the subjects presented unhealthy psychological characteristics that were "so pervasive that major disruptive events in their lives were ignored and interpreted as part of a normal existence."[24]
- A study of Jehovah's Witnesses confirms previous findings that the rate of mental illness among these followers is "considerably above average." Problems were attributable to a likelihood that people with emotional problems tend to join the faith, as well as the faith's subculture and teachings, such as fear-based teachings regarding Armageddon.[25]
- According to *The Psychology of Religion*, there have been instances where "the requirements of chastity and celibacy [are] too much of a psychological burden for Catholic priests and nuns to bear, and abnormal expressions of anxiety and other undesirable behaviors may result."[26]
- A study that looked at problems of perfectionism concludes that religions such as Orthodox Judaism might emphasize "superficial behavior" to the point that believers feel sinful for having 'normal' emotions."[27]
- There have been concerns that Mormons are under great stress, since studies show that the population of Utah—which is 70 percent Mormon—has an inordinately high rate of depression and greatly relies on psychotropic drugs. One study finds Utahans experience depression at a higher rate than any other state, and more than 14 percent suffer from serious psychological distress.[28]

Experts believe that some of the reasons for religion's negative psychological effects might include devoutly religious persons being prone to condemn themselves for being inferior;[29] believers needing but avoiding traditional mental healthcare;[30] religious beliefs portraying God as distant, uninterested, punishing, or vindictive;[31] religious beliefs being at odds with scientific knowledge; and using religion as a way to avoid dealing with unpleasant situations like illness and death.[32]

RELIGION AND THE MENTAL HEALTH OF CHILDREN

Very little study has been done on religion's effects on the mental health of young people. However, what information is available suggests, again, that most effects are good. This is especially true in terms of family interactions. A number of studies show that religious families tend to have strong, supportive relationships. For example, one study finds that parents who are more religiously active have fewer conflicts between the two parents, more cohesive family relationships, and fewer problems among their adolescent children. Another study suggests that religion supports responsible fathering. Spirituality can help families deal with children who have disabilities.[33] One study shows that adolescents who participate in faith-based activities get into less trouble than those who do not engage in such activities.[34] Yet another study defies the wide-reaching assumption about Catholic guilt in finding that Catholic teenagers are generally *not* guilt-ridden.[35]

According to Birkbeck College at University of London psychology professor Stephen Frosh in *Handbook of Parenting*, there is evidence that religious parents are "more likely to have harmonious family relationships rather than the converse."[36]

But we also know that a religious upbringing can be detrimental, even though empirical data—which has largely addressed only cults—is lacking. In an article written for the International Cultic Studies Association newsletter, cult expert Leona Furnari writes that the controlling nature of these groups interferes with children's development, beginning in infancy. More specifically, Furnari observes that former cult members experience learning deficiencies and problems reading social cues.[37] A workshop for people raised in cultic groups revealed serious problems. For example, dire, supernaturally based threats and regular criticism of the children's failings led to insecurity, self-hating, and dependency upon the leaders of the group. A paper detailing the result of the workshop remarks, "Such an environment is the opposite of what the psychological community would recommend for the rearing of children." Here, the authors state, "Children raised in such environments cannot develop confidence in themselves, or their immediate environment, because they can be criticized even when they obey. . . . Because the belief system by definition is unassailable, the child will always be 'wrong.'" The study also calls attention to the "black-and-white" ideologies, where members are taught to adhere to only one set of beliefs—beliefs held by the leadership.[38]

Children in cults can experience such negative consequences as isolation from outside influences, "psychological depletion" through forced repetitive tasks, guilt and anxiety, degradation, and intense peer pressure to give "all" to the cult.[39] One study of former members of high-demand religious groups finds that people who are raised in such environments, compared to those who join later in life, experience "significantly more psychological maltreatment and physical victimisation in childhood" and have "significantly higher levels of psychological distress" after leaving their sects.[40]

In an Australian study on cults, researchers note that some subjects suffered from dissociative identity disorder and that this disorder was the result of chronic trauma experienced during childhood, such as being made to engage in age-inappropriate behavior, including sexualization, and enduring severe punishments "often carried to the point of the child's emotional breakdown."[41] Another study finds that those who grew up in and eventually left a particular worldwide cult known as the Exclusive Brethren suffered from a variety of psychological symptoms, including alienation from society, a lack of interpersonal skills, and difficulty forming relationships.[42]

But experts also point to potential problems in mainstream religions, not only in cults. The previously noted study on perfectionism shows how Orthodox Jewish adolescents can suffer with the disorder.[43] The aforementioned study on Jehovah's Witnesses shows that the rules imposed on members, such as prohibiting the celebration of holidays and birthdays, requiring members to spend many hours each week in meetings, and controlling how Witnesses interact with non-Witnesses, negatively affect children. The researchers state, "It is very difficult for a child raised [as] a Witness to develop into a normal, socially aware, well-adjusted adult. They are taught that all of those of the world are evil, and even though worldly people may appear to be kind, this is one of Satan's tactics to lure people out of God's organization."[44] The same criticism has been raised regarding mainstream Christianity. In *Deadly Doctrine: Health, Illness, and Christian God-Talk*, Wendell W. Watters, MD, opines that families are unlikely to develop to their full potential due to Christian teachings that "are uncompromisingly antithetical to the development of self-esteem."[45]

While Stephen Frosh believes faith generally is beneficial to young people, he also notes that maternal depression is "quite common" in large families that are guided by faith to abstain from birth control and marry young. While the mental health effects on children in these families has not been studied, writes Frosh, "given the strength of the link between maternal depression and children's problems, difficulties are likely to be substantial."[46]

Religion and American culture expert Jason C. Bivins worries about what he calls a "fear regime" operated by evangelical Christian churches and communities that target young people. In *Religion of Fear: The Politics of Horror in Conservative Evangelicalism*, Bivins gives two examples, Christian comic books and church-sponsored "hell houses," both of which profess that eternal damnation awaits those who do not subscribe to certain beliefs and lifestyles.[47]

In *The Child's Song*, retired Princeton Theological Seminary pastoral psychology professor Donald Capps writes, "I believe that many religious ideas that children are taught cause them emotional torment and are therefore inherently abusive." What's more, he adds, "Religious ideas are more tormenting than torturing, since they are unlikely to cause acute emotional pain of the sort that occurs as the child awaits physical punishment, but are fully capable of harassment and persecution through repeated infliction of suffering or annoyance."[48]

Louise Anne Owens, the author of *Train Up the Child*, maintains that all six previously mentioned maltreatment categories can be manifested in a religious context.[49] Taking Owens's lead, I have attempted to provide detail within each category from a religious viewpoint:

1. *Spurning*: rejecting or degrading the child by making him or her feel unworthy of God's love, bound for eternal damnation, or sinful, wicked, or evil
2. *Terrorizing*: threatening the child with severe punishment for violating religious rules; threatening the child with harm due to supernatural forces, such as an angry god, the devil, or demons
3. *Isolating*: preventing the child from interacting with people based on their religious affiliation; denying the child access to media that does not reflect a particular religious viewpoint
4. *Exploiting or corrupting*: inculcating or indoctrinating the child into a faith at the expense of a well-rounded education; having the child work for a faith or place of worship, such as through proselytizing
5. *Denying emotional responsiveness*: failing to express affection and love, in keeping with the child-rearing norms of a religious community or faith group

6. *Neglecting mental health, medical, and educational needs:* denying children mental health or medical services or education as a way to conform to the norms of a religious community or faith group

This section on emotional maltreatment focuses on the first four categories— all forms of religious emotional abuse.

Chapter 10

SINFUL, DISOBEDIENT, EVIL, AND DEPRAVED—
RELIGIOUS SPURNING

As its name implies, *spurning* includes such acts as belittling, degrading, shaming, and publicly humiliating children.[1] In a religious context, the number one way spurning occurs is when children are told they are sinful. Jason Wilkinson, who was introduced earlier as having received a great deal of corporal punishment in school, learned about his own supposed sinfulness when he attended a small Christian school in central Texas. As mentioned earlier, Wilkinson says many kids were sent to the principal's office to be paddled. But those paddlings were also often accompanied by what Wilkinson calls "indoctrination."

"I remember sitting in this person's office for fifteen, twenty, thirty minutes as they would go on about the Bible and how children should be punished and how they think children should act and how they should behave and how they should be seen and not heard and a whole lot of minutia that I really just didn't absorb at all," singsongs Wilkinson. However, what he did "absorb" were school administrators' belittling comments. In particular, Wilkinson says the staff would quote Isaiah 64:6 about humans' deeds being akin to "filthy rags." He also remembers being warned of feeling pride. "Anything you do for yourself is for Satan," he recalls school administrators saying.

Looking back on those experiences, Wilkinson concludes that such spurning sharply contrasted with what many people in his church community said about children. "The general message is that, even though we are 'God's children' and these 'amazing beings of eternal light,' the flip side is that we're also taught we have no value and that we are sinners and are evil. So how to equate that? We're so 'amazing,' but we're also such absolute failures?"

Another victim of religious spurning is Louise Anne Owens, who writes about her abusive childhood in *Train Up the Child*. In the book, she discusses how her father, a fundamentalist Christian preacher, physically, sexually, and emotionally abused her, frequently using religious ideas to assist in his torture. With his religious teachings about hell and sin, the man both spurned and terrorized his daughter, two forms of abuse that often go hand in hand. Owens writes,

> My father's hell was a certain and terrible place; sins such as polishing my shoes on the Sabbath Day could send me there forever if I died or if Christ returned in the Rapture before I had a chance to repent. He so convinced me that I was a sinner who deserved to spend eternity in hell that, although I know now that I am a good person, the feeling that I am evil sometimes still returns.[2]

What makes religious spurning particularly insidious is that adults have long been of the mind-set that convincing children they are sinful is spiritually good for them. Back in 1908, a weekly magazine called the *Outlook* contained a six-part series called "On the Training of Parents." In its final piece, entitled "The Beginning of Wisdom," the magazine's assistant editor, Ernest Hamlin Abbot, praises a letter that he believes is a "narrative of a complete and orderly religious experience." The letter is from a father who talks about the pains he and his wife took in raising their daughter Marion so that she was "seriously exercised with religious things." As Abbot tells it, Marion's parents read to her from "leaflets for Sabbath-schools" when she was eight months old. When she was a year and a half old, her parents explained to her about "the origin and use of the Bible." In addition, her early indoctrination also included some damaging ideas. When she was two years old, Marion was made to kneel down and was told she should "ask God to make you good and give you a new heart." When Marion asked for clarification, writes Abbot, her parents then informed her "of the way of salvation by Jesus Christ, and the steps God had taken to save sinners." Abbot quotes the father's letter: "We endeavored to impress upon her mind that she was a sinner and needed forgiveness, and God would forgive her sins and give her a new heart through Jesus Christ." (Two years later, Marion died of a "disease of the brain," so no one will ever know what effect this religious spurning had on the child's mental state.)[3]

Does such well-intentioned religious spurning happen today? Without doubt. I was struck by a blog written by a woman from the United Kingdom who seems to be indoctrinating her young daughter in just the way the parents of Marion did. The woman explains how, first thing in the morning, her four-year-old daughter usually promises her mother that she is "going to be a good girl today." The mother writes that the girl "really means it, and I can see how she longs to finish even just one day in her life without doing anything wrong." However, writes the mother, "within at the least an hour of saying she is going to be good, that promise will be broken." Convinced of her child's propensity to sin, when the girl asks her mother if she has been good, the mother says she sometimes praises her but also tells her what she has done wrong. "I have never said to her she has been a perfect little girl who has done nothing wrong all day. . . . I do not believe in teaching children self-esteem or that they should feel good about themselves, because they should not. . . . The problem is sin. . . . We are all born God-hating and evil."[4]

Another example of religious spurning appears in the 2006 Academy Award–nominated documentary *Jesus Camp*, which documents what goes on in a charismatic Pentecostal children's summer camp run by a preacher named Becky Fischer. Throughout most of the movie, Fischer and her staff use various tactics to turn the children into a troupe of fanatical Christians. In one scene, Fischer speaks to the campers in such a way that some are brought to tears:

> I sense in my heart tonight what I heard the Lord say is that there's some kids here that say that they're Christians that go to church all the time, but you're one thing when you're at church, and you're another thing when you're at school with your friends. You're a phony and a hypocrite. You do things you shouldn't do. You talk dirty just like all the other kids talk dirty, and it's time to clean up your act. Come up here and get washed because we can't have phonies in the army of God. [*Fischer has the children wash their hands with bottled water.*][5]

Kelly, the woman who grew up with an abusive stepfather, remembers what kind of reaction children in her Jehovah's Witness community would get when they so much as questioned a faith doctrine. "It would be lovingly explained to them how 'simple' that thought is. Some parents would smack their kids. It depends on the parent, but I think that the child would definitely figure out very quickly that that line of thinking is considered wrong." And, Kelly says, if young children are told such thinking is wrong "over and over and over again, you don't even begin to question it as you grow old. It's hard for me to explain specific examples because it is so much the tapestry of the life."

Part of one teenager's life "tapestry" was listening to Christian rock music. When Daniel Sawtelle and I spoke on March 21, 2009, he explained that he grew up in the charismatic Church of God of Prophecy in Pennsylvania. Back then, says Sawtelle, he loved listening to religious tunes with a hard-driving beat that would get him pumped up before basketball games. But when he listens to those same songs today, Sawtelle hears something very different. He says the songs are rife with messages such as "I'm not worthy" and "I'm sinful." Looking back, Sawtelle says, "To constantly sing this as your, quote, 'fun music,' I think subconsciously gets into your mind, 'I really am a horrible, horrible person, because I tell a white lie, because I'm not Jesus. I am, by default, awful.'"

In addition to being considered sinful for being disobedient and harboring religious doubts, children can be made to feel sinful for engaging in sexual acts or even just thinking about them. This was the case with Kelly.

> If you're a kid and you masturbate, oh God, that's sin, which is, of course a particularly natural, normal, and healthy thing to do, to explore one's own sexuality. But due to one interpretation of scripture, masturbation is a big no-no. It's "freeing temptation into your heart," so that if you follow through on a natural physical urge, then you are sinful and dirty and bad. They won't say you're dirty and bad, but it sure as hell was implied.

Sawtelle's youth was also plagued with ideas about sinfulness and sex. When he reached puberty, he began having sexual thoughts, which he had been taught to believe were wrong, since sex is reserved for marriage: "The first time I masturbated, I cried myself to sleep." Sawtelle remembers thinking, "I'm awful. I'm this horrible, horrible person. Why am I doing these bad things?" Despite the fact that Sawtelle was a model student in high school, a talented athlete, and never in trouble, he never felt good about himself.

> I just assumed everyone was better than me. Everyone was a better Christian than me. No other Christian teenage boy was looking at porn except me. No other Christian teenage boy was hiding and masturbating and doing these things. "I'm the only one, and God is super upset with me. So I've got to right it before anyone finds out. I can't let anybody find out, because if they find out then they're gonna know that I'm this evil sinner and their opinion of me will fall. They'll ostracize me or whatever." It's all a direct line from hating myself for sinning then to hating myself and wanting to end my life.

When he began dating a devout Catholic girl in high school, Sawtelle says the two were miserable together in their sexual "sinfulness." "After we made out, we would cry," he says. When he consulted his pastor, the man told him that Sawtelle and his girlfriend should agree that if they were to be physically intimate again, they should break up. "I was on an emotional rollercoaster just for getting to second base."

Young people who grow up in a religious community that teaches that homosexuality is sinful—even, as in many cases, an abomination—and realize they are gay or lesbian (or merely question their sexuality) can grow to hate themselves, sometimes to the point of being suicidal. On a website devoted to former Christians, a woman named Melenie, who grew up Baptist, writes about how she learned at the age of four that "homosexuality was wrong" and that gay or lesbian people would "go straight to hell." This was a problem for Melenie because, at around the age of ten, she realized that she "liked girls." She writes about worrying that "god wouldn't love me anymore because I was an abomination." What's more, other church members ostracized Melenie for being gay.

> I struggled with the issue for a year before coming out to my best friend. She said she did not agree but swore to never tell anyone. I felt better finally letting someone know that I am a lesbian. That Wednesday I went to church like I always had since I was eleven, and I walked over to the preacher who was a friend of mine and said "Hello," and he would not speak to me. He looked through me like I was not even there. I walked over to my best friend and sat down beside her, still hurt. To my surprise she got up, and everyone in my youth group followed her. I left, and went home crying. The next Sunday the preacher told us about the evils of homosexuality, and how no matter what you did you were no longer a child of god, but of Satan.[6]

The reason why spurning hurts is due to the fact that perpetrators are castigating not simply victims' actions but who they are as people. Unfortunately, Christian teachings about sinfulness can accomplish this same harm. Wendell Watters makes this point in *Deadly Doctrine*. Watters says such teachings focus on a child's "innate badness," rather than the inappropriateness of a child's behavior. "Many parents fail to see the difference between saying to a child, 'You are a bad, naughty boy for doing that,' and telling the child that a particular mode of behavior is unacceptable and will not be tolerated in the family," he writes. "Children growing up in families relatively untainted by Christian notions of self-loathing will be more likely to develop self-esteem than children in a 'good' Christian home."[7]

Not surprisingly, children who are religiously spurned often suffer persistent pangs of low self-esteem. And they usually suffer in silence, as feelings of unworthiness prevent them from seeking help when they need it. For instance, when John was growing up in a fundamentalist nondenominational Christian community in Mississippi, he was paralyzed by fears, partly due to mental illness. But he kept these fears to himself. As the twenty-eight-year-old told me on March 7, 2009, he was tormented by frightening visions of demons, yet he never told his parents about them.

"I thought I was the sinner, and I was wrong. I felt so guilty about it, why would I want to talk about it? Why would I want to tell my parents and incriminate myself? I was an insane parent- [and] people-pleaser. The last thing my heart could stand was for my parents to be worried for my soul and to be disappointed in my faith."

Chapter 11

SCARING THEM INTO FAITH— RELIGIOUS TERRORIZING

S ome say that love and fear are the two most basic emotions from which all other feelings are generated. While a certain amount of fear is healthy in our lives, most people would agree that it's a lot more important to feel love—and plenty of it.

"Fear stifles love and constricts our ability to feel and live," writes Philip Greven in *Spare the Child*. "Fear also limits our ability to put ourselves in the place of others, to have empathy, to feel compassion, to know pity, and to extend ourselves openly and freely toward other lives and other people."[1]

According to Jason Bivins in *Religion of Fear*, "Fear chokes the very air of our culture like smog that, while it can be seen from afar, we breathe in unknowingly with deep gulps."[2]

Religious teachings speak to both love and fear. Fortunately, you hear more talk about love these days than fear, as opposed to the days when most churches engaged in "fire and brimstone" threats. Interestingly, a search for the words *fear* and *love* in old versions of the Bible compared to new versions produces results that are a testament to this improved outlook. For example, the King James Version tallies 501 mentions of the word *fear* and 442 mentions of the word *love*, while the New International Version brings up 326 *fear* mentions and 697 *love* mentions.

Even so, much of religion is still rooted in fear-based teachings. Worshippers continue to be bombarded by scary ideas: that they must fear God, that eternal damnation or spiritual death awaits apostates, that demons and the devil are eager to possess them, or that end times, Armageddon, or other apocalyptic events are imminent. All this makes for many a white-knuckled worshipper.

CHILD TARGETS OF FEAR

Given this bed of fear laid by many of the pious, it is not surprising that children fall prey to *religious terrorizing*. Examples of terrorizing include placing a child in an unpredictable or chaotic or recognizably dangerous situation; setting rigid or unrealistic expectations with the threat of loss, harm, or danger if those expectations are not met; and threatening or perpetrating violence against a child or a child's loved ones.[3] And these same abusive acts also happen in a religious context.

Religious adults have long engaged in the religious terrorizing of children. One of the first textbooks to be put in the hands of American colonial children was *The New England Primer*, which included religious and moral lessons.[4] The book presents both loving and frightening messages to attract children to faith and prevent them from straying. For example, it says God is "good and kind to me," and he is also "angry every Day with wicked ones which go astray."[5] While the book discusses "a Heaven full of Joy," it also makes it clear that "There is a dreadful fiery Hell, Where wicked ones must always dwell."[6] The primer uses little sayings to help teach the alphabet. For example, the letter Y stands for "Youth forward flips, Death soonest nips."[7]

Another notable textbook, *Tracts for Spiritual Reading*, was published in the United States in 1884. The book, written by British priest and youth minister John J. Furniss (and approved by the Catholic Church), provides children with a house of horrors tour in which the reader is taken through various dungeons, each offering one terrifying image after another of what happens to sinful children. For example, in the chapter entitled "The Sight of Hell," Furniss describes a girl who wears a bonnet of fire that "is pressed down close all over her head."

> It burns her head; it burns into the skin; it scorches the bone of the skull and makes it smoke. The red hot fiery heat goes into the brain and melts it. You do not, perhaps, like a headache. Think what a headache that girl must have. But see more. She is wrapped up in flames, for her frock is fire. If she were on earth she would be burnt to a cinder in a moment. But she is in Hell, where fire burns everything, but burns nothing away. There she stands burning and scorched; there she will stand for ever burning and scorched! She counts with her fingers the moments as they pass away slowly, for each moment seems to her like a hundred years. As she counts the moments she remembers that she will have to count them for ever and ever.[8]

Church literature has continued to target children with terrifying imagery. A friend of mine named Judy showed me her first-grade Catholic catechism correspondence course from the 1940s, the Confraternity of Christian Doctrine Course workbook. The course, published by the Diocese of Oklahoma City and Tulsa, speaks of God's love but also frequently reminds children of God's incredible and intimidating power: "God sees and knows all things. God knows **what you think.** God knows **what you say.** God knows **what you do.** You cannot hide anything from God."

Former Jehovah's Witness fifty-two-year-old William H. Bowen explains that when he was growing up in the Midwest, children's Jehovah's Witness literature frequently featured a picture of Armageddon showing the mass killing of people around the globe. On December 15, 2009, Bowen told me that as a child, "I lived in fear of Armageddon. That day was going to happen, and I thought it was going to happen at any time."

Religious children's books published today have softened their messages yet still invoke fear-based ideas, even for the tiniest of readers. For example, during a recent trip to the bookstore, I picked up a book entitled *Hail Mary*. The cutely illustrated text, intended for very young Catholics, speaks about the Virgin Mary's goodness and, for the most part, is a delight to read. However, at the end, authors Xavier Deneux, Sabrina Bus, and Leslie Matthews utter the plea, "Mother of God, pray for us sinners, now and at the hour of our death."9

TERRORIZED PARENTS, TERRORIZED CHILDREN

Many parents are themselves victims of religious fears. For example, Jennifer Gordon, the woman whose fundamentalist Christian parents suddenly clamped down on house rules when she was a child, says her mother and father harbored many fears. They worried about the devil encroaching on their lives at every turn. "Sneezing was the work of the devil," and her parents were frequently taking part in exorcisms; her father even tried to "cast out the spirit of a lack of vitamin C." He also believed that the broken vacuum cleaner was "demon possessed."

Some of these fears would be funny, except for the fact that children can grow afraid just by observing their parents being consumed by fear. "Children raised by fearful parents learn to be fearful," writes John Bradshaw in *Reclaiming Virtue*. "Fearful and anxious parents and teachers can destroy young children's courage to learn. They do so by making them afraid of not doing what other people want, of not pleasing adults. They also make them afraid of failing. They often create fear by shaming and threatening physical punishment. And even when they don't create children's fears, they use whatever fears their children already have to manipulate and control them. Cultures of obedience use fear to control their subjects."[10]

Take Mary Casey, the woman who, growing up, was not allowed to watch television or go to dances for fear that she would be exposed to evil forces. Casey says her mother's paranoia about her "growing up and getting pregnant or doing anything that had anything to do with sexual stuff" left Casey feeling terribly guilty for feeling sexual lust. In fact, Casey was afraid that "masturbating would send me to hell."

In an e-mail sent to me on May 19, 2008, forty-seven-year-old Joanne describes what it was like to grow up with a very anxious mother who belonged to the Church of the Nazarene in Georgia. According to Joanne, her mother "wore herself to a frazzle keeping the parsonage and her three children neat and clean and was constantly fearful that she was not 'measuring up.'" Simmons adds that her mother "found discipline through guilt inducement very effective, particularly with me." She continues,

> Sensitive as I was, I think I assimilated much of her fear and negativity just by watching her expressions and behaviors and hearing her pray out loud daily that God would forgive her for her sins, my brothers for theirs, and me for mine. Seeing the careful, devout nature of my mother's life, then hearing her beg God for mercy—well, I figured if she was worried, I should be all the more worried! This seriousness and fear surrounded every part of my life except when I was outside playing with my friends. There, I seemed able to set my fears aside long enough to do the impish and exploratory things that kids often do, but the fears would come again with a vengeance when I returned home. To compound the guilt, I developed rheumatic fever at age five which, in my young mind, was definitely a result of my bad deeds.

Susan, the mother who earlier described having raised her children as Jehovah's Witnesses, has great regrets for instilling in her children fears that she had come to believe herself:

> I think there was a certain amount of psychological terror with the kind of things that we were taught to teach our children about the future—what God was going to do, the destruction he was going to bring on mankind, fear of spirit creatures, fear of the devil, fear of demons—because we were taught that those were real beings—and that had a real influence on day-to-day life. And that terror is transmitted to your children. I really, really regret that.

A SCARY GOD

One of the most common forms of religious terrorizing is depicting God as a frightening deity, as opposed to one that is all loving. Such teachings portray God as being angry, vengeful, uncaring, and ready to punish ne'er-do-wells. As Eli Chesen notes in *Religion May Be Hazardous to Your Health*, "The child who sees his God as punitive lives with unneeded fears and begins to generalize his fear of God to include other things. In other words, he begins to perceive the world as angry and harsh."[11]

My friend Judy, who lent me the first-grade Catholic catechism course workbook, was terrified of—and hated—God growing up in Oklahoma. She developed these emotions from having been emotionally and physically abused by her father. "I saw tyranny and cruelty at home and believed that's what God wanted," Judy told me on August 5, 2008. Yet, Judy had been led to believe that God always knew what she was thinking and feeling. The realization that she did not love God as she was supposed to traumatized her: "I would try to hide what was in my heart. When I was praying I would say, 'I love you, God,' but in my mind I was saying, 'I hate you,' and then think that I was going to hell."

Images of a terrifying god are taught not only in Western faiths. In a report that discussed abuses that took place in *gurukulas*, schools run by the International Society for Krishna Consciousness (ISKCON) in the United States and elsewhere, an unidentified young woman was quoted describing how she was emotionally abused by being made to fear the god Krishna:

> The teacher used to say, "Oh, you don't know when you are going to die. You could die in your sleep." And one day I was really bad and one of my teachers said, "Who knows, you might die tonight. Krishna might be punishing you. He might be taking away your life. . . ." And from that night on I used to pray every night, "Krishna please don't kill me. I promise I will be a good girl tomorrow. Please let me get fixed up enough so I can go back to Godhead. Don't take me in my sleep." And for years I had insomnia. I was too afraid to go back to sleep.[12]

THE NEXT LIFE

Sometimes children can be comforted by believing in an afterlife, because they are taught they will be rewarded with everlasting peace and surrounded by their loved ones. Former Jehovah's Witness William Bowen recounted in our interview inspiring words he was told as a boy:

My parents regularly told me—as I told my children when they were raised in the religion—that someday you'll live in a "Paradise Earth," and you'll have a big lion or tiger to play with. All the animals will be at peace with man. They'll be just like big pets, and you'll reside in this paradiselike park where you'll have friends, and you won't have to fear the world or fear Satan, and you'll have this parklike existence in a happy place for eternity.

In her book, *Escape*, Carolyn Jessop writes about growing up in the FLDS. When she was a girl, Jessop was told that she had the chance to become a goddess if she "lived Polygamy and proved worthy. It was our own version of the Cinderella story. Just having the opportunity to live in a plural marriage was sold to me as a special blessing that few would ever have." And she adds, "I felt like the luckiest little girl to be one of God's elite and a spirit who was the most chosen of all his spirits before I came to earth."[13]

But beliefs about the afterlife can backfire and prove terrifying for children. For example, when I spoke with Joanne, the woman who grew up in the Church of the Nazarene and whose mother held intense religious fears, she explained that when she was a child, she suffered bouts of rheumatic fever and was bedridden for long periods of time. When Joanne was ten, her family left her alone after she had fallen asleep. Later, Joanne awakened to a dark house and panicked, thinking that Jesus had returned to Earth, taken her family to heaven, and left her behind. Fortunately, a kind salesman knocked on the door and was met by the terrified, crying child. When he asked what was wrong, she told him, "Jesus has come and taken my parents, and they're gone forever." After that, she says, the man waited with her until her parents returned, at which time "he chewed them out royally."

Daniel Sawtelle, who was introduced in the previous chapter, tells a similar story, one that happened on a number of occasions when he was in elementary school. Sawtelle says he would sometimes come home and not be able to find his parents. Like Joanne, Sawtelle thought the worst—that he had been left behind *forever*. Sawtelle says one time his mother came in from outside, only to find him in tears. "I thought the Rapture came and I missed it!" he cried.

In *Religious Abuse*, Presbyterian pastor Keith Wright tells a tragic story about a boy who mutilated himself as a result of fear-based notions of hell. The story, contained in a letter Wright received from a colleague, describes a boy who goes outdoors to play and finds the family's toy wagon sitting by itself. Thrilled to be able to have the wagon all to himself rather than share it with his brother, the boy takes the wagon to the top of a hill, climbs in, and pushes off. Wright continues:

All by himself! A glorious ride! Drunk with joy, the little boy said, "I'm going like hell!" The words had no sooner left his lips than the little boy saw his father—not in person, probably, but in his mind. With the vision of his father, a dark shadow fell on his day. The little boy had forgotten himself in gladness. He had used an evil word, a "Devil's word." The ride came to an end in a gloom of guilt. The boy tugged his wagon around behind the house to the manure pile that was there, found a piece of broken bottle, and, in an extravagance of self-blame, tried to cut off his toes.[14]

Gail, the woman who grew up and raised her children in the Church of Jesus Christ of Latter-day Saints, told me in our interview that the church's belief system is focused on the afterlife, to the detriment of many young people. Gail says fear-based ideas "wear down teenagers' psyches" by frequently warning that they will not be with their families in the next life due to not living righteously. "Parents often implement obedience in their children by continually putting the image in front of them that God is watching, and if you don't do things right, there will be consequences in the next life. The fear-based stuff is very subtle, but it's always there. It can cause extreme depression," says Gail.

In more insulated, conservative cultures, the "fear-based stuff" is not so subtle. In *Unchosen: The Hidden Lives of Hasidic Rebels*, Hella Winston describes how one girl grew up in a world in which "everything was 'based on fear.'" Winston writes that if Leah did something that was against the rules, "even by accident, she was immediately threatened with going to hell. Performing the commandments was never about expressing gratitude to God, or love, or joy, but only about fear. If she forgot to make a blessing over her food, for example, she got a smack. And the same thing happened if she was caught reading a secular book, or if she didn't keep her hair in braids, as she was supposed to." Winston discusses how Leah was "filled with terror" on family outings, such as a trip to the zoo: "There were so many things on the street she wasn't allowed to look at, like couples holding hands, or immodest clothing displayed in store windows, that it got to the point where she actually preferred to stay at home."[15]

Twenty-five-year-old Karis Huot says that when she was growing up in her Mormon home in New Mexico, she, like Leah, was terrorized by religious fears of both sex and hell. On March 18, 2009, Huot said when she was five, she began to compulsively masturbate. She now believes her behavior was prompted by anxiety—the result of living with an abusive father—but when her mother discovered her secret, the woman did not consider the possible psychological causes, just the theological repercussions.

My mom sat me down and told me that was against the religion. "Masturbation is a huge sin. You can't go to temple if you do it. You just cannot do
that in the religion." She told me that you can go to hell and yelled, got angry,
and then had me clean the entire house. I'm talking vacuum, sweep, mop. I
remember I was falling asleep cleaning the house as punishment. But as a kid,
I just couldn't stop [masturbating]. It was just a compulsion for me, and I was
always getting in trouble to the point where I remember they actually openly
started talking about it at church when I was maybe nine, ten, eleven. They
were talking about how this is a sin, and I would always sit there and think,
"I'm going to hell."

Former Jehovah's Witness Susan remembers one incident when her son
was seven. She feels guilty about it still.

I don't even remember what he did, but he did something that really pissed me
off, that was really horrendously bad and naughty, and I just remember telling
him things like, "Do you know, if you don't straighten out, you're not going to
be a part of God's heavenly kingdom? You're not going to be part of that. You
will get destroyed in Armageddon, because you're being so rebellious." I was
very angry in telling him that. He cried. He cried. I remember [knowing] when
the words came out of my mouth that it was wrong to do. I had that much
sense, to know that was wrong. I don't think I ever did that again.

DEVILS AND DEMONS

I have spoken to a number of people who described being terrorized by images
of demon possession or the devil coming to "get" them. Mary Sundeen, aged
forty-six, describes the small, rural Catholic church of her childhood in New
York State as a "fear-based bubble." In our December 5, 2008, interview, Sundeen said priests and lay teachers in children's educational programs at church
frequently threatened that "if you do something wrong, the devil is going to
get you. He is always testing your free will." Sundeen adds, "As a kid, you
really think that he's somebody with hooves, a tail, and a pitchfork that's
going to get you." While Sundeen has moved away from the church of her
childhood, she says, "Some of that fear always stays with you."

John, who could not tell his parents about his frightening hallucinations,
says the subject of the devil came up often in church: "I heard just as much
about Satan as I did about Jesus in church. It made for a very fearful vibe. I
felt like I was physically in danger, never mind just spiritually in danger. *Physically* in danger. Poltergeist getting me, you know." John, who says he had a
very vivid imagination as a youngster, had "uncontrollable" visions. "When

other kids were seeing ghosts and monsters, I was seeing the devil and believing it." Demons also haunted John. He describes one incident that drove him to hide under the covers of his bed and pray:

> I was in the third grade. My brother and I lived in this converted garage. We had windows on every wall. Every night, I would be so afraid to look at any of the windows because I could swear I saw demon eyes in the windows. I always thought I saw demons' eyes, but, on one particular evening, the shutters started going crazy. I don't know if I really believe that now, but in my mind, I remember it as such. It was weird.

In the newsletter *Freethought Today*, Sarah Braasch describes the fears that plagued her childhood Jehovah's Witness community. Besides the fact that Armageddon was "regarded with frenzied anticipation," demonic forces were believed to be lurking just about everywhere. For example, the cartoon characters the Smurfs were "capable of murder, rape, violence and general mayhem and, as such, all Smurf paraphernalia had to be either banished or burned or both from any respectable Witness's home." Writes Braasch, "When news of the Smurfs' demonic nature had come to light, I had to rid my bedroom of Smurfs, and I wasn't able to sleep for months thereafter. I was convinced I had inadvertently invited demons into my life."[16]

INSTILLING FEAR TO CONTROL AND DOMINATE

Sometimes, however, the real bogeymen are adults.

As has already been touched on, religions can spawn powerful leaders—leaders who can abuse that power through the abuse of children. One way is by terrorizing them. A shameful example is illustrated in Jack Hyles's *How to Rear Children*. The Baptist preacher appears to gloat in writing about how he terrifies a child who commits the "sin" of calling Hyles by his first name:

> The other day I was walking down the alley behind our church. A little boy about six years of age said, "Hi, Jack." I turned, picked him up by the collar, held him up to where our noses touched, and I said, "What did you call me?"
> He said, "Br-br-br-br-other Hyles."
> I said, "Let it always be so."[17]

In another example, a religious leader is said to have frightened a group of teenagers by having them witness his abuse of a child. The scene was described in a 2007 televised interview with Kathy Jo Nicholson, a former member of the FLDS. Nicholson describes how the sect's leader, Warren Jeffs, attempted to teach high school students a lesson in obedience:

> There was a little boy. He was in second grade, and he was a naughty little boy. He was a funny little boy, but the teacher kept having problems with him. So Warren went and got him, brought him to the high school, picked him up by his ankles, and shook him upside down for several seconds in front of our class. It was quite a large class of teenaged kids in the high school, and he told us, "I'm shaking the evil out of him. I hope this will work."[18]

This type of public humiliation can involve an entire congregation. Alex Byrd describes his Pentecostal Christian community as being fanatically homophobic. When Byrd was in his early teens, he witnessed a group of young people endure a public humiliation he will never forget. The incident took place during a large church revival. Byrd remembers church leaders marching six boys in front of the congregation, at which time the pastor explained that they had been caught having homosexual sex in the bathroom. Byrd says he could see on the boys' faces "sheer terror, pure unadulterated terror." Then Byrd says the deacons grabbed the boys by the arm while the preacher screamed at them in tongues and smeared vegetable oil on their foreheads. The purpose of this exorcism, says Byrd, was to "cast out the 'demons of homosexuality' and the 'demons of rebellion' while claiming that Satan was trying to establish a bench hold in the church via these horrible closet homosexuals."

There is no question that adults use fear-based religious ideas to control children. Indeed, studies show that introducing God to children as a punitive force helps ensure obedience; it is also associated with children blaming themselves for things that go wrong.[19] Louise Anne Owens, the author of *Train Up the Child*, told me on March 6, 2009, that she believes parents find threats about a punitive God to be a particularly effective backup for getting children to comply with their wishes. "Children cannot argue against a God that no one can see," she says.

Sometimes just being made to go along with certain religious rituals can be terrifying for children. (The subject of child ritual abuse will be addressed further later.) For example, thirty-five-year-old Mark Casey, Mary Casey's son, remembers his family joining a new, particularly charismatic Assembly of God church in Texas when he was ten years old. As Casey told me on June 5, 2008, no one had told him what to expect, and his mother was not there to protect him because she was up front playing the piano. Suddenly, Casey recalls, a group of adults surrounded him and began strongly urging him to speak in tongues. Terrified, Casey faked speaking in tongues just to make the group go away. "They would just keep on praying for you and very aggressively, praying with their hands on you," he says. "I felt very scared and pressured."

Chapter 12

IN THE WORLD, NOT OF THE WORLD— RELIGIOUS ISOLATING AND EXPLOITING

On January 18, 2009, Amanda Kurowski started going to public school in Meredith, New Hampshire. Normally, there would be nothing unusual about a ten-year-old entering the fifth grade, but this situation gained media attention because it was court ordered. A judge determined that Amanda's fundamentalist Christian mother, Brenda Voydatch, had to stop homeschooling her daughter and enroll her in public school, partly based on complaints made by Amanda's father, who is divorced from Voydatch. Martin Kurowski had told the family court that his daughter's schooling had left her "extremely isolated." Not only was Amanda not interacting much with other people, Kurowski told the court, he was disturbed by the religious teachings she was getting at home. For example, Kurowski testified that Voydatch told Amanda that he was a sinner who didn't want to be with his daughter in heaven, a claim that was backed up by a counselor. A guardian *ad litem* reported that the child appeared to reflect her mother's "rigidity" concerning her religious views.[1]

Naturally, the case was controversial. According to court documents, Amanda was a well-adjusted girl, and the judge had no problem with the academic curriculum she had been receiving under her mother's tutelage. Voydatch's supporters said the court was biased against Christianity. Her attorney told the press that it was doubtful a public school would broaden Amanda's views, since "the schools are the number one censors of religious thought."[2]

But the judge sided with Kurowski, who argued that Amanda needed to be in public school, where she would be exposed to a wider range of people

151

and ideas. "I want her to be able to make her own decision about what she believes in, what she wants to do," Kurowski told the court. "But I want it to be an educated decision based on a lot of different experiences, not just her religion and the kids from her church."[3]

Essentially, Amanda's father was accusing her mother of committing two forms of emotional maltreatment, *isolating* and *exploiting*. Examples of isolating include placing unreasonable limitations on children's freedom of movement within their environments and on social interactions with peers or adults in the community. Examples of exploiting include micromanaging a child's life and living vicariously through one's child.[4] This chapter deals with isolating and exploiting together because they often work in tandem, with one reinforcing the other, and the combination can greatly interfere with a child's cognitive development.

All good parents want to keep their children safe from harmful societal influences, such as drugs, pornography, and violence. There is good reason for mothers and fathers to scrutinize the television shows their children watch, the Internet sites they visit, and the people with whom they come in contact. In addition, parents naturally want to pass on to their children their values and ideals. But problems arise when parents are too protective and overbearing, wanting to control all aspects of a child's life.

Perpetrators of isolating and exploiting fit this description. In a religious context, isolated children are greatly limited in their interactions with those who do not subscribe to the same faith as the child's family or community and are denied exposure to media containing a variety of worldviews. Meanwhile, children can be bombarded with religious teachings, what many call "indoctrination," often beginning at birth. Adults who engage in religious isolating and exploiting seem to look upon themselves in the way God is depicted in Isaiah 64:8, in that parents are "potters" forming and molding children who are "the clay."

As an example of isolating, Karis Huot, the twenty-five-year-old woman whose Mormon mother told her she was going to hell for masturbating, says it was "a huge sin" to learn about other faiths and read anti-Mormon material. Huot adds, "They'll tell you, 'Be *in* the world, but don't be *of* the world,'" which is based on biblical passages in the book of John, as noted in the chapter on religious authoritarianism. "They don't want you to be friends with anyone that's not Mormon, or really close friends. They don't want you to adapt to the other person's lifestyle at all."

It is my belief that exploiting is the most common type of religious child maltreatment. But it's also one of the hardest to identify, because it happens gradually over time, and many people join in. So religiously exploited children hear the same religious messages from parents, teachers, religious leaders, and others day in and day out. Obviously, these children do not get to choose their own spiritual path. Rather, it is assumed that young people will worship the same way as the adults around them do. Everyone "lives and breathes" the same faith together.

In this way, perpetrators live their faith "through" their children without taking into account those children's individual psychological needs. On his website, psychologist Benzion Sorotzkin gets to the core of exploiting when he warns of "parents who believe that their children's purpose in life is to fulfill their own, often immature, emotional needs. They do not hesitate to manipulate their children's emotions to this end. Even this type of overt abuse is not always obvious to others, since these same parents are often very pleasant to other people as they have a strong need to gain the approval of others."[5]

Mary Casey, who grew up in the Pentecostal Assembly of God Church in New Mexico, remembers experiencing this kind of subtle, ongoing inculcation. As a child, she says, "every part of my whole life, other than getting to go to school during the day, was centered around religion and church. Nothing was ever really fun." Casey and her family went to services every Sunday morning, Sunday night, and Wednesday night, and if there was a revival within fifty miles of her home, Casey says her family would attend it every night it was open. "I was picked up from school and did my homework in the backseat on the way to the revival, sometimes not getting home until midnight. Our entire life revolved around church and religion," she said. "Every service revolved around the fact that we had to pray every day, hour on end. We needed to read the Bible every day. We were supposed to be at church every time the church door opened."

Former Jehovah's Witness Kelly describes the religious teachings of her childhood as "black and white":

> Everything was life or death. Everything that you did that could be bad was going against Jehovah. It wasn't you finding your way in the world. It wasn't you figuring out your personality. It wasn't you developing as a child naturally. You were either obeying Jehovah or you were going against the creator of all things. There was such a heaviness to that. It was life or death. It was fight or flight. It was survival.

Twenty-year-old James Chatham, who, as described earlier, was brought into the Remnant Fellowship Church when he was ten years old, says, "I cannot express to you enough how indoctrinated I was." Chatham was somewhat skeptical of the church's religious beliefs, but after a period of "steady indoctrination," there came a point when "even I believed all the BS." That

"BS," according to Chatham, included the idea that the church's founder, Gwen Shamblin, "suddenly started the one real church in the entire world (of what, three million people?) and we're the only ones getting it right. She's the only modern-day prophet and things like that. Some of that stuff is so extreme that I just find myself disappointed at myself for believing it."

But who can blame him? Chatham says these ideas were promulgated in church services, in Sunday school, and in his home. "It was day in, day out. 'This is the truth. We know it better than you do. Just believe us. Don't question it.' Over and over again until your only thought was, 'Why question it?'" What's more, Chatham's mother was a fervent Remnant Fellowship follower. "It's not hard for a kid to believe something that his parents are so passionate about. All the adults in my life at that point were so passionate about it [the church's teachings], so to not believe it would actually seem the absurd thing [to do] at the time. You didn't question the 'truth.' Unfortunately, that also meant that when people would come up to you with reason, you would attack it with pigheaded devotion."

As mentioned earlier, children commonly experience religious exploiting and isolating together. It's clear to see that adults can better indoctrinate youngsters when they are kept away from outside influences. Likewise, it's easier to keep those youngsters from wandering toward those outside influences through steady indoctrination. This double-whammy effect is what so concerned the father of Amanda Kurowski. Most people who suffer both forms of maltreatment, especially from birth, have a hard time sorting out just what was done to them later in life.

However, one young man spoke eloquently about this very thing. In September 2006, twenty-five-year-old Nicolas Jacquette testified before the French Parliament when the government was looking into problems of child abuse in cults. Jacquette, who had been raised in the faith of Jehovah's Witnesses, explained that the children in his community were kept separate from non-Witnesses as much as possible until they attended school. In anticipation for the children mixing with outsiders, Jacquette said he and other children were carefully and meticulously prepped: "We knew the content of every course in advance, and we were warned about some of them." Jacquette commented on how he viewed his fellow classmates following the indoctrination: "I was laughing inside when I was taught about *Homo sapiens*, thinking, 'They are so dumb, they don't even know man is only 6,000 years old.'"[6]

LIVING TWO LIVES

As much as some pious adults would like to isolate children from "the world," this is usually impossible. Except for children whose parents are wealthy enough to send them to private school, many attend public school, where they rub shoulders with nonbelievers. Interacting with "worldly" people can leave the isolated, exploited child feeling awkward, embarrassed, and frightened.

In our interview, William Bowen told me that the need to live two lives is a common problem among children growing up Jehovah's Witnesses. Bowen grew up in the religion, became a high-ranking church official, and then left after discovering leaders were mishandling cases of child sexual abuse. On the one hand, says Bowen, children are supposed to live the life of a dutiful Witness, but they must also interact with the "sinful" in general society. "They feel tremendously guilty about that," Bowen says, "and they know that 'God is watching them.' They feel like they're not measuring up to the standard of what they should be to be a 'real' Jehovah's Witness."

For instance, Witness children do not celebrate birthdays and many holidays that other children do. During his testimony in front of the French Parliament, Nicolas Jacquette described just how difficult this can be for those growing up in the faith. Jacquette explained, for example, that he does not know how old his parents are because birthdays in his household were never celebrated. Also, each year, children "see Christmas and the New Year pass as if they were ordinary days and then hear their friends talk about their presents. As a reaction to their pain, they have to reply that Santa Claus doesn't exist, that they know the truth, and that that [the belief in Santa Claus] is a lie." In school, where children so desperately want to be accepted by other students, religious demands can make life unbearable. Jacquette stated, "As teenagers, we don't even need to be a Jehovah Witness to be bullied, so imagine that for someone who can't dress in a fashionable manner, has to go door-to-door in a suit and tie, and is not allowed to celebrate his own birthday or go to parties. That's quite a heavy load." Jacquette added that children grow to believe that "extremely painful and unbearable" abuse, like school bullying, is normal, because they are told that being persecuted by outsiders is part of being one of "the chosen."[7]

Adults might relish the idea of being some of the martyred "chosen," but for children who are thrust into this role, it can be unbearable. Mark Casey says he was terribly afraid that someone he knew from school would one day pop into his church and witness the members practicing their strange, charismatic rituals of speaking in tongues and conducting "altar calls," where preachers urge members to come to the front to be converted. Casey remembers, "I spent a lot of time worrying, terrified that some kid from my school would be invited as a visitor. I was always looking over my shoulder to see if someone was stupid enough to have brought a visitor. I was afraid I would be found out, because I knew our church wasn't like other kids' churches."

SPREADING THE FAITH

Using children for the purposes of spreading faith is one of the most common forms of religious exploitation. And it has been going on for a long time. Back in 1944, the US Supreme Court ruled in *Prince v. Massachusetts* that a Jehovah's Witness had violated child labor laws by having a nine-year-old girl pass out religious pamphlets. In deciding the case, the high court stated, "The zealous though lawful exercise of the right to engage in propagandizing the community . . . may and at times does create situations difficult enough for adults to cope with and wholly inappropriate for children, especially of tender years, to face."[8] One inappropriate example of such "propagandizing" is the case of Rose, who spent hours hiding in the bathroom in kindergarten because she was being made to convert people to her family's fundamentalist Christian faith.

An extreme example of this kind of religious exploiting is illustrated in the documentary *Jesus Camp*. As was discussed in the chapter on spurning, the film concerns a camp in which a Pentecostal preacher named Becky Fischer trains children to be devout, fundamentalist Christians. Right from the get-go, we learn through an interview with Fischer that she is indoctrinating campers to meet her own religious agenda—to win an ideological battle against Islam:

> I can go into a playground of kids that don't know anything about Christianity, lead them to the Lord in a matter of just no time at all, and just moments later they can be seeing visions and hearing the voice of God, because they are so open. They are so usable in Christianity. . . . Where should we be putting our focus? I'll tell you where our enemies are putting it. They're putting it on the kids. They're going into the schools. . . . And they're putting hand grenades in their hands. They're teaching them how to put on bomb belts. . . . It's no wonder with that kind of intense training and disciplining that these young people are ready to kill themselves for the cause of Islam. I want to see young people who are as committed to the cause of Jesus Christ as the young people are to the cause of Islam. I want to see them as radically laying down their lives for the Gospel as they are in Pakistan, Israel, and Palestine, and all those different places. Because we have, excuse me, but we have the truth.[9]

Most of the time, this kind of religious exploitation is harder to pinpoint. Like Rose, thirty-five-year-old Mark Casey was also uncomfortable having to convert people to his Assembly of God faith. His mother, Mary Casey, told me that when her son was in a youth group in the seventh grade, the teenagers met with a "very strong" youth pastor who told the kids that "they were responsible for the salvation of their friends." Casey adds that the pastor instructed the children that they must "witness" to others in school: "You need to tell them about Jesus, you need to ask them to come to church." She adds that her son Mark was greatly conflicted because on the one hand, "he felt like it was his responsibility to save other students from going to hell, but of course, he couldn't do that because it was the seventh grade, and they would think he was crazy. So he internalized all of that. He said it was driving him crazy. It was."

Some children are encouraged or coerced to take on the role of religious leader. Often, pious parents love the idea, unaware that there can be psychological implications. That would seem to describe the parents of Daniel Sawtelle, the man who worried that he had missed the Rapture when he was a boy. Sawtelle began preaching at a very young age, and he did it with gusto: "When I was five, I told a guy he was going to hell because he was smoking. Just balls-to-the-wall complete honesty. At school, my teacher called me her 'little Jimmy Swaggart.' I would be preaching to the kids at the bus stop, saying, "You're going to hell for this." Sawtelle was encouraged by many adults in his community to be a "little preacher." He says, "I was like the golden child." Church leaders publicly praised him when he began bringing his Bible to school in the seventh grade. "At whatever church I went to, I was always the one to please my father and please the pastor. So with that came the attention and, I guess, the glory of being 'the good kid.'"

But what many of those adults failed to realize was that Sawtelle's efforts to save souls were not due to a spiritual "calling" but his need to win approval and love from his father. Sawtelle had always admired his gregarious father, who was a deacon in the family's church and would not hesitate to chastise people for not acting in a "Christian" way. "I could see he was very proud when I would speak out and preach. He would always talk about me in glowing terms. Now that I look back on it, that was a great motivator."

Sawtelle told me something else that was quite interesting. When he was born, his parents already had five children. It was after having raised the fifth child that his mother and father became "born again." Sawtelle says his parents' reason for having him as the sixth child was tied up with their newfound religious beliefs: "The whole reason they had me was to raise a child in the church."

Given all this, his parents were blinded to the possible psychological pitfalls of Sawtelle being a preacher prodigy. Instead, they subtly put pressure on him to perform. When Sawtelle was thirteen, they took him to a tent revival, where a church leader prophesized that Sawtelle could bring his older brother to Jesus. After that, Sawtelle made a concerted effort to convert his brother. In the back of his mind, the young Sawtelle knew that if he succeeded, it would be a "crowning achievement" in his parents' eyes.

When Sawtelle entered his teens, he was lonely. Not many wanted to be friends with someone who was so judgmental. He joined a faith-healing ministry, and when he was unable to heal people, he was plagued with self-doubt and became depressed. "I'd always felt that I was supposed to be like a Paul or an Elijah. There were Christians, and then there were the people that I was supposed to be, this incredible man of God, right?" When he was older and living on his own, he contemplated suicide. Finally, he got help after calling a suicide hotline.

John, the man who was terrorized by demons as a boy, also spread his community's faith as a "little preacher." John says the reason he worked to make people break down and give their lives to Jesus was to somehow ease his own gnawing guilt about being a bad person. And yet, all the while, his parents encouraged his rantings. John says his father still talks about how "my boy brought two hundred and fifty people to Jesus."

NOT BEING GOOD ENOUGH

A typical problem in fervent religious communities is that members are expected to be perfect. Not only is their faith to be pure, but they must prove it by devoting a great deal of energy and time to their religion and place of worship. There are also many rules and prohibitions governing how one lives one's life, from how many times a worshipper attends church to what he or she should wear to whom he or she can date. Children are made to comply with these unreasonable demands too, and so, like many adults who cannot possibly measure up, these young people are drowning in guilt.

As child advocate Rita Swan told me on April 13, 2009, "Guilt comes from never being able to meet the standards of perfection that are set out in a religion. Most religions teach that God never makes a mistake and never does anything wrong, and they lay on their members tremendous demands for perfection."

Mark Casey understands this effect. On June 5, 2008, the thirty-five-year-old said about his Assembly of God upbringing:

> We were always in fear of not being good enough. There was a lot of guilt about doing things that were natural, like listening to rock-and-roll music, masturbating, watching an R-rated movie. They were always talking about Jesus coming back. The way of thinking was that, if Jesus came back suddenly and you were sinning in any way—even speeding in your car—you could go to hell. There was always this fear of going to hell. It was a very fearful environment.

"You're constantly re-evaluating everything that you're doing and feeling guilty if you make a mistake," Karis Huot, who left the Church of Jesus Christ of Latter-day Saints when she was in her early twenties, says, adding:

> They tell you that no one can be perfect, but you're still supposed to work towards being perfect, so you never feel good enough. You're constantly trying to be better, better, better, and for some people, like me anyway, it just snapped. I was like, "I'm tired of this. I'm tired of feeling guilty all the time. I can't be better if I try my hardest." And then I was finally like, "Screw this."

Like many other children, Alex Byrd, who grew up in a Pentecostal Christian community, agonized over his inability to speak in tongues, a sign that the worshipper has a direct connection with God. Other kids faked it, says Byrd, but he never could master it. To make matters worse, adults responded to this failure by making him feel as though something were wrong with him. "They told me that I wasn't wanting it hard enough and that I needed to pray more and read my Bible more." Byrd adds that when he was twelve, he began to doubt his religious beliefs, so he regularly took part in "rededication services," a process by which the already-converted prove they are still faithful. But all the prayer and church services failed to ignite the faith he was expected to possess. By the time Byrd reached the age of twelve, he says, "I felt alone as hell."

It is no wonder that when children are removed from such oppressive situations and allowed to lead more normal lives, they feel a euphoric sense of freedom. Take, for example, Jason Wilkinson, who was told he was "sinful" at his Christian school. When he entered high school, Wilkinson was taken out of that confining environment and allowed to attend public school. He was ecstatic. No longer did he have to follow all the rules and prohibitions he was used to.

> I thought I'd gone to heaven. I thought it was a blessing. I was like, wow, there's a lot of kids here. You can choose your own classes. There's sports teams. There's a marching band. There's girls who can dress pretty, and I got a hug today. You know what I'm saying? I thought I'd died and gone to heaven, and all of the kids there [complained], "Oh, it's horrible. Oh my God, I got to ride a bus. Oh, my parents won't let me watch the R-rated movie. Aw, I can't go to the Marilyn Manson concert, wah." I just thought all these kids were retards after so many months of being there.

Wilkinson says he went through a "little rebellion phase" of cutting his hair "all weird" because it was the first time in his life that he could decide how to wear his hair. For Wilkinson, attending public school was the beginning of a life of freedom he had never known, and so even little things like his haircut were important. "It was like my allowance to be me," he says.

SABOTAGING INTELLECTUAL AUTONOMY

One harsh effect of isolating and exploiting is a breaking down of, or failure to develop, critical thinking skills. Children can be emotionally and intellectually stunted through what some call "brainwashing." Essentially, children are denied opportunities to ask questions, express their creativity, and explore.

David Jensen of Austin Presbyterian Theological Seminary is critical of oppressive child rearing that inhibits intellectual development. In our interview, Jensen said child abuse begins "when the child feels unable to ask questions" or the child's questions are considered to be "inappropriate or misguided or somehow out of the bounds of what the faith community needs to accept."

Mary Sundeen, the woman who grew up in a rural Catholic community, knows what it is like to be stifled in this way because the church of her childhood did not encourage children to ask questions or think for themselves. She told me about one incident when she was thirteen, when she asked a lay teacher in her Catholic high school a question about Genesis. Sundeen asked, "Where did humankind come from if, at one time, the only people on Earth were Adam and Eve, who only gave birth to two sons?" Rather than commend the girl for asking an insightful question, the teacher led her to the principal's office.

Sundeen says, when it came to religious teaching, this denial of acceptance led to her mentally shutting down. She was naturally curious and wanted to ask a lot of questions but instead had to remain in a "larvae stage" for a long time. "The inability to ask questions stunted me tremendously," she says.

In more totalistic environments, children are hardly permitted to think for themselves. I remember asking a woman who grew up in a conservative Amish community how adults reacted when she expressed her opinion about something when she was a child. "I don't think I ever had an opinion," was her reply.

In some groups, children who express individual thought—especially thought that seems to contradict the religious collectivist mind-set—even risk being punished. One religious group that has gained cult status is Twelve Tribes, which, as was explained earlier, has been accused of using harsh physical punishment on children. As it turns out, Twelve Tribes has also been criticized for what it does to children's psyches.

Much of that criticism came out in the 1980s, when the group was investigated for physically abusing children. One journalist, Barbara Grizzuti Harrison, was allowed to spend some time with the isolated sect and provided a particularly vivid depiction of intense religious exploitation. Harrison's findings were published in a 1984 issue of the *New England Monthly*. Back then, the group was called the Northeast Kingdom Community Church. What Harrison learned is that the group had strict rules about how children *think*. Namely, children were reportedly not allowed to fantasize or imagine about most things, and if they showed signs of having done that, they were punished. For example, Harrison heard that a three-year-old boy had been kept in a dark closet for half an hour because he pretended that a block of wood was a car. "Fantasies steal the person you are," a member of the group told Harrison.[10]

During her stay, Harrison observed many children in the group, and her descriptions of them are eerie. "The children standing nearby express no curiosity. They are without animation. They do not speak," she writes. Harrison soon understands that "None of the children may ask a direct question or make a choice. If they are offered an apple or an orange, their response must be, 'I'll have what you know it is good for me to have.'"[11]

Twelve Tribes has continued to receive criticism. In 2001, the *New York Post* reported that former members of the group say that children in the sect may sometimes be allowed to play physical games, like basketball, but toys are forbidden because of the group's belief that children should be rooted in reality.[12] In another article, a researcher who studied Twelve Tribes says that children can be disciplined for using their imagination, such as playing with dolls or trucks.[13] Another report states that the group considers "independent thought" to be sinful.[14]

Some belief systems force upon children outrageous psychological demands, such as those that promote faith healing. Children, as well as adults, in these communities who get sick and then do not get better with prayer can be made to feel as though they are spiritually unworthy. Perhaps, they might be told, they did not pray hard enough, or they did not *believe* hard enough. The Christian Science Church has been criticized for its rigid teachings about spiritual healing. According to Christian Scientists, health problems do not really exist. Rather, they are delusions caused by faulty thinking and the inability to comprehend God's goodness.

What does this mean, then, for a child who gets sick? Caroline Fraser wrote about growing up in the church in *God's Perfect Child: Living and Dying in the Christian Science Church*. She describes, for instance, how she and other children learned about "Mortal Mind," a deprecating term for human thought. "Mortal Mind was thinking we were hurt when we fell down. Mortal Mind was accidents. Mortal Mind was forgetting to go to the bathroom before Sunday school and wetting our pants. Mortal Mind was being jealous or hateful or nasty. Mortal Mind was having a tantrum. Mortal Mind was crying." As much as she studied, prayed, and went to Sunday school, Fraser says she and other children "couldn't keep our Mortal Minds on the Divine Mind. We were full of Error."[15]

Fraser was further plagued when she became ill, which happened often because she had a sensitive stomach (which could have been brought on by her family's faith teachings). Her family often drove to visit her grandparents, which always made her carsick. Fraser remembers trying to apply Christian Science teachings when she became nauseous: "I would have trouble *knowing* I wasn't carsick. Car sickness was Mortal Mind. Throwing up was Mortal Mind." But she lost the mental battle every time: "I waited for God to fill up the world like the air in a balloon, but the air in the car just got worse and worse. Then I threw up, a horrible explosion of Error, the vomit snaking down my Sunday dress and the seat of the car. Now I was Error. Error was in me. *Error was me.* My father thought so too." She writes that her grandparents were even more devout Christian Scientists than her parents, so any evidence of "Error" had to be hidden from them: "We had to pull over by the side of the road and clean the vomit out of the car, with hankies, so they wouldn't see it. When Error came calling, we weren't supposed to tell."[16]

Fraser also became sick at school, vomiting "all the time." One non–Christian Science teacher rebuked her for not letting on she was sick. Not being a Christian Scientist, Fraser writes, the teacher "didn't realize that I couldn't have told anyone that I was sick. You couldn't *say* 'sick.'" Feeling ill left Fraser racked with feelings of guilt and self-doubt. In her book, she remembers asking herself, "What was the matter with me? Why wasn't I God's Perfect Child? Why couldn't I Know the Truth? If There Was No Spot Where God Was Not, where was I?"[17]

Children who are religiously isolated and exploited are made to be what their pious caretakers want them to be—often because such compliance affirms for those adults that their belief system is "right." Such children are put in a very difficult position, according to cult expert and psychologist Michael D. Langone. Writing for the International Cultic Studies Association news-letter, Langone states that these children find themselves either "submitting totally or risking severe psychological, and sometimes physical, punishment. Neither of these options—suppression of natural tendencies to test limits and assert individuality vs. exposure to possibly severe and persistent punish-ments—is conducive to the growth of self-esteem and a secure sense of belonging to a caring community."[18]

In addition, says Langone, children who are not allowed to express honest feelings might be expected to put on a positive front. Bethany Fenimore, the woman who wrote the online letter to spanking advocate Roy Lessin, knows what it's like to be so controlled. She says she, along with the children in her southern California church, were supposed to act like "happy robots. So if I was bummed about something and I was kind of mopey, that was grounds for a beating. I was to be happy about all things."

Fenimore remembers an illustration her artist father drew for a Christian publication. The illustration, called *Joy*, featured a girl who had skinned her knee: "She's pointing to the knee, and she's smiling this big, glowing smile. It was all about how you're joyful no matter what is happening to you and that was part of what God's plan was for us."

CONCLUSION

The damage caused by religious emotional maltreatment can be most clearly seen when children or adults try to extricate themselves from the faith. Depending on how authoritarian the religious environment is, leaving the flock and venturing out on one's own can be extremely difficult. Many of those I've interviewed have done well with their adult lives. However, they say they will always struggle with the long-term psychological effects of having grown up with oppressive faith.

Daniel Sawtelle, for instance, went to live on his own as a young adult, but after having devoted so many years to evangelism, he felt that his life had no meaning. After his engagement to a young woman ended, he became depressed and suicidal, and going to church did not help. That's when he began to think seriously about the beliefs he was raised with and to question whether he had been a victim of emotional abuse. He turned to acting, which became therapeutic; made friendships with people outside the church; and maintained a blog that tracked his spiritual journey. Today, he is an atheist and believes that the world would be a better place without any religion.

John, the man who was petrified of demons as a boy, was diagnosed with a number of mental illnesses as a teenager. When I interviewed John, he had been in therapy for two years and was making good progress. Still, he continues to struggle with a negative self-image due to a fear-based religious upbringing. "I am just forever guilty," says John. "I will be a guilty person when I die because of that. I just always have this knot of guilt, you know? And I don't even know what for anymore." However, when I checked in with John a year after our interview, he was doing well. He and his wife were expecting a baby boy, and he was excited at the prospect of becoming a father. When I asked him his thoughts on teaching his child religion, John said he would only take his son to church if he asked to go.

For Mary Sundeen, the woman who called the Catholic church of her youth a "fear-based bubble," a whole world opened up in high school. That was when she attended a girls' college preparatory school run by the Catholic order the Sisters of St. Mary of Namur in Kenmore, New York. Unlike the priests of her youth, who often instilled fear through threats of punishment for "sinners," the sisters were devoted to teaching young women the value of Christianity and social justice. And they led by example. Sundeen says the women not only served their local impoverished community, they also traveled to war-torn Rwanda, where they offered a safe haven for rape victims and those disfigured by machete attacks. Today, Sundeen is president of the national nonprofit organization the HealthWell Foundation, which provides financial assistance to patients struggling to pay for high-cost medication. Sundeen says her lifelong work assisting people in need was inspired by the Sisters of St. Mary of Namur: "They were one of the greatest significant influences of my life."

Bethany Fenimore's teenage years, however, went the opposite way. Fenimore, who had been raised by fundamentalist Christian parents who frequently spanked her, lived in virtual isolation. When she was a young teenager, Fenimore says her parents moved to a house in a rural part of southern California, did not allow Fenimore to socialize with people outside their church, and homeschooled her and her siblings. At the age of seventeen, however, Fenimore was permitted to live with her grandmother, who allowed Fenimore more freedom. Having made this break, Fenimore felt a tremendous sense of freedom, but she also remembers feeling very lost:

> Society now expects me to do something with myself, but I don't even know how to talk to people. And people are reporting back to me that I'm strange and I have a weird way of talking. I've got a body I can't stand, and I have no idea about sexuality. I don't know how to date. It was a miracle that I didn't get date raped. Men [in the culture of her upbringing] were people you didn't say no to.

Fenimore began living on her own when she was eighteen. She says that was when "I literally took my first step in trying to be a human in American society." Today, Fenimore has her own apartment, is self-employed, and has good friends. But her troubles are not over. For example, she gets flashbacks: "I'll be going along in my life and, all of a sudden, I'll feel impending doom or a sadness or grief." Also, Fenimore says she still sometimes cannot believe she is actually free of the control of her parents: "I was allowed at eighteen to take off my prison garb, and I have been waiting ever since to be told that I have to go back."

Part 3

VIOLATING A SACRED TRUST
Religious Child Sexual Abuse

INTRODUCTION

For a number of years, forty-five-year-old Cheryl Cooney operated a website called Clergy and Educator Abuse Survivors Empowered, or CEASE.org. Its purpose was to reach out to people who had been sexually abused as children by clergy in the Seventh-Day Adventist Church. But when Cooney first began posting information, it was for her own healing. As she explained on the site, Cooney had been a victim herself: "This charismatic minister used the Bible to manipulate and control me sexually for more than ten years." Soon after publicizing her own experiences, Cooney learned her story was far from unique within the denomination.

Cooney's abuse began when she was fourteen years old. As she told me on October 15, 2008, the perpetrator, whom we'll call Stephen, was a respected teacher at her Seventh-Day Adventist private school and lived in her Long Island, New York, neighborhood. Stephen was thirty-two years old, was married, and had three children, and he would soon became a senior pastor at Cooney's church. It was Cooney's mother who decided that her daughter and Stephen should spend one-on-one time together. Cooney had to take the train to school, and her mother thought it would be safer if she went with a school faculty member than if she rode alone. So it was arranged that the teenager would ride to school every day with Stephen.

"We started traveling together, and he built up a relationship of trust," says Cooney. She saw Stephen a lot, not only on the train but also in school where he taught. She also heard him give sermons in chapel, and she did office work for him.

"He was a cool teacher by all the other students' standards," says Cooney. "He was the one that everyone wanted to hang out with, and here I had this time with him on the train. He built up a really strong friendship and spiritual connection where, when he started to cross over the line, I had already gained so much trust in his relationship with God and his 'holiness,' if you want to call it that."

Cooney truly was convinced that the man was holy: "I did believe a hundred percent that he was called by God to do what he was doing in terms of his ministry, and I saw my fellow students were spiritually impacted by his message. It influenced me a lot." Stephen did not make a sexual advance right away. In fact, it would be two years before he made a move. During that time, he did what is called "grooming"—that is, gaining Cooney's trust and reliance as a confidante over time. Cooney recalls:

> He would tell me stories about his own high school experiences that were really inappropriate to be sharing with a student. About girlfriends, and about, you know, licentious behavior. I remember thinking, "I could never tell my mother that he told me this story." Slowly, he eroded all of the protections around me and got me more and more isolated from other friends and family and trusting really only him at that point. It was very, very gradual and very, very "brainwashing."

When Cooney was sixteen, Stephen kissed her.

"I flipped out," Cooney says, yet she didn't feel she could tell anyone about it. "The only person I talked to about it was *him* to try and make myself feel better that he would never have done anything wrong." At first, Cooney tried to convince Stephen that he *had* done something wrong, but she says he claimed to have been "led by God, so, therefore, it wasn't wrong."

Given his skilled ability to manipulate her, Stephen was able to convince Cooney to go along with other types of sexual activities. When the confused and guilt-ridden teenager expressed worry, Stephen's advice was to pray, "which I proceeded to do because I was so freaked out. I didn't know what else to do. I had never had a physical relationship. I had never had a boyfriend. I had never been kissed. I had only seen my parents kiss on the lips, and that was, to me, sacred. It wasn't casual. It was huge to me. And here this person had done that."

Stephen also quoted scripture to calm Cooney, choosing passages that he claimed justified their sexual activities. Cooney says, "As I got past each freakout point, he would take it a step further. Within a year, it was full-blown oral sex," although Stephen did not have intercourse with her since "that was saved for marriage."

The secretive sexual abuse continued even after Cooney went to college. In fact, she was not able to extricate herself from the relationship until she was twenty-six years old. Two years later, she saw a therapist for a different matter, and the subject of her relationship with Stephen came up. Cooney had referred to it as "an affair"; through therapy, she learned that she had been a victim of sexual abuse by a man who used his religious status to manipulate her into doing whatever he wanted.

Now that so many child sexual abuse scandals involving clergy have made the news in recent years, it is no surprise that many, many other children have, like Cooney, been molested or raped by those holding religious power. This section is about *religious child sexual abuse*, which is abuse perpetrated by a religious authority. But first, what is *child sexual abuse*?

CHILD SEXUAL ABUSE

David Finkelhor, codirector of the Family Research Laboratory and professor of sociology at the University of New Hampshire and one of the country's renowned experts on the subject of child sexual abuse, describes this form of maltreatment as *the exposure of a child to sexual experiences that are inappropriate for his or her level of physical and emotional development, coercive in nature, and usually initiated for the purpose of adult sexual gratification*.[1] According to the federal government's Child Welfare Information Gateway (CWIG), child sexual abuse is

> the employment, use, persuasion, inducement, enticement, or coercion of any child to engage in, or assist any other person to engage in, any sexually explicit conduct or simulation of such conduct for the purpose of producing a visual depiction of such conduct; or the rape, and in cases of caretaker or interfamilial relationships, statutory rape, molestation, prostitution, or other form of sexual exploitation of children, or incest with children.[2]

Furthermore, CWIG states that child sexual abuse includes "activities by a parent or caregiver such as fondling a child's genitals, penetration, incest, rape, sodomy, indecent exposure, and exploitation through prostitution or the production of pornographic materials."[3]

How pervasive is child sexual abuse? Federal statistics show that 9.5 percent of those found to have suffered maltreatment—approximately 67,000 children—were victims of sexual abuse in 2009.[4] These statistics, of course, only include *reported* cases and so they likely only represent a fraction of how much abuse actually occurs. According to one study, 25–30 percent of women and

10–20 percent of men say they were sexually abused as children.[5] Surveys show that 44 percent of victims of sexual assault and rape are under the age of eighteen. Both girls and boys are victimized, although more victims are female.[6] Most abusers are men, although abuse by women appears to be increasing.[7]

As far as risk factors are concerned, child sexual abuse is unlike other forms of abuse. For example, unlike nonsexual physical abuse, a perpetrator's history of child sexual abuse[8] and victims' income level[9] are not significant predictors. Rather, other factors come into play, such as a victim's lack of proper supervision and support.[10] Child sexual abuse is more prevalent in homes where there has been a disruption of the relationship of the victim's biological parents. Also, children who live with a stepfather are more at risk.[11] Many but not all incidents of sexual abuse involving victims who are below the age of thirteen are committed by individuals who meet the diagnostic criteria for *pedophilia*, a psychological condition marked by an adult's sexual desire for a prepubescent child, whether or not the adult acts on those desires. Perpetrators who are strongly sexually attracted to postpubescent children are known as *hebophiles* (in cases in which the victims are female) and *ephebophiles* (in cases in which the victims are male).

Just as Stephen was with Cooney, many sexual abusers are manipulative, skillfully able to "groom" victims to get them to comply with their demands and keep the abuse secret. These perpetrators tend to be smart, well liked, and charming, according to an editorial written by former volunteer prison chaplain and judicial vicar Father Thomas Brundage. But, as Brundage notes, it's all a front:

> They tend to have one aim in life—to satisfy their hunger. Most are highly narcissistic and do not see the harm that they have caused. They view the children they have abused not as people but as objects. They rarely show remorse and moreover, sometimes portray themselves as the victims. They are, in short, dangerous people and should never be trusted again. Most will recommit their crimes if given a chance.[12]

Incest is largely defined as sexual contact between persons who are so closely related that their marriage would be illegal.[13] However, some experts say incest always should be defined as abuse and identified as such even when the perpetrator is not a relative. According to one definition, *incest* is "any use of a minor child to meet the sexual or sexual/emotional needs of one or more persons whose authority is derived through ongoing emotional bonding with that child."[14]

The public has only recently begun to understand how common incest is. For a long time, people assumed that the so-called incest taboo prevented incest from occurring. More likely, however, an aversion to the idea of incest has simply prevented it from being *reported*. In fact, there's reason to believe that incest is the most common form of child sexual abuse, since more than 70 percent of perpetrators are immediate family members or someone very close to the family.[15] (This fact belies another myth—that children are most commonly victimized by strangers.) According to the Rape, Abuse, and Incest National Network (RAINN), the perpetrator-victim relationship in most incest cases makes this form of maltreatment especially harmful. "It disrupts the child's primary support system, the family," states the organization's website.[16]

HARM TO VICTIMS

Child sexual abuse can be extremely harmful, both physically and psychologically. Physical consequences can be lacerations and bleeding, damage to internal organs, neurological damage, and venereal disease and infections.[17] Pregnancy is also a serious concern, since the death rate from complications of pregnancy and childbirth is much higher for minors than for adults.[18] Negative short- and long-term psychological effects include depression, posttraumatic stress disorder, eating disorders, dissociative identity disorder, substance abuse, self-destructive behavior such as mutilation, and suicide.[19] Child sexual abuse victims commonly suffer from depression, anxiety, dissociation, conduct disorders, and aggressiveness. They can also engage in inappropriate or early sexual behavior; experience interpersonal problems, educational difficulties, and loss of self-esteem; and contemplate and commit suicide.[20] Many victims turn to religion for healing, but others detach themselves from faith. For example, in one study, victims said they felt alienated from God and were left with a sense of powerlessness and meaninglessness.[21]

Father Brundage, who talked to about a dozen people who had been victimized by one notorious pedophilic priest in the 1990s, writes in his editorial that those interviews were gut-wrenching: "In one instance the victim had become a perpetrator himself and had served time in prison for his crimes. I realized that this disease is virulent and was easily transmitted to others. I heard stories of distorted lives, sexualities diminished or expunged. These were the darkest days of my own priesthood."[22]

In his memoir, *Lost Boy*, Brent W. Jeffs accuses his uncle of repeatedly raping him, beginning when the boy was five years old. Jeffs writes that his life was changed forever after the first incident:

> I was never the same after that. At some point, everything went away—my feelings, but also all sensitivity, any sense that the world was a good place. I

just went numb. When he was done, I put my clothes back on. I had no idea what had just happened. I didn't know there was such a thing as rape—or that it could happen to a boy. In kindergarten, I didn't even know where babies came from.[23]

RELIGION AND CHILD SEXUAL ABUSE

It might seem strange to include child sexual abuse in a book that looks at maltreatment influenced by religious belief. After all, most religious organizations—despite all their problems preventing child sexual abuse—openly condemn this form of maltreatment. For example, the United States Conference of Catholic Bishops has concluded that the sexual abuse of minors is "an evil" and that knowingly allowing abuses to continue is "cooperation with evil."[24] The late president and prophet of the Church of Jesus Christ of Latter-day Saints, Gordon B. Hinckley, called child sexual abuse an "insidious evil" and referred to the "exploitation of children . . . for the satisfaction of sadistic desires" as "sin of the darkest hue."[25] And according to the official website of Jehovah's Witnesses, child sexual abuse is "animal," "demonic," and "among the vilest perversions."[26]

So why talk about this abuse in the context of religion? There are three reasons: One, while they are in the minority, some religious factions condone and openly practice what general society considers to be child sexual abuse. Two, perpetrators of religious child sexual abuse commonly use faith-based messages to dominate victims and procure their silence. And three, a great deal of child sexual abuse happens—and continues unabated—due to the fact that religious authorities are sometimes bestowed with great power.

Chapter 13
MURDERED SOULS

As mentioned earlier, religious child sexual abuse occurs when perpetrators are religious authorities. Often these authorities are members of the clergy, such as priests, ministers, church elders, rabbis, and imams, but they can also be principals or teachers in faith-based schools, religious youth group and camp leaders, and the heads of pious households.

Research is scant on this form of maltreatment, so there is a lot we don't know about how frequently it happens. Despite the problems that have plagued so many religious institutions, "no interfaith central clearinghouse exists for religious child abuse cases," declares Kibbie Ruth in her chapter in *Child Maltreatment*.[1] And, Ruth adds, there is no centralized record keeping of insurance company payouts after lawsuits are settled. "With such limited information about the legal settlements in even a single judicatory, one can understand how the actual number of offending clergy and wounded children seems impossible to calculate," says Ruth.[2]

Yet we can draw a few conclusions. For one, the vast majority of religious authorities do not sexually abuse children. According to a 2004 report of clergy-perpetrated child sexual abuse in the Catholic Church conducted by the John Jay College of Criminal Justice in Washington and commissioned by the United States Conference of Catholic Bishops, 4,392 members of the clergy had been accused of sexually abusing minors during that time. That figure represents approximately 3–6 percent of all priests in the United States. It is unclear how the percentage of abusers in the priesthood compares to that in the general population, as no reliable comparison studies have been conducted.[3]

173

However, while the percentage of abusers appears to be low, many victims are left in their wake. Some religious authorities have each managed to abuse dozens, even hundreds, of victims. The John Jay College report finds that during the period studied, more than ten thousand individuals filed claims against the priests, and nearly one-fifth of those people had siblings who also alleged abuse. Those allegations emanated from 95 percent of dioceses and approximately 60 percent of religious communities. In evaluating these numbers, the report concludes that the problem of child sexual abuse in the Catholic Church is "indeed widespread."[4]

Child sexual abuse is almost always traumatic for victims, but when perpetrators are religious authorities, victims are left with a unique set of psychological burdens.

"Those harmed within a religious institution—especially if abused by religious authorities—suffer trauma, shame, and guilt in a way that is different from the emotional, social, and physical injury of all abuse victims," writes Kibbie Ruth. Ruth notes that some victims refer to this abuse as "soul murder."[5]

University of Illinois at Chicago researcher Bette Bottoms expresses the same sentiment in one of her studies: "Because religious leaders are thought to be moral or holy, their sexual advances are likely to be particularly confusing, guilt-inducing betrayals for victims."[6] She adds that such abuse "may be psychologically damaging for children who have been raised to fear God and revere the church and its leaders. To child (and adult) parishioners, clergy are inherently powerful, trustworthy, and free by definition of mortal vice in much the same way as is God."[7]

The trust breakdown can have serious spiritual implications. As Thaeda Franz of Liberty University states in a paper on power, patriarchy, and sexual abuse, in cases where a clergy member has molested a child, "God begins to be associated with the experience of molestation, and can keep the victim from seeking out religious spiritual help later in life."[8]

Carla, a forty-seven-year-old woman I interviewed on March 12, 2010, experienced this loss of trust and spirituality after she was molested by her stepfather, who was also her family's Lutheran church choir director in Texas: "I grew up feeling like I had an inside, behind-the-scenes view of reality. Seeing my stepfather allied with my minister and all the other muck-a-mucks in my church made me think church is corrupt, that it is not a place you can trust or believe in."

"My ability to pray and believe that there's a God listening was impacted by the abuse," says Cooney, who was abused by her church's senior pastor for years. "I don't trust that anymore, so I have a problem from that very basic sort of spiritual level that you need to be able to connect with God."

When the abuser is a religious authority in the home, the negative effects can be particularly devastating. Flora Jessop, the former member of the Fundamentalist Church of Jesus Christ of Latter-day Saints (FDLS), writes in *Church of Lies* about enduring years of sexual abuse perpetrated by her father from the time she was eight years old. In the FLDS, men are considered to be the high priests of their households. Jessop explains that FLDS children are taught that "sex is bad and your body is evil. We were never supposed to touch our own body or even look at it." So, for Jessop, "Taking my clothes off and getting naked with my father was not only extremely humiliating, it was damning." After the first time her father molested Jessop, she remembers thinking that she would "go straight to hell."[9] The confusion, says Jessop, overwhelmed her: "Dad took my soul and twisted it."[10]

LESSER-KNOWN CASES

By now, the public is well aware of child sexual abuse scandals that have plagued religious institutions and faith groups. The Catholic Church has spent billions of dollars on costs related to lawsuits in the United States alone. A full-scale raid on the FLDS in Texas and subsequent criminal trials of numerous members have landed the polygamous sect firmly in the spotlight. But while both the Catholic Church and the FLDS have been embroiled in scandal, many other religious institutions and faith groups have also been accused of failing to stop—and even covering up—cases of religious child sexual abuse. Examples include the Church of Jesus Christ of Latter-day Saints, Jehovah's Witnesses, Baptist churches, and Amish and Orthodox Jewish communities. And yet there are obscure cases that fly even further below the public's radar.

Take, for example, the case of Mario "Tony" Leyva, a self-ordained Pentecostal Christian minister who turned out to be one of the most notorious pedophiles in American history. Leyva began victimizing young boys soon after he began preaching as a teenager in Georgia. He targeted boys, many of whom were being raised by single mothers, and was skillful at convincing parents to allow him to spend time with their sons after church revivals. As Mike Echols notes in *Brother Tony's Boys: The Largest Case of Child Prostitution in U.S. History*, Leyva decided he would trap victims by "prayin' with 'em, quotin' the Bible to 'em, and prophesyin' to 'em. And then I'll promise to teach 'em how to drive!" Echols writes that one of Leyva's first victims was a thirteen-year-old boy whom Leyva enticed into his car by letting him drive. Once the two got to a remote area, Leyva performed fellatio on the boy, telling him that what they had done was "God's special way for His people to love each other."[11]

Leyva traveled the country, abusing boys in more than a dozen states; he eventually confessed to molesting at least a hundred boys, although authorities believed that he had victimized several hundred. Most of Leyva's victims did not report the abuse because they were embarrassed and ashamed; some who did come forward were rebuffed by law enforcement.[12] However, the law finally caught up with Leyva, and he was arrested on sexual assault charges. On October 11, 1988, he pleaded guilty to transporting minors in interstate commerce with intent to engage them in criminal sexual activity and prostitution (since he had offered boys to two other men)[13] and was sentenced to twenty years in federal prison.[14]

Another notorious case occurred in one family's home. The perpetrator was Douglas Guill of Heron, Montana, who, in March 2008, was convicted on five counts of rape, incest, and sexual assault and sentenced to fifty years for each count with no possibility of parole. All charges related to Guill's daughter, whom he molested when she was a child. Guill repeatedly raped her over a fourteen-year period until she ran away from home at the age of twenty-two. The girl's stepmother also participated in the abuse. Guill kept his daughter like a prisoner, isolating her in the home and forbidding her to interact with outsiders.[15] The man used his religious power in the home to carry out the violations. The victim told authorities that Guill largely limited her reading to only the Bible. She also said Guill proclaimed that God had directed him to molest her and that she would go to hell if she told anyone about what they had done.[16] At Guill's trial, witnesses testified that he controlled his daughter and others in the household by convincing them that he had a special relationship with God and would determine who would go to heaven or hell.[17]

RELIGIOUSLY SANCTIONED CHILD SEXUAL ABUSE

While they are in the minority, some religious factions condone and openly practice what general society considers to be child sexual abuse. While this might seem shocking, religious cultures have permitted child-adult sex for a very long time, albeit with certain regulations. In ancient Judeo-Christian cultures, males from puberty on were officially permitted to have sex with girls, even very young ones. Of course, no one back then used the terms *sexual abuse* or *pedophilia*; those terms did not gain prominence until the 1900s. Instead, the ancient Hebrews and early Christians called it *marriage*.

According to the late social worker, child advocate, and feminist Florence Rush in *The Best Kept Secret: The Sexual Abuse of Children*, the ancient Hebrews considered marriages to be "consummated" in a number of ways, such as forming contracts. But another way was by sexual intercourse. As Rush makes clear, it was most common for girls in ancient times to be married once they became pubescent and could conceive. However, there was no minimum age requirement. In fact, as Rush notes, in the Talmud, Sanhedrin 69a states, "A maiden aged three years and one day may be acquired in marriage by coition."[18]*

Child rape among the ancient Hebrews was recognized in ancient times, but it was not seen as a violation against the child so much as the child's presumed owner, her father. Deuteronomy 22:28–29 reflects this attitude in its laying out of penalties for a man who rapes a girl. The text states that a man who "seizes" a virgin and "lies with her" must pay the girl's father "fifty shekels of silver" and marry her and never divorce. While the passage acknowledges that the act of rape leaves a girl "humbled" (translated in later versions of the Old Testament as "violated"), this did not pertain to the victim's psychological state but rather her reduced eligibility for marriage.

"The feelings of the victim of rape are not really that important under biblical law," writes government researcher Mark E. Pietrzyk on InternationalOrder.org. Rather, Pietrzyk notes that rape was considered a crime because it "violated the property rights of the father and the rules of social order. The virgin status of a young girl was a valuable asset to a father hoping to obtain a suitable bride-price from the man who would marry his daughter. If this asset was destroyed before marriage, it was an economic loss to the father."[19]

Things did not change much once Christianity came into being, writes Pietrzyk. He notes that Christian canon law followed Roman law in setting the minimum age of marriage at twelve for females and fourteen for males—ages that signaled a "readiness for procreation." Pietrzyk writes that it was not uncommon for girls to be wed to partners generations older. In fact, writes Pietrzyk, the third-century theologian Saint Augustine married a ten-year-old girl when he was thirty-one. Tormented with guilt for wanting to consummate the marriage, Augustine converted to Christianity and became celibate.[20]

Pietrzyk reveals that popes in the Catholic Church ruled that intercourse with girls "had the effect of sealing a marriage contract, as long as such intercourse took place after the age of discretion, which was seven. Once intercourse had taken place, the marriage could not be annulled. . . . Thus even for very young partners, the act of intercourse bound the two of them together for life."[21]

Parents continued to arrange marriages for prepubescent children into the Middle Ages, and, even though physicians warned of the dangers of impregnating very young girls, Pietrzyk notes that "the Catholic Church continued to bless marital bonds with twelve-year-old girls." While these marriages required the consent of the child, "the child was usually not in a position to challenge his or her parents and resist an unwanted union. This led to a number of abuses which went unchallenged by the [Catholic] Church." Pietrzyk adds that critics lobbied to have the church raise the age of consent to marry in the sixteenth century, but the church didn't change the twelve/fourteen rule until 1918, when it raised the minimum ages to fourteen for girls and sixteen for boys.[22]

Over the years, Western society grew more resistant to the idea of marrying off the young. In the United States today, different states grant people the legal authority to agree to various sexual activities at ages ranging from about fourteen to eighteen. Federal law dictates that the age of consent be eighteen in most cases.[23]

Still, there have been recent cases in the United States in which faith communities have ignored these laws. Two particularly notorious faith factions are the Family of Love and the FLDS.

THE FAMILY OF LOVE

The Family of Love was started under the name the Children of God in 1968 in Huntington Beach by traveling minister David Berg. During the 1970s, Berg went into hiding and communicated to members only through letters until his death in 1994. It was around this time that he developed his "Law of Love," a doctrine that mixed Christian beliefs with sexuality, and changed the name of the group to the Family of Love. An example of the "Law of Love" was the infamous "flirty fishing," an evangelistic practice that promoted sex between members and potential converts.[24]

In the memoir *Not without My Sister: The True Story of Three Girls Violated and Betrayed*, three sisters who grew up in the movement—Celeste Jones, Kristina Jones, and Juliana Buhring—describe how they and others in the group were sexualized as children. They were made to dance provocatively (sometimes naked), participate in orgies, and perform sexual acts with adults. Write the women, "Berg told his followers that the Ten Commandments were now obsolete. Everything done in love (including sex) was sanctioned in the eyes of God. Adultery, incest, extramarital and adult-child sex were no longer sins, as long as they were done 'in love.'" Berg told members that his nanny had performed oral sex on him when he was a toddler and that he had enjoyed it. "He said that it was normal, natural, and healthy and that there was nothing wrong with it, which gave everyone so inclined carte blanche to follow suit," write the authors. Furthermore, Berg continued to reinforce the idea that "children should be allowed to enjoy sexual contact among themselves as well as with adults—and many adults in the Family [of Love] embraced and carried out these suggestions."[25]

These problems came to light in 2005 when Berg's adopted son Ricky Rodriguez murdered his former nanny and then committed suicide. In a video he made the night of the killings, Rodriguez is seen loading a gun and waving around a knife and other weapons as he explains how he was molested by the nanny and his mother, Karen Zerby. What also was made public was a parenting book by Berg called *The Story of Davidito* that contains photographs of naked adults and children in compromising positions.[26]

The organization, which today calls itself the Family International (TFI), has denied allegations that Berg and Zerby, TFI's current leader, abused children or promoted abuse. But, in 1995, Zerby stated in an internal publication, "Because of the insight Dad [Berg] gave into the scriptures which granted us a great deal of sexual freedom, without clearly stated explicit restrictions that prohibited all sexual activity between adults and minors, it resulted in actions that caused harm to some children. He must therefore bear responsibility for the harm. . . . But this doesn't mean that everyone else is completely blameless. Anyone who attempted to use the Law of Love to justify any unloving, selfish or hurtful behavior is responsible before God for it."[27]

Today, TFI's website admits to having had a "colorful history," although it makes no mention of "flirty fishing" or any other of Berg's sexual teachings.[28] The website describes children as "priceless treasures and gifts from God" and vows to "amply and competently" meet children's physical, emotional, psychological, and spiritual needs.[29] Former members say the group no longer sexually abuses children but that those guilty of wrongdoings of the past are still in leadership positions.[30]

THE FUNDAMENTALIST CHURCH OF JESUS CHRIST OF LATTER-DAY SAINTS

Until fairly recently, some members of the FLDS were able to perpetrate child sexual abuse without many on the outside finding out. The polygamous sect of some ten thousand people lives in isolated communities, mainly in Utah, Arizona, Texas, and British Columbia, Canada. The FLDS dates back to the mid-nineteenth century as one of a number of polygamous, fundamentalist Mormon sects that continued to practice polygamy (more specifically, *polygyny*, marriage between one man and multiple wives) after the mainstream Church of Jesus Christ of Latter-day Saints renounced plural marriage in 1890. The FLDS believes that through polygamy, men and women can ascend to the highest level of the "celestial kingdom" in the afterlife.

Unlike many of the other polygamous, fundamentalist Mormon groups, the FLDS has conducted underage marriages where girls as young as twelve have been married to men (often much older). Evidence obtained during criminal investigations shows that sect leader Warren Jeffs proclaimed such marriages to be mandated by God.[31] Such a belief system is rooted in Mormon scripture, which speaks to plural marriage with virgins. Specifically, the Doctrine and Covenants, a text that Mormons believe contains divine revelations as told through church founder Joseph Smith, condones men marrying many virgins. Section 132:61–62 declares that even "if he have ten virgins given unto him," he is not an adulterer, "for they belong to him."

In the documentary *Damned to Heaven*, a middle-aged man and former FLDS member named Edward explains that many FLDS men are eager to marry underage girls. Edward says it's problematic to wait to marry a girl once she reaches the age of eighteen, since "there's a slim chance that she'll still be a virgin." Older girls make for a tougher marriage, says Edward, since they tend to "get restless" or "go wild." He adds, "Of course, all men prefer to marry a virgin. It's kind of like buying a new car instead of a used car."[32]

The FLDS saw the beginning of the end of its practice of underage marriage on April 3, 2008, when state officials raided the 1,700-acre Yearning for Zion Ranch, the group's Texas community located outside the small town of Eldorado. Investigators had received a phone call made by a female claiming to be a sixteen-year-old FLDS member living in an abusive polygamous marriage. Texas authorities were alarmed to see teenage girls who were pregnant and caring for children. When several underage girls were questioned, they explained that they had been "spiritually united" with adult men and that no age was too young to be married. Furthermore, the girls said that the group's leader, known as "the Prophet," determined when and to whom a girl should be married. Social workers ultimately removed 439 girls and boys from the compound and placed them in foster care and shelters.[33]

Many saw the raid as drastic and intrusive, especially given that most of the children taken away had never lived outside their FLDS community. Furthermore, the phone call that prompted the raid turned out to be a hoax. On May 22, 2008, a Texas appeals court ruled that the state lacked sufficient evidence to keep the children in the care of the state, and nearly all of them were returned to their homes. However, despite the legal bungles, the investigation uncovered child maltreatment problems that few outside the sect knew about. A report released on December 22, 2008, by the Texas Department of Family and Protective Services concluded that the case was about the "sexual abuse of girls and children who were taught that underage marriages are a way of life," "parents who condoned illegal underage marriages," and "adults who failed to protect young girls."[34]

More specifically, the report found:

- Of 146 families investigated, 62 percent had a confirmed finding of abuse or neglect involving one or more children in the family.[35]
- Twelve girls who ranged in age from twelve to fifteen had been "spiritually" married and had been victims of sexual abuse with the knowledge of their parents.
- Seven of the girls who were removed had one or more children. Based on the total number of girls who had been removed, state officials concluded that more than one out of every four pubescent girls was in an underage marriage.
- Those girls plus 262 other children had been subjected to neglect because their parents had failed to remove them from a situation in which they or other children were exposed to sexual abuse.
- One hundred twenty-four adults were designated as perpetrators, including men who engaged in underage marriages and parents who agreed to the marriages or failed to take reasonable steps to prevent them from taking place.[36]

At a congressional hearing to learn about abuses in the FLDS, Senator Ben Cardin of Maryland stated, "What is happening here is as bad as anything I've seen in the world: Children and families who have been denied basic human rights because of the activities of those involved in these polygamous colonies. It is difficult to understand how this can occur in the United States."[37]

In addition to shedding light on these problems, the investigation ultimately led to a string of arrests, indictments, and convictions of male members of the FLDS on child sexual abuse and bigamy charges. By February 2011, seven men had been convicted and five were still in the pipeline awaiting trial. By that time, the fate of sect leader Warren Jeffs was still undecided. In 2007, he was convicted for being an accomplice to rape for presiding over a marriage between a fourteen-year-old girl and her older cousin. However, the Utah Supreme Court overturned the conviction due to improper jury instructions.[38]

But Jeffs's troubles were far from over. As of February 2011, Jeffs was sitting in a Texas county jail awaiting trial on charges that he had sex with two girls, one under fourteen years of age and one under seventeen years of age. A court entered a not guilty plea on Jeffs's behalf. These charges were based on evidence that turned up in the raid, such as DNA samples taken from children that could prove paternity and a 2006 photograph marked "anniversary" showing Jeffs kissing a twelve-year-old girl.[39] Even more damning, Jeffs got caught up in an international child-smuggling scandal in which as many as thirty-one FLDS girls in Canada allegedly had been brought into the United States to marry Jeffs and other men in the sect.[40]

The Texas raid brought about another change—the sect's renunciation of marrying girls of minor age. On June 2, 2010, a spokesperson for the FLDS made this announcement: "The church commits it will not preside over the marriage of any woman under the age of legal consent in the jurisdiction in which the marriage takes place."[41]

Chapter 14
RELIGIOUS POWER AND CHILD SEXUAL ABUSE

The factors that lead religious authorities to sexually abuse young people are complicated. In addition to theories that explain why anyone sexually abuses a child, two theories are commonly discussed as to why those with religious authority commit this act: a failure on the part of religious institutions to properly prepare, screen, and supervise religious leaders;[1] and requirements of celibacy and chastity imposed upon clergy members, which critics say stunt psychosexual development.[2] But there is another important risk factor to be considered: the power held by many religious authorities.

When religious authorities who interact with children are bestowed with great power, those children become particularly vulnerable to sexual abuse. Comedian Bill Maher pointed to this problem when he discussed child sexual abuse in the FLDS and the Catholic Church on the April 11, 2008, episode of his HBO television program *Late Night with Bill Maher*. As Maher told his audience, "Whenever a cult leader sets himself up as God's infallible wingman here on Earth, lock away the kids."

In fact, power plays a huge role in most cases of child sexual abuse, according to CWIG, which states,

> The child has little knowledge about the societal and personal implications of being involved in sex with an adult; in contrast, the adult has sophisticated knowledge of the significance of the encounter. The child's lack of power and knowledge means the child cannot give informed consent. Finally, although in some cases the adult may perceive him/herself providing pleasure to the child, the main object is the gratification of the adult.[3]

Interestingly, some child advocates liken clergy-perpetrated child sexual abuse to father-daughter incest, a form of maltreatment that is greatly enabled by the power imbalance between perpetrator and victim.[4] In *Child Maltreatment*, Kibbie Ruth opines that abuse by faith leaders "most closely correlates with the dynamics of incest," as "the vulnerability children experience in their families is similar to their vulnerability in the 'family' of faith."[5] Carol Delaney agrees in *Abraham on Trial*: "Roman Catholic priests, referred to as 'Fathers,' are the very men who represent God the Father, or at least his will, on earth." These leaders, according to Delaney, "are channels for God's power; they act in his name; they are revered, respected, trusted, and looked up to for moral guidance; the abuse of that trust is, therefore, all the more reprehensible."[6]

Many children have been primed—usually from birth—to revere, fear, and trust these authorities. "Children have been taught to trust adults, especially one who has a dominant leadership role in the church or in the community," writes Ron O'Grady in *The Hidden Shame of the Church: Sexual Abuse of Children and the Church.*[7]

It is likely that Cheryl Cooney would never have been abused by her minister were it not for the power imbalance that existed between them. Stephen was able to take advantage of both his revered status and Cooney's naïveté about sex to satisfy his sexual needs. (All this was aided, of course, by the fact that Cooney's mother arranged for the minister to spend a great deal of one-on-one time with her daughter.) Stephen's method of coercion was subtle—he did not violently force himself upon her—yet as in father-daughter incest cases described by Herman, Cooney still felt vulnerable and unable to refuse Stephen's advances.

Carla, the woman whose choir director stepfather molested her when she was eleven years old, felt powerless to object to anything her abuser did. She was confused. After all, she liked the man, who was much more affectionate than her biological father. Also, Carla knew that he was popular in their church community. "When he started touching me I was uncomfortable about it, but it was a completely inarticulated feeling, you know? I was completely shut down. There was no way for me to even put it into thought. I just remember feeling uncomfortable but I didn't even really avoid him," she says.

Another frightening example of this kind of manipulation is illustrated in the National Geographic documentary *Inside a Cult*. The film profiles a New Mexico cult called Strong City, led by Wayne Bent. Bent's followers believe that he is the Messiah. He appears to believe it himself. "I am the embodiment of God. I am divinity and humility combined," he tells the filmmaker. In another scene, a teenage girl tells her friend what it was like to lie naked with Bent: "We went to the bedroom and laid down, and he held me, and somehow it was, like, all of heaven was open to me somehow. I started to see God. Well—'somehow'—it was the son of God holding me!"[8]

As has been noted, fathers in pious households also can hold tremendous power over children they choose to victimize. In her memoir *Church of Lies*, Flora Jessop describes the first time her FLDS father molested her at the age of eight: "'Sit down and open your legs,' he said. Obediently, I dropped down to the filthy barn floor and opened my legs, the lips of my vagina spread wide open. . . . I couldn't imagine why he would ask me to do this. But he was my dad—the priest of our home. What he did was commanded by God, so he must have a reason."[9]

USING RELIGIOUS MESSAGES

As indicated earlier, sexual abusers often justify child sexual abuse with religious messages and use those messages to dominate victims. These messages carry the greatest weight when delivered by religious authorities, whether they command from the pulpit or in a classroom or home.

"Many survivors remember that the Bible was used to coerce them into abusive submission or feeling they were responsible for the abuse," writes Carolyn Holderread Heggen in *Sexual Abuse in Christian Homes and Churches*. She adds that scripture that speaks to honoring and obeying parents is commonly used by sexual abusers to dominate child victims.[10]

In *Child Maltreatment*, Kibbie Ruth notes that such pedophiles "may tell children that their sexual relationship with them is God's will" or "use prayer and other sacred ritual to close the abuse with religious power." Furthermore, they might quote religious texts in such a way as to "assure the victims of the appropriateness of their harmful activity."[11]

On August 26, 2010, Kathryn Goering Reid, who heads a domestic violence shelter in Waco, Texas, and is the former associate general secretary of the Church of the Brethren, told me how she once counseled a man who justified his sexually abusing his daughter with scripture. The man, who was mentally ill and had been the victim of sexual abuse as a child, told Reid the reason he had had sexual intercourse with his daughter "was to teach her to honor her father and mother." According to Reid, the man was an "extremely" religious Christian who suffered from delusional mental illness. "His faith supported his delusion," she says. "So he takes the scripture I love, twists it on its head, and uses it to support behavior I abhor."

Cheryl Cooney remembers a similar form of manipulation. She says one tactic her minister used to get her to comply with his sexual demands was telling her that God had predicted his wife would die and he would then marry Cooney. Religious authorities who abuse children and claim to have God on their side, says Cooney, have "an extra tool in their arsenal that a regular high school teacher doesn't have."

In a notorious case that took place in the Catholic Church, a Wisconsin priest named Lawrence Murphy used religious messages to dominate some two hundred boys who were students at a school for the deaf. One victim said that Murphy coaxed him at the age of fourteen into a closet and molested him. When the boy told Murphy that what was happening was wrong, he says the priest replied that God had sent him and that "this is confession."[12]

Brent Jeffs did not grow up Catholic, yet he says he experienced that same victimization. In *Lost Boy*, he accuses his uncle, FLDS sect leader Warren Jeffs, of repeatedly sexually assaulting him from the time the boy was five years old. Brent Jeffs writes that the religious leader invoked spiritual messages to get him to comply with his wishes and not tell anyone about the abuse:

> The first time, Warren brought me over by the tub. He knelt down so he could see my face. He took on a very serious tone. He said that God had chosen him to help me become a man and that what was about to happen was God's will for me. This is how a boy becomes a man, he stressed. This is "God's work." His voice was calm, matter-of-fact, and patronizing—as if he was explaining a key point of doctrine to a kindergartner in the simplest possible way. But then, he got colder and sharper.
>
> "You cannot tell anyone or say anything to anyone—because this is between you and God. If you do tell, you will burn in hell," he said, trying to make me feel the flames. He had this mean, vicious look in his eyes. It was like he was looking through me.[13]

In faith groups whose customs allow for adult-child sex, religious messages are used to support such acts. A former member of the Children of God, who grew up in the religious group that used to mix Christian teachings with sex, described the group's culture in a media interview: "Everything was backwards, the way we were growing up. . . . Everything that was wrong, we were taught was right. Everything that was really evil and wicked and perverted was done in the name of Jesus."[14]

VICTIMS KEEP SILENT

Many victims keep silent after having suffered sexual abuse. When perpetrators are religious authorities, victims are all the more reluctant to tell another person what has happened to them. Not only do they feel shame but, if a perpetrator is revered in a community or family, victims may fear that no one will believe them, or worse, that they will be punished for making such an accusation or blamed for the abuse.

Bette Bottoms writes in one study, "Because victims may be aware of parental and community veneration of religious authorities and of the church and religion they represent, victims may be particularly reluctant to disclose abuse, believing (perhaps rightly) that their claims will be ignored."[15]

"A religious leader's 'holy aura' and the assumed level of ultimate trust blinds parents to potential dangers for their children and muffles the children's voices of protest when abuse has taken place," writes Kibbie Ruth.[16]

Child sexual abuse attorney Tim Kosnoff believes parents' reverence for Catholic priests, in particular, is unmatched in any other occupation or profession: "Doctors, lawyers, I am hard pressed to think of anybody that would come close to the way in which priests are perceived by parishioners." Kosnoff notes that the fears and anxieties child victims harbor after having been molested by a religious authority lead them to believe that no one will believe them if they tell and no one will protect them from further abuse. "The best thing they can do to protect themselves is to try and bury it, forget about it, and not tell anybody," says Kosnoff.

That describes Joel Engelman, the man who discussed corporal punishment in Orthodox Jewish yeshivas. In 2010, Engelman went public with allegations that a rabbi in his yeshiva, the principal, molested him when he was eight years old. "It was very shocking to me that a rabbi of his considered piety would do something like that," Engelman told me. "It was very overwhelming." So overwhelming, in fact, that he did not speak of the abuse for ten years. The principal was, after all, a well-respected rabbi, says Engelman, adding, "Who am I, as the minor or the young adult, to be saying things of this nature, of this terrible nature about him?"

Brent Jeffs writes in his memoir that he too kept quiet immediately after his uncle brutally raped him.

> I didn't want anyone to see me or say anything to me. I felt like I must have been a bad person for this to have happened to me, like it was some kind of punishment. I'd been told that it was what God wanted, so I must have done something terrible. Why would God do that to a good boy? I felt like it was all my fault, that I should have done something to stop it. I felt filthy and disgusting and repulsive. . . . I couldn't even explain it to myself, let alone tell an adult. He had so much power in the church that even if I had started kicking and screaming when he tried to take me out of the classroom, it probably wouldn't have made any difference. All I could do to protect myself was leave my body—but it seemed like every time I did that, I was less able to bring myself back.[17]

Carla, the woman who was molested by her stepfather, who also served as her church's choir director, remembers those same feelings of helplessness: "There was no one to go to and say, 'Excuse me, my stepfather's a creep.' There was no way in that environment I was going to go to his buddies and friends in the church and accuse him."

In many Muslim communities, it is unthinkable for a child to accuse a religious authority of sexual abuse. Salma Abugideiri of the Peaceful Families Project told me that children who tell their parents or others that they have been sexually abused by an imam are likely to get little or no support: "The least likely believed accusation of child abuse would be if it was directed against an imam. People would really have a hard time believing it, and I think the child would probably get severely reprimanded, if not punished, for making that kind of accusation in most communities."

Tim Kosnoff says children who were abused by Roman Catholic priests and came forward to make an accusation have also been met with cruelty. Remembering parents of victims whose cases he has handled, Kosnoff says, "It was completely unthinkable that a priest could be a sexual predator of their sons and daughters. I have had dozens and dozens of clients who were abused by Roman Catholic priests who reported that they tried telling their parents, and they were beaten. They were beaten by their parents for saying such a 'vile' thing about Father O'Malley or Father O'Donnell."

THE ENABLING PARENT

By now, the stories are common: Parents find out that their child has been molested by a member of the clergy, and they are aghast. Commonly, they say they never once thought that the religious leader who abused their child could have been a pedophile. "What parents wouldn't be thrilled to have a faith representative visit the family home and show a sincere interest in their children?" asks Ruth in *Child Maltreatment*.[18]

There is no question that most mothers and fathers are devastated to learn that a religious leader inappropriately touched their child. These parents commonly were raised to revere religious authorities, and many sexual abusers are skilled at manipulating parents into trusting them with their children. Yet the fact remains that parents play an enabling role in allowing such abuses to take place. They buy into the idea that religious leaders can do no wrong, so abusive adults escape background checks and, as in the case of Cheryl Cooney, are permitted to spend lots of time alone with victims.

As Ruth notes, "When the adults who are in a position to protect children from an errant religious leader are convinced that the leader is above reproach, those adults may unwittingly encourage a relationship between the abuser and the victim."[19]

This naïveté was brought out in *Brother Tony's Boys*, in which Mike Echols chronicles the abuses perpetrated by serial pedophile Mario "Tony" Leyva. Echols explains that many parents "felt truly blessed" to have their sons spend time with a so-called prophet of God. One mother, in fact, says how pleased she was "to have Brother Tony bring my boy up straight in the ways of the Lord."[20] In another family, a father laments that he allowed his son to stay with Leyva in a hotel room: "We trusted him. We were told to trust him. We just trusted the guy implicitly!"[21]

Barbara Dorris, the national outreach director for Survivors Network of those Abused by Priests (SNAP), told me how, when she was nine years old, her mother agreed to send her to work for a priest in her St. Louis neighborhood. She says this led to him repeatedly sexually abusing her for several years. Dorris's mother never questioned whether the priest could be trusted to be alone with her child: "I think my mother was proud of the fact that the priest picked me. It marked me as being special. It marked me as being good. I think Mom was proud of the fact that Father liked me and would ask me to come in and count mission money, that Father would ask me to come and help at church."

And some parents apparently do not want to know the truth. Karis Huot, the woman who was made to feel guilty for masturbating as a child, says her Mormon missionary molested her while her parents were in the room as the group watched videos. Like many children in the Church of Latter-day Saints, Huot was eight years old and assigned a missionary to help her prepare for baptism.

"He [the missionary] would take his hand and put it, you know, under your butt, up to your vagina kind of go along like that through your clothes. And it took me a while until I started thinking 'this is weird.' And then I would get up and move to another spot. But then, usually, he would just kind of mosey over like [it was] nothing . . . like it was natural, just like affection. But, of course, he would do that when no one else noticed."

Huot says that the missionary took things further when they were alone. One time, when the two of them were in her room with the door closed, he offered to give her a massage. "I was laying down, and he was giving me a full-body massage, and I remember thinking it was weird, that he was massaging my butt and around my hips. I was kind of uncomfortable, but I was thinking—I was eight, you know—'I guess he knows a different kind of massage.'" At that point, Huot's father opened the door and saw what was going on, but instead of ordering the young man out and reporting him to the church or outside authorities, he simply yelled, "Don't come in here with the door shut!" and then walked off.

"I don't know what my parents thought," says Huot. "They were just blind, like they just didn't want to see it."

It might seem unfair to attribute blame to parents of children who have been victims of religious sexual abuse. Mothers and fathers, like the victims, often have also been betrayed by these leaders. But by subscribing to beliefs that religious leaders are not capable of harming a child—and by passing on those beliefs to their children—they put their loved ones at risk.

Chapter 15
FAILING VICTIMS

Americans have been inundated with news stories about religious child sexual abuse. All major religious organizations seem to have been touched by scandal, and the same goes for many independent places of worship. But, in the spring of 2010, just when many Americans thought they had heard it all, along came the story of Tina Anderson.

In 1997, when Anderson was fifteen, she was allegedly raped twice by the deacon of her church, the Baptist Trinity Church in Concord, New Hampshire. Anderson became pregnant and told then-pastor Chuck Phelps that it was the deacon, a thirty-eight-year-old man named Ernest Willis, who impregnated her. After hearing this, Phelps reported the incident to law enforcement and social services. But Phelps apparently felt his job in responding to the case was not done. According to Anderson, who decided to speak to the press about the matter when she was twenty-eight, Phelps announced to other churchgoers that Anderson was pregnant, after which she had to read a letter Phelps ordered her to write, asking forgiveness for "allowing a compromising situation to occur" that led to "immorality." At the same service, Willis, too, stood up and confessed that he had been unfaithful to his wife. There was no mention of the two issues being related.[1]

None of this came to light until 2010. Police reopened the case after being alerted to a Facebook page with information about Anderson's plight, arrested Willis, and charged him with two counts of rape and two counts of having sex with a minor.[2] Part of the reason the story had been kept quiet was that when Anderson's pregnancy became known, she was sent to Colorado to live with a Baptist family. In media interviews, Anderson has said that this was done against her wishes, and that while she was in Colorado, she was kept cloistered until she had her baby. After that, according to Anderson, church members there forced her to give the baby up for adoption and warned her not to talk to anyone about her troubles. Back in Massachusetts, with Anderson out of the picture, nothing happened to Willis. He was never arrested because, according to authorities in Concord, police closed the investigation after they were unable to find Anderson.[3] Furthermore, the church allowed Willis to remain a member until he left in 2004.[4]

When interviewed by the media, Phelps, who is no longer at Trinity, blamed law enforcement for dropping the ball in 1997 and admitted no wrongdoing. Also, while he admitted to arranging for the public church confession, he maintains that it was not a disciplinary act but an attempt to help the teenage Anderson. "This was a chance for people in the church assembly to embrace her, and they did," Phelps told the press.[5]

But Anderson has maintained that she was a victim not only of rape but also of "systemic brainwashing" as church officials made her believe the rapes were her fault.[6] She has said she was berated for her "immoral" behavior by Phelps and others. For example, according to Anderson, Phelps told her she was lucky not to have been born during the Old Testament, when adulterers were stoned to death.[7]

As of the fall of 2010, the case had not yet been prosecuted, yet it raises some important issues. Namely, if what Anderson and others say really happened, it shows just how far religious leaders will go to deny, ignore, or cover up cases of religious child sexual abuse. The current pastor of Trinity, who arrived one year after Anderson made her public confession, has conceded that the church acted immorally. In June 2010, Rev. Brian Fuller told reporters, "We have heartfelt regret for the victim, that she ever stood in front of our congregation, as well as absolute regret and . . . disgust that the perpetrator remained so long in our congregation."[8]

The case also shines light on how poorly congregants can respond to such allegations. It was not only church leaders who failed Anderson after she was impregnated by a man more than twice her age. For example, Anderson has said that Phelps's wife responded by asking the girl, "Did you enjoy it?" What's more, Anderson's mother allegedly went along with church officials' suggestion that she be sent to Colorado. "My mother is very much a follower," Anderson told the media. "She believes she needs to do what [the church] tells her because they are men of God."[9]

At least one member of the laity did object to the way Anderson was treated. Matt Barnhart has told the press that his family left the church after

Anderson had to give her public mea culpa. "It nagged me for years. They blamed her. They shipped her off," Barnhart said.[10]

Later, this section will discuss how the upper ranks of religious organizations abuse their power to keep cases of child sexual abuse secret. This chapter looks at how the less-powerful members of faith communities—victims' relatives, friends, and others—are just as likely to fail victims.

FAITH COMMUNITIES TURN THEIR BACKS

Child sexual abuse is a difficult topic for anyone to deal with. Many people do not know how to respond when a child confesses that someone has touched him or her "down there." Many would simply like the problem to go away. But the way adults react to children who have been sexually abused greatly affects the victims' ability to recover emotionally from that trauma. As one study notes, one of the most important factors in reducing the intensity and duration of a child's response to trauma is "the availability of a healthy and responsive caretaker to provide some support and nurturance."[11] Specifically, girls who have been sexually abused have a better chance of psychological recovery if they enjoy a warm and supportive relationship with a nonoffending parent.[12]

Unfortunately, faith communities have often not responded well to children who have been sexually abused. Much of this has to do with denial. "People of faith are hesitant to admit that the very communities that claim to value children can also be responsible for their harm," writes Kibbie Ruth in *Child Maltreatment*. "Abuse of children occurs in all faith traditions—by clergy, congregational leaders, religious education teachers, youth ministers, and others trusted by the children. The harm done by abuse within the faith community is amplified by its denial."[13]

This denial is potentially harmful for all children, according to Keith Wright. "We are naïve when we assume that a clergyperson or leader or member in any denomination or religious group is above abusing a child," states Keith Wright in *Religious Abuse*. "While we must guard against cynicism that leads us to suspect every clergyperson or choir director or youth worker of the worst, we must also be alert to the *potential for abuse* which is always present when children are in the care of adults—especially adults who have the opportunity to build close and intimate relationships with those who are too young and too powerless to defend themselves." Wright adds, "Only when we are aware of the possibility of danger, can we take the steps which will lessen the likelihood of child abuse in our religious community."[14]

As stated earlier, it can be devastating for a child who has been victimized to be denied comfort or to be ignored. But that is what happened to Brent Jeffs. In his memoir, *Lost Boy*, the former member of the FLDS alleges that, on a number of occasions beginning when he was five years old, the sect's leader, Warren Jeffs, removed the boy from the classroom, raped him, and then returned him to the classroom. Brent Jeffs writes that no one questioned these disappearances nor seemed to notice him becoming more withdrawn. Jeffs describes the first time his alleged abuser brought the injured, terrified boy to the classroom: "I quickly scurried to the farthest, most isolated corner I could find. Immediately, I was in tremendous pain again, bleeding and unable to talk. I tried to curl up into myself and rock and hide." Jeffs adds, "My feelings of shame were confirmed when no one even noticed there was anything wrong with me. I just went home after class and changed my clothes," where "the physical evidence of Warren's crimes left in my soiled and bloodstained underwear simply disappeared into our massive laundry pile."[15]

One girl, unlike Jeffs, had the courage to come forward and talk about her abuse, only to be met with brutality. In *Unchosen: The Hidden Lives of Hasidic Rebels*, Hella Winston talks about a young woman named Leah, who, when she was ten years old, was repeatedly molested by a man in her Orthodox Jewish community. After Leah told close friends about the incidents, her school principal found out and expelled Leah, claiming she would be a bad influence on the other students. "If this weren't punishment enough," writes Winston, "Leah's father then threatened to burn her with a hot pan if she ever spoke up about the molestation to anyone again."[16]

According to Asher Lipner, a psychologist and rabbi who works in the Orthodox Jewish community in Brooklyn, well-meaning friends and family members of an abuse victim often stand in the way of healing. On the blog *The Un-Orthodox Jew*, Lipner says community members are sometimes "concerned more for the victim's own reputation, since the stigma of being a survivor is so debilitating in our community." He adds that some members of the community even "have more compassion and concern for the molester and his family's reputation or the reputation of the institution that harbored him, than for the victim." He notes, "One of the bravest people I know had several psychiatric hospitalizations after her family refused to take her side against a family member who molested her for years. She had multiple therapists from our community during this time but has only found healing by going outside of the community for help."[17]

This failure to support victims becomes even more intensified when the alleged perpetrator is a religious authority. In fact, the status of accused perpetrators of child sexual abuse probably has a lot to do with why many pious individuals won't report cases, according to one expert who commented on a

2002 survey. This survey reveals that Protestants are more likely than Catholics to have sexually abused children in a religious setting. While this could be true simply because Protestants outnumber Catholics in the United States, Indiana University sociology professor Anson Shupe opined to the media that Protestants are less reluctant than Catholics to come forward and report such crimes "because they don't put their clergy on as high a pedestal as Catholics do with their priests."[18]

"Even adults who notice a suspicious relationship between a religious professional and a child may be very unlikely to question it," writes Bette Bottoms in one of her studies. "The special circumstances of abuse by religious authorities may make it particularly likely to go unreported and keep recurring, and to promote painful confusion in young victims that make its long-term psychological consequences difficult to bear."[19]

Earlier it was explained that some closed Muslim communities will respond poorly to children who allege that an imam has sexually abused them. As Salma Abugideiri explained it to me, many Muslims fail victims in this way.

> It creates a crisis of faith for everyone. It's a lot easier to say to the kid, "How dare you make up this story? This is a man of God. How could you say that?" It's a lot easier to do that than to say, "Oh my gosh, this person that we have trusted, who's led the community, who performed our marriages, who made the call to prayer in my infant's ear—that this person has violated everything that we stand for." And so it makes everyone have to do a lot of soul searching, coming to terms with things. It's a very painful experience.

In addition, says Abugideiri, there is a belief within Muslim communities that "if the abuse stops, then there are no lasting repercussions for that child." She continues,

> So, a lot of times people will take action, maybe they'll move to another community, maybe they'll pull their kid out of that Sunday school or youth program. They'll do what they think would protect the kid from further abuse. But because there's a lack of understanding that that damage has long-term psychological implications for the child and that the perpetrator could also be hurting other kids, people don't do any more than that, and they feel like that's enough, and they will deal privately with whatever agony it's caused them.

A failure to report sexual abuse allegations is particularly problematic in closed communities, as many fear being persecuted by governmental agencies, even those that are designed to help curtail child abuse, such as law enforcement and child protective services. This fear of persecution is somewhat understandable given that some religious groups have, and continue to be, persecuted to some degree. Examples include Jews, fundamentalist Mormons who practice polygamy, and Muslims. However, it is likely that, for a number of groups, these fears are overblown and could be mitigated with more communication between religious leaders and outside authorities. In the meantime, reluctance to report child abuse allegations frequently serves to allow abuse to continue.

For example, to protect themselves from possible persecution, Jewish communities commonly adhere to cultural laws that forbid the spreading of gossip, slander, and bringing of shame upon other Jews. However, this "keep to ourselves" approach has harmed children who are victims of sexual abuse, as laws against negative talk about the race are sometimes interpreted to mean Jews should not report known or suspected cases of abuse to outside authorities. Jewish leaders have tried to explain to community members that these laws do not apply when children are in danger and need help. In an editorial for the *Jewish Star*, Ben Hirsch argues that using such principles to prevent reports of abuse is "little more than a form of self-protection." Hirsch, who founded Survivors for Justice, an advocacy organization to support Orthodox Jewish survivors of sexual abuse and their families, adds that such self-protection has "come at the expense of the protection of our community's children."[20]

In an e-mail sent to me from Asher Lipner, he describes a patient of his who "had the experience of being retraumatized when he told a frum [observantly Jewish] therapist that he had been sexually abused by a prominent rabbi." Lipner says the therapist refused to believe the patient "because 'rabbis don't act that way.' Even when he accepted the patient's account (because he found another rabbi to believe his story) the therapist told me that he still did not want it publicized due to the potential '*Chillul Hashem*' [casting shame or bringing disrepute to belief in God]."[21]

Many worshippers instinctively feel compelled to protect the reputation of their faith. One woman I interviewed, who wanted to go by the name of Sarah, says she was sexually abused by her pastor when she was a teenager. In trying to get her abuser fired, Sarah thought she could turn to her mother for support. But instead, her mother seemed more worried about how the allegations would affect the church's image. Sarah says when the abuse was happening, her mother told her she had heard a rumor that "something was happening" between Sarah and the pastor. Sarah says her mother only said, "I don't like that it looks like that, so you might want to be careful what you do." So, says Sarah, "That was putting it all on me and caring about what people think more than my well-being."

Years later, Sarah summoned up the courage to tell her mother while the two were in a therapy session that she wanted to get church officials to fire her abuser. Sarah says she still hoped her mother would respond by saying, "Let's get him. It's horrible what happened to you." But instead, her mother's first reaction was, "Are you really sure you should go public with this?"

Other victims have also struggled to gain their parents' support. The documentary *A Twist of Faith* concerns a man's struggle to sue the Catholic Church for his having been sexually abused by a priest in his youth. The man, Tony, longs for his mother to stand by his side and to give up her ties to the church. But the mother is torn between her allegiance as a mother and as a worshipper. In one scene, Tony and his mother discuss his legal troubles:

> MOTHER: Well, Tony, lookit. I can deal with what I believe was being told a little by the bishop. I can deal with that. The church is like to me like any large company. Sometimes the right hand doesn't even know what the left hand's doin'.
>
> TONY: They know. They fuckin' know. They damn well know that this is tearin' up marriages, that this is tearin' up individuals. That this is—they know and they are the pillars of society and the sons of bitches don't do anything to stop it.
>
> MOTHER: Watch your language.
>
> TONY: And you know what? You run around with those guys. It's guilt by association. You—you—you—I'm sorry, mom, but you're talkin' out of two sides—
>
> MOTHER: No.
>
> TONY: You're wantin' to—you so *vehemently* want to hang on to what you need to, and I don't [begrudge] you that, but, for God's sakes, what is it gonna take?
>
> MOTHER: Are you asking me to leave the Catholic Church?
>
> TONY: No, I'm not asking you to leave the Catholic Church. I'm asking you to stand up.
>
> MOTHER: What!
>
> TONY: I'm askin' you to stop writin' checks.
>
> MOTHER: What in hell's bells do you think I've been doin' or trying to do? I'm not hiding. I'm not hiding. But I am—
>
> TONY: Do you put money in the basket every week?
>
> MOTHER: Yeah.
>
> TONY: Yeah.
>
> MOTHER: I think that's my obligation.
>
> TONY: The money you're givin' them is payin' the attorneys that are fightin' me![22]

Remarkably, when cases come to court, it is not uncommon for faith communities to come to the aid of perpetrators over victims. For example, religious leaders and congregants sometimes raise money for the criminal defense of alleged abusers or sit in the courtroom expressing support for the defendant. Mary Byler, who grew up in a conservative Amish community in Pennsylvania, was first sexually abused by her father and two older cousins and, later, by her two older brothers, Johnny and Eli. Byler's story is poignantly told in an article written by Nadya Labi for *Legal Affairs*. Labi explains that Johnny and Eli repeatedly raped their sister from the time she was eight until she reached the age of seventeen. "Once, Eli climbed on top of her while Johnny held her down," writes Labi. It was impossible for Byler to escape the abuse: "Her brothers waited for her in the outhouse, the milkhouse, the barn. They climbed in her window if she locked the door to her room. When she locked the window, they took the door off by its hinges."[23]

Byler told her mother but received no support. According to Byler, her mother believed the matter was settled because Johnny and Eli had confessed in church and had been banned from church activities for a number of weeks. Also, Byler said her mother blamed her daughter for not "fighting or praying hard enough" and for being unforgiving. What led Byler to notify authorities was when she suspected another brother was abusing her four-year-old sister. Rather than come to her aid, Byler's church voted unanimously to excommunicate her. But, as a result of Byler's bravery in coming forward, all three brothers were indicted, pleaded guilty on sexual assault charges, and received sentences ranging from ten years' probation to eight years in prison. At the 2004 trial of one of the brothers, more than one hundred Amish men and women sat in the courtroom in support not of Byler, but of the defendant. This so infuriated the judge that he asked the crowd, "How many of you have ever cried for Mary Byler?"[24]

But to cast all the blame onto parents or congregants would be a mistake. Powerful religious institutions and leaders of faith groups have at best consistently failed, despite their proclamations that child sexual abuse is sinful, to acknowledge the existence of these crimes. At worst, they have tried to protect perpetrators and left victims out in the cold.

Chapter 16
SECRECY AND SILENCE AT THE TOP

M any religious institutions put in place safeguards that aim to eradicate sexual misconduct on the part of clergy members and other employees and volunteers. These safeguards typically include conducting background checks on anyone who comes in contact with children and instituting policies and procedures that determine how those organizations handle cases of alleged abuses. In addition, many religious organizations pride themselves on their willingness to address issues of child sexual abuse with their members and the public. For instance, the Jehovah's Witnesses organization says on its website that it has produced articles "to educate both Witnesses and the public regarding the importance and the need to protect children from child abuse." Furthermore, the site states that "anyone in a responsible position who is guilty of child abuse would be removed from his responsibilities without hesitation. . . . We regularly review our procedures to ensure that they are in compliance with the law."[1]

The website of the Church of Jesus Christ of Latter-day Saints maintains, "The church has long encouraged families to talk about child abuse, to educate themselves on how to recognize and prevent such tragedies." The church states that since 1976, more than fifty news and magazine articles have appeared in church publications condemning child abuse or educating members about it; church leaders have spoken out on the subject at international church conferences; and child abuse is the subject of a "regular lesson" taught during Sunday meetings. The church claims to have also developed "extensive training materials" to educate church leaders on how to identify and respond to allegations of abuse, and professional counselors man a twenty-four-hour help line to answer local leaders' questions.[2]

In 2010, the Rabbinical Council of America drew up its "Convention Resolution: Condemning and Combating Child Abuse." The resolution states, among other things, that the rabbinical authorities acknowledge that sexual and physical abuse of children goes on in the Jewish community; that some Orthodox rabbis have been indicted or convicted for child abuse or child endangerment; and that such abuse poses great harm to victims.[3]

Similarly, in 2006, the United States Catholic Conference of Bishops (USCCB) issued a revised Charter for the Protection of Children and Young People, a document that instructs dioceses and parishes to reach out to victims and their families and demonstrate "a sincere commitment to their spiritual and emotional well-being," as well as report allegations of child sexual abuse to public authorities and cooperate with investigations.[4]

It would seem that religious institutions are doing all they can to prevent child sexual abuse from happening within their jurisdictions. "The Catholic Church is probably the safest place for children at this point in history," states judicial vicar Thomas Brundage on the website Catholic Anchor Online.[5]

However, the battle is far from over.

For starters, simply having policies and procedures in place is not enough to prevent abuse. No matter how well thought out these plans are, they can do little unless church officials who directly oversee the operations of places of worship are committed to enforcing those polices.

Episcopal priest and pastoral psychotherapist Sarah Rieth is one of a group of task force members who developed sexual misconduct policies and procedures for the Episcopal Diocese of Western New York in 1999. The next year, those policies earned the archdiocese a Polly Bond Award, a national ethics award that acknowledges excellence and achievement in the ministry of church communication within the Episcopal Church. As Rieth said in our interview, there are policies and procedures in many churches, but they are "only as good as the person charged to implement them and as good as that person is committed to implementing them and committed to learning about proper pastoral response." Rieth says that, for some churches, officials in charge "have no actual desire to do anything," in which case such plans are nothing more than "window dressing."

In addition, while many religious organizations have done a good job of trying to prevent abuse, they continue to let victims down because of how poorly they respond to victims *after* actual abuse takes place. In many cases, the response has been to silence victims, handle the cases internally, not report abuses to outside authorities, and fail to provide victims adequate mental health services. Given these problems, religious officials' claims about being committed to speaking out about child sexual abuse, rooting out perpetrators, and caring for victims' needs often fall flat.

FAILURE TO REPORT ABUSE

Some religious organizations are clear that all suspected or actual cases of child sexual abuse must be reported to local authorities. For instance, those originally drawn up by Rieth and other task force members for the Episcopal Diocese of Western New York state that all allegations of abuse are to be reported to the bishop of the archdiocese, who, in turn, is required to "cause" those allegations "to be promptly reported to the appropriate criminal or civil authorities."[6]

But very often, clergy do not report suspected or actual cases of child sexual abuse. A typical situation occurred in Phoenix in 2010. That summer, police arrested a man for allegedly molesting his two daughters, both of whom were teenagers at the time of his arrest. According to one of the daughters, the acts included sexual intercourse. Police said that the man admitted to numerous counts of sexual abuse with both victims over a period of years. But the father was not the only adult involved in the case. Police also arrested pastors Daniel and Laura McCluskey because they knew about the molestation and failed to report it as required by law. According to police, the older daughter told the pastors about her father inappropriately touching her, after which the McCluskeys only told the girl that because the father had repented, she should forgive him and restore their relationship.[7]

According to national statistics, clergy as a professional group are some of the least likely reporters of child abuse. In fact, the percentage of clergy who report allegations each year in the United States is so abysmally low that clergy do not even show up in national statistics as a separate category of reporting professionals. Instead, cases that are reported by clergy get lumped into an "other" category that also includes cases reported by sports coaches and camp counselors.[8] There are a number of reasons for this, but a big one appears to be a failure on the part of religious institutions to train clergy on such laws, since many clergy are ignorant of such mandates.[9] While most religious organizations claim to abide by local civil mandatory reporting laws, it's often unclear just what those laws require. Some statutes exempt clergy from reporting, and others do not explicitly state that clergy are required to report. In fact, a 1998 survey of clergy members shows that nearly one-third of the clergy had no education about child abuse and neglect, and nearly one-quarter falsely believed that evidence, rather than the suspicion of abuse, is required before a report should be made.[10]

What's more, many states provide clergy and religious institutions with a loophole that exempts the reporting of information if it is obtained as part of "privileged communication," such as during confession.[11] Church officials maintain that priest-penitent confidentiality is critical to provide a safe place for congregants to discuss private matters with clergy. Rev. Marie Fortune agrees, but to a point. The founder of the FaithTrust Institute writes on the organization's website, "It provides a context of respect and trust within which help can hopefully be provided for an individual."[12]

But Fortune adds, many confuse *confidentiality* with *secrecy*, which, she says, is "the absolute promise never under any circumstance to share any information which comes to a clergyperson." Confidentiality, on the other hand, "means to hold information in trust," while allowing for the sharing of information if it means protecting someone from harm. "Confidentiality is not intended to protect abusers from being held accountable for their actions or to keep them from getting the help that they need. Shielding them from the consequences of their behavior likely will further endanger their victims and will deny them the repentance which they need," writes Fortune. The ultimate cost of requiring secrecy in cases of alleged child abuse, Fortune warns, is that it may "support maintaining the secret of the abuse of a child which likely means that the abuse continues."[13]

On a more cynical note, critics believe that religious institutions abuse the "privileged communication" provision. For example, one attorney who represents victims told the *New York Times* that many church officials have argued that the exception relieves them of having to report to outside authorities evidence of child sexual abuse that is discovered among their ranks. According to the lawyer, when a priest informs his bishop that he has acted in a sexually inappropriate way with a minor, church officials claim that the interchange was an inviolate confession and keep the information secret.[14]

"The word 'confidentiality' has by now become a means of covering up a multitude of questionable and often dangerous practices," writes Fortune. "Confidentiality may be invoked for all the wrong reasons and not truly in the interests of a particular congregant or of society."[15]

Critics say it is not just low-level clergy who tend not to report abuse but also those at the top of most religious organizations. Officials in those positions have been particularly reluctant to turn in accused or actual pedophiles and other abusers to authorities. One reason, say critics, is the perceived need to protect the faith or institution from getting caught up in scandal. According to Marci Hamilton, a professor at the Benjamin N. Cardozo School of Law at

Yeshiva University, religious entities including the Roman Catholic Church, the Church of Jesus Christ of Latter-day Saints, Jehovah's Witnesses, and Orthodox Jewish communities have rules or theological principles that forbid scandal.[16]

"The incentive to prevent the appearance of tarnishment is powerful," writes Hamilton on FindLaw.com. She adds, "The [religious] institution will work hard to keep the damning information inside the organization and away from outsiders."[17]

Many religious institutions and communities also prefer to "prosecute" abuse cases internally. Despite the fact that most priests, bishops, rabbis, imams, ministers, and church elders have next to no professional experience investigating crimes of child sexual abuse, many religious officials advocate for letting their own institutions and communities handle such matters. Officials in the Catholic Church have gone so far as to suggest that they are superior to civil authorities when it comes to looking into such cases. For instance, in 2001, then-Cardinal Joseph Ratzinger—who was made pope in 2005—stated in a letter he cowrote that "the functions of judge, promoter of justice, notary and legal representative can validly be performed for these [child sexual abuse] cases only by priests."[18] The cowriter of that letter, Archbishop Tarcisio Bertone, who was then secretary of the Vatican's Congregation for the Doctrine of the Faith (CDF), said in a 2002 interview with the international magazine *30 Giorni*, "In my opinion, the demand that a bishop be obligated to contact the police in order to denounce a priest who has admitted the offense of pedophilia is unfounded."[19] Even more troubling, in March 2010, the Vatican announced that a priest who confesses sexual abuse in the sacrament of penance should be absolved; also, the confessor should not feel the need to encourage the priest to disclose his acts publicly or go public with that information himself.[20]

Child advocates oppose religious organizations' failure and refusal to report child abuse. They maintain that such cases must be promptly handed over to public authorities so they can be properly investigated and so perpetrators no longer are a threat to victims. The aforementioned Phoenix case illustrates how abuse continues when perpetrators are not reported. According to police, the older sister was no longer victimized by her father after she told the pastors about the abuse, but the father continued to abuse the younger sister for two more years.[21]

"We strongly urge that clergy report any disclosure of sexual abuse of a child," writes Marie Fortune on the website of the FaithTrust Institute. "None of us have the capacity to handle these situations in isolation and without outside collaborative intervention. Professionals to whom sexual abuse is disclosed need help in protecting a child and holding an abuser accountable." Fortune writes that the Arizona pastors' failure to report the abuse that a victim brought to their attention represents "savage ignorance with dreadful and unnecessary consequences for victims. . . . Let this be a wake-up call for spiritual leaders: We need the help of our secular colleagues to work in concert with our pastoral guidance to stop sex offenders."[22]

Sarah Rieth agrees. As she explained in our interview, "If we have reasonable suspicions that a child is being maltreated, moral law requires that any person report abuse to the civil authorities." The criminal justice system is not perfect, she concedes, but "it's the best system we have, and it's the child's best chance for the abuse to stop and for the child to get the help that he or she needs."

In light of criticism that dioceses have not been forthcoming with information about abuse cases, the Vatican seems to have softened somewhat on the position of reporting abuses to outside authorities. In the summer of 2010, Pope Benedict XVI stated that child abuse cases should be handled by *both* civil and canon law "with respect for their reciprocal specificity and autonomy."[23] Later that year, the Vatican announced that it was planning to issue a set of guidelines to bishops around the world that would address the need to obey civil reporting requirements. While the church did not indicate it would require all abuse allegations to be reported, church officials said they discussed the need for bishops to collaborate with civil authorities in reporting abuse. Advocates for victims, however, said the Vatican was still not doing enough to protect children, since church officials had not turned over to authorities the names of all known pedophile priests.[24]

CONDUCTING INTERNAL "INVESTIGATIONS"

It's not that religious institutions do absolutely nothing when allegations of sexual abuse arise. Most have well-established, detailed policies for how these cases must be handled. The thing is, most of these policies concern the *internal* handling of such cases. But as critics point out, while religious leaders can help in many ways—for example by providing pastoral counseling to victims— most priests, bishops, rabbis, imams, ministers, and church elders have no expertise in investigating matters of child sexual abuse. This can cause a myriad of problems, especially if cases are internally reviewed before or in lieu of being turned over to outside authorities. The sooner secular authorities get their hands on evidence, the better. If these internal reviews cause delays, victims' memories can fade, DNA evidence may no longer be retrievable, and the statute of limitations can run out.

On June 24, 2010, I spoke with Houston attorney Daniel Shea, who has sued the Catholic Church for allegedly covering up child sexual abuse allegations. Shea says church officials have "mucked up" plenty of cases by conducting internal investigations before prosecutors have gotten involved, which Shea asserts constitutes an obstruction of justice. "As soon as the crime is committed, you report it to the police and get out of the way," says Shea.

Sarah Rieth agrees that churches conducting internal investigations is a bad idea, especially if done before outside authorities are done with a case. "It would be like an incest family trying to heal itself," she says.

It is now well known that the internal system employed by the Catholic Church has, in many cases, amounted to nothing more than a shell game of moving pedophilic clergy from parish to parish, sometimes permitting them to again have contact with children. When the USCCB convened in 2002, it issued a 140-page indictment of the ways bishops had failed in their duty "to protect the most vulnerable among us from possible predators."[25] Incredibly, after US bishops formed a national review board to address the scandal, its chief enforcer, former Oklahoma governor, FBI agent, and federal prosecutor Frank Keating, himself a Catholic, quit the board and left the church in disgust. Keating likened some Catholic bishops to the Mafia, who "hide and suppress" information. As Keating wrote in his resignation letter, "To resist grand jury subpoenas, to suppress the names of offending clerics, to deny, to obfuscate, to explain away; that is the model of a criminal organization, not my church."[26]

From victims' perspectives, religious organizations' own internal investigations of alleged child sexual abuse crimes have been harmful. Many victims have said they were not satisfied with the way religious officials evaluated their cases. For example, in one 1994 case, a fifteen-year-old girl talked to Jehovah's Witness elders about how she had been repeatedly molested by an adult Witness from ages ten to thirteen. Years later, the woman told the *New York Times* that the elders had asked explicit questions about the abuse that made her uncomfortable. And it was all for naught, since the elders ultimately agreed with the perpetrator that the girl had misinterpreted his actions. To make things worse, the elders warned the victim against reporting the abuse to outside authorities or talking about it to other members, according to the woman. As she told the *New York Times*, if she were found to have been guilty of "gossip or slander," she stood to be disfellowshipped or excommunicated.[27]

As Marci Hamilton writes in the *William and Mary Bill of Rights Journal*, "Religious groups have demonstrated no superiority to secular organizations in protecting children [from sexual abuse] and have harmed their own reputations through these failures."[28]

REBUFFING VICTIMS

This historical failure to keep cases of child sexual abuse secret has gained religious organizations a reputation that hardly squares with many claims that they care about the needs of victims. Instead, these institutions appear more concerned about their own financial bottom lines. Attorney Tim Kosnoff, who has sued numerous religious institutions on behalf of abused victims, told me the ultimate goal of these entities is not to help victims but rather to "do what is necessary to protect the church from scandal." He adds, "There is this almost autonomic impulse to deal with the matter through denial, concealment, cover-up, and minimization."

Canon lawyer Thomas P. Doyle describes the Catholic Church's collective response to victims as "wave after wave of deception, stonewalling, outright lying, intimidation of victims and complex schemes to manipulate the truth and obstruct justice."[29] One example of such stonewalling is convincing courts to seal employment records.[30] For instance, as late as May 2010—five years after the USCCB passed its revised Charter for the Protection of Children and Young People—the Norwich Diocese of Connecticut was alleged to have refused to hand over hundreds of documents pertaining to a child sexual abuse case involving a priest at St. Joseph's Church in New London. One of those documents, attorneys say, is a letter that was sent to then-Cardinal Joseph Ratzinger, the current pope.[31]

The more recent unveiling of a large set of internal church documents reveals just how potentially damaging such exposure can be and, therefore, why religious organizations want to keep such information secret. In October 2010, attorneys for 144 plaintiffs who claimed to have been sexually abused by Roman Catholic priests affiliated with the Diocese of San Diego released some ten thousand pages of church personnel files that had previously been sealed. The documents revealed abuses by priests that attorneys say church officials knew about well before they were made public. One of those cases involved a priest who, despite having been the target of complaints, was made director of a Roman Catholic residential facility for troubled boys. Some of the plaintiffs in the recent lawsuit had been residents of that facility and claimed that same priest abused them.[32]

Religious institutions have been accused of dragging out court cases in hopes of legally and psychologically exhausting victims so they will give up the fight. Cheryl Cooney believes her Seventh-Day Adventist church tried that tactic with her. In the late 1990s, she tried to get church officials to fire the minister who had abused her and to pay for her mental healthcare and legal expenses. But instead, she says, the church only offered to have the minister quietly resign. "They said the statute of limitations had expired, so they wouldn't do anything," she says, adding that the church finally fired the minister—but only after she threatened to go public about her case.

"Silence has been a standard condition of financial compensations to victims," states Kibbie Ruth in *Child Maltreatment*.[33]

Carol Delaney writes in *Abraham on Trial* that children who are sexually abused by religious authorities such as priests often suffer "a double betrayal" —after they suffer the sexual abuse itself, they are violated by the overseeing religious institution, which, Delaney notes, has often not believed the child and has "taken the side of the priest."[34]

A key reason behind this failure to attend to victims' needs comes from a determined effort on the part of religious institutions to avoid scandal and keep cases of child sexual abuse secret. Some religious organizations and communities that have been highly criticized of such secrecy include the Catholic Church, Jehovah's Witnesses, and Orthodox Jewish communities.

THE CATHOLIC CHURCH

No religious institution has excelled at secrecy like the Catholic Church, and this mastery is reflected in at least two official church documents. The first, dated March 16, 1962, provides bishops with instructions on how to handle "crimes of solicitation," which are "obscene" acts perpetrated by a cleric or "attempted by him with youths of either sex or with brute animals."[35] The document calls for information regarding such crimes to be "pursued in a most secretive way" and that the crimes are to be "restrained by a perpetual silence."[36] The document further states that officials faced with a case involving an errant priest may remove him from his ministry, but they can also "transfer him to another [assignment]."[37] It also orders that documents describing unfounded accusations be destroyed.[38]

The term *perpetual silence* is extraordinarily important. It refers to a strict code of secrecy that is known in canon law as *the pontifical secret*. As the 1962 document explains, those subjected to such secrecy—the offending clergy, their victims, and witnesses[39]—must "promise sacredly, vow and swear" to keep the matter secret. In fact, they are even forbidden to communicate confidential information "directly or indirectly, by means of a nod, or of a word." The secret must be kept "under whatever type of pretext" even "for the purpose of a greater good."[40] The penalty for violating the "perpetual silence" is excommunication—a penalty that can be lifted only by the pope.[41]

Church officials say that this ironclad secrecy was—and some say, still is—

necessary to protect victims and alleged perpetrators. Supporters contend that the policy has allowed victims and witnesses to come forward and speak freely, knowing that their responses would be kept confidential, and protected the name of the accused until the church determined if he was, in fact, guilty. These supporters say that extending the pontifical secret to "crimes of solicitation" was not meant to cover up abuses. They point out that the 1962 document *requires* victims to denounce priests who have abused them, partly because these crimes carry with them "inestimable detriment to souls."[42] Also, say supporters, canon law does not prohibit church officials from reporting crimes to outside authorities.[43]

However, such serious codes of confidentiality have had negative consequences. For example, because members of the church are sworn to the pontifical secret even in situations that involve the "purpose of the greater good," an individual would be barred from reporting a known pedophile to authorities, even knowing that that pedophile was abusing scores of children. Former professor of canon law and oblate priest William Woestman told *America Magazine* that holding church authorities to the pontifical secret was probably interpreted as barring those authorities from notifying civil law enforcement of allegations of abuse by priests.[44] Not surprisingly, the 1962 document says nothing about turning abusive priests over to law enforcement or about providing victims spiritual or psychological counseling. Instead, it simply lays out penalties for those found guilty of crimes of solicitation, such as being suspended from celebrating Mass and from hearing sacramental confessions, and being deprived of "all benefices and dignities."[45]

"It screams by its silence," says Houston attorney Daniel Shea, who strongly refutes the stance that holding victims of sexual abuse to the pontifical secret is done on their behalf. Rather, he says, it is meant to procure their silence and protect the church's image. Imposing such fears about violating the secret is an example of mind control, says Shea.

Vatican officials say that the 1962 norms no longer apply, that they have been superseded by later codes. However, the aforementioned 2001 letter cowritten by then-Cardinal Ratzinger makes it clear that little had changed. At the time, Ratzinger headed the Congregation for the Doctrine of Faith, a body that oversees, interprets, and updates church doctrines. In the letter, Ratzinger orders that certain moral crimes, including sex crimes involving a minor, "are reserved to the apostolic tribunal" of Ratzinger's department. Furthermore, the cardinal states that cases of child sexual abuse are "subject to the pontifical secret," noting that the 1962 "crimes of solicitation" order has been "in force until now." Like that 1962 document, nowhere in Ratzinger's letter does he indicate that bishops should turn perpetrators over to civil authorities or reach out to victims.[46]

In 2011, a letter surfaced that seemed to back up critics' claims that the Vatican has consistently tried to keep child abuse cases secret from outside authorities. The letter, written by the Vatican's top diplomat in Ireland, told bishops that their mandatory reporting of abuse cases "gives rise to serious reservations of both a moral and canonical nature." A Vatican spokesperson said that people had misunderstood what the letter meant, that the Holy See was only emphasizing that Irish bishops follow church law meticulously. Still, critics say the letter from Rome put the kibosh on reporting priest-perpetrated sexual abuse cases to authorities. Prior to having received the letter, Irish bishops, having been hit by the first lawsuits filed by victims, had pledged cooperation with law enforcement.[47]

"The obsession with secrecy though the years has been instrumental in preventing both justice and compassionate care for victims. It has enabled the widespread spirit of denial among clergy, hierarchy and laity," writes Thomas Doyle in a paper on the church's policies concerning confidentiality. Ironically, though, Doyle points out that the church's modus operandi of secrecy has backfired: "The secrecy has been justified to avoid scandal when in fact it has enabled even more scandal."[48]

JEHOVAH'S WITNESSES

According to public statements made by Jehovah's Witnesses, their organization does not have much of a problem when it comes to clergy-perpetrated child sexual abuse. A press release that appears on the Witnesses' official website states that only eleven elders—out of a total of eighty thousand—have been sued for child abuse, in thirteen lawsuits filed in the United States over the last hundred years. "The incidence of this crime among Jehovah's Witnesses is rare," concludes the announcement. Furthermore, writes the site, "We do not silence victims. Our members have an absolute right to report this horrible crime to the authorities."[49]

And yet, despite their theological differences, there are many similarities between the way the Catholic Church has handled—or not handled—cases of religious child sexual abuse and the way the Jehovah's Witnesses organization has: In both cases, while no one is directed to violate abuse reporting laws, there is still a palpable desire for the matter to remain within the church. For one, the organization has a complex internal system for handling such cases.[50] Also, there is a unique rule that the church applies when internally investigating child abuse cases—one that makes a victim's life so difficult, it might explain why incidents of child sexual abuse among Jehovah's Witnesses are "rare."

Evidence of the church's resistance to make abuse cases public is embedded in the very website articles that the church touts as ones that "show our concern for protecting children from sexual abuse."[51] While these articles provide a great deal of information about prevention, it is difficult to find any that explicitly discuss what to do *after* a child says he or she has been molested. Most speak in generalities. For example, one article stresses that child victims must be given love and support and not be made to feel at fault, and that "the accused molester will have to be confronted."[52] Another article suggests that parents get abuse victims professional help, while making sure that "any such professional will respect your religious views."[53] But there is something important missing from these articles—the suggestion that parents should report these crimes to law enforcement or child protective services.

And while Jehovah's Witnesses have been criticized along with other religious organizations for failing to address victims' needs, this religious entity has a particular rule that has gained it some notoriety. The rule comes into play when Jehovah's Witnesses conduct internal investigations of abuse allegations and is based on Deuteronomy 19:15, which prohibits a witness in a court proceeding to "rise against a man concerning any iniquity or any sin that he commits" unless the matter can be resolved "by the mouth of two or three witnesses." Despite the fact that just about all sexual abuse happens in secret, Witness officials adhere to the verse and require victims to produce *at least two witnesses* to prove their case if the alleged abuser does not confess or repent. According to the organization's website, "As a Bible-based organization, we must adhere to what the scriptures say."[54]

Critics rebuke the two-witness rule, as well as the fact that the church, like other religious organizations, resists expelling abusers from the faith if they repent. "If a person can cry a good tune, there are virtually no repercussions and nobody besides the elders ever knows," Jean Kraus told the *New York Times*. Kraus said her former husband confessed to abusing their daughter, but elders in their Queens congregation let him off with only a reprimand. "They told me that he wasn't a wicked man, that it was a weakness," said Kraus.[55]

Indeed, the church admits that it remains committed to keeping most members in the fold, even those who have molested children. As one church spokesman told the media, "We view such judicial hearings as an extension of our shepherding work as ministers. In other words, we're there to save a person's soul. In these cases we are not going to be vindictive because these are our brothers, and we would hope that they would change."[56] Meanwhile, however, the way the Jehovah's Witnesses organization has handled cases of alleged child sexual abuse has made it difficult for many victims to believe that, as the church proclaims, "Jehovah's Witnesses worldwide are united in their abhorrence of this sin and crime."[57]

ORTHODOX JEWISH COMMUNITIES

According to critics, one stronghold of power in Orthodox Jewish communities are the rabbis who run yeshivas. Joel Engelman, who earlier alleged that his yeshiva principal molested him, explained to me that Orthodox Jewish parents are subject to a "constant fear of how the community is going to perceive [their] child. And yeshivas play a huge part in that. The rabbis play a huge part in that." Engelman says the biggest concern among parents is that their children will have stellar reputations so that they can marry into a good family. Therefore, children are expected to behave themselves, says Engelman:

> There's a mold and everybody needs to fit that mold. If anybody steps out of line, they automatically lose their chance of a marriage prospect. So if you speak out on anything, on any given issue, especially an issue like this, these yeshivas have enormous power in saying, "We'll kick your kid out of school. And then everybody is going to look and say, 'Oh, this kid got kicked out of school. What's going on?'"

Unfortunately, there have been numerous cases where yeshivas have abused that power to keep pedophiles' actions secret. A notorious case in point is that of Rabbi Yehuda Kolko of Brooklyn. Kolko was accused of molesting as many as twenty victims in the Yeshiva Torah Temimah in Flatbush over several decades. At least five lawsuits have been filed against the yeshiva concerning accusations against Kolko.[58] In April 2008, Kolko pleaded guilty to two counts of child endangerment and was sentenced to three years' probation.[59] What was so disturbing about the case, in addition to the facts surrounding the abuses themselves, was the alleged intimidation of victims by yeshiva officials. One lawsuit accused yeshiva administrators of orchestrating "a campaign of intimidation, concealment and misrepresentations designed to prevent victims from filing lawsuits." For example, the lawsuit stated that when the case was to come before a rabbinic hearing, school administrators told family members of alleged victims that if they came forward, they would be shunned by the Jewish community and their children would later have a hard time getting accepted into yeshivas in the area.[60]

Engelman knows full well what it is like to be the target of such intimidation. As has been mentioned, Engelman has gone public with allegations that he was molested by his yeshiva principal, a rabbi. But according to Engelman, the man was not his first abuser. When he was in elementary school in his Hasidic community in Brooklyn, Engelman says an older boy in school first molested him. When Engelman's parents complained to the principal, he seemed to put a stop to it. But, in an insidious turn of events, that rabbi apparently had pinned Engelman as a potential victim for himself. Shortly after Engelman's parents told the principal about the abuse, Engelman says the principal summoned the eight-year-old to his office. The principal, Rabbi Avrohom Reichman, was, as Engelman puts it, "one of the scary dudes" at the school. The man never cracked a smile, says Engelman, and was very strict. So when the young Engelman was told to go to Reichman's office, he was understandably afraid.

"I remember him telling me, 'Close the door behind you,' and he motioned for me to get on his lap." Begrudgingly, Engelman did as he was told, and, after that, Engelman says, Reichman's demeanor changed. Engelman says the man seemed concerned in a grandfatherly sort of way, asking Engelman how his day was going and if he liked school. And, while the principal was asking him these questions, he began to swivel his chair from side to side. Engelman says he does not recall whether Reichman became sexually aroused from this encounter; however, it was the first of many. "This started becoming a pattern of him calling me into the office, telling me to get on his lap, starting to swivel the chair, and talking to me in this manner," says Engelman. "And he would sort of caress me, my shoulders, and then every now and then, his hands would sort of find themselves a little lower on my body and sometimes on my genitals." Engelman says this would go on for about fifteen or twenty minutes, after which Reichman would often get the boy to assure that he would not tell his parents about what had gone on. Engelman says the molestation continued about twice a week for two months, after which he was taken out of the school because of another matter.

Engelman did not tell anyone about the molestation until he was eighteen years old, when he divulged to his mother what had happened. Both she and his father were supportive, and when Engelman was twenty-two years old, they decided to confront Reichman and school officials about the abuse. Their single purpose was to get the school, United Talmudic Seminary, to fire Reichman. At first, they thought they would be successful. Engelman says school officials assured his family that they would get to the bottom of it, that this was not the first incident involving Reichman, and that he would most certainly be fired. But that is not what ended up happening. According to Engelman, the officials dragged out the case until Engelman was twenty-three years old, at which time New York's statute of limitations ran out. The school told Engelman's family that a panel of rabbis had determined that Reichman would not be removed. One official indicated that the abuse was not severe since there had not been any skin-to-skin contact.

To get their side of the story, I tried to contact both Reichman and school officials at the United Talmudic Seminary on October 7, 2010. A message I left for Reichman was not returned. When I asked to speak to a school official about the case, a secretary curtly said that it was the school's policy not to disclose information to the media.

Engelman's story is not unique. He has learned about a number of other men who say they, too, were victimized by Reichman in their youth. But the abuse continues, says Engelman, because yeshivas have "always managed to shut up the victims" who want to stay in the community. Engelman says he was not as vulnerable because he had left his community when he was eighteen.

As in other religious organizations, Orthodox Jewish communities have ways of handling cases of child sexual abuse that do not involve outside authorities—an internal court system known as the *beth din*. But many victims are fed up with that system, having seen some of the same ineptitude that victims in other faith communities have experienced. As a result, more and more victims are reporting their abuses to secular authorities. Still, many conservative Jews are reluctant to challenge rabbinical leaders and contact outside authorities. In a case involving one of Kolko's victims, a father flew to Jerusalem to ask a prominent rabbi if he was committing a sin by reporting his six-year-old son's alleged abuse. The rabbi gave the father his blessing,[61] but one wonders whether the son would have ever seen justice done had the rabbi given his father a different answer.

CONCLUSION

Many victims have felt the "double betrayal" that Carol Delaney refers to in *Abraham on Trial*, when religious institutions and communities rebuff victims instead of caring for their needs. In *Sexual Abuse in Christian Homes and Churches*, Carolyn Holderread Heggen writes, "If victims' pleas to get the church they love and respect to discipline the abusive pastor are disregarded, profound hopelessness may set in. Sometimes when pastor and church turn their backs, the victim is left with a sense of terrifying abandonment. When abuse survivors feel deserted and betrayed by the pastor, the church, and God, it is no wonder their despair sometimes finds tragic, poignant expression in suicide."[62]

Cheryl Cooney told me after she discovered her Seventh-Day Adventist church was fighting her efforts to have her abuser fired and be compensated for her pain, she "felt totally betrayed by the church. Until that point, I felt that the church had nothing to do with what happened. It was this random case where this man had been the bad one and the church was still good. The fact that the church should have protected me never entered my thought because I really grew up believing it was the 'true' church." The church's ill treatment of Cooney was contrasted by how her employers reacted when they were told about the abuses. When Cooney took her case public, she alerted her employers that she might be on the news, and she says they were "wonderfully supportive."

Tina Anderson, the woman who was made to say a mea culpa in front of her Baptist congregation for having gotten pregnant, has stated that she wants to move on with her life and not dwell on the abuses that took place when she was a teenager. Still, she has made clear that she cannot forget that feeling of abandonment when church officials failed to support her in her time of need. "There's always heartache there," Anderson told the media.[63]

As a result of so many years of failing to address the problem of child sexual abuse, faith communities and those in leadership positions have a long way to go to win back the favor of those who once held them in high esteem, especially the victims of those crimes. As one woman told the media after hearing the pope apologize for the child sexual abuse scandal in the Catholic Church, she did not need to hear about his "sense of shame." She needed him to "correct the situation." As she put it, the pope's shame is "a far cry from the shame that victims have had to live with our entire lives."[64]

How have religious institutions in America been able to maintain such a thick wall of secrecy for so long? Why don't faith communities do a better job of coming to the aid of victims who are abused by religious authorities? The answers are not difficult to see. Shockingly, many followers continue to revere, admire, and worship religious authority figures, even those who have been criminally charged and convicted for abusing children or have failed to protect children from abuse. Despite the paper trail that has followed the pope, raising suspicions that he, personally, has been involved in covering up abuse cases,[65] he remains popular. On May 26, 2010, more than a hundred thousand people filled Saint Peter's Square to show support for the scandal-beleaguered pontiff.[66]

It is this kind of blind devotion to religious leaders, institutions, and communities that continues to leave children vulnerable to sexual abuse.

We might then ask: Who gives religious leaders the power to protect abusive clergy and other pedophiles? And who gives clergy the power that enables them to abuse?

The answer is simple: We do.

Part 4

SIN OF DENIAL

Religious Child Medical Neglect

INTRODUCTION

No child should have to suffer the way Robyn Twitchell did.

On April 3, 1986, it was obvious that something was wrong with the two-year-old when he began crying and then screaming and vomiting. Robyn's parents, David and Ginger Twitchell of Boston, were worried and sought help right away. But they did not call a doctor. Instead, they contacted a Christian Science "practitioner"* to pray for Robyn. The Twitchells were members of the Christian Science Church, which teaches that spiritual-healing techniques administered by church members are superior to medical care.[1]

Over the next few days, Robyn's symptoms grew worse; he refused food, became weak, and appeared to be in pain. A Christian Science nurse prayed for Robyn, sang him a hymn,[2] bathed him, and tried to get him to eat. The nurse's notes reveal that, at times, Robyn's condition appeared to be improving; yet, at other times, he was "moaning in pain, vomiting, and listless," and he could not walk on his own.[3] As the hours wore on, Robyn suffered excruciating pain; neighbors later said they shut their windows to block out the toddler's screams. Yet Robyn's parents held firm to their Christian Science beliefs that spiritual-healing practices—not medical treatments—would end their son's agony.

The Twitchells were wrong. On April 8, Robyn died from a bowel obstruction, a condition that is normally quickly and effectively treated with medication. Without medical care, however, Robyn developed peritonitis, an often painful inflammation of the membrane that lines part of the belly. Later, after he and his wife were charged in the death of their son, David Twitchell testified on the witness stand that his son had died in his arms. Breaking down in tears, Twitchell said that during Robyn's last moments the toddler was "shaking, not something violent, just a quiet shaking and that wasn't very long."[4] Some two hours after Robyn died, David Twitchell called 911 on the advice of a funeral home.[5]

Although Robyn's parents deeply loved their son, they were still responsible for his suffering and death. Because they held to their religious beliefs in refusing to provide him with the medical care that he needed—help that was only a phone call away—Robyn suffered from *religious child medical neglect*.

This form of maltreatment is just one form of *neglect*, the failure of a parent, guardian, or other caregiver to provide for a child's basic physical, medical, educational, or emotional needs.[6] Neglect is the most common form of child maltreatment. In 2009, nearly 80 percent of all children who suffered maltreatment—some 540,000 children—were neglected.[7] More than half of all child fatalities due to maltreatment were the result of neglect.[8] Child neglect is often difficult to identify and, therefore, tends to be underreported, note Martha Farrell Erickson and Byron Egeland in the second edition of *The APSAC* [American Professional Society on the Abuse of Children] *Handbook on Child Maltreatment*:

> Although the bruises and scars of physical abuse are more readily apparent, the quiet assault of child neglect often does at least as much damage to its young victims. Typically defined as an act of omission rather than commission, neglect may or may not be intentional. It is sometimes apparent . . . and sometimes nearly invisible until it is too late. Neglect is often fatal due to inadequate physical protection, nutrition, or healthcare. Sometimes, as in the case of "failure to thrive," it is fatal because of a lack of human contact and love.[9]

RELIGION AND CHILD NEGLECT

Religious belief contributes to many forms of child neglect. For example, children raised in cults can suffer serious psychological problems when they are placed in the care of surrogates and kept alienated from their parents.[10] Some religious groups and communities deny children educational opportunities, such as the Amish, who often take their children out of school after the eighth grade, making it difficult for those who leave the sect to find work. Earlier, this book explained how clergy and religious communities shy away from reporting cases of child sexual abuse; this same kind of neglect applies to situations involving other forms of child maltreatment.

Kibbie Ruth speaks to this problem in *Child Maltreatment*, as she highlights a number of faith-based ideas that abuse victims are told, such as "suffering is a virtue," the importance of "suffering in silence," and "God never gives you more than you can bear."[11] Critics refer to faith communities' "culture of forgiveness," in which abuse victims are discouraged from feeling anger and instead are told to forgive their perpetrators.[12] In one particularly troublesome case, a teacher—who was mandated by law to report abuse—refused to report the physical abuse of a student. Even after a student told her that her father had been abusing her and her brother, the teacher struggled with the decision to report the crime. In deciding against the idea, the teacher told a friend that she did not do so partly because during prayer she "heard Jesus saying that we are not to pass judgment."[13]

Then there is neglect of mental health services. In many faith communities, mental illness is considered to be a weakness and is written off as a failure of devotion to God. Many religious leaders who are untrained in psychology "counsel" young people struggling with psychological conditions and resist recommending that they see a mental health professional. Some members of the clergy even take it upon themselves to tell worshippers to get off needed psychotropic medication.[14] One person who has run across such problems is Rev. Douglas Ronsheim, executive director of the American Association of Pastoral Counselors (AAPC), which trains in pastoral counseling clergy who are also licensed in mental health services. As Ronsheim told me in a May 26, 2010, interview, there are Christian and "biblical" counselors who consider their counseling sessions an opportunity for conversion. Ronsheim says AAPC considers proselytizing in counseling sessions to be an ethical violation because counselors are imposing their values on clients. Yet, he says, many Christian counselors include in their services "bringing people to Jesus."

Sometimes the devout deny children even their basic physical needs. As an example, in 1989, a fourteen-year-old boy in Pennsylvania died of starvation after his father, a former Seventh-Day Adventist minister, refused to spend the little money the family had on food because he designated it as "tithe" money that "belonged to God."[15] In addition, some faith groups harm children through the promotion of strict, unhealthy diets.[16] When mothers and fathers engage in dangerous rituals, they risk leaving their children parentless. One such ritual is snake handling, an obscure tradition still practiced in some churches in Appalachia and other parts of the United States.[17] (Snake handlers follow Mark 16:17–18, which claims that believers "will take up serpents" as a way to cast out demons and not be harmed by the venom.) In a particularly tragic 1999 case, five children in Tennessee were orphaned after both of their parents died from handling snakes during church services.[18]

Keith Wright, author of *Religious Abuse*, is a victim of this kind of neglect. As he notes in his book, he lost his mother to tuberculosis when he was young. But her death might not have happened had she not listened to fellow Christian Scientists who discouraged her from getting medical care, as Wright explains:

> As a small child, I remember hearing my father late at night pleading with my mother to seek medical treatment for her illness. At one point, she *did* agree to enter a sanitarium in the higher, drier climate of west Texas. With medical attention and a favorable climate, she might have recovered, as did her sister who had the same illness and who stayed at the clinic. However, members of the Christian Science Church traveled to west Texas to persuade her to return home near the coast and to trust that God would heal her. She died when I was seven.[19]

As troubling as these problems are, this section deals specifically with one form of religious child neglect—the withholding of needed medical care due to beliefs about divine intervention, faith healing, and doctors—because this particular form of neglect is pervasive and potentially deadly, as in the case of Robyn Twitchell.

Chapter 17
WHY NO ONE CALLS IT *NEGLECT*

At the outset, most perpetrators of religious child medical neglect do not appear to be truly neglectful. On the contrary, when a child is sick, parents and other caretakers seem to be doing all they can to get the child well. They pray, anoint the child with oil, employ the laying on of hands, or conduct exorcisms.[1] In one case, in which an eleven-year-old girl was dying from untreated diabetic ketoacidosis, her father sent out an e-mail to an online Christian ministry pleading, "Help, our daughter needs emergency prayer!"[2]

The faith-healing practices that these often well-intentioned believers employ are usually not harmful in and of themselves; in fact, some likely have salutary psychological effects.[3] The problem is that these rituals are conducted *in lieu of medical care*. The authors of the *Handbook of Religion and Health* note that a host of psychological and theological factors come into play when worshippers refuse to treat health problems with medical care:

> Members of some religious groups may decide to stop lifesaving medications in order to prove their faith. Likewise, some aggressive faith healers encourage followers to stop medical treatments as a way to demonstrate the faith necessary for divine healing. Such recommendations are based on isolated biblical passages taken out of context that emphasize the need to depend entirely on God—not on human methods—for cure. Consequently, diabetics may discontinue their insulin, hypothyroid patients their thyroid hormone, asthmatics their bronchodilators, and epileptics their antiseizure medications, all in the name of faith, and often with disastrous consequences.[4]

The refusal to call a doctor or take a sick child to a hospital in a timely fashion causes children immense suffering, long-term health problems, and death. Many times, child victims of religious medical neglect appear to endure health problems as if they were living in the Middle Ages: broken bones are not set, ruptured appendixes are not removed, and cancerous tumors grow to mammoth sizes. In many cases, children die from treatable conditions, such as infections, meningitis, bowel obstruction, diabetes, and pneumonia.[5]

Sometimes children are denied important preventive procedures based on adults' across-the-board religious opposition to medical care. For example, a refusal to vaccinate has led to children contracting such diseases as polio, measles, rubella, whooping cough, and Type B Haemophilus Influenzae.[6] In 1991, eight children in Pennsylvania died during a measles epidemic—children whose parents were members of two fundamentalist Christian churches that shunned medical care. Children are also denied health insurance and disability services on religious grounds. Because mothers do without prenatal care or choose not to have medical professionals on hand at births, babies are born unhealthy, are stillborn, or die during or soon after birth. Also, a failure to do genetic testing on parents or children leads to children being born with or developing mentally and physically crippling diseases.

The few national statistics available show that the Twitchells are not alone in remaining stoic and adhering to faith-healing beliefs, only to watch a sick child die. According to one news report, 126 children in the United States died between 1973 to 1988 because their parents withheld medical treatment "out of doctrinal conviction that prayer is the most allowable treatment for illness."[7] A 1998 study that looked at more than 172 child deaths in the United States that were attributable to "religiously motivated medical neglect" finds that most of the victims would likely have survived had they received timely medical care.[8] Experts estimate that hundreds of American children have died in faith-healing cases since the 1980s,[9] and that, on average, about a dozen children die each year.[10]

While the public is likely to hear about only egregious cases, critics point out that many more children suffer in various ways on a daily basis. Rita Swan, who founded Children's Healthcare Is a Legal Duty (CHILD), a national membership organization that promotes the rights of children to receive medical care, writes in a 2000 article for the *Humanist* that untold numbers of children "have suffered needless fear and pain or have become permanently disabled. Illnesses and injuries left untreated can produce a host of outcomes." As an example, Swan cites a case in which a child became "profoundly deaf at age seven after a series of ear infections for which her Christian Science parents wouldn't secure medical treatment."[11]

Around the time Robyn Twitchell's parents were being brought to trial, Norman C. Fost, who had headed the American Academy of Pediatrics (AAP) committee on bioethics, was quoted as saying, "We're interested not just in kids who die. What we're concerned about are the hundreds and hundreds more who suffer from inadequate medical treatment."[12]

Sometimes, courts have intervened and ordered parents to provide ill children medical care, such as chemotherapy for leukemia or surgery to remove a tumor. In 1996, the federal government extended the authority of child protective services agencies to prevent adults from withholding medical care from seriously ill children. As the act now reads, social workers may intervene—with court orders if necessary—to provide children with "necessary" medical care or treatment or to "prevent the withholding of medically indicated treatment from children with life-threatening conditions."[13]

However, as is all too common, authorities, such as social workers and prosecutors, find out about problems after a child dies or is left permanently disabled. A large reason is politics, as many states have passed laws that grant prosecutorial immunity to parents who deny their children needed medical care on religious grounds. Without fear of punishment, adults essentially have been permitted to cause their offspring unfathomable suffering.

RELIGIOUS EXEMPTIONS

At first blush, general medical neglect does not seem to be a very serious problem in the United States. This form of maltreatment is defined as a parent or guardian's denial of, or delay in, seeking needed healthcare for a child.[14] In 2009, only 2.4 percent of children who suffered maltreatment—about 16,000 children—were reported to have been victims of medical neglect.[15] But these numbers do not tell the whole story. For one, only egregious cases tend to be reported.[16] And two, these figures leave out many cases in which religious belief is a key motivator.

Why is this? In part, social workers, law enforcement, medical examiners, and others have only recently become aware of these cases. Many times, faith healing–related child deaths have occurred in obscure, isolated religious sects. A 1998 study that looked at this problem explains, "Deaths of children in faith-healing sects are often recorded as attributable to natural causes and the contribution of neglect minimized or not investigated."[17]

Even more so, though, there have been laws put in place that mask these crimes. Since the 1970s, many states have passed "religious exemptions," provisions written into child abuse laws that grant some degree of prosecutorial immunity to adults who withhold medical care from children based on beliefs about the power of faith healing. According to the way these laws are written, courts are often prohibited from considering these parents to be, officially, neglectful. For example, when Robyn Twitchell died in Massachusetts, that state's religious exemption read: "A child shall not be deemed to be neglected or lack proper physical care for the sole reason that he is being provided remedial treatment by spiritual means alone in accordance with the tenets and practice of a recognized church or religious denomination by a duly accredited practitioner thereof."[18]

Most religious exemptions came into being as a result of federal legislation known as the Child Abuse Prevention and Treatment Act (CAPTA), which was signed into law in 1974. While CAPTA was one of the key pieces of legislation to prevent child abuse, it also included a new regulation imposed by the US Department of Health, Education, and Welfare (HEW) that required states to enact religious exemptions in order to receive federal grants for child protection work. Spearheading this move were prominent Christian Scientists, some of whom were high-ranking officials in the Nixon administration.[19] According to Rita Swan, HEW officials admitted that the Christian Science Church was the only party that asked for the regulation. With the financial incentive put before them, most states quickly enacted the exemptions. In 1983, the federal government lifted the regulation, but by then nearly every state had religious exemptions on the books.[20] As of 2010, about thirty states had faith healing–based religious exemptions.[21]

As a result of these exemptions, many parents who deny their children needed medical care—even in cases that involve horrendous suffering—are not held accountable.

"Parents have been successful in using the exemption to defend against criminal charges, even in cases in which the child has died," writes Robert W. Tuttle of George Washington University Law School on the website for the Pew Forum on Religion and Public Life. There are legal maneuverings that courts sometimes use to get around these exemptions, such as charging alleged perpetrators with crimes that are not subject to religious exemptions. Also, in states where religious exemption laws are vague, defendants generally have had a harder time using religious belief as a defense. However, even in those states, writes Tuttle, some parents still have managed to prevail because "courts generally interpret legal uncertainty in favor of the criminal defendant."[22]

Critics say these exemptions have taken a great toll on children's health. Seth Asser, the Rhode Island pediatrician who coauthored the aforementioned 1998 study on child fatalities, wrote a paper entitled "Legalized Child Abuse: Faith Healers and Child Deaths" that was posted on the Internet in 2005. "We know of nearly three hundred children that have died since passage of CAPTA when parents who belonged to faith-healing sects have denied them lifesaving medical care," Asser writes. "We suspect that there are many others unreported to authorities or reported as being from 'natural' causes. Many other children have been permanently disabled due to medical neglect."[23]

In 1997, the AAP committee on bioethics formally opposed states adopting religious exemptions. The organization declared that a failure to seek medical care for children who are seriously ill is "child neglect, regardless of the motivation." In summary, the proclamation reads, "To these ends, the AAP calls for the end of religious exemption laws and supports additional efforts to educate the public about the medical needs of children."[24]

THE ROLE OF POLITICS

Since the federal government rescinded its religious exemption mandate, some states have repealed or modified their religious exemptions. For example, Massachusetts did away with its exemption in 1994, eight years after Robyn Twitchell died. As of February 2011, Oregon, which still allowed exemptions for some homicide cases, stood poised to completely repeal its religious exemption. Yet, by that time, the number of states to have made such a move amounted to only a handful, and a few states, such as Arkansas and West Virginia, still granted broad immunity to parents in such cases, even if children died as the result of their parents relying on prayer over medical care.[25] Even tragic cases of child suffering have not been enough to get lawmakers to do away with exemptions. For example, in 2010, Wisconsin lawmakers failed to repeal or modify that state's broad religious exemption even though legislative discussions took place on the heels of a highly publicized trial, in which a faith healing–believing couple had allowed their eleven-year-old daughter to die from untreated diabetes.

The Christian Science Church, a religious organization that has most heavily lobbied to retain these exemptions, has continued to say that exemptions are necessary to prevent religious discrimination. According to the church's official website, the organization wants to "ensure that laws provide every citizen a choice of healthcare, including the system of spiritual prayer that Christian Scientists have found to be effective."[26]

But others say politics has had more to do with why so many states have adopted faith healing–related exemptions. The subject is "one of these untouchables," says Wisconsin state representative Terese Berceau, who led the 2010 fight in her state to repeal its religious exemption. As she explained in our September 6, 2010, interview, "The discussion of religion in our country catches fire really fast. Legislators do not want to go near religion, or at least they don't want to go against mainstream religion." Furthermore, she notes, the powerful Christian Science Church strongly opposes the repeal of these laws. "I think we have a church that has unusual, disproportionate clout," says Berceau. (This holds especially true in Berceau's state of Wisconsin, whose medical licensure law actually bears the impress of the church's fingerprints: "No law of this state regulating the practice of medicine and surgery may be construed to interfere with the practice of Christian Science. A person who elects Christian Science treatment in lieu of medical or surgical treatment for the cure of disease may not be compelled to submit to medical or surgical treatment.")[27]

The third-rail aspect of criticizing religious medical neglect has had more far-reaching implications. For instance, in 1996, the federal government expanded CAPTA, which accomplished two things. On the positive side, the new stipulations give social workers more autonomy to intervene in abuse cases, but another stipulation essentially hamstrings that autonomy when those cases involve religious child medical neglect. Specifically, the new provisions state that nothing in the act may be construed

> as establishing a Federal requirement that a parent or legal guardian provide a child any medical service or treatment against the religious beliefs of the parent or legal guardian . . . [or] . . . to require that a State find, or to prohibit a State from finding, abuse or neglect in cases in which a parent or legal guardian relies solely or partially upon spiritual means rather than medical treatment, in accordance with the religious beliefs of the parent or legal guardian.[28]

Political sensitivity surrounding the issue of religious child medical neglect has even led some child advocates to downplay faith's contribution to such problems. For example, the second edition of *The APSAC Handbook on Child Maltreatment* defines *medical neglect* as "a caregiver's failure to provide *prescribed* medical treatment for their children" [italics added].[29] This virtually excludes the worst perpetrators of religious child medical neglect from being found to be neglectful, since they are unlikely to take sick children to a doctor in the first place; therefore, no medical treatment would be prescribed. In explaining the political minefield that surrounds this topic, the authors of the chapter on medical neglect, Martha Farrell Erickson and Byron Egeland, acknowledge that the subject "has raised some of the most controversial legal issues in the field of child protection, particularly in regard to cases in which the parents' religious beliefs conflict with the recommendations of the medical community."[30] (The third edition of the handbook does away with this definition of medical neglect. Instead, author Howard Dubowitz simply and correctly states that "neglect of healthcare occurs when children's basic healthcare needs are not met.")[31]

But while some shy away from the subject of religious child medical neglect, others have no compunction to voice their opposition. In light of high-profile, egregious cases often involving the death of a child, the Internet is abuzz with passionate commentary often by individuals demanding to know why children are made to suffer from what are usually easily treatable conditions. Critics from the faith community often make the case that God *wants* people to make use of physicians, not shun them. Posting to his website, Dr. R. Albert Mohler Jr., president of the Southern Baptist Theological Seminary, refutes the position that many perpetrators of religious child medical neglect state—that scripture supports using faith healing in lieu of medical care:

> The Bible never commands any refusal of legitimate medical treatment. I am unspeakably thankful for modern medicine, for antibiotics and anesthesia and chemotherapy and dialysis and diagnostics. The list goes on and on. There is no Christian prohibition against legitimate medical treatment. I believe that God heals, that we should pray for healing in Christ's name, and that our lives are in God's hands. I believe that all healing comes ultimately from God, but that He has given us the blessings of medicine for the alleviation of much suffering and the treatment of disease. There is no conflict here.[32]

Similarly, in 2009, when a judge was sentencing the Wisconsin couple for allowing their daughter to die of diabetes, he told the defendants, "God probably works through other people, some of them doctors."[33]

Chapter 18
THE HAZARDS OF BLIND FAITH

When children get sick, it's not unusual for mothers and fathers to turn to their faith to help them understand their children's illnesses. According to an article on spirituality, religion, and pediatrics that appeared in the journal *Pediatrics*, "Caregivers may . . . use religious and spiritual worldviews to make sense of, and find meaning in, their children's experience of illness, particularly in cases of chronic or life-threatening illness, or cases of disability, where parents may see themselves as being tested or even punished. The family's understanding of why their child has become ill may draw on religious roots."[1]

Many Americans also pray over a sick child or even conduct unconventional faith-healing methods. However, these rituals are usually done in conjunction with—not in place of—medical care. The vast majority of fundamentalist and faith healing–believing parents are not guilty of medical neglect, writes George Washington University public interest law professor Jonathan Turley in a commentary that appeared in the *Washington Post* in 2009. Most believers "avail themselves of a doctor's care when faced with a dire medical condition," he writes.[2]

Caroline Fraser, one of the most outspoken critics of the Christian Science Church, notes that a majority of its believers are sensible. Fraser states in the *Atlantic Monthly* that

> most Christian Scientists strike a balance between their faith and their children's welfare. Christian Scientists willingly obey this country's laws requir-

ing the presence of a physician or a licensed midwife during childbirth; some have cesarean sections. . . . My own recollections and interviews with those currently practicing suggest that some Christian Scientists are willing to have their children vaccinated. Moderate Christian Scientists say, "C. S. stands for Common Sense," and a number of those I interviewed insisted that the individual parent must decide which children's illnesses or injuries can or cannot be "handled in Science."[3]

Many religious leaders, including some from the 1800s, have advised against followers relying solely on spiritual practices to cure the body. For example, in the mid-nineteenth century, Brigham Young criticized those who relied purely on spiritual healing to overcome illness. While Young derided medical care—back then, medical standards were atrocious—he did promote midwifery and the use of herbal remedies. Young encouraged people to use both natural and spiritual treatments in a sermon delivered in 1856:

> If we are sick, and ask the Lord to heal us, and to do all for us that is necessary to be done, according to my understanding of the Gospel of salvation, I might as well ask the Lord to cause my wheat and corn to grow, without my plowing the ground and casting in the seed. It appears consistent to me to apply every remedy that comes within the range of my knowledge, and to ask my Father in heaven, in the name of Jesus Christ, to sanctify that application to the healing of my body.[4]

Of all the criticism that Christian Science has received, the church's founder, Mary Baker Eddy, did not advocate a dogmatic adherence to utilize spiritual healing. In fact, Eddy stated that Christian Scientists "may consult with an MD on the anatomy involved."[5] In addition, Eddy advised members who believed they could benefit from "certain ordinary physical methods of medical treatment" to seek out such treatment.[6]

Yet sprinkled throughout this landscape of reason is a minority of believers who throw themselves into blind faith and rely solely on religious practices, such as prayer or other forms of faith healing, to cure the ills of children. These devout individuals are usually taken by the idea of divine intervention; that is, they are convinced that God will cure their sick children and they can summon the deity's help through faith-healing rituals. According to Turley, "some religious parents continue to maintain that belief in God means belief in His power and discretion to heal." Furthermore, writes Turley, these extremists take to heart Exodus 15:26, which states that God promises not to infect with disease anyone who obeys him, "For I am the LORD who heals you."[7]

In some criminal trials involving faith healing–believing defendants who have been charged with medical neglect, it is common for the defendants to say that they did not think their children were very sick. While this might serve as a convenient legal position, it might also speak to the kind of blind faith many of these parents hold. Some parents have allowed their children to develop grotesque and disfiguring maladies because of their adherence to beliefs about faith healing.

One such egregious case is that of four-year-old Natali Mudd. The child's parents, Ron and Martha Mudd, were members of a now-defunct Indiana-based religious group called the Faith Assembly that believed that faith-healing practices alone could cure illness. Natali died in March 1980 from a tumor that grew out of her eye and became so large it equaled the size of her head. Instead of alerting a doctor, Natali's parents prayed. Police who later visited the home found blood trails along the walls where the child had tried to support her head as she made her way from room to room. One investigator, aghast at what he saw, remarked to the media, "It's hard to comprehend a little toddler going through all that because of religion with all the treatments available."[8] Ron and Martha Mudd never faced criminal charges, as they were protected by Indiana's religious exemption law.

Even more startling, Natali was not the Mudds' last victim. Two years after she died, a court ordered the couple's five-year-old daughter Leah to receive an operation to remove a basketball-sized tumor from her abdomen, but the surgery failed to save her life. What's more, the Mudds were not alone in their fanatical views. Other members of the Faith Assembly, adults and children alike, suffered and died from treatable illnesses. One public health nurse named Barbara Clouse used court orders to get children of Faith Assembly families the medical treatment they needed. When Clouse approached church members, she says they told her, "Get out of here. We don't need your help. The Lord's here."[9]

In contrast, the Christian Science Church claims that its members do not adhere to its tenets out of blind faith.[10] In fact, supporters proclaim that disease is the result of a "mental blindness" to God's presence.[11] Yet the many cases of children who have died agonizing deaths under the watch of Christian Science caretakers prove that those believers are just as likely to succumb to blind faith as other believers. Consider what happened to twelve-year-old Ashley King of Phoenix in 1987. After she had missed an excessive number of school days, police visited Ashley's home to find her bedridden, with a tumor on her leg the size of a watermelon. State child welfare workers intervened and, through a court order, got Ashley admitted to a hospital, where she was diagnosed with bone cancer. But by then it was too late, and Ashley died in 1988. During her prolonged stay at home—in the course of which her parents had prayed for her and not sought medical care—the cancer had progressed to the point that the flesh on her leg had begun to decay and had such a foul odor that it reportedly permeated the entire floor of the hospital.[12]

Then there is the case of Nancy Brewster. On September 29, 1963, Nancy died of what her death certificate listed as "probably malignant lymphoma." A photograph of Nancy shows a pretty seven-year-old girl with wavy blond hair, a broad smile, and a large lump protruding from the right side of her neck. Nancy's mother, Ruth Price Brewster, was a Christian Scientist who called in a practitioner to pray for her daughter after she developed lumps on her neck and vomited repeatedly. After Nancy died, her mother went on to become a Christian Science practitioner. Two decades after Nancy's death, Brewster published a testimony in a Christian Science journal in which she stated that "rearing four children with total reliance on God for healing was a joy. I cannot remember an activity missed because of illness." But, in fact, Brewster had borne five children, not four. By failing to mention the pretty blond seven-year-old girl who died, the woman seemed to have blinded herself to her daughter's very existence.[13]

A district attorney who has had quite a bit of experience with religious child medical neglect understands this mentality. John S. Foote, the district attorney of Oregon's Clackamas County, has prosecuted criminal cases where parents in the faith healing–believing group the Followers of Christ have allowed children to die due to medical neglect. On September 29, 2010, Foote explained that such zealous believers are different from most abusive parents. Talking about the Followers of Christ, Foote says, "These are people who are very committed parents but have this glaring gap in their willingness to [provide medical] care." According to Foote, these parents "are very involved with their children and otherwise are taking care of them, so it's got a little different flavor. Their faith creates this tunnel that bores right through what is otherwise good parenting and creates these tragedies."

"WE WANTED TO BELIEVE"

What leads some Americans to tenaciously hold on to beliefs that faith healing—more so than doctors—can save their children from getting very sick or dying? For some parents, the refusal to provide a sick child with medical care simply comes from a desperate attempt to both save the lives of the sons and daughters they love and adhere to their own glorified ideals about faith.

"We wanted to believe," a father named Larry Parker told *People* magazine in explaining why he and his wife took away the insulin that their eleven-year-old diabetic son, Wesley, had been taking. In the early 1970s, the Parkers belonged to the First Assembly of God Church of Barstow, California, and when they heard a man speak in church about how God had cured him of a "painful spine condition," they allowed Wesley to step forward to receive the man's prayers. Remembers Parker, "We began telling ourselves, 'Okay, we're going to believe it [that Wesley would be miraculously cured], and that will make it true.' All my life I'd been taught that if you could get enough faith to ignore external circumstances, your faith would be complete."[14]

But that "complete" faith cost Wesley his life; he died from diabetic shock. Even after Wesley showed telltale signs of diabetic duress—vomiting, having headaches and stomach pains, urinating excessively, and, finally, going into a diabetic coma—the Parkers did not call a doctor or an ambulance. "We were fighting ourselves," Larry Parker told *People* magazine. "Because of our love for our son, we wanted to give him insulin. But we were fighting that, thinking our faith demanded we not do it."[15]

As mentioned earlier, some parents insist on praying for sick children and forgoing medical care to prove their piety. This motivator seems to have been a factor in the aforementioned Wisconsin case in which the parents of eleven-year-old Madeline "Kara" Neumann refused to take the ailing diabetic to a doctor. According to a police chief, Kara's parents, Dale and Leilani Neumann, attributed their daughter's death to the fact that they "didn't have enough faith."[16] A family friend who was at the house when Kara died told police that he implored Dale Neumann to get medical help for his daughter, but the man refused, saying Kara's illness was "a test of faith."[17]

There are many other factors that drive parents to commit religious child medical neglect—factors that are socially and theologically based.

SOCIAL PRESSURES

Worshippers can be greatly influenced by the words of religious authorities who proclaim the "miracle" of faith healing. Unfortunately, children have been harmed as parents have bought into these claims. One such case helped to end the career of Jack Coe, who ran a traveling tent ministry after World War II. The heavyset, larger-than-life preacher was famous for claiming his revival tents were the largest in the world and able to seat more than twenty thousand people. However, in 1956, Coe was arrested in Florida and charged with practicing medicine without a license for his role in causing a child to suffer. Coe had told the parents of a polio-afflicted three-year-old boy that he had healed their son and instructed them to remove the boy's leg braces, leaving him in constant pain.[18]

Religious authorities use a myriad of techniques to pressure parents into going along with certain faith healing–related practices. For Rita Swan, who grew up in the Christian Science Church, such pressures cost her young son his life. In 1977, Swan's sixteen-month-old son, Matthew, developed what she learned later was bacterial meningitis. In staying with Christian Science teachings, Swan and her husband called a church practitioner on whom Swan says the couple had become "very emotionally dependent." On April 13, 2009, Swan told me how, after the practitioner prayed for Matthew, he seemed to have "just a fantastic healing. One day he was immobilized and couldn't lift his arms, and then the next day he was bouncing around, his normal self again. And so that to us was very powerful proof of God's power and a faith healer's power, and a message that you shouldn't go to a doctor."

But as such "recoveries" are typical in patients with meningitis, Matthew's fever returned. After more healings and more episodes in which Matthew's fever subsided, the toddler finally developed a fever that would not go away. Still, the Swans did not take Matthew to a doctor, largely because of what practitioners were telling them. Swan says they made the couple believe the boy's failure to recover was their fault, that their fear was the cause of the problem. She adds,

> Fear shows "a lack of trust in God" and "a lack of gratitude to them [the practitioners]." And they repeatedly told us that we needed to detach ourselves as parents from the situation. The first practitioner even told us not to pray for Matthew. She said that Matthew would get confused if there were more than one person trying to address his thought. And she would lean over him and talk to him and she'd say, "Matthew, you cannot be sick. You live in the kingdom of God, and God made you as his perfect spiritual idea." And she just openly told us not to pray for him, because we were interfering with her work, and that was very agonizing to be cut off from your child that way.

One night, when Matthew was up for many hours screaming, the Swans decided they would take their son to a doctor. When they told a practitioner that they wanted to dismiss her and why, the practitioner responded coldly. According to Swan, the woman said she would no longer be able to pray for Matthew and that the Swans would have "a long, hard road" back to Christian Science for seeking medical care. Reluctantly, the Swans changed their plans and followed the practitioner's advice that they call for a church nurse. Three days later, however, the Swans did take Matthew to the hospital. This occurred after the practitioner told them that Matthew might have a broken bone. It was their ticket to get Matthew medical help, since broken bones are one of a handful of medical conditions for which Christian Scientists are allowed to seek medical care. Unfortunately, however, Matthew's health had deteriorated so greatly by that point that doctors were unable to save him.

While religious leaders today are probably far less likely to take such chances with a child's health, they continue to strongly promote faith healing as a cure-all. One particularly charismatic self-proclaimed faith healer, for example, is evangelical Christian Cindy Jacobs, the cofounder of the Generals International ministry of Red Oak, Texas. In a YouTube video, Jacobs can be seen preaching to a concert hall–sized crowd, animatedly pacing the stage and yelling above eerie music:

> If you need any kind of miracle at all, you just get up and start to move towards the front, because the cloud of glory is gonna come! Backs are being healed! Feet are being healed! God is taking away migraines! Discs are being replaced! Somebody needs a healing of Hepatitis C! You are being healed right now! There's somebody else! You have AIDS? You are being healed right now, right at this moment! . . . Hallelujah! Just when I count to three, I want you to do something you could not do! . . . Are you ready? When I count to three! If you couldn't bend over, bend over! If you couldn't move your arm, move your arm! If you had a tumor, see if it's gone! Whatever it is! Are you ready? Are you ready? Are you ready? Are you ready? Are you ready? Here we go! One! Two! Three! Move! Move! Move! Move! Move! Move! Move! Do it now! Do it now! More! Put your hands up! Bend over! Touch the floor! Come do it! Move! Move! Move! Move![19]

Peer pressure is also a powerful motivator that enables worshippers to refuse children medical care. In the *Handbook of Religion and Health*, the authors explain how fellow worshippers can subtly manipulate others to doubt themselves before doubting the power of faith healing:

> If a religious person becomes physically ill, members of his religious group may pray for his healing. If the person is healed, this reaffirms the religious beliefs of the group. If the person is not healed, however, he may be blamed for the illness, which may be viewed as the sufferer's fault (it can't be God's fault, since he wishes to heal people and has the power to do so). Perhaps the person's faith isn't strong enough, or there is unconfessed sin in his life.[20]

Critics of the Christian Science Church call attention to its use of member testimonials. These personal stories often declare that someone's medical condition has been cured through spiritual healing. Despite the fact that experts have questioned the validity of these testimonials, Caroline Fraser, who grew up in the church, writes in *God's Perfect Child*, "It is impossible to exaggerate the effect such testimonies have on Christian Scientists." Fraser notes that these testimonies "validate not only their beliefs but [also] their entire lifestyle, bolstering and supporting a profound reliance on Christian Science to the exclusion of other methods." She adds, "All Christian Scientists have their own fund of such testimonies that they fall back on in moments of doubt or trouble when they are questioned by curious or skeptical outsiders. These testimonies encourage and confirm Scientists in their faith, as [founder Mary Baker] Eddy knew they would."[21]

ILLNESS IS NOT A BIOLOGICAL PROBLEM

Some worshippers do not see illness and death as caused by biological factors. Rather, other influences are believed to be at work, such as evil forces or the sufferer's moral failures. Therefore, to these believers, it only stands to reason that the best way to rid the body of illness is to attack the problem spiritually rather than medically.

"Illness and emotional distress are not viewed in scientific terms but rather in religious terms," says one report that looked at faith healing among American fundamentalist and Pentecostal Christians. The report goes on to note that disease and mental problems "are not expected occurrences in life" but "'works of the devil' and a reflection of personal error and sin." Therefore, the paper concludes, those who maintain this worldview are unlikely to seek the help of a physician. Instead, they look for "religious healing for being a bad person."[22]

The Bible contains numerous stories in which Jesus "heals" people of possession by demons and evil spirits, so it is perhaps not surprising that some worshippers see illness as the handiwork of evil forces, such as the devil or demons. For example, Unleavened Bread Ministries, from which the Neumanns sought help when their daughter Kara was near death, promises that faith healing can cure all sorts of ills. The church's pastor, David Eells, has referred to "corporal sickness" as "a curse" that only God can remove.[23]

Apparently, Kara Neumann's parents also held similar beliefs. In writing about their unwavering faith, Erik Gunn of the *Isthmus* newspaper explains that the couple saw Kara's body as "a battleground in a spiritual war between Jesus Christ and the forces of hell. Only by resisting worldly medicine, they believed, could she be saved." Leilani Neumann told police of Kara's condition, "We just thought it was a spiritual attack and we prayed for her."[24] One relative told police that Leilani Neumann believed Kara died because the devil was trying to stop Leilani from starting her own ministry.[25]

The principles behind Christian Science beliefs about spiritual healing are unique, yet, like the other examples given here, Christian Scientists are guided by a particular view of disease in which illness is not understood to be a physiological problem. Rather, Christian Scientists believe that while disease seems real to the mortal senses, it is, in actuality, an illusion. As one Christian Scientist described the ideology in a media commentary,

> Christian Scientists hold that behind all diseases are mental factors rooted in the human mind's blindness to God's presence and our authentic relation to God, revealed in the life of Christ. They hold that treatment is a form of prayer or communion with God in which God's reality and power, admitted and witnessed to, become so real as to eclipse the temporal "reality" of disease and pain. Such treatment they see as actively and specifically ministering to human need.[26]

In cases of young children becoming ill, Christian Scientists tend to view those health problems as the product of their parents' faulty thinking—specifically, their fears, ignorance, and sins.[27]

Seeing illness not as a serious biological problem but as one that can be relatively easily "fixed" with prayer may explain why some parents whose children are very sick or seriously injured seem eerily calm. In the *Atlantic Monthly*, Caroline Fraser refers to a "bizarre unflappability" among Christian Scientists who are faced with a medical emergency involving their children. "That infuriating, smug calm in the face of crisis is part of what makes Christian Science so dangerous," writes Fraser. She adds,

> Fixated on their rote readings and prayers, Christian Science parents and practitioners are apt to be unmoved by the visible signs of any disease or accident. I remember the hypnotic voice of the practitioner my mother phoned to talk to me when I was sixteen and had a fever so high that I had been delirious; the practitioner was interested in hearing not how I felt but what I had been studying in *Science and Health* [Christian Science religious text].[28]

WAITING ON DIVINE INTERVENTION

Another influential belief is that sickness can be cured by a supernatural force, such as God or Jesus. A case in point is that of a Tennessee woman who allowed her teenage daughter to die of a rare form of bone cancer. In May 2000, Jacqueline Crank of Tennessee took her fifteen-year-old daughter, Jessica, to a clinic after Jessica developed a tumor on her shoulder. Failing to heed the clinic's advice to take her daughter to a specialist, Crank prayed instead. At her trial, Crank, a fundamentalist Christian, held up a Bible she had brought with her and stated that she had decided "to turn to Jesus Christ, my lord and savior, for her [Jessica's] healing."[29]

"Fundamentalists tell us their lives are in the hands of God, and we, as physicians, are not God," a physician told *Time* magazine when it reported on the death of Kara Neumann.[30] One study that examined parents' beliefs in divine influences found that the stronger those beliefs are, the more likely parents of symptomatic children are to endorse seeking spiritual guidance, although those beliefs do not preclude them from also seeking help from physicians, friends, and relatives.[31]

One-year-old Patrick Foster from Pennsylvania suffered greatly from his parents' adherence to the idea that God, not doctors, would cure him of what later turned out to be cancer. Patrick's health problems began in 1996, when he caught a bad cold that would not go away. Week after week, Patrick's fundamentalist Christian parents, Daniel and Anne Marie Foster, responded by praying. Some months later, Patrick became lethargic and gaunt. Then his parents noticed a growth bulging from his left side, so they stepped up their prayers and church attendance, as described by *Oregonian* reporter Mark Larabee in his extensive series on faith healing–related deaths in America.

> As the growth swelled, the Fosters increased their prayers. Four times each week they attended services at Faith Tabernacle Congregation Church in north Philadelphia, asking their pastor to pray aloud for Patrick. Regardless of how sick Patrick got, there would be no visit to a doctor. And no medical treatment, not even an aspirin. Members of Faith Tabernacle, like thousands of faith-healing Christians across the United States, trust that God, inspired by the prayers of true believers, will heal sickness and disease. To seek a doctor's care would be to turn their backs not only on their faith, but [also] on God himself. Patrick was in the Lord's hands, Anne Marie Foster would tell police.[32]

In early May, a neighbor saw the boy sitting on his father's lap. By that time, Patrick's growth weighed six pounds—almost one-third of the child's weight. Larabee notes that the listless boy "needed his father's help just to lift his head."[33] A social worker who visited was alarmed by what he saw. In addition to the growth protruding from his abdomen, Patrick appeared to be in pain. Also, one eye and one hand were swollen, and his face was covered with mucus, saliva, and a rash. The social worker urged the Fosters to rush Patrick to the hospital. When they refused, the social worker returned with the police and a court order demanding that the Fosters release Patrick to a doctor's care.

When Patrick arrived at the hospital, doctors estimated that he was within twenty-four hours of death. He was diagnosed with a malignant Wilms' tumor, a common form of childhood cancer that has a high survival rate if treated early. The tumor—the most advanced case the doctor had ever seen—was growing from one kidney to the liver. It had also attached itself to a vein leading to the heart, severely restricting blood circulation. Patrick was treated with chemotherapy, intensive life support, and, finally, surgery to remove the tumor. After that, Patrick's condition dramatically improved.[34]

Back at the Fosters' church in Philadelphia, Larabee writes, the sermons delivered by Kenneth Yaeger included a prayer that authorities would stop persecuting members of the church who refused to give their sick children medical care. "We know it's God's work to trust him with the healing of our body," Larabee quotes Yaeger as saying. "Man didn't make these bodies, God did. Sometimes we hinder God's ability to help us by using human efforts." Yaeger went on to urge parishioners to put "every bit" of their faith in God so that they would be "saved from the power and hold of Satan and be delivered to an eternal life."

One couple in the pews, Dawn and Roger Winterborne, stated that they were still devout believers even after five of their children, all younger than two, died of cystic fibrosis, and a sixth child, a four-day-old baby girl, died of pneumonia between 1971 and 1982 after being denied proper medical care. "There was no medical cure for them," Dawn Winterborne said. "God could have cured them." Although she neglected to provide a reason as to why her deity failed the family, she added, "We still believe the same way."[35]

"GOD'S WILL"

As indicated earlier, many parents look to their faith to understand children's health problems. The aforementioned *Pediatrics* article on spirituality, religion, and pediatrics states that there are times that "parents may define major losses as part of a great picture or divine plan."[36] Taken to an extreme, some believers are convinced that everything in life, including illness and death, is part of that divine plan, or, as many call it, "God's will." Based on this belief, some worshippers feel that medical intervention in the case of illness or as a way to prevent illness would be pointless, if not an affront to the deity.

Religious parents who subscribe to the "God's will" mantra have caused undue suffering and death for children and adults alike. Take, for example, a Colorado sect known as the Church of the First Born, which has been criticized for severely neglecting the health of its infants and its children. In one tragic 1990 case, a newborn died and the mother nearly lost her life as well due to her certainty that everything is "God's will." When Ruth Berger Belebbas went into labor, her baby got stuck inside the birth canal. With no medically trained professionals present, the baby died. Hours later, paramedics who arrived on the scene found the dead child still lodged inside Belebbas's body. One paramedic implored Belebbas to allow for medical help, but she refused, saying, "It's all in God's hands." An investigator even warned Belebbas that she was probably going to die if she did not get to a hospital; still, Belebbas could not be dissuaded. According to the investigator, Belebbas said she understood the risks and, "if she died, it was God's will, and that she was prepared for whatever God had planned for her."[37]

The concept of "God's will" is common among conservative Amish clans and has led to court orders requiring parents to allow doctors to treat young people.[38] One health issue that is particularly problematic in closed communities like the Amish is genetic disorders. Because the Amish intermarry, their children have a relatively high likelihood of being born with rare, severely debilitating diseases. The Amish could stem this trend through genetic testing, but many refuse to do so, often because they believe so doggedly in "God's will."[39] For example, one such disease is maple syrup urine disease, a hereditary metabolism disorder that prevents the body from breaking down certain parts of proteins, giving urine a sweet smell. If caught early, the disease can be treated. However, if children are not tested and the disease progresses, it can lead to severe brain damage and death.

On September 16, 2010, I interviewed fifty-six-year-old Iva Byler, who grew up in the conservative Old Order Amish clan in Ohio. For not having any medical training, Byler knows a great deal about a rare genetic disorder called Cohen syndrome, which has plagued some Amish communities. In 1996, when Byler left her Amish community with her daughters, she did not know exactly what was wrong with them, as they suffered with many mental and physical disabilities. After becoming involved with the DDC Clinic in Middlefield, Ohio, which was founded to study rare genetic disorders among the Amish, all three of Byler's girls were diagnosed with Cohen syndrome.

Byler explained to me that, even though her daughters were receiving treatment, they required twenty-four-hour care. Betty Ann, at age thirty-one, has the mentality of a nine-month-old; Irma, at twenty-seven, functions as a six-year-old; and Linda, at twenty-five, has the mentality of a three-month-old. Due to a low white blood cell count, the women got sick often. They also had seizures and were going blind, both common symptom of Cohen syndrome. But as difficult as life is for Byler, she is glad to have gotten clear medical information about her daughters' conditions. "Once you know something, it helps you cope so much more," says Byler. "You have a name for it. There might not be much you can do about it, but there's something about knowing."

Byler says when she was living among the Amish, it was accepted that many children are simply born "slow." "No one questioned that it could be due to inbreeding," she says. Byler says many young Amish people continue to intermarry and refuse to get tested to see if they are likely to pass on genetic diseases, based on their belief that anything good or bad that happens is "God's will." As one Amish man who would not undergo premarital tests told the media, "Our lifestyle is that way. We trust God to take care of that, you know?"[40]

RESURRECTING CHILDREN

Some faith-healing fanatics believe that if a child dies, that child is not gone forever but will be resurrected. This mind-set is described in an article about the First Assembly and Church of the First Born. As Eileen Welsome writes in the *Denver Westword*, the Colorado-based group believes "wholeheartedly in the power of prayer" and holds on to those beliefs even after children die from medical neglect:

> While their grief is as intense as that of any parent who loses a child, the sorrow is tempered by the unerring conviction that the child's death was God's will. Sanctified through their parents and utterly free of sin, the children—or "little dolls," as one church member calls them—are believed to be merely asleep until Judgment Day, when they will awaken and join the Lord and their families in heaven.[41]

The belief in children being resurrected was also apparent in the case of Kara Neumann. Writing for the *Isthmus*, Erik Gunn describes the scene at the hospital after county medical examiner John Larson arrived to investigate:

> Larson examined the dehydrated, emaciated body of 11-year-old Madeline Kara Neumann. Lines snaked into the lifeless girl's body. Larson stepped away so the young girl's parents, Dale and Leilani Neumann, could be alone with her and their grief. Then he took them aside, asking what funeral home they preferred. "We won't need one," he was told. "She will be alive tomorrow." Larson pressed further. He explained that the body would be taken to Madison for an autopsy. Again the couple waved away the facts lying before them in the hospital bed. "You won't need to do that," they assured him. "She will be alive by then."[42]

Certainly, devout parents who maintain beliefs about mortal resurrection and lose a child are often terribly devastated by such a loss. However, conjecturally speaking, it's possible that parents who think that death is only a temporary condition might not be as motivated to pull out all the stops—including summoning medical care—as parents who do not maintain this belief. When eleven-year-old Wesley Parker died of untreated diabetes, his father, Larry Parker, did not act at all like a normal parent who had just lost a child would act. As he told *People* magazine, Parker remembered thinking, "Nothing to get excited about. He's going to rise from the dead." After that, the family conducted a "resurrection service" at the funeral home. "I look back and sometimes think, 'I must have been crazy,'" Parker told *People*. "But you can't undo things you've done."[43]

UNTRUSTWORTHY DOCTORS

Faith healing–related abuses occur not only because of how believers perceive illness and spiritual ways to cure illness but also because of how they look upon medical professionals. While the Christian Science Church says it does not prohibit members from seeking medical care,[44] that has not stopped church leaders from making derogatory statements about medicine.[45] Christian Science practitioners typically do not make it a practice to pray for Christian Scientists who are also employing medical treatments, since church founder Mary Baker Eddy stated that a belief in medicine's potential to cure "works against Christian Science."[46]

Some extremist groups believe that obtaining medical care leaves a person vulnerable to satanic influences. This was what the now-defunct Indiana-based Faith Assembly believed. According to the group's leader, Hobart Freeman, Satan works through those promoting medicine, science, and education. Members believed that obtaining medical care actually causes sickness and death as the patient weakens against Satan's grip. Thus, members did without medical care—choosing instead to pray and fast—and pregnant women did without prenatal care and gave birth without the assistance of medical personnel. As a result, children and adults needlessly died. Critics of the group blamed more than ninety deaths in eight states—a majority of which were deaths of mothers and babies in childbirth—on the Faith Assembly faith-healing practices.[47] In two Indiana counties, concerns about the deaths led to investigators being brought in from the US Centers for Disease Control (CDC) to study the situation from 1975 to 1982. The investigators came away with very troubling results: Women—mostly expectant mothers—died at a rate that was one hundred times the statewide rate, and the fetal mortality rate was nearly four times the state's. Most deaths were due to a failure to seek obstetric care during pregnancy and childbirth.[48]

Another influential and controversial voice among pro–faith healing Christians has been Carol Balizet, a former nurse from Florida. As Shawn Francis Peters explains in *When Prayer Fails: Faith Healing, Children, and the Law*, Balizet stresses in her writings the need to withdraw from "worldly" systems, such as government, education, and medicine, because of her belief that they are, as Peters says, "inherently satanic." Meanwhile, writes Peters, Balizet argues that women who follow her teachings "free themselves from 'the stronghold of deceptions about medical care' and enter into the realm of 'kingdom healing.'"[49] Peters notes that Balizet has urged people to "refuse medical care completely" and instead rely on prayer, or as she describes it, the "valid, workable, God-given alternative to submission to the medical system."[50] Furthermore, Balizet has advocated for babies to be delivered at home without the assistance of medically trained professionals. According to Balizet, writes Peters, "women were to give birth at home and rely solely on prayer for support, even in the most complicated deliveries."[51] Balizet has also maintained that suffering in childbirth is good.[52]

Balizet's ideas have been strongly criticized. For instance, Adrian van Leen, the director of Concerned Christians Growth Ministries of Australia, told the media that birthing mothers who have followed Balizet's principles and then made a last-minute decision to head for a hospital have narrowly avoided serious problems: "There have been birth complications, breech births, and so on where, if medical assistance hadn't been brought in, there could have been tragedy."[53]

At least two cases influenced by Balizet's teachings—as well as by Balizet herself—did end in tragedy. One involved a baby named Jeremiah Corneau, who was born into the small Massachusetts religious group called the Body, which, as was earlier noted, allowed a baby named Samuel to starve to death. Jeremiah had no life outside the womb, for he died from complications in childbirth when no medically trained individuals were present. According to the New England Institute of Religious Research, a nonprofit organization that studies cults, the Body was heavily influenced by Balizet's writings.[54] Another case involved two-year-old Harrison Johnson of Florida, who died after sustaining 432 wasp stings in 1998. Harrison's family knew Balizet personally. Not only had she attended his home delivery,[55] but she was present after he was stung, at which time caregivers treated the boy with prayer and an oatmeal bath and did not call for an ambulance until seven hours after the attack. Balizet testified at the trial of Harrison's parents that Harrison did not show symptoms that would have warranted medical care.[56]

A CHRISTIAN ISSUE?

While many believers, including Jews and Muslims, see God as responsible for mental and physical health, the term *faith healing* is most commonly used in Christian circles. In addition, some researchers say that religious child medical neglect is largely committed by Christians. A recent article that appeared in the *Southern Medical Journal* states,

> We have been unsuccessful in finding any English-language literature to document religion-based medical neglect in the other great religions of the world [besides Christianity]: Buddhism, Islam and Hinduism. . . . One assumes that child abuse and neglect, including medical neglect, may be associated with religions other than Christianity, but there is not empirical literature available to document that assumption.[57]

One can reflect on different theories for why these cases tend to occur in Christian communities. One possible explanation is that the New Testament includes many stories of Jesus conducting faith healings. In the Bible, Jesus makes the blind see, the deaf hear, and the disabled walk. Jesus also cures people of such health problems as paralysis, fevers, leprosy, epilepsy, and the skin condition dropsy. In Luke 22:51, Jesus even reattaches a man's severed ear. In Mark 5:22–34, before Jesus heals a woman who is dying from hemorrhaging, he learns from the woman's father that doctors have tried to heal her and only made the situation worse. In contrast, two figures who loom large in Judaism and Islam—respectively, Moses Maimonides and Ibn Sina or Avicenna—were physicians.

Regular folks, too, can practice faith healing, according to the Bible. In Mark 16:17, the resurrected Jesus declares that those who believe in him "will lay hands on the sick, and they will recover." James 5:14–16 states that church elders can cure a sick person by praying over him and anointing him with oil. The passage also explains that the faithful can be healed by confessing their sins and praying for each other. "The effective, fervent prayer of a righteous man avails much," notes the passage.

Many Christians who believe in faith healing commonly refer to these Bible stories. Such passages provided inspiration to Mary Baker Eddy in beginning the Christian Science Church, which places the practice of spiritual healing at the core of its teachings. According to Virginia S. Harris, former chair of the Christian Science Church's board of directors, the Bible was Eddy's "constant companion" and the scriptural accounts of Jesus healing the sick "were alive and real to her." In a 1997 speech, Harris explained that Eddy asked, "If those healings occurred then, why can't they be happening today?"

Harris also tells the famous story of Eddy being close to death following a serious injury when she fell on an icy sidewalk. Eddy "asked for her Bible. She opened it to one of the accounts of Jesus' healings. She had a profound spiritual insight and was healed right then."[58]

Various Christian churches see faith healing as an important part of their doctrine. The Vatican, for example, has a special congregation dedicated to the investigation of the validity of alleged "miracles" that have been attributed to prospective saints, and those miracles often involve recovery from illness.[59] Recently, a French nun claimed to have recovered from Parkinson's disease after writing down the name of the late Pope John Paul II. Many Catholics proclaimed this "miracle" as evidence that the pontiff should be canonized. (Later, the nun's symptoms returned, leaving doctors to presume that she had not been afflicted with Parkinson's but a similar disease of the nervous system that can go into sudden remission.)[60]

Pentecostalism's charismatic movement, which began at the start of the twentieth century, is renowned for its beliefs in divine intervention and healing. Ever since the 1930s, Pentecostal preachers have drawn large crowds as they demonstrate their self-proclaimed abilities to heal people on the spot. Some of the Pentecostal movement's best-known faith-healing leaders have been Smith Wigglesworth, Aimee Semple McPherson, Jack Coe, and Oral Roberts. The Church of Jesus Christ of Latter-day Saints considers the laying on of hands to be a "procedure revealed by the Lord for performing many priesthood ordinances," including administering to the sick.[61]

In trials in which parents have used faith healing in lieu of medical care for their sick children, the defendants and their supporters have sometimes justified their actions by referring back to those early days in the Bible. "We believe in Jesus Christ . . . and he tells you to anoint them [the sick] with oil and pray for them. So that's what we believe in," said one faith leader at a court hearing after his group had been found to have harmed many members through medical neglect.[62] The same argument was made by supporters of the parents of Kara Neumann when they were on trial for allowing her to die from undiagnosed diabetes. David Eells, the pastor of Unleavened Bread Ministries, an online church with which the Neumanns were affiliated, posted on the church's website, "We are not commanded in scripture to send people to the doctor but to meet their needs through prayer and faith."[63]

But according to scholars, these scripturally attached believers have a skewed view of history. In *Medicine and Health Care in Early Christianity*, Gary B. Ferngren writes that it is erroneous to assume that early Christians saw medicine only through a supernatural lens. Rather, writes Ferngren, toward the end of the first century of the Christian era, Christians employed a variety of healing methods. Those methods included spiritual ones, such as prayer and anointing with oil, but they also included "healing by natural means," therapies that ranged from "the physician's repertoire to folk remedies, home cures, traditional treatments, and herbal recipes." And, Ferngren notes, these methods were not used exclusive of one another: "None was thought incompatible with the others."[64]

In fact, Ferngren asserts that the early Christians' regard for medicine and healing was not that different from the rest of the Greco-Roman world. Over a number of centuries, Christians "did not attribute most diseases to demons, they did not ordinarily seek miraculous or religious cures, and they employed natural means of healing, whether these means involved physicians or home or traditional remedies."[65] False assumptions, writes Ferngren, date back to the Enlightenment and were later popularized in North America by books that characterized Christianity as a faith that opposes science.[66]

In an article for *Pediatric Nursing*, Dónal P. O'Mathúna and Kellie Lang point out that the New Testament and a great deal of Christian literature promote "an integrated view of physical and spiritual worlds." For example, they state, the New Testament encourages the sick to both pray and "use a little wine for their stomachs. . . . In the same way, most Christian interpreters see no conflict with praying for healing while calling the doctor or going to a pharmacist." The authors note that passage 38:1 from the ancient Hebrew text of Ecclesiasticus instructs people to honor doctors because doctors are part of God's creation.[67]

Chapter 19
FATAL PRAYERS

Does faith healing ever actually work? Looking at empirical data, some studies seem to show that faith healing—or, as some call it, "distance healing"—does cure. However, critics have found flaws in most of these studies, many of which have not been subject to peer review. Also, a number of other studies have shown that prayer has no benefit on patients and in some cases can even make patients fare worse.[1]

The baseline problem is that it is exceedingly difficult to empirically prove that prayer can heal the body. For one thing, it's hard to measure something as amorphous as prayer. Also, how can researchers be assured that prayers are genuine or that prayers coming from those involved in a study are not skewing the results? Compounding the problem is that most studies examine patients who are simultaneously receiving medical care, so it's impossible to determine whether a "miraculous" recovery is truly due to prayer or to medical treatment.

Advocates of faith healing most often point to what they claim to be anecdotal evidence of its value, but these have been called into question. For instance, a Harvard Medical School professor and physician who reviewed Christian Science testimonies has stated that he rarely found such self-reported diagnoses to be "even approximately correct."[2] When prayer does seem to bring about a cure, skeptics point out that there is no proof that it happened by supernatural means. After all, prayer can have salutary effects, since it can relax the believer,[3] and the placebo effect can come into play.[4]

But here is what cannot be disputed: While medical care does not cure 100 percent of the time, failing to treat children's illnesses medically greatly increases the chance that they will not recover and, most likely, will get worse. According to studies and investigations conducted among pro–faith healing religious groups, the evidence is ironclad.

The first widely known cases of religious child medical neglect took place in England in the early 1900s, when children were discovered to be dying at an inordinate rate in a small religious sect called the Peculiar People. The group, which was begun in 1838 in Essex, promoted faith-healing practices while eschewing medical care. As a result of child fatalities—a problem that worsened after a 1910 diphtheria outbreak—some parents were imprisoned. The first comprehensive study to examine such problems in the United States was conducted nearly a century later.

In 1998, "Child Fatalities from Religion-Motivated Medical Neglect" was published in the journal *Pediatrics*. Its authors were critical care pediatrician Seth Asser and Rita Swan, whose young son Matthew died from bacterial meningitis after being prayed over by Christian Science practitioners. Using information from newspaper articles, public documents, trial records, and personal communications, the study examined the records of 172 child deaths that had occurred between 1975 and 1995 in which there was sufficient information to determine the cause of death and where the history indicated that "failure to seek medical care was primarily based on a reliance on faith healing."[5] The study evaluated cases that had come from a total of twenty-three religious denominations in thirty-four states. A majority of the cases—83 percent—came from five religious organizations: the Indiana-based Faith Assembly, the Pennsylvania-based Faith Tabernacle, the Church of the First Born in Oklahoma and Colorado, the South Dakota–based End Time Ministries, and the Christian Science Church.[6]

The results show that, of the 172 cases, 140 of the children died from conditions for which survival rates with medical care would have exceeded 90 percent; 18 of the cases had expected survival rates of more than 50 percent; and all but 3 of the remaining cases would likely have had some benefit from clinical help.[7] The study reveals other disturbing statistics:

- Nearly all of the ninety-eight children who did not have cancer "would have had an excellent prognosis with commonly available medical and surgical care," while four would have had a good outcome. Only two of the noncancer cases would not have "clearly benefited from care."[8]
- "Many histories revealed that symptoms were obvious and prolonged," and "parents were sufficiently concerned to seek outside assistance, asking for prayers and rituals from clergy, relatives, and other church members."

- In one family where the mother had been a nurse before joining a church with "doctrinal objections to medical care," five children died of pneumonia before the age of two.
- For children who had tumors, "available medical care would have given them a reasonable chance for long-term survival and reduction of pain and suffering."
- Of the fifty-nine cases of prenatal and perinatal death, all but one of the newborns would have had a "good to excellent expected outcome with medical care."[9]

Some of the cases described in detail revealed an unusually strict reliance on faith healing. For example, when a two-year-old child choked on a bite of banana, "her parents frantically called other members of her religious circle for prayer during nearly an hour in which some signs of life were still present." In another case, a faith healing–believing father allowed his five-month-old son to die of bacterial meningitis despite the fact that the father held a medical degree.[10] The study notes how births attended by unlicensed midwives ended in tragedy. In one highly disturbing case in which both child and mother died, a young woman was brought to the emergency room after having endured fifty-six hours of active labor. During that time, the infant's head was at the vaginal opening for more than sixteen hours. The authors write,

> The dead fetus was delivered via emergency cesarean, and was in an advanced state of decomposition. The mother died within hours after delivery from sepsis because of the retained uterine contents. The medical examiner noted that the corpse of the infant was so foul smelling that it was inconceivable anyone attending the delivery could not have noticed.[11]

Swan and Asser note that more than one-quarter of the evaluated cases occurred since 1988, leading them to be concerned that "this form of preventable child mortality continues unchecked."[12]

The study has limitations. For instance, the authors admit they were not able to calculate overall incidence and mortality rates based on how data was collected. Also, predictions of survival rates were based only on Asser's evaluations, leaving some to question whether the study is subjective and biased.[13] Still, Asser and Swan's study reveals a significant problem occurring within faith healing–believing sects and religions, as the authors note in their conclusion:

> We think that the comparison with outcomes expected in ordinary medical settings is a valid indicator that death and/or suffering were preventable in virtually all of these children. These fatalities were not from esoteric entities

but ordinary ailments seen and treated routinely in community medical centers. Death from dehydration, appendicitis, labor complications, antibiotic-sensitive bacterial infections, vaccine-preventable disorders, or hemorrhagic disease of the newborn have a very low frequency in the United States. We suspect that many more fatalities have occurred during the study period than the cases reported here.[14]

Other investigations of religious groups by governmental agencies, researchers, and the media confirm Asser and Swan's finding—that many religions and faith communities that refuse to summon medical care are endangering children's lives. While Asser and Swan studied nearly twenty faith groups, three organizations are worth special mention.

THE CHRISTIAN SCIENCE CHURCH

The Church of Christ, Scientist, the official name of the Christian Science Church, is the largest faith to make spiritual healing a core belief. However, Christian Scientists appear to have gone more "mainstream" in recent years. Of the handful of high-profile criminal cases that have come to light in the last decade, none involve perpetrators who harmed their children due to Christian Science beliefs. But the potential is still there. The religion continues to attract believers throughout the world, even though its membership is said to be dwindling.

The church has made it a policy not to divulge the size of its membership, but there is no question that, during a period of time, it enjoyed huge popularity. In 1941, the organization was large enough to accommodate more than eleven thousand Christian Science practitioners in the United States alone.[15] At its estimated peak in 1955, there was a branch church in nearly every sizable city.[16] Founder Mary Baker Eddy's "bible," *Science and Health with Key to the Scriptures*, has been published in seventeen languages and remains a companion text to the Bible for Christian Scientists.[17] The church has long been a powerful political influence, with a membership that has been made up largely of middle- to upper-class citizens, a number of whom have held high-level positions in government. The church has also spent lavishly on legal fees in court cases and advertising campaigns to promote its positions.[18]

Eddy created the church in 1879 in Boston after claiming that her life had been saved by reading the Bible following a near-fatal fall.[19] In 1875, Eddy wrote the "bible" of Christian Science, *Science and Health*—later called *Science and Health with Key to the Scriptures*. Eddy remained committed to the movement until her death in 1910, although she spent the last years of her life in seclusion.

For a long time, the reputation of the Christian Science Church remained one of purity and beneficence, especially concerning spiritual healing. For decades after the founding of the church, it was commonly believed that Christian Scientists lived longer than the average person.[20] But a number of studies have tarnished that reputation. At least two studies that compared longevity of alumni of a Christian Science college with alumni at a college that was not meant for Christian Science students show that Christian Scientists generally had a shorter lifespan than the control subjects.[21] The findings were particularly revealing given the fact that Christian Scientists tend to maintain healthy lifestyles by not smoking or consuming alcohol, tea, or coffee.[22] The church's spiritual-healing methods were further called into question in the 1980s as a number of child death cases were publicized by the media—children for whom Christian Science prayers had failed, Robyn Twitchell being one example.[23] In fact, of the religions and faith groups Rita Swan and Seth Asser examined in their 1998 study, the second-highest number of child fatalities from failed faith healing—twenty-eight—emerged from the Christian Science Church.

In 1992, the church knew it had to take action to curb the number of criminal cases that were entering courtrooms and reduce its liability, so its board of directors issued a statement. It reminded members that using spiritual healing might not always be "legally respected" by prosecutors; it suggested that Christian Scientists who relied on spiritual healing "should consider well their individual spiritual readiness, their own past experience and record, and the mental climate in which they live"; and it stated that decisions pertaining to "the appropriate care of children are always made by the parents—not by a Christian Science practitioner or the church."[24]

Christian Science is still a religion that gives many members hope and meaning, but the church is no longer the powerful organization that it once was. Back in 1995, there were fewer than two thousand Christian Science practitioners worldwide.[25] One estimate puts US membership at 106,000 people who worship at some 1,300 churches.[26] The church's diminishing numbers are likely due to a host of factors, such as a national attrition trend among major religious denominations, advances in medical science, and bad publicity generated from medical neglect cases.

In recent years, it certainly has softened its traditionally pro–spiritual healing stance. In February 2011, as Oregon was poised to get rid of its faith-healing religious exemption in all homicide charges, the church, in an uncharacteristic move, did not lobby against that effort. As he was quoted in the *Oregonian*, Christian Science media and legislative liaison John Clague admitted that the numerous deaths coming from the Followers of Christ had "reached a critical mass." He added, "We should never risk the life of a child through the practice of spiritual care."[27]

Wisconsin state representative Terese Berceau, who has battled the church in trying to repeal her state's religious exemption, told me she believes that Christian Scientists are now less dogmatic about adhering to church tenets about spiritual healing than they have been in the past. Plus, recent criminal convictions of faith-healing parents in other faiths are a reminder that some courts are getting tougher in prosecuting these individuals. "Not only do they [Christian Scientists] not want their children to die," says Berceau, but "maybe also knowing that if a child dies that they are going to go to trial" affects parents' actions. Yet Berceau still worries that children in Christian Science families are not getting adequate care. She says pediatric doctors have told her that they have occasionally treated a Christian Science child in a crisis situation, "but the thing that concerned them was that the child wasn't going to come back."

JEHOVAH'S WITNESSES

Jehovah's Witnesses do not reject all medical care outright. However, because of legalistic adherence to certain biblical passages, the organization has instituted policies that have jeopardized the health and lives of children. These policies stem from passages that prohibit the "eating" of blood (including Genesis 9:4, Leviticus 3:17, Leviticus 17:14, and Deuteronomy 12:16 and 23) or "abstaining from" blood (including Acts 15:20 and 29). Witnesses' attempts to live according to these passages have, for example, led to a faith-wide ban on vaccinations from 1931 to 1952 due to a belief that inoculation was "a direct injection of animal matter in the blood stream." Later, the leadership announced that members could decide for themselves whether they should accept vaccinations and, finally, began to support the use of vaccines.[28] In the same way, the organization strongly advised against organ transplants from 1967 to 1980.

Jehovah's Witnesses continue to stir up controversy with their refusal to accept blood transfusions or certain blood products, such as parts of whole blood that can be used for testing and in treating various health problems. This viewpoint was made clear by a Witnesses spokesperson who told the press in March 2008 that the transfusion of blood or a major component of blood, such as plasma, is "contrary to what is stated in scripture."[29] Many Witnesses take this rejection of blood seriously. One San Francisco Witness told the media, "If I violate God's law on blood simply to gain a few more days—or years—of life, I would be dead spiritually, and my relationship with God would be damaged beyond repair."[30]

"Jehovah's Witnesses are well known for taking these Bible commands [concerning blood] to heart," boasts the official website of Jehovah's Witnesses.

"They reject all transfusions involving whole blood or the four primary blood components—red cells, plasma, white cells, and platelets."[31] Many Witnesses carry a "blood card," a wallet-sized advance directive to physicians in case of emergencies. One version of the card quotes Leviticus 17:14 and instructs that the patient wants no form of blood to be "fed into [his or her] body," although it says that blood substitutes may be used in case of extreme blood loss.[32]

The prohibition is so widespread among Witnesses that many hospitals accommodate their needs by developing "bloodless" procedures that can involve giving patients transfusions using their own blood. Sometimes, the patient's blood is mixed with a solution to expand its volume, or doctors use devices that collect and recycle a patient's blood. Jehovah's Witnesses are quick to point out that blood transfusions have been associated with the transmission of viruses and bacteria, among other complications, although these transmissions are rare. One study suggests that patients who accept blood transfusions stay longer in hospitals and are readmitted at a higher rate than those who undergo surgeries where no blood is accepted.[33]

Still, many object to the faith's no-blood policy. One problem, say critics, is that the faith's controlling organization, the Watchtower Bible and Tract Society (WTS), has changed its blood policy throughout the years.[34] And its latest stance is confusing because it allows some blood products while prohibiting others. The WTS also states that Witnesses should decide for themselves whether to accept "minor blood fractions," such as clotting factors used by hemophiliacs, or the "immediate reinfusion of a patient's own blood during surgery" because "the Bible makes no clear statement" about such transfusions.[35] Doctors, too, are confused. As one physician remarked in a paper on Witness policies, "Since this biblical law is said to be absolute, it is unclear why the WTS does not simply refuse all medical use of blood."[36]

The advocacy group the Associated Jehovah's Witnesses for Reform on Blood (AJWRB), made up of Witnesses from around the world, aims to educate fellow believers about, and to bring an end to, what the organization calls "the irrational aspects of the Watchtower Society's policy on the use of blood and blood products."[37] The group believes that church officials endanger Witnesses' lives by discouraging blood transfusions and other procedures. The AJWRB and other critics question whether many Witnesses fully understand the consequences of refusing blood transfusions or are being manipulated into agreeing to the no-blood policy. These opponents point out that Witness literature contains horrifying stories of blood transfusions gone wrong but does not discuss the benefits, and Witnesses may feel obliged to refuse blood and carry the "blood card" due to pressure from peers or elders.[38] According to critics, the WTS has apparently kept true to Leviticus 17:14, which states that whoever eats "the blood of any flesh . . . shall be cut off." That is, Witnesses who accept a prohibited blood-based treatment and do not sufficiently repent are believed to have betrayed God; as a result, these "apostates" have been disfellowshipped.[39]

Most tragically, adult members and children have died due to the no-blood policy. The AJWRB states that objecting to blood transfusions and other procedures is "a tragic and misguided policy that has claimed thousands of lives, many of them children."[40] The organization's website lists "a small sampling" of dozens of names of Witness adults and children from around the world who have died from being denied needed blood.[41] In fact, a 1994 issue of WTS's *Awake!* magazine glorifies children who died after turning down blood transfusions. The cover of the magazine shows twenty-six photographs of children with the title "Youths Who Put God First."[42] The article lovingly describes four children, all of whom faced life-threatening illnesses and battled doctors and courts that wanted them to receive blood to save their lives. Two of those children "won" their battles and died.[43]

Courts have generally sided against Jehovah's Witnesses who have wanted to deny children medical treatments on religious grounds. For example, in a 1968 class action lawsuit, the Supreme Court ruled that the state of Washington could order blood transfusions for minor children over the objections of the minors' parents.[44] However, in 2007, a judge allowed a fourteen-year-old Seattle boy with leukemia to reject a blood transfusion, even though the teenager, Dennis Lindberg, knew he most likely would not survive. Lindberg died on the evening of the judge's decision.[45]

While hospitals and physicians have made concessions to try to accommodate adult Witnesses, they are less tolerant when the patients are children. In a paper published in the *Western Journal of Medicine*, Dr. Osamu Muramoto of the Regional Ethics Council of Kaiser Permanente's Northwest Division writes, "Children of JW parents should be given treatment independently from their parents' religion." Muramoto adds, "In emergency situations where there is risk of harm to the child by withholding blood-based treatment, immediate danger should be relieved, including, if necessary, giving blood-based treatment."[46]

THE FOLLOWERS OF CHRIST

One of the most dangerous sects in regard to extremist faith healing–related beliefs has been the Followers of Christ. The Pentecostal congregation in Oregon City, Oregon, began in the early 1900s and was led by an authoritarian, Apocalypse-preaching pastor by the name of Walter White, who died in 1969.

Today, the group of approximately 1,200 to 1,500 members appears to remain committed to its doctrines that promote faith healing and discourage, if not prohibit, conventional medical care.[47] So, when a child in the sect falls ill, members attempt to summon divine intervention through prayer, fasting, anointing with oil, and the laying on of hands.[48] Some members believe that turning to scientific medical methods reflects a lack of faith in God.[49]

Children living in the church community have paid dearly so that adults can maintain this ideology. In 1998, an investigation by the newspaper the *Oregonian* found that, of nearly eighty minors buried in the church's graveyard over several decades, about one-quarter probably would have lived had they been allowed medical care. In some cases, that care could have been as simple as administering antibiotics. The Followers' cemetery contains graves of many infants, some who lived for such a short time that they never received first names. Around the time the *Oregonian* completed its study, the state's medical examiner, Larry Lewman, concluded that twenty-five children from the group had died over a ten-year period beginning in the late 1980s and that many had suffered "painful, torturous deaths that sometimes lasted days, if not weeks."[50]

Lewman talked to me on September 3, 2010, about his findings, which show that Followers of Christ children have a death rate that is twenty-six times that of the general population. Lewman spoke of deaths caused by such treatable conditions as diabetes, strangulated hernias, and infections. In addition, four mothers and three babies died during and after childbirth from a bacterial infection that Lewman says appears only in textbooks discussing health problems from the 1900s. "I don't know what century they're living in, but it's certainly not this one," says Lewman.

Among the headstones are those of two children whose deaths recently made the national news. One is fifteen-month-old Ava Worthington, who died on March 2, 2008, from pneumonia and a severe blood infection that could have been treated with antibiotics.[51] The toddler also had a softball-sized mass of cysts in her neck that may have suffocated her. Instead of summoning medical care, family and church members prayed for her, administered small amounts of wine,[52] and anointed her with olive oil.[53] For his role in her death, Ava's father, Carl Brent Worthington, was convicted of criminal mistreatment and sentenced to sixty days in jail followed by five years' probation. The judge also ordered Worthington and his wife to provide medical care for their other children.[54]

Soon after Ava died, her uncle, sixteen-year-old Neal Beagley, died on June 17, 2008. Neal died from heart failure caused by a urinary tract blockage. Over the course of two months, Neal's symptoms grew worse until he was having trouble breathing and felt a tightness in his chest, and yet his parents,

Jeffrey and Marci Beagley, performed prayer rituals rather than seeking medical care.[55] A pediatric urologist who testified at the trial of Neal's parents said the teenager's case was the worst he'd ever seen, that the urinary tract was completely destroyed, and that he found it "mind boggling" that Neal lived as long as he did. The urologist added that a doctor could have saved Neal's life as late as the day he died by simply installing a catheter.[56] In March 2010, Neal's parents were sentenced to sixteen months in prison followed by three years' probation, having been convicted of criminally negligent homicide.[57]

Followers of Christ cases continue to make their way through the criminal justice system. In July 2010, Timothy and Rebecca Wayland pleaded not guilty to charges of first-degree criminal mistreatment after their daughter, seven-month-old Alayna, developed a tennis-ball-sized growth over her left eye. The condition, known as hemangioma, threatened to cause Alayna to lose her vision in that eye.[58] According to court testimony, Alayna's mother treated her daughter by anointing her with oil and wiping the yellow discharge that continually seeped from her eye.[59]

That same month, it was reported that Dale and Shannon Hickman were arrested in the death of their infant son, who was born about six weeks premature and lived nine hours. An autopsy determined the baby, who weighed less than four pounds, died of staph pneumonia and complications from a premature birth, including underdeveloped lungs. No one with medical training reportedly attended the birth, and no one called a doctor.[60]

Seth Asser, the Rhode Island pediatrician who joined Rita Swan in publishing the study on child deaths in faith healing–focused religious orders, notes in a paper he wrote for an educational foundation that the risk of children dying in the Followers of Christ is significantly higher than that of the general population. Asser adds,

> The stories of prolonged suffering were each uniquely grotesque: uncontrolled fevers, excruciating pain, convulsions, choking on a bite of banana for an hour, and tumors larger than basketballs. Some were home from school with teachers' knowledge of their plights, folks who failed to report because of their interpretations of the religious exemption laws. Some had diseases preventable with routine vaccinations such as measles or the now rarely seen diphtheria. Newborns died from lack of trained assistance at delivery. Many who were otherwise normal-appearing term babies, did not have coroner inquiries because, never having taken a breath, they were classified as "stillborn" not persons.[61]

A judge overseeing a trial involving a Followers of Christ defendant echoed these concerns when he addressed sect members with this dictum:

"The fact is, too many children have died unnecessarily—a graveyard full."
Said the judge, "This has to stop."[62]

CONCLUSION

Despite the fact that some Americans hold potentially dangerous beliefs about
faith healing, we should not be too dismayed in thinking that such beliefs will
increase. Recent cases have been confined to small, socially isolated religious
communities, such as the Followers of Christ. While most states still have
laws that grant exemption from child abuse laws to parents who withhold
medical care from children for religious reasons, some prosecutors have been
able to circumvent those laws by charging neglectful parents with more serious
crimes for which no exemptions apply. And while some courts have required
that a child's life be in danger for social workers or doctors to intervene, that
has not been true across the board. For example, in deciding a 1987 case
involving Christian Science parents, a California appeals panel ruled that
courts may order medical examinations to protect minors from the recurrence
of life-threatening diseases over parental objections. In other words, the disease needs only to pose a *threat* of harm.[63]

We can also be assured that most people of faith reject zealous claims that
faith healing should replace medical care. Such a criticism was clearly stated
on Amazon.com, when a devout Christian woman reviewed a book that
advocated for prayer and keeping doctors at bay during childbirth. The
reviewer says she agrees with the book's author that "the FIRST response
should always be prayer" when complications in childbirth arise. However,
she writes, "Sometimes God may use 'conventional' methods to perform His
'miracles,'" such as "a doctor, a midwife or even an ambulance ride leading
to emergency surgery to perform the miracle of life!" The woman goes on to
say that blindly following the ideas in the book "can be dangerous. . . . God
gave you a brain—use it."[64]

And yet, it would be naïve to think that cases of religious medical neglect
are going away. The same court battles such as those waged by the Peculiar
People go on today. Shortly before this book was published, a mother and
father who were members of the Philadelphia-based First Century Gospel
Church, a fundamentalist Christian group that believes that seeking medical
care reflects a lack of faith in God, were convicted of involuntary manslaughter and child endangerment after they failed to seek medical care for
their two-year-old son who died from pneumonia.[65]

George Washington University Law School professor Jonathan Turley notes in the *Washington Post*, "Today, the Old Peculiars are largely gone (their faith-healing views thinned their numbers considerably), but many other sects . . . have prospered."[66] In *God's Perfect Child*, Caroline Fraser also reminds us not to be fooled into thinking that cases of religious child medical neglect are a thing of the past: "We may smile and shake our heads over the folly of the seventeenth, eighteenth, and nineteenth centuries, their healers, mesmerists, hypnotists, and layers on of hands, but there is very little difference between the credulity of those times and that of the present. We are an ahistorical people."[67]

As the daughter of a physician and a holistic health writer, I see the benefits of both medical care and unconventional treatments. However, as a parent, I owe it to my child not to take on faith everything that is said, regardless of the source. When children are ill, parents must do their part to conduct thorough research to determine what is the best way to help their sons and daughters get better. And if a particular treatment is not working, they should try something else. In this day and age, there is no excuse for allowing a child to suffer—or, certainly, to die—when much of the information parents need to make good decisions is at their fingertips.

Chapter 20

SORTING OUT THE DEMONS
OF CHILD RITUAL ABUSE

During the 1980s and early 1990s, this country was gripped by a bizarre and overwhelming fear that children were being brutally and sadistically tortured and killed in ritualistic ceremonies. The perpetrators were commonly thought to be part of a large network of satanic cults or groups that immersed themselves in other occult beliefs. There were rumors that devil worshippers were kidnapping children and babies and forcing them to take part in abusive, bloody rituals. Many people fomented those fears, including social workers, law enforcement, prosecutors, psychiatrists, the media, and religious leaders and their organizations.

It was a time known as the satanic panic.

Investigations of these alleged abuses ultimately proved that people's fears were largely unfounded. There was no satanic network crisscrossing the country. While some abuses took place, they were hardly on the level of severity that had been believed. In other words, people had become scared out of their minds for no reason, thanks in part to what can only be described as devil phobia.

There were two awful outcomes of the satanic panic. For one, it ruined people's lives. Innocent people were accused of atrocious crimes against children. They were stigmatized, and some went to prison. Meanwhile, alleged child victims were manipulated into making outrageous accusations against adults; some of these youngsters were needlessly removed from their homes for months and even years.

The other fallout was that many Americans became convinced that child ritual abuse was a complete fallacy. In fact, child ritual abuse does happen in this country. What's more, perpetrators most often subscribe to "mainstream" faiths, not Satanism. But before going further, it's important to first understand the religious, social, and political influences that have clouded the issue of child ritual abuse.

THE SATANIC PANIC

In the early 1980s, an anticult movement was under way in America. Many strange new religious groups had sprouted during the 1960s and 1970s, and mainstream religious America did not know what to think of them. Americans worried that cults would corrupt young people, and in fact, parents were "losing" their sons and daughters to cults. Some cults, like the Manson Family and others, were dangerous, killing both outsiders and members.

At the same time, America was growing more aware of the seriousness of child abuse. In 1974, Congress passed the Child Abuse Prevention and Treatment Act (CAPTA), which established new regulations for mandatory reporting of allegations and provided funding to child abuse prevention programs. Then, in 1980, a book called *Michelle Remembers* was published, which chronicled a woman's recovered memories of having been a victim of satanic ritual abuse. Later, several investigations would discredit the allegations made in *Michelle Remembers*, but before that happened, all these factors contributed to create a cultural paranoia powder keg.

The spark that ignited those fears was a child abuse case in Manhattan Beach, California. In 1983, a woman named Judy Johnson filed a complaint with police that her preschool-age son had been sodomized by his teacher, Ray Buckey. Buckey worked at a preschool called the McMartin School, which was run by his mother, Peggy McMartin Buckey. Some of Johnson's allegations were quite bizarre. In addition to accusing Buckey of sexually abusing her son, she reported that Peggy McMartin Buckey "drilled a child under the arms" and that Ray Buckey "flew through the air."[1] As part of their investigation, police called upon the services of a Los Angeles child advocacy group. After a social worker interviewed the children, she determined that 360 youngsters at the McMartin School had been sexually abused. In 1984, Ray Buckey, Peggy McMartin Buckey, and three other staff members were charged with 321 counts of child abuse.

It was a weak case. Police had uncovered no forensic evidence of abuse. At a preliminary hearing, when a child was asked to identify his abusers, the young witness pointed to photographs of actor Chuck Norris, a city attorney, and four nuns.[2] Later it would be learned that Judy Johnson, the woman who made the initial allegations, was mentally ill. (In 1985, Johnson was diagnosed with paranoid schizophrenia, and in 1986, she died from alcohol poisoning.) In 1986, a newly elected district attorney found the McMartin School case to be so weak he dropped charges against all the accused except Ray Buckey and Peggy McMartin Buckey.[3]

The trial against the Buckeys began in 1987. Prosecutors contended that the two sexually molested eleven children over a period of five years. But the allegations were too bizarre to be believed. Nine children testified that they were molested and photographed and then frightened into silence by being forced to watch bloody animal mutilations. Children talked about seeing witches fly, traveling in a hot air balloon, and being flushed down toilets to secret rooms, where they would be abused before being handed back to their parents.[4] The youngsters told of seeing a parakeet squeezed to death and being forced to watch a rabbit sacrificed on a church altar. Two children claimed that Ray Buckey killed a pony in front of them, and one testified that the man dressed as a witch in a satanic ritual.[5]

Prosecutors were botching the case. Some were accused of misconduct, such as withholding evidence, and one member of the team quit in disgust. Most damaging to the prosecution, jurors were shown videotapes of the children being interviewed by the social worker, who appeared to be manipulating the children into making their allegations.[6] Years later, one of those children, as an adult, told the press, "I lied. . . . Anytime I would give them an answer that they didn't like, they would ask again and encourage me to give them the answer they were looking for."[7]

In 1990, Peggy McMartin Buckey was acquitted on all counts. Following a retrial that resulted in a hung jury, the prosecution dropped the case against Ray Buckey. In the end, Buckey and his mother spent a total of nearly seven years in jail waiting for the case to draw to its conclusion. The McMartin School was forced to close. The two-and-a-half-year, $15 million trial became the longest and most expensive criminal trial in US history. After the "not guilty" verdict was announced, Peggy McMartin Buckey told the media, "I've gone through hell and now we've lost everything."[8]

But the McMartin School case was only the beginning. Soon after it made headlines, more than one hundred preschools became the targets of similar accusations. Rumors spread across the country that children were being tortured and killed in rituals performed by a coast-to-coast network of Satan-worshipping cults. Allegations included acts of necrophilia and cannibalism, the sacrifice of animals and babies, orgies, and the forced ingestion of semen, blood, and feces. One magazine article reported, "Victims—some as young as three—spoke of hooded ceremonies, animal mutilations, weird potions, murders, and 'baby breeders,' female cult members who bore children for the sole purpose of ritual sacrifice."[9] There were more arrests, including stings that rounded up dozens of people. A wave of hysteria was sweeping the nation.

Therapists were deluged with stories from adult patients who, through repressed and recovered memories, claimed to have been ritually abused in childhood. There were estimates that fifty thousand to sixty thousand children were being ritually abused annually, most of them in satanic rites.[10] A survey conducted for the National Center on Child Abuse and Neglect looked at investigations performed by more than eleven thousand clinical social workers, psychiatrists, psychologists, district attorneys, police departments, and social service agencies. The researchers found more than twelve thousand accusations of group cult sexual abuse based on satanic ritual. (Not one case showed substantial corroborating evidence of well-organized satanic cults that engaged in the sexual abuse and physical torture of children.)[11] According to one news article, 70 percent of Americans believed that "at least some people who claim they were sexually abused by satanic cults as children, but repressed the memories for years, are telling the truth."[12]

In 1984, social worker Kee MacFarlane, who interviewed the children in the McMartin School case, testified before Congress that "an organized operation of child predators"[13] was committing "bizarre rituals involving violence to animals, scatological behavior and what they perceive as magic, and children [were being] threatened into silence with the use of weapons, threats of harm and death to family members, and observing the slaughter of animals."[14] Convinced that it had a sweeping occult ritual abuse problem on its hands, Congress doubled its budget for child protection programs.

State governments sprang into action, too. For instance, a 1998 Illinois law declared that a person would be found guilty of ritualized abuse of a child if that person "tortures, mutilates, or sacrifices any warm-blooded animal or human being"; "forces ingestion, or external application, of human or animal urine, feces, flesh, blood, bones, body secretions, nonprescribed drugs or chemical compounds"; "places a living child into a coffin or open grave containing a human corpse or remains"; or "unlawfully dissects, mutilates, or incinerates a human corpse."[15]

Many self-proclaimed experts on Satanism fanned the flames of fear. Most were evangelical and fundamentalist Christian leaders who gave seminars and conferences urging audiences to begin Christian psychotherapy, join antisatanic support groups, and undergo exorcisms. In *Satanic Panic: The Creation of a Contemporary Legend*, published after the panic had subsided, Jeffrey S. Victor wrote about these "moral crusaders" who exacerbated the panic by "promoting unnecessary fear of imaginary deviants: secret, conspiratorial Satanists." Victor adds, "Regardless of their motives, their organizing and lecturing activities function to aggravate widespread fear in society."[16]

The media stepped up the panic, too. In 1987, national television talk show host Geraldo Rivera told his audience, "Estimates are that there are over one million Satanists in this country." Rivera also stated that the majority of perpetrators "are linked in a highly organized, very secretive network. From small towns to large cities, they have attracted police and FBI attention to their satanic ritual child abuse, child pornography and grisly Satanic murders. The odds are that this is happening in your town."[17]

It did not help matters much when, in 1989, police found real evidence of a small serial-killing religious group that dealt in the occult. Buried on a ranch in Matamoros, Mexico, were fifteen adult bodies, including that of an American student who had gone missing when he went to Mexico on vacation. When police searched the property, they found cauldrons in which floated human blood and animal parts. At a press conference, some cult members who had been dealing drugs said they believed human sacrifice would protect them from being discovered by the police.[18]

The panic finally began to die down in the early 1990s, as people began to realize that many of the claims of abuse were baseless. It was discovered that most criminal cases lacked physical evidence, and social workers, law enforcement, and prosecutors had relied mostly on unsubstantiated, and often coerced, child testimony. FBI and state investigations failed to uncover evidence of a satanic conspiracy.[19] A study of thirty-six criminal cases involving allegations of ritual sexual abuse of children showed that only about one-quarter resulted in convictions and most of the convictions had little to do with ritualism.[20]

In 1992, Kenneth V. Lanning, who worked for the FBI as Supervisory Special Agent of the Behavioral Science Unit at the National Center for the Analysis of Violent Crime, wrote a report after conducting intensive investigations of claims of satanic networks abusing children. His conclusions helped shut the door on rumors of such abuse:

> In none of the cases of which I am aware has any evidence of a well-organized satanic cult been found. Many of those who accept the stories of organized ritual abuse of children and human sacrifice will tell you that the best evidence they now have is the consistency of stories from all over America. It sounds like a powerful argument. It is interesting to note that, without having met each other, the hundreds of people who claim to have been abducted by aliens from outer space also tell stories and give descriptions of the aliens that are similar to each other.[21]

Around this time, two evangelical Christians, Bob and Gretchen Passantino, were also debunking claims of satanic ritual abuse on their website and in Christian publications. In an article entitled "The Hard Facts about Satanic Ritual Abuse," the Passantinos warn about the dangers of unsubstantiated fears:

> There is no evidence that SRA stories are true. There are alternate hypotheses that more reasonably explain the social, professional, and personal dynamics reflected in this contemporary satanic panic. The tragedy of broken families, traumatized children, and emotionally incapacitated adults is needless and destructive. Careful investigation of the stories, the alleged victims, and the proponents has given us every reason to reject the satanic conspiracy model in favor of reason and truth.[22]

As the satanic panic came to look more and more like a bogeyman scenario, some people who had promoted the fear began uttering public apologies. In 1995, Geraldo Rivera spoke on a television program called "Wrongly Accused and Convicted of Child Molestation" on CNBC: "Now I am convinced that I was terribly wrong. . . . And many innocent people were convicted and went to prison as a result . . . and I am equally positive [that the] 'Repressed Memory Therapy Movement' is also a bunch of crap."[23]

Having realized that there was, in fact, nothing to fear, many Americans concluded that child ritual abuse was a made-up phenomenon. In writing for the *New York Times Magazine*, Margaret Talbot explains how people were ready to put the events of the satanic panic out of their minds:

> When you once believed something that now strikes you as absurd, even unhinged, it can be almost impossible to summon that feeling of credulity again. Maybe that is why it is easier for most of us to forget, rather than to try and explain, the satanic-abuse scare that gripped this country . . . the myth that devil worshippers had set up shop in our daycare centers, where their clever adepts were raping and sodomizing children, practicing ritual sacrifice, shedding their clothes, drinking blood and eating feces, all unnoticed by parents, neighbors and the authorities.[24]

But to think that child ritual abuse never happens is a mistake. In fact, child ritual abuse is a reality that goes on in many religious communities. What's more, the perpetrators are much more likely to be worshippers of God than of the devil.

CHILD RITUAL ABUSE IN AMERICA

Let's cover some basics. A *ritual* is an established rite or ceremony. It does not have to be religious but often has a religious component. In fact, one study on the mental state of people engaging in religious belief shows that ritual is a crucial component of the religious process because "it is the primary technique whereby followers gain access to the state of dissociation, which makes religious belief and experience possible."[25]

The practice of rituals is as old as religion itself. Leviticus 1:5–13, for instance, gives detailed (and gory) instructions on how to sacrifice a "bullock" or castrated bull. After the animal is killed, its blood is sprinkled around the altar. After that, the carcass is cut up into pieces, and its entrails and legs are washed. Finally, everything is burned on the altar, which creates "a sweet aroma to the LORD."

Religious rituals can be a good thing. Whether they involve lighting candles, saying prayers, reading from religious texts, anointing with oil, singing hymns, or performing baptisms, rituals are a concrete way for people to express their piety and spirituality. Rituals bring people psychologically closer together; provide a structure for celebrating life's happy times, such as births and weddings; and help people through times of tragedy and grief. "Ritual distances a person from emotions and permits him or her to return to the world— a process that obsessive self-concern hinders," say the authors of *The Psychology of Religion*.[26]

But some people become obsessed with ritual. For these believers, ritual becomes more than just a symbolic gesture. Instead, it takes on huge meaning, such as proof of piety before God. Some believe the rituals themselves have supernatural powers. Religious or spiritual rituals, in and of themselves, can be dangerous. Examples include Christian self-flagellators and the New Age sweat lodge ceremony that went awry in October 2009, leading to three people dying and numerous others being rushed to the hospital.[27]

What is *ritual abuse*? According to the website ReligiousTolerance.org, *ritual abuse* is a "psychological, sexual, spiritual and/or physical assault on an unwilling human victim, committed by one or more people whose primary motive is to fulfill a prescribed ritual in order to achieve a specific goal or satisfy the perceived needs of their deity."[28] Since rituals are often of a religious nature, so is ritual abuse.

Children have long been made the victims of religious ritual abuse, the most egregious being child sacrifice. As noted earlier, during the Renaissance, children in Europe were whipped on Innocents' Day. Children have been brutally murdered at the hands of fundamentalist Mormons practicing "blood atonement." Even today, some Shiite Muslims slice the foreheads of boys—some as young as infants—in a ritualistic bloodletting that is supposed to commemorate the suffering of Hussein, the son of a cousin of Muhammad, who was killed in battle, thereby preventing him from taking power. Shiites believe Hussein should have been Muhammad's successor.[29]

Child ritual abuse is not only physically and sexually abusive—it is almost always emotionally abusive. Many times religious rituals make children feel uncomfortable and unsafe. Often, adults are so caught up in their own need to perform rituals that they fail to comprehend how those rites affect children. An example is what happened to Mark Casey, who, as was explained in the chapter on terrorizing, was frightened when adults in his church laid their hands on him and urged him to speak in tongues. I am also reminded of a young woman who spoke to an audience of social workers at a conference I attended in Utah in 2010. The woman, who did not want to be named, had left the FLDS. She described what it was like for her to be baptized at the age of eight:

> I remember my mother telling me exactly what would happen, how I would feel once everything had occurred. Well, after I got baptized and they were doing the laying on of hands, I just remembered thinking, I am not feeling what my mother told me I would feel. And I just felt really uncomfortable, like there was just these men standing around me with their hands on my head and I just—it wasn't a feeling of enlightenment, it was an awkwardness for me.

It's impossible to say how often child ritual abuse happens, but Ariel Glucklich states in *Sacred Pain: Hurting the Body for the Sake of the Soul* that abusive rituals are frequently performed on young people:

> Around the world, children have been subjected to pain, from whipping to circumcision (boys and girls), subincision, or superincision; piercing noses, ears, or cheeks; scarification; knocking out teeth; kneeling in hot coals; getting beaten by sticks; hanging from hooks; and so forth. This violence ranges from the Americas to Africa, Asia, and Europe, and at all known times in human history.[30]

While it's impossible to say how many children are ritually abused in this country, there is enough anecdotal evidence to indicate that child ritual abuse is pretty common and is not confined to any one faith, including Satanism and Christianity. The motivations run the gamut. Of course, mental illness can be a factor. Also, just like all religious child maltreatment, ritual abuse can feed an adult's desire to overpower and dominate a child. An occult type of example is what Anne A. Johnson Davis suffered as a child. In her memoir, *Hell Minus One: My Story of Deliverance from Satanic Ritual Abuse and My Journey to Freedom*, Davis chronicles the ritual abuses perpetrated by her mother, stepfather, and acquaintances. The group donned black robes while they subjected Davis to a host of horrific violations. "They used me as an object to torment and torture. In their sick minds, I was property—a 'Satanic sacrifice,'" she writes.[31]

Davis writes of having been subjected to abuses from the time she was a small child. For example, when she was four years old, she describes being tied with ropes, hung upside down, smeared with her mother's menstrual blood, being forced to watch a live dog be disemboweled and then have her head placed inside the animal.[32] Future abuses include having her nails pulled on with pliers, having her chest tightly bound with a leather strap that stopped her breathing, and being vaginally and anally penetrated.[33] Davis recalled these memories later in life. When she was in her thirties and experiencing episodes of rage against her husband, she sought therapy and began to remember what had been done to her.[34] The whole thing would seem implausible except for the fact that Davis's parents actually confessed to the abuses through letters to their daughter and to the police.[35] The cover of Davis's book shows a photograph of the author at the age of three with bruises on her face.

Barbara Dorris, too, says she was victimized by those acting on prurient desires, but her perpetrators were Catholic priests. As discussed earlier, Dorris says she was repeatedly raped by her neighborhood priest, beginning when she was six years old. A few years later, she says, her abuser got other priests to join in, and they brought in other child victims. Dorris says she and the other children were physically and sexually abused in bizarre Catholic-based rituals. As Dorris explained on March 12, 2009, the priests first met at a church and then went to a farmhouse where they dressed up in altar-boy garments.

"Obviously, it was planned, because when we got to the church, everything was laid out, ready to go," Dorris says. She adds that the priests used religious messages in abusing the children. For example, she says they burned the soles of the victims' feet to "purify your soul." She also remembers her abusers telling the children, "'If you pray with a pure heart, this won't hurt.' Sexual abuse is about power and control, and they certainly had power and control over us."*

Some child ritual abuses are done as rites of passage. For example, one high-profile case of ritualistic murder by Satanists occurred in 1995, when fifteen-year-old Elyse Pahler of San Luis Obispo, California, was killed by three teenage boys as part of a satanic initiation rite. Jacob Delashmutt, Joseph Fiorella, and Royce Casey choked and stabbed Pahler to death and returned later to have sex with her corpse. According to the boys' confessions, killing Pahler was a "sacrifice to the devil" to give their heavy metal band "craziness" to "go professional."[36]

Believers of non-Western faiths also commit these crimes. Such was the case of Marie Lauradin of Queens, New York, who, in 2009, was charged with forcing her six-year-old daughter to undergo a Haitian Loa voodoo ceremony that left serious burns over 25 percent of her body. According to prosecutors, Lauradin allegedly poured rum over her daughter and then forced her to walk through a ring of fire on the floor, which lit her ablaze.[37]

But what is the most common theological motivation behind child ritual abuse in America? By simply perusing criminal cases, the answer becomes obvious: Perpetrators are attempting to spiritually extract from a young person's body an undesirable influence, usually the devil or demons. Consider these recent cases:

- On November 13, 2001, Sabrina Wright of Washington Heights, New York, was charged in the drowning death of her four-year-old daughter, Signifagance Oliver. According to investigators, Wright said that the drowning took place as she was trying to exorcise the child of demons.[38] Two years later, Wright—who had a history of mental illness—confessed to a judge that she killed her child while trying to "bless" her. The woman reportedly believed that Signifagance was evil and possessed by the spirit of Wright's dead mother.[39]
- On July 3, 2002, twin brothers who operated a summer Bible camp in Austin, Texas, beat eleven-year-old Louie Guerrero so severely that the boy needed a blood transfusion. At the trial of the twins, Joshua and Caleb Thompson, Louie testified that Joshua was praying "to get the devil out of me" as he beat him. Louie's father stated that after Caleb Thompson brought the boy home, Caleb said they had not been able to "get the devil out."[40]
- On August 22, 2003, eight-year-old Terrance Cottrell died at the Faith Temple Church of the Apostolic Faith in Milwaukee, Wisconsin, during the last of a series of exorcisms designed to rid the boy of autism. Pastor Ray Hemphill and church members, including the child's mother, held Terrance down. In describing the incident in *God vs. the Gavel*, Marci Hamilton writes that Terrance fought the hands that restrained him while Hemphill pressed his knee against the boy's chest. "After three weeks of meetings, the child quieted down," Hamilton writes, "but when the twelfth ceremony ceased, the boy could not be revived, because he had died of suffocation."[41]
- On July 29, 2007, police in Phoenix, Arizona, said they had responded to

a call that an exorcism was taking place. When they arrived on the scene, they found Ronald Marquez choking his three-year-old granddaughter, who was bloody, crying in pain, and gasping. According to police, Marquez was trying to "release demons" from the girl. The girl's mother, naked and bloody, was also in the room, chanting. Police subdued Marquez with stun guns, after which he stopped breathing and died.[42]

- On January 9, 2008, police found Banita Jacks in her home along with the decomposing bodies of her four daughters: five-year-old Aja Fogle, six-year-old N'Kiah Fogle, eleven-year-old Tatianna Jacks, and seventeen-year-old Brittany Jacks. Police also found religious scribbling on the walls and no food in the house.[43] Autopsies revealed that the victims had probably been strangled, bludgeoned, and stabbed. In an interview with police detectives, the mother told them that the oldest daughter, Brittany, was a "Jezebel" who was possessed by demons and a bad influence on her sisters, and that starving the children was a way to remove their demons.[44] The crime scene photos were so horrific, the judge in the case stated that they would "probably haunt me for the rest of my life."[45]

- On April 14, 2008, authorities said that twenty-five-year-old Nelly Vasquez-Salazar of Waukegan, Illinois, confessed to brutally slashing to death her six-year-old daughter, Evelyn Vasquez, because she believed that the child was possessed by the devil. The child reportedly had been stabbed eleven times. What apparently led the mother to suspect demons was her daughter's habit of sleepwalking. According to police, Vasquez-Salazar told her mother that she would wake up and find Evelyn standing by her bed. Her mother then reportedly told her that the child was possessed.[46]

- On December 2, 2008, a young Texas couple was charged with capital murder for killing thirteen-month-old Amora Carson in what investigators called an exorcism. Authorities said Blaine Milam attacked the baby with "numerous objects, including a hammer," in a bedroom over an eleven- or twelve-hour period, allowing the child's mother, Jesseca Carson, in only once. The baby was found with severe trauma to her head and bite marks all over her body. (Later evidence showed she had also been sexually assaulted.) According to authorities, Jesseca Carson could hear what was going on in the bedroom, and Milam told her it was "the different voices of the devil" coming out of the child[47] as he attempted to "beat out the demons."[48] (Milam was later sentenced to death; Carson was sentenced to life without the possibility of parole.)

In all these cases, adults were attempting to cast out negative or evil forces from children's bodies, acts that caused injury and sometimes death through the ritual of exorcism.

EXORCISM: A POPULAR RITE

What is *exorcism*? Dictionary.com defines it as "to seek to expel (an evil spirit) by adjuration or religious or solemn ceremonies." Is exorcism a ritual? Yes. According to Catherine Bell, author of *Ritual: Perspectives and Dimensions*, there are six categories of commonly practiced "life-cycle" rites. One of them is the *rite of affliction*, whose purpose, Bell says, is to "seek to mitigate the influence of spirits thought to be afflicting human beings with misfortune." Bell adds, "Rituals of affliction attempt to rectify a state of affairs that has been disturbed or disordered; they heal, exorcise, protect, and purify."[49]

Considering the aforementioned criminal cases, it appears that most cases of child religious ritual abuse in America fall under the category of rites of affliction, specifically through the practice of exorcism. Or, as Kibbie Ruth describes it in *Child Maltreatment*, acts committed by "overzealous parents" who "believe that they must purify their child through physical torture."[50] For that matter, repeated corporal punishment designed to "beat the devil" out of children, as was described in the section on physical abuse, can constitute a form of ritual abuse.

One reason why exorcistic religious ritual abuse is not immediately recognized as abuse is that perpetrators often believe they are doing something spiritually beneficial for children. For example, they may feel that their actions are chasing away evil spirits. Of course, the irony here is these well-meaning, fearful adults end up injuring—even sometimes killing—the very children that they aim to protect. The other reason exorcistic ritual abuse is not apparent is because perpetrators are committing abusive acts not through Satan-worship but through God-worship. It probably would surprise many to know that child ritual abuse more often occurs not through the worship of evil forces but through efforts to get rid of them.

"What is particularly ironic in acknowledging this kind of ritual crime is that it is performed, not out of *devotion* to organized evil (demons, Satan, witchcraft), but rather to *expel* it," writes David Frankfurter in *Evil Incarnate: Rumors of Demonic Conspiracy and Satanic Abuse in History*. Frankfurter goes on to say,

Historically verifiable atrocities take place not in the ceremonies of some evil realm or as expressions of some ontological evil force, but rather in the course of *purging* evil and its alleged devotees from the world. . . . It is the discourse of evil and monstrosity and of their *annihilation* that most consistently moti-vates participants—in moods of determination and ebullience—to unspeak-able violence, evil.[51]

Exorcisms are an age-old rite. Back in Jesus' time, the religious leader was kept busy casting out "demons" from people's bodies (although it appears that many subjects were actually afflicted with mental illness or epilepsy). While some Americans see exorcism as archaic, the religious ritual has been gaining in popularity both in the United States and elsewhere, largely due to the same kinds of fears that spread the satanic panic.

In *Satanism Today: An Encyclopedia of Religion, Folklore, and Popular Culture*, James Lewis writes, "Belief in the reality of demonic possession and exorcism is still very widely accepted by many conservative Christians, both Roman Catholic and Protestant. The Bible contains so many accounts of exorcisms that anyone who wishes to interpret Christian scripture literally is compelled to accept the reality of demonic possession and exorcism."[52] According to Lewis, exorcism "can be a formal, ritual procedure, or a less formal process, depending on the tradition."[53] He adds that in Western religions, in particular, "exorcism is often dramatic and even violent."[54]

"I have met with hundreds of people, from various walks of life, who are convinced not only that demons exist but also that they routinely cause trouble in the lives of ordinary women and men," writes Michael Cuneo in *American Exorcism: Expelling Demons in the Land of Plenty*.[55] Cuneo notes that this resurgence is a fairly recent phenomenon. He says exorcisms were "all but dead and forgotten" in the late 1960s, but by the mid-1970s, "suddenly count-less people were convinced that they themselves, or perhaps a loved one, were suffering from demonic affliction; and exorcism was in hot demand."[56]

A 2001 Gallup poll shows that more than 41 percent of Americans believe people are sometimes possessed by the devil, although this is down from 49 percent a decade before.[57] A 2007 Pew Research survey shows that two-thirds of Americans completely or mostly agree that angels and demons are active in the world.[58]

According to Caroline Fraser, writing for the newsletter of the organiza-tion Children's Healthcare Is a Legal Duty (CHILD), "Exorcism is univer-sally popular, not only in Christianity but [also] in virtually every faith. . . . People love to believe that evil can be driven out—of the temple, of the church, of their bodies and minds. Exorcism is a dramatic, theatrical, and highly entertaining act, possibly one of the most diverting rituals ever devised to enliven dull religious services." Fraser notes that Pentecostalism—a faith that strongly subscribes to the value of exorcism—is one of the fastest-growing Christian groups in the world, with 115 million adherents.[59]

Cuneo believes that the 1973 movie *The Exorcist* helped to give birth to exorcism ministries across the country.[60] According to Cuneo, the satanic panic, too, played a big role in fostering a renewal of interest in exorcism. "It was the Satanism scares [of the 1980s and 1990s], above all else, that constituted the real breakthrough for exorcism within American evangelicalism," as "significant numbers of Americans, evangelical and otherwise, became convinced that a clandestine cult of Satan-worshippers was spreading menace across the land."[61]

Many church groups now regularly perform exorcisms throughout the United States and around the world. In fact, interest in the topic was deemed sufficient to warrant the release of a newly restored version of *The Exorcist* in 2000. And in 2011, Anthony Hopkins starred in *The Rite*, whose plot is similar to *The Exorcist*, except Satan's supposed victim is a pregnant teenager instead of a little girl.

"If you're determined to get an exorcism, chances are you'll succeed in getting one," writes Cuneo. "Exorcism is more readily available today in the United States than perhaps ever before. It's not a procedure you'd necessarily brag about undergoing. It's not something that's generally spoken of in polite company. But it's most certainly available, and within certain sectors of the population, it's in hot demand."[62]

The Vatican has helped to foment the craze. Citing a shortage of priests who know how to perform exorcisms—and despite having on staff hundreds of "official exorcists"—Pope Benedict XVI has ramped up an exorcism training program for priests and has recently updated exorcism guidelines.[63] Meanwhile, Roman Catholic dioceses throughout the United States have been overwhelmed with requests to evaluate claims of possession by evil supernatural forces. As a way to beef up the number of priests capable of performing exorcisms, in November 2010, bishops sponsored a two-day conference in New York on how to conduct exorcisms, which included teaching priests about the origins of exorcism and how to evaluate if a person is, indeed, possessed.[64]

Protestants perform exorcisms, too, although theirs are not as regulated as those conducted within the Catholic Church. In this way, Protestant exorcisms are usually performed by ministers or laypeople from fundamentalist or evangelical Christian churches and tend to take on a more do-it-yourself approach. Many religious leaders talk about "spiritual warfare" against demonic forces. As an example, Real Deliverance Ministries sells a book called *The War Manual* that, according to the organization's website, promises to show how "demons have real-for-sure, planned-out battle strategies for defeating you."[65]

"My church was very big into satanic panic," says thirty-six-year-old Alex

Byrd, who was raised in the southeastern United States in the Pentecostal church known as the Assemblies of God. As Byrd told me on November 23, 2009, "Almost all media that was not church-approved was condemned as being satanic." Byrd remembers that his church believed that a number of popular consumer items boded evil. For example, the popular dolls Cabbage Patch Kids "could open doorways to Satan," says Byrd, "because the adoption certificates were seen as too much like real children." This pervasive paranoia, Byrd says, led to his church's operational model of "spiritual warfare," in that worshippers were led to believe that exorcism was necessary to cast out the ubiquitous demons.

Such fears keep some purported exorcists very busy. For example, Bob Larson of Spiritual Freedom Church in Denver, Colorado, speaks about exorcism on popular television talk shows and performs exorcisms all over the world.[66] Many tune in to his deliverance sermons over the radio and pay a lot of money at his mass exorcism rallies.[67] Those who wonder if they are possessed by evil forces can take Larson's twenty-one-question "demon test." Larson, who calls himself "The Real Exorcist," provides on his website videos of him exorcising people. In performing his exorcisms, Larson has his subjects personify their own "demon," after which they often get very emotional.[68]

Byrd says he witnessed exorcisms every Sunday during church services, where church leaders would cast out the "demons" of homosexuality, alcoholism, heart disease, and the like. "And sometimes they would have people who didn't exactly want to come up, and they [church leaders] would forcibly make them come up and try to cast, like, the 'demons of rebellion' out of them," says Byrd. In fact, exorcisms were performed "for just about everything. If you had a cold or you skinned your knee in Sunday school, they would pretty much get over you and start praying in tongues and would drive out the demon of the common cold. This was normal and accepted in that church." Byrd says that exorcism was also used as a means of oppression; if members were perceived as disagreeing with a point of church doctrine, "they were convinced that you were possessed," at which point "they would start praying over you forcefully."

Rose, the woman who spent hours in the bathroom in kindergarten because she was too scared to fulfill her parents' expectations that she lead people to Jesus, was part of a "deliverance ministry team" in her church. Starting in 1978, when Rose was eighteen, she and her team made house calls, performing exorcisms on adult church members who requested the service. When I spoke to Rose on July 27, 2009, she explained that her fundamentalist Christian church was one of many that were part of a newly burgeoning deliverance ministry movement. Rose maintains that, for those living in a culture that fears evil, the devil, and demons, exorcism is considered to be a reasonable solution to many perceived sins. She says she exorcised people of every sin from greed to gluttony. She adds that these notions are cultivated and encouraged by sermons, church meetings, and audio and video materials that warn churchgoers about satanic possession.

According to an article written by Agnieszka Tennant for *Christianity Today*,

> Besides headaches, addiction to smut, and hearing voices, deliverance manuals list alcoholism, chronic fatigue syndrome, homosexuality, nightmares, persistent anger, and jealousy among the possible symptoms of demonization. Increasingly, even the most common ills and sins are being linked to demonic sources and healed by demon expulsion. The magic takes place when demons are—depending on whom you turn to—confronted, expelled, driven out, dismissed by the Lord Jesus, sent to the pit, coughed up, spewed, vomited, disgorged, cast out, dispossessed or exorcised. Or so some believe.[69]

Even after exorcisms have been found to be injurious, proponents continue to justify the importance of this practice. Take the case of Laura Schubert, a woman who won a court settlement after proving that in 1996, she was injured and psychologically traumatized at the age of seventeen after having undergone two elongated exorcisms at the Pleasant Glade Assembly of God in Fort Worth, Texas. (The case was later dismissed by the Texas Supreme Court, which determined that church members had not acted maliciously and should not be penalized for conducting exorcisms.) Lloyd McCutchen, the senior pastor of the church, wrote in a court filing, "It is our belief that the holy spirit is not the only spirit that can influence a person. Evil spirits can move and can torment [a] person." Speaking of the exorcism that was performed on Schubert, McCutchen says,

> Many people did "lay hands" on Laura Schubert and pray for her. . . . This type of activity happens on a very regular basis in our church. . . . Within our church, it is not unusual for a person to be "slain in the spirit." . . . When this happens, a person often faints into semiconsciousness, and sometimes lies down on the floor of our church. It is our belief that this is a positive experience in which the holy spirit comes over a person and influences them.[70]

HARM TO VICTIMS

Certainly, most exorcisms are performed on adults, not children, and do not turn violent. Many adults who undergo exorcisms, and perhaps some young people, find the experience cathartic. Michael Cuneo believes that abusive exorcisms are exceptional.[71] But given how fervently people believe in the value of exorcism, how frequently the ritual is performed, and how many justify the ritual as being beneficial for subjects, it's appropriate to consider the ritual's potential for harm.

Alex Byrd's parents frequently performed exorcisms on him, partly as punishment. They also used the threat of exorcism as a way to scare the child they accused of having a "demon of rebellion." Byrd remembers that when he was a teenager, he was beginning to question the truth of his church's dogma and the ethics of religious leaders. Usually, he kept these feelings to himself, but when he was about fifteen years old, he saw his mother watching a preacher on television. When he accused the preacher of espousing anti-Semitic remarks, Byrd's mother told him not to "question a man of God," to which Byrd replied that he did not think the televangelist *was* one.

"She went off," says Byrd. "She grabbed the bottle of Wesson oil then and there, smeared it on my forehead, grabbed my head, and started praying and screaming in tongues." Byrd said the haranguing by his mother went on for about a half hour. "She said if I didn't fly right, she was going to call the deacons and have them perform a full-blown exorcism on me, and she was going to send me to a faith-based mental hospital where they would straighten me out. It was a very serious threat."

Jennifer Gordon, the woman whose parents became extremely strict once they converted to Christian fundamentalism, also underwent exorcisms in her youth. On December 6, 2009, Gordon explained that her church regularly performed exorcisms, during which time people became "emotional and weird." When Gordon was thirteen or fourteen, she was sometimes accused of having a "sassy mouth," and this made her father "afraid that I was filled with the devil." So, on several occasions, Gordon says her father took her to church, where a group of men performed exorcisms on her:

> There would be four to eight of the elders who would start praying and praying, and I was just kind of trapped there. And then, eventually, they'd all be laying hands on me, and the more I squirmed, the more hands, the more praying, the longer it went on with them touching me all over, and 'praying the devil out of me.' And eventually you learned (or I learned) to fake it and say or do whatever it was that would convince them that either the devils were coming out or that I was all good and clean now, because then they would stop and leave me alone. It was terrifying.

Laura Schubert, the teenager who was held down by church members during two exorcisms in her Texas church, has stated that she suffered serious psychological problems as a result of those rituals. According to court documents, Schubert had nightmares and hallucinations, believing that demons were coming into her room at night. She mutilated herself and became depressed and suicidal. Unable to function in everyday life, Schubert dropped out of high school in her senior year and abandoned plans to attend Bible college and pursue missionary work. Mental health experts diagnosed her with post-traumatic stress disorder that they associated with the exorcisms.[72]

A 1995 study calls attention to exorcistic rituals. In examining "religion-related child abuse," the study looked at alleged incidents of abuse told to therapists by their patients, who were children or else adults remembering childhood abuse committed against them or others. In some cases, it was alleged that children had been beaten by perpetrators attempting to rid them of evil. In one case, an "eyeball was plucked out of a youth's head during an exorcism ceremony." The researchers state that psychological abuse was common in the child ridding-of-evil cases.[73]

While we can't believe all alleged cases of ritual abuse, one wonders how many abusive exorcisms are being performed on children behind the closed doors of homes and churches. A YouTube video provides a glimpse of one disturbing exorcism that took place at the Manifested Glory Ministries in Bridgeport, Connecticut. The nine-minute video shows a large group of church members standing around a young man who is about to have his homosexuality "cast out" of him. At one point, a man yells, "You homosexual demon, get up on outta here!" Then the man places his hand firmly on the face of the boy who writhes around. Afterward, the teenager is so exhausted he has to be held up, and then he vomits.[74] According to a news report, the boy was sixteen and one of at least five teenagers who had undergone the same kind of antigay exorcism at the church.[75]

We should also be concerned that children with special needs or behavioral or psychological problems are not getting help because they are mistakenly viewed as being possessed by demons. In these cases, children may be denied access to specialists and instead undergo exorcisms. An example is the aforementioned case of Terrance Cottrell, where a church tried to exorcise the boy of autism, which led to his being suffocated by the pastor.

Parents who frequently spank their children due to beliefs that this treatment can rid a child of evil spirits can cause serious, even deadly, injury. The section on physical abuse described the tragic death of Josef Smith, the eight-year-old boy who died from having been physically abused by his parents. As it turns out, the parents' fear of Josef being possessed by a demon likely played a role in his death.

While it's unclear just how Josef died, witnesses say Josef's parents believed him to be demon possessed. The boy even called himself "Legion," a demon mentioned in the Bible. The boy exhibited erratic and violent behavior, which the parents responded to, not by getting him mental healthcare, but by beating him and isolating him in his room.[76] According to Josef's brother, who testified at their parents' trial, on the day that Josef died, the brother put Josef in a wooden chest as his parents had instructed after the child began "screaming, cursing, and carrying on." The brother said he then kept the chest shut with an extension cord. Ten or fifteen minutes later, after Josef stopped yelling, the family opened the chest to find Josef unconscious. He died a few hours later in a hospital.[77] It is cases like these that lead child advocates to conclude that America no longer needs worry too much about children being ritually abused by devil worshippers. As the researchers of the aforementioned 1995 study on religion-related child abuse conclude, "Our study leads us to believe that there are more children actually being abused in the name of God than in the name of Satan."[78]

CONCLUSION

The satanic panic happened many years ago, yet America is no less fearful of Satan and demons as it was at the height of the panic.

"For a significant minority of Americans, Satan and his henchmen are still very much alive, working double-time spreading misery and menace across the land," writes Michael Cuneo in *American Exorcism*. For these Americans, writes Cuneo, exorcism "isn't just some medieval hand-me-down, or a scream-in-the-dark B-movie contrivance. Rather, it's a spiritual weapon of utmost, life-and-death importance."[79]

Such fears are blinding, as America's pious refuse to admit that child ritual abuses are being committed by members of their own faith. FBI agent Kenneth Lanning addresses this blindness in the 1989 article he wrote for *Police Chief* magazine. A quote from that article appears in Carl Sagan's *The Demon-Haunted World*: "Christianity may be good and Satanism evil. Under the Constitution, however, both are neutral." Lanning adds, "The fact is that far more crime and child abuse has been committed by zealots in the name of God, Jesus and Mohammed than has ever been committed in the name of Satan. Many people don't like that statement, but few argue with it."[80]

Unlike what happened during the satanic panic decades ago, where fears of evil spirits led people to demonize individuals by falsely accusing them of abusing children, today's satanic panic poses a different kind of problem altogether: the refusal to believe that child ritual abuse exists. Such blindness caused problems for Don Wall, the assistant district attorney of Tangipahoa Parish, Louisiana. On August 28, 2009, Wall explained that he had discovered that members of the small Hosanna Church had sexually abused several children. As in the McMartin School case, Wall lacked forensic evidence, but he had other solid proof that the crimes had taken place. For instance, the pastor of the church had kept a journal detailing acts of ritual sexual abuse. And also, unlike the McMartin case, social workers and therapists used appropriate interviewing techniques with the child victims, and videotapes of those interviews were shown to the jury.

Wall says he was careful to downplay the ritualistic aspect of the case because he worried that others would assume the case was weak, given its similarity to those that had taken place in the 1980s. "I had McMartin thrown in my face a lot during all this," Wall told the media, as defense attorneys kept comparing his case to that one in the press. Naysayers said the allegations were nothing more than "a hysterical reaction" and that the ideas of sexual abuse were planted in the children's minds. Still, Wall was successful in convicting the defendants. "Worshipping the devil is not illegal. Child molestation is. That's what I focused on," said Wall.[81]

As in any abuse case, we should be careful about alleging that anyone has abused a child. However, it would also be irresponsible to assume that ritual abuse never happens because of false allegations having occurred in the past. Considering how many exorcisms are done in this country, we should assess whether these rituals involve children and if they are ever physically or emotionally harmful. We must also accept the fact that anyone is capable of child ritual abuse—whether he or she worships the devil or God.

Chapter 21

IS MALE OR FEMALE CIRCUMCISION RELIGIOUS CHILD MALTREATMENT?

It took me a while to decide whether to include a chapter on circumcision in this book for a number of reasons. My thinking was, one, male and female circumcision are often performed for cultural, rather than religious, reasons. Two, female genital cutting—also known as female genital mutilation—is illegal and is rarely performed in the United States. And three, a majority of Americans circumcise their male babies. Given its popularity, it can't be abusive, can it?

Then I did some research, and what I found shocked me.

Regarding the first point, while parents circumcise their sons and daughters for many reasons, religion can be a big factor. Second, many girls in the United States are at risk for being genitally cut, as they come from immigrant families who intend to take their daughters to their homeland to have the procedure done. Third, while male circumcision has some health benefits, it carries serious risk, even the risk of death.

There is one other reason that led me to write this chapter, and it is based on information that I still find hard to believe. Initially, I, like most Americans, thought that female genital cutting was, and has always been, virtually nonexistent in America—that it is a custom followed only in other countries. I was wrong. As it turns out, for a number of decades in the nineteenth and twentieth centuries, doctors in this country performed clitoridectomies—surgeries that involve the excising of the clitoris—on girls and women. What's more, there were religious influences that compelled physicians and parents to have girls undergo circumcision, and these influences were neither Muslim nor Jewish. They were Christian.

But my main reason for wanting to cover male and female circumcision is this: For whatever reasons, cultures around the world—including ours—have been cutting off parts of children's genitalia for a very, very long time. Furthermore, while the procedures are justified in a myriad of ways, most people do it for no other reason than that it is customary. Despite where one stands on the issue of genital cutting, the fact is, all medical procedures carry risk. We owe it to the recipients of these procedures—most of whom have no say in the matter whatsoever—to consider those risks carefully and then decide whether circumcision is truly in the best interest of the child.

MALE CIRCUMCISION AND RELIGION

Male circumcision is an age-old practice, one that is mentioned numerous times in the Bible. Joshua 5:2–9, for example, describes a mass circumcision of boys and men that is ordered by God. No one is quite sure how the practice of male genital cutting got started. Various theories suppose that it began as a sacrificial offering to ensure fertility, as a tribal mark, as a rite of passage, as a means of humiliating enemies and slaves, or as a hygienic measure.

According to hospital surveys, more than one million male babies are circumcised in the United States every year—a rate of one every seven seconds.[1] As of 2005, the procedure was the third most common inpatient surgery performed in the United States.[2] At its peak, 80 percent of male newborns were circumcised in hospitals in the early 1970s.[3] Since then, the rate has been gradually, but consistently, declining. Based on government surveys of hospital circumcisions, 55.4 percent of newborns were circumcised in 2007, the most recent statistics available.[4] This is down from 56 percent in 2005.[5] However, the country's overall circumcision rate is higher than that figure shows because statistics include only circumcisions that take place in hospitals soon after birth. Therefore, they do not include traditional Jewish circumcisions and procedures done in doctors' offices. A nationwide survey conducted by the National Health and Nutrition Examination Survey, collecting data from 1994 and 2004, concludes that the overall circumcision rate is 79 percent; of all ethnic/racial groups, the highest percentage of circumcised males were non-Hispanic whites.[6]

There are several different techniques used to circumcise newborns, although all procedures basically do the same thing—stretch out the foreskin and remove all, or nearly all, of it. Circumcisions typically are performed in hospitals, including those requested by Muslims; however, traditional Jewish circumcisions take place in the home, at catering establishments, or in synagogues.[7]

The United States remains the only country to routinely perform the procedure for nonreligious reasons.[8] One survey of new American mothers finds that two major reasons given for having newborns circumcised were hygiene and appearance. Many mothers thought that their sons would be more attractive to future sexual partners if they were circumcised.[9] Others studies show the major factors influencing parental decision making in the United States are the father's circumcision status, opinions of family members and friends, a desire for conformity in their son's appearance, and the belief that the uncircumcised penis is easier to keep clean.[10]

While cultural factors greatly influence parents' decisions to circumcise, religion also plays a big role. In fact, many Jews, Muslims, and, surprisingly, Christians, assume that their faith requires them to remove the foreskin of the penis. However, it's worth questioning this position in the cases of all three faiths.

Beginning with Judaism, the Old Testament implies that circumcision is a requirement for all Jewish males. In Genesis 17:9–14, God tells Abraham that he and his descendants must be circumcised to "keep My covenant." In addition, God orders that all male children be circumcised when they are eight days old; anyone who is not circumcised will be "cut off from his people." The website JewishMohel.com states that "more than any other Jewish ritual, the *Bris Milah* represents Jewish identity" and "is performed as a symbol of our commitment to transmit our values to the next generation." In other words, to become a true Jew, a male must be circumcised.[11]

However, the idea that Jews are required by their faith to have their sons undergo circumcision as it is practiced today is up for debate. Scholars state that the type of circumcision performed in Abraham's time was much more conservative that what is done today. That is, in biblical times, the foreskin was merely snipped at the end. The purpose was to provide a physical mark that identified males as Jewish. However, authoritative rabbis later decided more—and eventually all—foreskin should be removed.[12] As medical research writer James E. Peron writes in a Christian parenting magazine,

> The original biblical circumcision of Abraham's time was a relatively minor ritual circumcision procedure in which only the redundant end of the foreskin extending beyond the tip of the glans was removed. This was called *Milah*. It is from this term that the Jewish Religious Covenant circumcision ritual *Bris Milah* or *Brith Milah* got its name. Following *Milah*, a penis so circumcised would still contain a considerable portion of the foreskin and the penis would have continued to go through its natural development since most of the foreskin would have remained intact.[13]

Because of their understanding of the minor procedure that took place in Abraham's time, some Jews do not believe that they are required to circumcise. Many also find the painful procedure abusive and do not want to inflict it on their sons. In addition, these circumcision opponents maintain that Jewish law considers all boys born to Jewish mothers to be part of the faith, thereby making circumcision unnecessary to fulfill this rite.[14] In keeping with this idea, "alternative mohels" (Jews trained in the practice of circumcision) perform symbolic ceremonies that take the place of circumcision. One such alternative mohel, Moshe Rothenberg, told the *Village Voice* that the first nontraditional *bris* he chose to perform was for his own son. The ceremony involved the washing of the infant's feet with water, "the way Abraham did when he welcomed visitors into his tent."[15]

Male circumcision is also greatly important in Islam. According to the World Health Organization, of the approximately 30 percent of males circumcised worldwide, an estimated two-thirds are Muslim.[16] In Islamic countries, male circumcision is usually performed during adolescence, although in America, Muslims often conform to the American custom of having the procedure done in infancy. Male circumcision is not mentioned in the Qur'an, but it does appear in the collection of sayings by and about Muhammad known as the *hadith*, leading some Muslims to conclude that circumcision is a recommended, if not obligatory, *sunnah*—ritual or activity that is based on how Muhammad lived his life.

But it is a fallacy that all Muslims follow this practice. For example, Muslims in Vietnam conduct a symbolic ceremony on fifteen-year-old boys in which the religious leader simulates the act of circumcision with a wooden knife without touching the skin. There is a small contingent of Muslims who oppose male circumcision, not only because they believe it to be cruel, but also because they feel, like Jewish opponents, that their faith does not require it. These opponents point out that not only is circumcision absent from the Qur'an, but also Islam forbids disfiguring the body. In fact, passages in the religious text speak against altering the human body, which is described as having been designed in its perfect form by God. For example, passage 25:2 in the Qur'an explains that Allah created everything "in exact measure" and "precisely designed everything." Similarly, 64:3 says that Allah "designed you and perfected your design." And 4:119 indicates that "distorting the creation of God" is evil. Finally, while many Muslims assume that passages in the hadith support or mandate male circumcision, opponents question the authenticity of those passages.[17]

The Christian motivations are less formalized and more varied. Some Christians believe that their faith forbids male circumcision.[18] In the fifteenth century, the Roman Catholic Church threatened Christians who practiced it with "loss of eternal salvation,"[19] although the church is neutral on the issue today. On the other hand, some European churches have been transfixed with the idea that Jesus' foreskin has been preserved and carries miraculous powers; a few places of worship all have simultaneously claimed to have had in their possession the "Holy Prepuce."

And yet some Christians assume that their faith *requires* them to circumcise males. That is what Matt Richardson believed when he decided to circumcise his son in Texas in 2000. Richardson, who was raised in the Lone Star State, explained to me on November 5, 2010, "I can't specifically say where, growing up, I picked up [the idea] that circumcision was the right thing to do, but I had a really powerful, deep belief that it was my responsibility to do that for my firstborn son as a Christian. I felt it was my responsibility to God." He says that he has asked other Christians about their viewpoint on circumcision in various churches, and many—congregants and ministers alike—sounded sure that Christians should circumcise their sons.

After Richardson agreed to have his son circumcised, however, he grew to regret that decision. His son suffered numerous complications following the procedure. Also, Richardson later took a closer look at scripture only to realize that numerous passages in the New Testament make it clear that Christians are in no way mandated to circumcise their sons. For example,

- Acts 15:11 states that uncircumcised gentiles shall be saved in the same manner as circumcised Jews "through the grace of the Lord Jesus Christ."
- Romans 2:28–29 says, "For he is not a Jew who is one outwardly, nor is circumcision that which is outward in the flesh; but he is a Jew who is one inwardly; and circumcision is that of the heart, in the Spirit, not in the letter; whose praise is not from men but from God."
- According to 1 Corinthians 7:17–19, those who are called by God and who are not circumcised should not feel compelled to undergo the procedure: "Circumcision is nothing and uncircumcision is nothing, but keeping the commandments of God is what matters."
- Galatians 5:6 says that a man who wants to be in Christ achieves that goal by means of "faith working through love," for "neither circumcision nor uncircumcision avails anything."
- Philippians 3:2–3 warns people to beware of "the mutilation! For we are the circumcision, who worship God in the Spirit."

Richardson says that had he known these passages existed, he would not have opted to have the procedure done, and he says it's important for Christians to gain a better understanding of church doctrine as it relates to circumcision. Richardson notes that many parents of faith are more likely to heed scripture than they are to heed, say, the AAP, which says that circumcision is medically unnecessary. But when it comes to scripture saying that circumcising is *theologically* unnecessary, that is another matter. "God is more important than what some medical association says," Richardson states. "And then to find out that the Bible doesn't actually say you need to do that—you're like, 'Why did we do it to begin with?'"

Richardson adds, "I think if you took the religious aspect out of circumcision, the percentage of people who have the procedure done would fall to the floor."

FEMALE CIRCUMCISION AND RELIGION

Like male circumcision, female genital cutting, too, is a very old practice, which some theorize was originally intended to prevent evil spirits from entering a woman's body.[20] In fact, the hadith contains a passage describing a conversation between Muhammad and a practitioner of female genital cutting. When the woman asks the faith leader if she should continue her profession, Muhammad gives her his approval but with this warning: "If you cut, do not overdo it, because it brings more radiance to the face and it is more pleasant for the husband."[21]

Female circumcision—or, as it is sometimes called, female genital mutilation—persists primarily in some parts of Africa, the Middle East, and Asia. The procedure is most commonly performed on girls between the ages of four and ten, although it can also be performed on infants and just before marriage. It is estimated that between four and five million procedures are performed annually on female infants and children worldwide.[22] The World Health Organization estimates that 100 million to 140 million girls and women worldwide have been victims of female genital mutilation. Parents have their girls cut for a host of reasons. Many see female genital cutting as a necessary part of raising a girl properly, a rite of womanhood, and a way to prepare her for marriage. Some believe it complies with cultural and religious beliefs about female purity and marital fidelity.[23]

The way girls are cut ranges in severity. At the mild end of the spectrum, only the clitoral hood is removed. Sometimes, the clitoris is also excised, along with the labia minora. A particularly controversial method, called *infibulation*, involves removing genital tissue, after which the labia majora are sutured together, leaving a small hole for urine to pass through, and, later, menstrual blood. After that, the girls' legs are tied together for weeks to allow for healing. According to a medical journal article on the procedure, "Infibulation replaces the vulva with an almost solid wall of flesh that joins the thighs from the pubis nearly to the anus, with the exception of a small orifice at the inferior portion of the vulva." The article goes on to note that the physical barrier created by infibulation makes consummation of a marriage "nearly impossible." therefore, "the husband or one of his female relatives will enlarge the vaginal opening with a small knife so that sexual intercourse can take place."[24]

Female genital cutting of minors has been federally banned in the United States since 1996, and at least seventeen states have passed laws making it illegal. The practice is also illegal in a number of other countries. Still, a large number of girls in the United States are at risk of being genitally cut. Those born into families that have emigrated from parts of the world where the practice is common are frequently taken back home to have the procedure done. According to the Population Reference Bureau, nearly 228,000 females in the United States are estimated to be at risk. Of those, more than 62,000 are believed to be younger than eighteen years of age.[25]

While no data is available on the prevalence of female genital cutting in the West, there is evidence that the procedure is performed illegally in the United States. There have been reports of family members taking girls to underground clinics in the United States to have the procedure done.[26] In addition, two individuals have been accused or convicted of carrying out the procedure. In 2006, an Ethiopian immigrant living in Atlanta was convicted of excising his two-year-old daughter's clitoris with a pair of scissors while another adult held her down, although he adamantly claimed to be innocent and accused his ex-wife of performing the procedure.[27] Then in 2010, a woman in La Grange, Georgia, was arrested for surgically removing the clitoris of her one-year-old infant.[28]

The question as to whether female genital cutting is religious is a controversial one. Most countries in which the practice is commonly performed are Islamic, yet many Muslims abhor the practice and insist that it is influenced by cultural, not religious, norms. Muslim opponents of female genital mutilation point out that the practice is not mentioned in the Qur'an and that it is occasionally performed in Christian communities. A number of Islamic countries in the Middle East, in fact, have outlawed female genital cutting.

"When one considers that the practice does not prevail and is much condemned in countries like Saudi Arabia, the center of the Islamic world, it becomes clear that the notion that it is an Islamic practice is a false one," writes

Haseena Lockhat, a child clinical psychologist at England's North Warwickshire Primary Care Trust, in *Female Genital Mutilation: Treating the Tears*.[29]

However, some Muslims believe that the practice is religiously condoned, if not required.[30] Writing for *Middle East Quarterly*, Thomas von der Osten-Sacken and Thomas Uwer state that, "at the village level, those who commit the practice believe it to be religiously mandated. Religion is not only theology but also practice. And the practice is widespread throughout the Middle East."[31] In a 2001 interview with international newspaper the *Independent*, an imam explained, "As far as female genital mutilation is concerned in Islam, it is permissible and not obligatory."[32] Some interpret the hadith's mention of female genital cutting—in which Muhammad permits a practitioner to continue a mild version of circumcision—to mean that, like male circumcision, the procedure is a religiously required sunnah.[33] One website—written by a Muslim woman—states that practitioners should follow Muhammad's command and not cut too severely.[34]

IS FEMALE CIRCUMCISION ABUSIVE?

Most Americans believe that any form of female genital cutting is abusive. Critics say, too, that the severity of abuse mounts when the procedure is done in places where it is illegal, since girls are circumcised in secret, under dismal medical conditions, and without anesthesia, sterilization, or proper medical instruments. The same is true when the procedure is conducted in outlying areas, where, for example, the outer labia might be stitched up with thorns.[35]

According to the World Health Organization, female genital cutting has no health benefits and can lead to such short- and long-term complications as severe pain, hemorrhage, tetanus, sepsis, urine retention, recurrent bladder and urinary tract infections, cysts, infertility, increased risk of childbirth complications and newborn deaths, and painful sexual intercourse. The procedure "involves removing and damaging healthy and normal female genital tissue, and interferes with the natural functions of girls' and women's bodies," states the organization's website.[36] Critics also note that the procedure robs women of sexual sensitivity.

There has been little study done on the psychological effects of female genital cutting. One anthropological paper states that in some cultures, circumcision is seen as "the machinery which liberates the female body from its masculine properties" and, as such, women interviewed see female genital cutting as a "source of empowerment and strength."[37] However, a 2010 study shows deleterious effects. In examining the psychological health of Dutch

African women who had undergone the procedure, the study shows that the women were "stressed, anxious, and aggressive," were more likely to have disagreements with their partners and, in some cases, refused to enter into relationships.[38]

Many believe that the practice of female genital cutting oppresses women and their sexuality. As Brigitte Gabriel notes in *They Must Be Stopped: Why We Must Defeat Radical Islam and How We Can Do It*:

> Young girls have their clitoris removed without anesthesia to eliminate their sexual drive and preserve them for a life of sinlessness and purity. . . . As so much rides on a woman's honor, including the livelihood and community standing of every member of her extended family, the practice is a kind of insurance policy. Female genital mutilation ensures that honor will be preserved because the girl will not have any sexual attraction to boys. It also will ensure that the girl, who is considered a financial burden to the family, will be prime property on the marriage market as a virgin.[39]

Some American doctors have been so concerned about the dangers of girls being cut in foreign countries or in illegal clinics in the United States that they have proposed performing a "ritual nick" on the clitoris. The purpose is to appease families so they will not seek to have girls undergo more severe, dangerous procedures.[40] In 2010, the AAP proposed, "It might be more effective if federal and state laws enabled pediatricians to reach out to families by offering a ritual nick as a possible compromise to avoid greater harm."[41] So far, "ritual nick" efforts have failed to take root, due to legal complications and opposition by human rights groups.

Still, the practice of female genital cutting has many supporters. One website written by a Muslim woman purports that female genital cutting has salutary effects. The writer states that the practice is harmful only when practitioners are not properly trained, use unsterilized instruments, or cut too severely, although she is vague about just how much tissue should be removed. The writer claims that female genital cutting provides such benefits as a reduction of infections "from microbes gathering under the hood of the clitoris" and attacks of herpes and genital ulcers. What's more, the woman believes that female genital cutting helps to improve the sex life of some couples: "Women of hot climates often have a large clitoris which arouses their desires when it rubs against the adjacent clothing. It may even grow to such a size that sexual intercourse is not possible. Therefore, circumcision reduces her desires and their effects in the first case, and makes intercourse possible in the second case." All in all, the site asserts, a properly performed female circumcision "produces health and psychological benefits."[42]

In an online forum in which Singapore women write in asking and answering questions about female genital cutting, one mother pipes up, "It will be very fast & quick! . . . My girl recovers very fast. She gave a quick shriek during the process but after that she's fine."[43]

FEMALE GENITAL CUTTING IN AMERICA: A SECRET HISTORY

Most Americans believe—as I did before I began researching this topic—that female genital cutting is a barbaric and abusive practice promoted and performed by uneducated populations in developing countries. The common belief is that American doctors would never perform the procedure, nor would they be legally permitted to do so.

Then I found out the truth: For quite some time, physicians in this country regularly promoted and sometimes performed clitoridectomies on girls and women. There were a number of factors driving this movement, such as financial gain; however, Christian ideas about female purity also fueled the trend.

The nineteenth century was a time of sexual prudery in America. While men were allowed to possess sexual desire—as it was necessary for procreation—the same was not true for women. "It was unthinkable that any decent woman should derive pleasure from sex," according to an article that examines that time period in the *Journal of the American Medical Association*.[44]

Driven by fanatical religious beliefs about female chastity and fears about sex leading to the breakdown of society, some medical authorities and health reformers forcefully condemned masturbation in adults and children. The problem was, however, that these so-called experts knew very little about medicine. As medical researcher John Duffy writes on the website for the Female Genital Cutting Education and Networking Project, the physicians sought to "compensate for their inability to deal with disease," and so they "increasingly began assuming the role of moral leaders" and seized upon the topic of masturbation. Duffy says that by the second half of the nineteenth century, the subject of masturbation "became one of general concern," one that first "came to public attention through the efforts of a few moralists." However, it became a significant issue when "the medical profession, seeking to bolster its status in society, transformed the moral question of masturbation into a medical condition."[45]

One strident masturbation abolitionist, for example, was Sylvester Graham, a vegetarian dietary reformer, Presbyterian minister, and inventor of the graham cracker, who railed against the medical dangers of masturbation in the 1830s. According to Graham, masturbation could lead to sexual fantasizing, at which point it became a problem of the brain, which then made every organ in the body vulnerable to disease. Meanwhile, Graham asserted, the act of reaching a sexual climax during masturbation would lead to insanity, idiocy, a breakdown of the body, and "a ruined soul."[46]

One prominent physician who was influenced by Graham was John Harvey Kellogg, a breakfast cereal mogul and staunch Seventh-Day Adventist. In his *Plain Facts for Old and Young*, which was published in 1877 and then reissued in 1891, Kellogg colorfully proclaims masturbation to be an "awful sin against nature and against God." He also opines that "this moloch of the species" is so addictive that it could make people "its slave to an almost incredible degree."[47] (Moloch is described in the Bible as a deity worshipped by pagans and reviled by God.) Kellogg does not stop there:

> The sin of self-pollution is one of the vilest, the basest, and the most degrading that a human being can commit. It is worse than beastly. Those who commit it place themselves far below the meanest brute that breathes. The most loathsome reptile, rolling in the slush and slime of its stagnant pool, would not bemean itself thus.[48]

Kellogg was particularly concerned about children masturbating. In speaking about boys developing the habit, Kellogg states, "A boy who is thus guilty ought to be ashamed to look into the eyes of an honest dog."[49]

Like some of his colleagues, Kellogg saw masturbation as the cause of a myriad of physical and mental health problems of boys and men, including clubfoot, spinal disease ("which could be traced to no origin but masturbation"), insanity, "religious insanity" (in which the individual is "conscience-smitten in view of his horrid sins" and, "ruined for both worlds . . . he becomes a hopeless lunatic"),[50] and dwarfism, "like a plant which has a canker-worm eating away at its roots."[51] Girls who masturbated could become afflicted by a host of maladies, including warts on the fingers, uterine disease, menstrual irregularity, sterility, breast reduction, and itchy genitals. Kellogg believed that girls suffered from the same general effects as boys; however, "in females the greatest injury results from the nervous exhaustion which follows the unnatural excitement." Kellogg continues, "Nervous diseases of every variety are developed. . . . Insanity is more frequently developed than in males. Spinal irritation is so frequent a result that a recent surgical author has said that 'spinal irritation in girls and women is, in a majority of cases, due to self-abuse.'" Kellogg also attributed to masturbation among girls the conditions of hysteria, neurological disorders, and epilepsy.[52]

In addition to denigrating masturbation, these authority figures recommended a host of abusive "cures," which included the male genital area being "treated" with blistering agents, mild acid solutions, and leeches, as well as bloodletting and cutting of the foreskin.[53] Kellogg proposed such antimasturbating solutions as bandaging children's genitals, tying their hands, and covering the private area with a cage. In addition, Kellogg notes that circumcision "is almost always successful in small boys" and states that the operation should be performed by a surgeon without using anesthesia, "as the brief pain attending the operation will have a salutary effect upon the mind, especially if it be connected with the idea of punishment."[54]

It's hard to say just when circumcision began to be touted as a remedy for masturbating girls. Nor is it possible to know how many were cut and at what ages. Apparently, the medical community sought to keep the practice of female genital cutting under wraps. In *Women under the Knife: A History of Surgery*, Ann Dally notes that, because the topic ultimately became a source of "deep shame" in medical circles, modern gynecological textbooks do not mention clitoridectomy.[55]

But the clitoridectomy was certainly promoted as an antidote for masturbating females, as well as a cure for insanity, which some doctors believed was caused by masturbation. Dally notes that European physicians first began talking about performing clitoridectomies on women in cases of visible diseases, such as tumors, but, in the second half of the nineteenth century, the clitoridectomy had become, for some doctors, "a common practice and even an ideological crusade."[56] Duffy writes that masturbation in women was seen as an even more grave problem than in men because females in the Victorian era were considered to be "delicate, sensitive, frail, and emotional creatures."[57]

One obstreperous physician who was particularly vocal about the benefits of the clitoridectomy for ending masturbation in females was British doctor Isaac Brown Baker. In 1866, an article appearing in an American medical journal explained how Baker claimed to successfully treat epilepsy and other nervous disorders by excising the clitoris.[58] Dally writes that Baker's theories were discredited in England, after which the doctor went to America, where he "found more sympathetic colleagues." After that, Dally writes, "the operation was part of standard treatment for many years and was done openly and with an air of respectability."[59] By the late 1800s, Dally writes, the clitoridectomy was believed to provide a host of benefits that coincided with religious and cultural ideas about how women should and should not behave. "There was no question of a surgeon operating on a clitoris simply because the woman masturbated or was psychologically disturbed," writes Dally.[60]

Some physicians called for the clitoridectomy to be used on girls. For example, in 1894, Dr. A. J. Bloch of New Orleans, who called masturbation "moral leprosy," describes the case of a fourteen-year-old schoolgirl who was cured of nervousness and pallor after doctors had succeeded in "liberating the clitoris from its adhesions and by lecturing the patient on the dangers of masturbation."[61]

According to John Duffy, Bloch was one of the last physicians to speak disparagingly about masturbation in normal individuals. By the late nineteenth century, "medical studies were beginning to demonstrate that masturbation caused no serious functional disturbances and that the psychological problems involved arose from the social attitude towards the practice rather than the act itself. As these ideas gained medical acceptance during the next thirty years, the subject of masturbation in normal individuals gradually disappeared from medical journals."[62] Ann Dally notes that the medical community began to see female circumcision proponents as strange, fanatical, and cultlike. Also, there were reports of girls and women going insane and committing suicide after being circumcised,[63] thereby debunking the assertion made by circumcision proponents that the procedure was a cure for insanity.

However, there is evidence that the clitoridectomy was both promoted and performed on girls as late as the 1960s and possibly even later. Dally says that information on clitoridectomies appeared in standard American textbooks until 1925. One medical textbook published in 1936 suggests that girls be treated with circumcision as well as the cauterization of the clitoris.[64] Furthermore, a 1951 Christian manual for girls both castigates masturbation and extols the virtues of female circumcision as a cure-all. *On Becoming a Woman*, written by a physician named Harold Shryock, states that masturbation "lowers a young woman's regard for her reproductive organs." Shryock adds that masturbation also makes a girl fatigued and stupid and even leads to immune deficiency. "There is an increased tendency to catch a cold," Shryock asserts. "Evidence of irritation of these tissues is sufficient reason for a young woman to consult a Christian physician. Oftentimes the remedy for this situation consists of a minor surgical operation spoken of as *circumcision*. This operation is not hazardous and is much to be preferred to allowing the condition of irritation to continue."[65] Shockingly, Blue Cross health insurance covered female clitoridectomies until 1977.[66]

Due to a dearth of statistics or any kind of systematic information gathering about female genital cutting performed by doctors in America, we may never know just how many girls in America have undergone clitoridectomies to be cured of masturbation, insanity, and other "ailments." But personal stories told by victims reveal the physical and psychological harm girls and women suffered.

For instance, in a 1997 issue of *Doubletake* magazine, Peter Feibleman describes how his mother's 1916 clitoridectomy psychologically affected her. When Feibleman was a teenager, he found out that his mother had had her clitoris removed when she was five years old to stop her from masturbating. The procedure—which was done at the request of the girl's mother—was performed in a "fashionable" part of Manhattan at the office of a distinguished gynecologist, writes Feibleman. He describes asking his mother if it had really happened: "I remember that day better than most days because it was the first time I'd ever seen my mother cry. She confirmed the mutilation . . . and added that we would not discuss the matter again."[67]

Years later, following two suicide attempts, Feibleman's mother, weakened with emphysema at the age of seventy-four, changed her mind and decided she would tell her son what took place in that gynecologist's office. She explained that she was scared because her parents left her alone with the doctor. She did not remember the procedure itself because she was sedated, but she did remember her governess treating the wound at home while her aunt Edna was present. "She soaked the cotton in iodine, separated my legs, and put the iodine on the raw incision. I don't remember any pain then. . . . All I remember is Edna asking why I was screaming so loud, and Fraulein saying, "Dorothy's been a dirty girl."[68]

Once the wound healed, Feibleman's mother continued to touch herself. "They thought they'd broken me, but they were wrong," she told her son. "The next time they caught me doing it, my bed was exchanged for a bed with bars on the side. . . . They tied my wrists and ankles to the bars at night with leather straps. . . . They put a metal brace between my knees and I slept that way. But I still found ways around them." One morning the girl's mother noticed her flushed face and guessed that she had been masturbating again. After that, her mother threatened to send her to an insane asylum. Six weeks after confiding in her son, Feibleman's mother made a third attempt at suicide and succeeded. "I can't say now that my mother's early mutilation led to her suicide," he writes, "but I do know this; it wounded her, wounded her body, wounded her spirit. She was a beautiful woman who had no belief in herself as a woman, and that lack of belief affected most of her life."[69]

Feibleman adds that he mistakenly believed his mother's case was unique. In investigating the matter, Feibleman spoke with an elderly gynecologist who explained that "the sexual mutilation of American women had been a lucrative industry in the United States from 1867 until at least 1927, and possibly much later—a thriving business few people spoke about afterward."[70]

In her memoir, *The Rape of Innocence*, which explores her experience receiving a severe clitoridectomy in the 1960s, Patricia Robinett remembers her mother frequently yelling at her to stop touching herself. When Robinett was around fifty years old, she figured out through a conversation with her mother and a physical examination by a nurse that she had had her clitoris and clitoral hood and part of her inner labia removed as a child but had forgotten the traumatic experience. In the memoir, Robinett describes how she remembers touching her "good-feeling place" often as a way to comfort herself, a kind of self-protection from her mother's frequent emotional abuse. But after kindergarten, the time she believes the circumcision was performed, "My source of comfort was gone. . . . All I could do was to curl up in my bed and cry. . . . There were no more good feelings. There was no more comfort. No more soothing. No more buffer from life."

Writes Robinett, "They hurt my body, but even worse they broke my spirit, my will to live and my ability to trust and love. I was not tamed—I was broken."[71]

IS MALE CIRCUMCISION ABUSIVE?

Unlike female circumcision, male circumcision is widely accepted in America as a safe procedure and hardly a form of child abuse. Proponents point out that a circumcised penis is easier to keep clean than an uncircumcised one. In addition, they attest that the procedure is often very quick, and, if properly performed, provides a number of health benefits, most of which come into play once recipients of the procedure are of adult age. For example, circumcision protects against the development of balanitis (inflammation of the glans penis) and phimosis and paraphimosis (inability to retract the foreskin, a condition that requires intermittent or chronic bladder catheterization) in elderly men. Uncircumcised males are at a higher risk for developing urinary tract infections, penile cancer, and HIV infection and other sexually transmitted diseases than circumcised males.[72]

Some studies show that circumcision has no substantial effect on sexual function and that circumcised men have more varied sexual activity. A study of American women suggests that they prefer circumcised penises, mainly for reasons of improved hygiene.[73] Furthermore, advocates state that the procedure has a negligible complication rate when properly performed by an experienced physician soon after the child is born. John Harkins, an obstetrician/gynecologist and assistant professor at the University of Texas Southwestern Medical School in Austin, says in the almost twenty years he has been practicing medicine, he has seen instances when a circumcision has been done too early and must be repeated to remove more foreskin. But, other than that, he has never once seen a complication due to circumcision. "It's *extremely* rare," Harkins told me in our November 19, 2010, interview.

The website JewishMohel.com calls circumcision "a wonderful beginning" for a newborn and "a warm and memorable experience, replete with significance and meaning for all those involved."[74]

Plus, having a newborn undergo circumcision saves him from being possibly ostracized for being different from other boys. Harkins says that was why he had his son circumcised: "Locker rooms are very nasty places for adolescents."

So, from the proponents' point of view, the benefits far outweigh the risks. But do they really? While the aforementioned health problems can be serious, most are very rare—even in uncircumcised men—including penile cancer,[75] which can likely be prevented with proper hygiene.[76] The magnitude of risk of urinary tract infection is questionable,[77] and such an infection is also a risk factor of having circumcision performed.[78] Experts point out, too, that behavioral factors are far more important determinants for acquisition of HIV and sexually transmitted diseases than is circumcision.[79]

As it turns out, the medical reasons given for performing male circumcisions are little more than rationalizations. This explains why the AAP and American College of Obstetricians and Gynecologists (ACOG), as well as many other medical associations throughout the world, do not recommend routine male circumcision in newborns.[80] In addition, many states have stopped allowing for Medicaid to cover the costs of routine infant circumcision.[81] According to the College of Physicians and Surgeons of British Columbia, "Routine infant male circumcision performed on a healthy infant is now considered a non-therapeutic and medically unnecessary intervention."[82] "It's not a necessary procedure," says John Harkins. "That, I think, we can all probably agree with."

Furthermore, it is hard to believe that the foreskin is an unnecessary piece of tissue, a mistake of nature. On the contrary, say circumcision opponents, it serves a very important purpose—to protect the delicate penile organ.[83] This function is especially important in newborns, whose foreskin is naturally adhered to the penis. The importance of allowing the penis of a newborn to remain intact goes a long way toward explaining why I have not come across a single scientific study proving that circumcision helps to improve or prolong life in a majority of males or why no medical association recommends that the procedure be routinely performed on newborns.[84]

The procedure of male circumcision becomes even more difficult to justify when one considers the many risks associated with the procedure. While many doctors remain confident that the risks are very rare, studies do not definitively confirm this. In fact, findings are all over the map, with purported complication rates ranging from .02 percent to 55 percent.[85] John Harkins says an ACOG committee opinion from 2001 states that the rate of complications due to circumcision is low; however, the opinion also states that the actual rate is not known.

Meanwhile, the risks can be serious and even life-threatening. They include hemorrhaging, amputation of the glans, acute renal failure, life-threatening sepsis, local infection, surgical trauma, urinary tract infections, bacteremia, and meatal inflammation.[86] One study shows that circumcision causes an ulceration of the urethral opening in 20 to 50 percent of circumcised infants, which can cause discomfort and pain during urination and requires surgery.[87] Meatal stenosis, a restriction of the urinary opening that often causes penile discomfort and pain and can require surgery to correct, is believed to possibly be the most common complication of neonatal circumcision.[88]

While many believe that death due to circumcision is exceedingly rare—a 1982 study estimates that the death rate is 1 in 500,000[89]—a recent study shows that death is, indeed, a factor to be considered. The 2010 study conducted by private researcher Dan Bollinger finds that approximately 1 of every 77 male neonatal deaths are due to circumcision in the United States each year—a total of about 117 deaths, which is more than neonatal deaths due to problems that have gained much greater attention, such as a mother's use of addictive drugs and sudden infant death syndrome in the first month of life. Because circumcision is almost always an elective procedure (aside from medical reasons such as to correct a birth defect or penile injury), circumcision-related deaths generally are avoidable, writes Bollinger.[90] In fact, male babies have died from complications such as hemorrhaging,[91] infections,[92] anesthesia overdose, oxygen deprivation, infection, and a failure to treat complications due to botched circumcisions.[93]

John Harkins vehemently takes issue with Bollinger's findings. "He's playing very fast and loose with his numbers," he says, noting that the 117 death count "sounds awfully high to me." Harkins makes clear that if the death rate is what Bollinger claims—which is about .01 percent or one in ten thousand—circumcision would not be performed. But again, it's impossible to know just what the death rate is, considering there has been so little study devoted to the issue. Also, death certificates only indicate how the body failed—heart failure, for example—rather than what medical procedures or other mishaps might have led to death.

Circumcision opponents see hemorrhaging as a particularly dangerous complication. The advocacy group Doctors Opposing Circumcision states that a blood loss of only 2.3 ounces in a newborn is sufficient to cause shock. The group also notes that life-threatening bleeding can go undetected since such a small amount of blood can easily be concealed in a highly absorbent diaper.[94] Many rabbis subscribe to the belief that they must draw "one drop of blood,"[95] and a minority of rabbis still practice the controversial ritual of sucking the blood, which has led to babies contracting herpes (from which one baby died).[96]

Pain is another issue. There is no question that circumcision, especially when performed without pain relief, is painful, and newborns may perceive pain more intensely than older children or adults. According to a Canadian medical report, unanesthetized circumcision on newborns can bring on such bodily changes as increased heart and respiratory rate, decreased oxygen in skin tissue, skin flushing, vomiting, increased crying, diminished responsiveness to parents, and choking. In addition, these infants have been found to be more sensitive to pain when receiving immunizations during the first six months of life.[97] Finally, there is postoperative pain—healing usually takes ten to fourteen days[98]—and some circumcisions can require follow-up surgeries.

The AAP and other medical organizations recommend that physicians use pain relief during circumcision,[99] yet many physicians and rabbis do not use it. Some claim it isn't necessary, while others believe that the administration of pain relief is itself harmful. John Harkins uses a topical analgesic cream or jelly when he performs circumcisions on newborns and refuses to use a common invasive method, injecting the anesthetic lidocaine hydrochloride into the penis. "I don't know if you've ever had lidocaine injected, but it burns like crazy," says Harkins.

It is debatable whether undergoing male circumcision as an infant leads to psychological problems. One study finds little scientific evidence of the procedure producing adverse effects on psychological or emotional health,[100] while other studies show that infants do retain memory traces of traumatic events.[101] However, there is no question that babies do not enjoy the experience. A patient pamphlet on male circumcision put out by ACOG says that the procedure of male circumcision is quick, but "the baby will cry during and for a short while afterward."[102] Most circumcisions are performed out of a parent's view, a likely reason why the procedure is so popular among parents. Some mothers who have witnessed their sons being cut have reacted with fear, anger, and horror. In one study, a mother even said that the procedure was so horrible to watch, she told the doctor afterward that had she had a gun at the time, she would have killed him.[103]

Finally, contrary to what circumcision proponents say, opponents believe that the procedure greatly affects sexual pleasure.[104] Without the protective foreskin, the sensitive glans of the penile head can become dry, leathery, and less sensitive, while an intact, mobile foreskin provides stimulation during intercourse.[105]

A NEED TO KNOW MORE

Even though it's rare that a girl is circumcised in the United States, opponents of the procedure believe more people should learn about it. Dr. Nawal Nour, director of the African Women's Health Center at Brigham and Women's Hospital in Boston, treats women who have been genitally cut and has expressed concern that, given the fast-growing Muslim population, more and more girls and women from immigrant families will undergo the painful, potentially dangerous procedure in their homeland and return to the United States to live. So Nour believes that medical professionals need a greater knowledge and understanding about how to properly care for and treat such victims.[106]

Is there also a sizable educational gap regarding male circumcision? For many Americans, probably not. John Harkins says a vast majority of parents he sees in private practice have done their due diligence and researched the procedure's pros and cons. "I have never in my experience had somebody be wishy-washy about whether they want a circumcision or not," he notes.

But Matt Richardson, the Christian father who believed his religion mandated that he have his son circumcised, and his wife, Michelle, say they wish they had known more about the procedure when they had it performed on their infant. Prior to arriving at the hospital for their son's birth, the couple had not agreed as to whether they would circumcise, and they were faced with making the decision at a bad time. It was late at night when Michelle Richardson gave birth. The two were exhausted, and she was on painkillers. So when a pediatrician came in to do an exam on their son, neither were in any kind of shape to make a well-thought-out decision.

Matt Richardson—who, at the time, believed his religion required him to have his son circumcised—remembers, "The first words from the pediatrician were, 'Have you decided to have your son circumcised?' And I looked at my wife and looked at the pediatrician and said, 'OK.'" The Richardsons say the pediatrician failed to tell them about the procedure's risks, about the different types of techniques that can be used, or that pain relief was an option. Matt Richardson says he remembers signing a consent form, but when he tried to get a copy of it years later, the hospital said there was no record of it.

Michelle Richardson believes her son was given no pain relief. As she told me on November 6, 2010, analgesic treatment is not in the medical records. Also, when she was handed her son after he underwent the circumcision, his body was swollen and purple from hypoxia, a condition in which the body is robbed of oxygen, caused in this case, Michelle Richardson says, from her son's continued crying. After being circumcised, "he was just a totally different person when he came to me. He was screaming when he came to me." Michelle

Richardson says she was then horrified when the pediatrician showed her the infant's penis, which was "raw and bloody. I didn't expect it. Right then, my heart sank, and I knew at that moment that I had made a huge, grave mistake."

In the days after the circumcision, the boy's pain continued when he urinated on the wound. His penis was buried inside his body, a condition his pediatrician said was not unusual; however, when the organ emerged three years later, the child was diagnosed with meatal stenosis, which means that his urine stream was deflected so that it shot up instead of down into the toilet, and this condition required the boy to undergo surgery at the age of four. And there was another problem. As was confirmed by the boy's pediatrician, the doctor who performed the circumcision removed an inordinate amount of foreskin, causing the Richardsons' son great discomfort and pain. "He would have screaming spells because he didn't have enough skin to accommodate the growth," says his mother. "He would pull his penis and scream, begging for the pain to stop."

Michelle Richardson says she blames herself "for not being educated, knowing what I was supposed to know. It seems like it's the responsibility of the parent to know this, but then we're not given any information."

Other circumcision opponents say there is a lot that both parents and physicians do not understand about male circumcision. Take, for example, the value and ease of good hygiene. Although a great many Americans choose to circumcise male newborns because they believe the uncircumcised penis is difficult to keep clean, ACOG contradicts this position. As the organization notes in its perinatal guidelines, "The uncircumcised penis is easy to keep clean. . . . Gentle washing of the genital area while bathing is sufficient for normal hygiene."[107] Due to a dearth of knowledge about hygiene and how it relates to circumcision rates, in 1996, the Canadian Paediatric Society expressed "an urgent need" for appropriate studies on the effectiveness of simple hygienic interventions among circumcised and uncircumcised boys and men.[108]

According to the Canadian Children's Rights Council, "A program of education leading to continuing good personal hygiene would offer all the advantages of routine circumcision without the attendant surgical risk. Therefore, circumcision of the male neonate cannot be considered an essential component of adequate total healthcare."[109]

Michelle Richardson believes that parents who are expecting a boy or do not wish to know ahead of time the sex of their baby should be taught about the risks of circumcision and other issues, including postoperative care, before they get to the hospital. An ideal time, she says, would be during prenatal visits and childbirth education classes. In addition, Michelle Richardson would prefer that hospital staff stop routinely asking parents if they wish to circumcise.

Ignorance on the part of the American public regarding foreskin care and the risks of circumcision bodes danger. For example, one patient pamphlet put out by ACOG says that it is normal for the infant's foreskin not to be able to be pulled back completely until the child is three to five years old.[110] However, some doctors strongly warn against pulling pack the foreskin in young boys because it can lead to injury. Instead, these physicians advise gentle cleaning and note that the foreskin usually does not become fully retractable until puberty.[111]

Some doctors have erroneously told parents that circumcision is necessary.[112] While the AAP believes parents should not be coerced by medical professionals to have the procedure done,[113] sometimes even if doctors and parents decide together to have a child circumcised, the decision leads to unnecessary tragedy. Such was the case in October 2010, when a doctor and mother agreed that her baby would be circumcised, despite the fact that he was recovering from surgery. According to the mother's blog, the baby began bleeding uncontrollably immediately after the circumcision was performed and died.*

Dan Bollinger is particularly concerned about Americans' ignorance of the fact that death is a possible risk of circumcision. "A survey of ten popular infant-care books found that none warn that circumcision could result in a baby's death," he writes. "Most websites and literature on circumcision also minimize or ignore the risk of death, and no contemporary study has attempted to learn the magnitude of this problem."[114] In fact, as of November 2010, statements and publications put out by the AAP[115] and ACOG[116] fail to mention death as a possible, if rare, risk.

Some doctors feel it's important to discuss with patients the pros and cons of male circumcision, but it's hard to know how often this occurs. A 2009 survey of AAP members shows that only 66 percent of pediatricians interviewed (not all of them had performed circumcisions) reported discussing the pros and cons of circumcision with all or most parents of healthy newborn males, a number that is down from 1997, when 74 percent reported having had this conversation.[117] One reason these discussions do not take place is that many parents have already made up their minds about whether to circumcise, but another reason has to do with when the procedure is performed. Most circumcisions are done in the hospital soon after the baby is born. As was seen in the case of the Richardsons, this is not an ideal time for parents to make such an important decision.

Doug Diekema, a pediatrician at Seattle Children's Hospital and a member of the AAP's Task Force on Circumcision, says most pediatricians try to have "a fairly extensive" conversation about the pros and cons of circumcision. However, as he told me on November 10, 2010, many circumcisions are done on newborns in the first days of life. In referring to the 2009

AAP survey, Diekema says he does not know why fewer pediatricians overall are discussing circumcision with parents, but the findings give him pause. "The survey makes it look like one-third of physicians are not talking about it. The conversation shouldn't be just a routine question, 'Would you like a circumcision, yes or no?'"

What to do? One solution, suggests Diekema, is to have the initial conversation in the hospital but allow for a waiting period. Then, after the parents come home from the hospital, those who decide to circumcise can make the appointment to have the procedure done in a doctor's office. "That would be more in keeping with the spirit of informed consent," says Diekema. "The decision should be thoughtful and not unduly mandated or coercive." This idea has been proposed in Florida, where advocates are seeking to ban unnecessary hospital circumcisions. The push came after a hospital mistakenly circumcised a baby against the mother's wishes.[118]

ARE WE HYPOCRITICAL?

Few can argue that routine female genital cutting is not abusive. The same should be said of male genital cutting. Just as with its female counterpart, the rationales given by advocates of male circumcision do not stack up against the many risks, and religious justifications are legalistic and exploitive. Some men feel wronged by having been circumcised. As one circumcised man in his fifties wrote to me in an e-mail, "I don't know what kind of an effect it has had because I don't have a foreskin." Nevertheless, he writes, "It is someone else's body. The decision should be made, and can be made, by the adult who lives in that body."[119]

Given what we know about the dangers of male circumcision, one wonders why Americans tend to be so accepting of the procedure. Many castigate all forms of female genital cutting, while the mildest form of that procedure—where only the hood of the clitoris (also called the *prepuce*) is removed—is essentially no different from male circumcision. Critics, therefore, see this stance as hypocritical.[120] In fact, while the AAP opposes all forms of female genital cutting, it concedes that "some forms of FGC [female genital cutting] are less extensive than the newborn male circumcision commonly performed in the West."[121]

Michelle Richardson believes that protecting girls from genital cutting but not boys violates the Fourteenth Amendment that guarantees everyone the same protection under the law. As she wrote in an e-mail dated November 11, 2010, "Intact genitals are the birth right of both genders, not just females." The

US federal law banning female genital cutting of minors makes clear that the practice "can be prohibited without abridging the exercise of any rights guaranteed under the first amendment to the Constitution or under any other law."[122] If that's the case, why can't the same be said of male genital cutting?

It is understandable that parents contemplating circumcision worry that their sons, if left intact, will suffer low self-esteem if they look different than other boys. However, as more and more parents are forgoing circumcision for their infant boys, the problem of looking different is on the wane.[123] This might especially be the case in areas with a growing Hispanic population, since that culture tends to circumcise less often than whites. Meanwhile, parents are learning ways to discuss those differences with their children to alleviate such stress. Michelle Richardson is such a parent. After her son suffered his circumcision complications, she left her next two sons intact and talks to all her boys about "embracing our differences."

But it will probably be a long wait until a majority of the country adopts this attitude. Unlike the Richardsons, a majority of Americans appear to embrace conformity, partly due to being unaware of circumcision's risks and the ease of caring for the intact penis. Still, many circumcision opponents hope that the country will soon look upon male circumcision in much the same way they view female circumcision: an unnecessary, potentially dangerous procedure that removes an important part of the body.

Chapter 22

TRAIN UP THE CHURCH AND EVERYBODY ELSE

So far, this book has revealed some of the worst aspects of faith, but, as explained in chapter 1, my purpose is not to disparage all faith. Rather, I have tried to identify certain forms of worship that are potentially harmful to children—forms that thrive and endure in religious authoritarian environments. The good news is that many Americans are working toward reducing religious child maltreatment by raising awareness of these issues. At the forefront of this movement are child advocacy groups, religious leaders, teachers, medical and mental health professionals, researchers, law enforcement personnel, social workers, prosecutors, and the media. In addition, victims of religious child maltreatment have helped the public better understand their suffering through their writings and advocacy.

However, there is still much more we can do. This chapter suggests changes that could be taken up by government officials, lawmakers, secular agencies, parents, and faith communities as a whole.

REPEAL FAITH HEALING-RELATED RELIGIOUS EXEMPTIONS

As was discussed in the section on religious child medical neglect, many states have religious exemption laws that grant some degree of prosecutorial immunity to those who have withheld medical care from children, even in cases where that denial leads to serious illness or death.

These exemptions should be done away with. They were largely put in place not because of overwhelming grassroots support but through the lobbying efforts of the Christian Science Church. And while supporters of such exemptions commonly claim they are needed to protect religious liberty, such a fear is unfounded. No child abuse statute denies anyone the right to pray for a sick child. Those laws simply aim to prevent parents from needlessly allowing a child's health to deteriorate by failing to provide medical treatment. The problem is, these religious exemptions state that, in certain cases, faith healing–believing parents, unlike other parents, do not have to provide that care.

The dangerous aspect of religious exemptions, say critics, is that they *encourage* the pious to forgo calling a doctor or 911 when a child is at risk of getting seriously ill or is close to death. These circumstances make it difficult for social workers to track children who are at risk so they can prevent problems from occurring. These concerns were raised at a 2010 legislative hearing in Wisconsin when that state was considering repealing its exemption. One person who submitted written testimony was Sarah Davis, an attorney, a law professor, and the associate director of the Center for Patient Partnerships at the University of Wisconsin–Madison.

"Wisconsin's religious exemptions tragically mislead parents to believe that they have a legal right to withhold medical care as long as they believe in the power of prayer," writes Davis. Furthermore, she asserts, by not classifying faith healing–related cases in which parents withhold medical care as neglect, the state is encouraging people not to report such cases to child protective services.[1]

Certainly, some religious extremists would continue to adhere to their faith practices even if such exemptions were repealed—some would probably adhere to them more tightly—but it's likely that most mothers and fathers, faced with the likelihood of imprisonment for neglecting their children's health, would rely more on doctors. One person who saw the value in such a deterrent is Russ Briggs. Briggs is a former member of the Followers of Christ, the sect earlier described as one in which members' religious medical neglect has led to great child suffering and death. In 1999, Briggs told the *Oregonian* that he supported repealing that state's religious exemption, not so much to punish neglectful parents, but to prevent the needless suffering. "I'd rather people just say, 'The state has spoken. I better listen,'" said Briggs.[2]

Despite what proponents assert, getting rid of these exemptions does not jeopardize religious liberty; rather, having them in place grants irresponsible parents of faith special privileges if they claim that their decision to withhold medical care from children was motivated by religion. As one prosecutor told *Time* magazine at the time Oregon was considering repealing its exemption, "If you or I had committed the same crime against our own child, we would be looking at twenty-five years in the penitentiary."[3] Repealing these exemptions would level the parental playing field because child maltreatment laws would then treat all parents who neglect their children's medical needs the same—regardless of their religious affiliations.

Keeping these exemptions on the books not only gives special treatment to faith healing–believing parents, it *discriminates against child victims of religious medical neglect.* Since perpetrators in these cases are treated with more leniency than other parents who neglect for nonreligious reasons, repealing these laws would afford all children—including those of devout parents—the right to needed medical care. This call for equality was made clear in a declaration issued by the AAP in 1997, when its committee on bioethics formally opposed religious exemptions:

> The American Academy of Pediatrics (AAP) believes that all children deserve effective medical treatment that is likely to prevent substantial harm or suffering or death. In addition, the AAP advocates that all legal interventions apply equally whenever children are endangered or harmed, without exemptions based on parental religious beliefs.[4]

The many states with religious exemptions are sending this simple yet dangerous message: The lives of children of religious parents are not as valuable and worthy of saving as are the lives of children of nonreligious parents. From the standpoint of a child victim, of course, there is no difference. It is the same suffering. It is the same crime.

As Russ Briggs told the media, "I've said all the way along, it doesn't have to do with the parents being punished, it has to do with saving the children."[5]

REQUIRE CLERGY TO REPORT CHILD ABUSE AND NEGLECT

Reporting suspected and actual cases of child maltreatment to governmental agencies such as child protective services and law enforcement is key to protecting children's safety. Unfortunately, though, the United States is not very good at this. A 1990 study found that only 40 percent of all child maltreatment cases were reported. What's more, the same study showed that only 35 percent of the most serious cases known to professionals who were mandated to report were, in fact, reported or otherwise finding their way into the child protection system. A 2000 study shows that 65 percent of social workers, 53 percent of physicians, and 58 percent of physician assistants were *not* reporting all cases of suspected abuse.[6]

Members of the clergy could do a great deal to increase these numbers by reporting reasonable suspicions of child maltreatment. After all, members of the clergy are often privy to the most intimate of family matters and are, therefore, likely to hear about cases where children are being harmed. But, as we learned in the section on child sexual abuse, clergy, as a professional group, rarely report known or suspicious cases of child abuse, often making the claim that they must protect "privileged communication"—a claim critics say is misunderstood or a red herring. Episcopal priest and pastoral psychotherapist Sarah Rieth is critical of clergy and religious organizations that fail to report actual or suspected abuse cases. As she said in our interview, "We talk about a culture of accountability, and we want accountability for abusers. If institutions are not willing to be held accountable themselves, then it means the domination is more important than protecting and healing these vulnerable children."

If religious institutions continue to fail at reporting abusive clergy to authorities or requiring that their employees do the same, then state mandatory reporting laws should be strengthened so that clergy are kept to the same standards as others who interact with children, such as teachers, doctors, and social workers. As was pointed out earlier, most current laws are inconsistent and vague and carry light penalties. Rewriting these laws so that they explicitly require clergy to report child abuse would be an important step to increasing the number of overall cases that get reported. One 2002 case in Tennessee illustrates how this can happen. There, a pastor reported his youth minister for possession of child pornography. As he told the media, the pastor would have liked to handle the case within the confines of his church, but he also felt he had done the right thing by reporting to outside authorities. In the end, said the pastor, "The law was clear, and it did play a role in our decision."[7]

EXTEND OR ELIMINATE CHILD SEXUAL ABUSE STATUTES OF LIMITATIONS

To prevent crimes of child sexual abuse, it is essential to remove legal barriers that stand in the way of holding perpetrators accountable and giving support to victims. A key way to accomplish these ends is to extend—if not eliminate—statutes of limitations for alleged crimes of child sexual abuse. These laws put a time limit on how long after the alleged crimes occur that they may be prosecuted or litigated.

As it stands now, many victims of child sexual abuse do not see justice done because many statutes of limitations are too short. It can take years—sometimes decades—for child victims of sexual abuse to feel courageous enough to come forward to accuse their abusers. Furthermore, many child victims of abuse block memories of those incidents from their memories, only to recall them years later. While some question the reliability of "recovered memories" (critics say many of these memories are false, that they are brought out in therapy through manipulative tactics), a range of studies contradict that criticism. For example, one study looked at women with previously documented histories of sexual victimization in childhood; nearly 40 percent were unable to remember the abuse. The study concludes that women who were younger at the time they were abused and those who were molested by someone they knew were more likely to have no recall of the abuse.[8]

Some statutes of limitations are unusually short, setting the cutoff of filing criminal charges or lawsuits at just a few years after alleged victims reach the age of majority. In *Justice Denied: What America Must Do to Protect Its Children*, Marci Hamilton asserts that the current system prioritizes the "comfort" of child abusers over child safety.[9] She says current laws have commonly worked against victims because if a legal deadline is not met, "the litigant or prosecutor is out of luck—it's just too late to go to court. The SOLs [statutes of limitations] are arbitrary rules, and they stop prosecution even when survivors have strong and just claims."[10]

This is not an issue that affects only religious institutions, yet some of the strongest lobbying forces to limit statutes of limitations have been religious organizations. Because of their wealth of resources, some religious institutions and groups have been able to defeat many bills that propose to extend or eliminate such statutes. An example is what happened to the Child Victims Act, which has been the New York Assembly's answer to extending its statute of limitations. The bill would extend the statute from five years past majority age to ten years past. That is, instead of the statute expiring when victims reach twenty-three, it would expire when they are twenty-eight. The bill also includes a provision that would allow a one-year window beginning on a particular date following the bill being signed into law, during which time any victim of abuse could come forward and file a legal claim against an abuser, regardless of how far in the past the alleged abuse occurred.

Had the Child Victims Act been made into law in 2008 or earlier, it would have greatly helped Joel Engelman, the twenty-five-year-old man who, as described in the sexual abuse section, accused the principal of his yeshiva of molesting him when he was eight years old. Two years before Engelman and I spoke in 2010, he and his parents had tried to get the school to fire the principal, but, according to Engelman, officials dragged out negotiations until Engelman turned twenty-three years old. At that point, New York's statute of limitations had run out and the school continued to employ Engelman's alleged abuser. Engelman says once he turned twenty-three, school officials bluntly told his family, "There's nothing you can do. If you put up a fight, we're a lot stronger than you. We're this huge institution, so just let it go." Engelman says, "And that was their response: 'We decided that he's [the abuser's] not so harmful. Go fly a kite.'"

The year Engelman and I talked marked the fifth consecutive year in which New York had failed to pass the Child Victims Act. Commenting on the demise of the bill, New York State Catholic Conference communications director Dennis Poust told the *New York Times* that the 9-to-6 vote by the state Senate panel that defeated the bill represented an emerging consensus that longer time limits on legal liability violated the civil rights of the church. "You cannot ask institutions to take responsibility for the failures of a few individuals whose actions took place forty and fifty years ago," said Poust.[11]

The state of Washington is much more accommodating to child victims than New York is. It gives victims three options by which they can sue or press criminal charges against alleged abusers and their employers: within three years of the alleged injurious act; within three years of the time the victim discovered or reasonably should have discovered that the injury or condition was caused by the alleged injurious act; or within three years of the time the victim discovered that the act caused injury.[12] Other states, such as Delaware, Oregon, and Connecticut, provide victims similar latitude.

It is statutes like these that give attorneys like Tim Kosnoff the ability to file lawsuits against religious institutions accused of wrongdoing, as long as they are located in those states. On June 3, 2010, Kosnoff told me that if it weren't for the handful of states that have passed these progressive laws, "we wouldn't know anything about this crisis because what would happen is, people would go to a lawyer, and the lawyer would say, 'I can't help you.' The person would leave, go home disappointed, and nothing more would come of it."

Kosnoff has little sympathy for religious institutions that complain that extending or eliminating statutes of limitations would unfairly penalize alleged abusers and organizations because they would open the floodgates to lawsuits involving decades-old crimes. For one thing, says Kosnoff, victims— not defendants—carry the burden of proof when such cases are litigated. Therefore, victims "are more prejudiced by the passage of time." What's more, says Kosnoff, addressing an imaginary prospective defendant,

> The reason it has taken the person this long to come forward—it is not their fault, it is *your* fault. What you did stigmatized them, shamed them, and led them through a life of denial and repression of this traumatic experience that they couldn't come forward earlier in time. So you should not get the benefit. You, defendant, you, perpetrator, you, enabling religious institution, should not benefit from your own wrongful acts.

SECULAR AGENCIES SHOULD REACH OUT TO RELIGIOUS COMMUNITIES

It is important for local governmental agencies such as law enforcement and child protective services to make inroads with faith communities as a safeguard to protecting children from abuse and neglect. "Building common understanding can only help to improve communication in the future if problems erupt. Reaching out to religious communities, especially those on the fringe, should be deliberate and part and parcel of an ongoing community-based policing model," writes Karel Kurst-Swanger in *Worship and Sin: An Exploration of Religion-Related Crime in the United States.* According to Kurst-Swanger, law enforcement and other secular agencies can bridge communication gaps between those agencies and faith communities by becoming familiar with the belief systems, customs, and rituals of faith groups. In addition, Kurst-Swanger says law enforcement can educate religious communities about the purpose and intent of the law. "It is important that both religious leaders and secular practitioners engage in an open dialogue whenever possible to prevent an escalation of fear and anxiety," she says.[13]

Some public officials faced with the challenges of trying to reduce abuse in closed religious communities have attempted bridge-building efforts. For example, in April 2010, Clackamas County, Oregon, district attorney John Foote sent out 415 letters to individuals and couples who were members of the Followers of Christ, the sect with the high child death rate that is apparently due to religious medical neglect.

"We know that you care deeply about your children and your faith," Foote's letter states. "But we also believe you want to do the right thing and that you want to protect your children from illness and death whenever possible." The letter goes on to say, "As a starting point towards a possible dialogue between members of the church and law enforcement, let me ask the following question. Is there an opportunity for us to agree under what circumstances parents should take their children to a doctor or a hospital for appropriate medical care?"[14]

When I spoke to Foote in September 2010, he said he was trying to send two important messages to the Followers of Christ: "You need to take care of your children. We're more than willing to help you do that. Human services in the county is more than willing to work with you. And that's what we want. But if you don't, we're going to prosecute you, and your life is going to change forever."

After sending the letter, Foote says he did not hear much from members of the group, but about one month before he and I spoke, he received a phone call from a man who only identified himself as a member of the Followers of

Christ who was married and had young children. Then, much to Foote's surprise, the man asked the district attorney for advice on seeking medical care for his children. "I don't believe in what the church is doing. I need you to tell me what I should do," said the man. Foote says he responded by telling the father that he, too, was a parent of young children. "This is what I do," Foote said. "I have developed a relationship with a pediatrician that I trust, and I rely on that pediatrician to tell me how to take care of my kids on a medical side. If I have any questions, I ask the doctor, and I always err on the side of protecting my kids. That's what I do. And that's what I suggest you do." Foote says he has no idea whether the man calling was genuine in his inquiry or a "plant" by the group, but he was glad to have had a positive conversation with a church member.

In the same way, Utah's attorney general, Mark Shurtleff, has reached out to polygamous fundamentalist Mormon clans by offering mental health services. In addition, while Shurtleff has not made efforts toward decriminalizing plural marriage, he has opposed raids on communities, such as the one conducted by Texas law enforcement officials in 2008 on the FLDS community, and he has vowed not to prosecute polygamists for violating antibigamy laws unless he suspects they are guilty of violating other laws, such as those pertaining to child abuse.[15] Shurtleff believes it would be a waste of resources to try to arrest the estimated ten thousand polygamists who live in Utah, and it would result in the destruction of thousands of families.[16] While Shurtleff has been criticized by antipolygamy groups of not being tough enough in following up on child abuse cases within fundamentalist Mormon communities,[17] in 2003, Shurtleff persuaded Utah's legislature to strengthen its law against child bigamy so that a polygamous adult caught taking a spouse who is under eighteen would be charged with a second-degree felony punishable by up to fifteen years in prison, instead of a third-degree felony punishable by up to five years in prison.[18] To encourage these communities to get social services—for instance, many are afraid to get counseling or report child abuse for fear they will be turned in to authorities for practicing polygamy—Shurtleff formed the Safety Net Committee. The group, composed of polygamists, government officials, and social service workers, is charged with opening up communication with closed polygamist societies.

Shurtleff has said trying to communicate more with polygamous groups is the best solution to protect abused children. "We ultimately succeed by getting people to trust us," Shurtleff told the media. "And it's working. We truly do not believe that there has been a child bride marriage in Utah since 2005."[19]

As of August 2010, information from Shurtleff's Safety Net Committee had not led to any prosecutions of child abuse among fundamentalist Mormon groups in Utah, but when I spoke to Safety Net Committee coordinator and psychotherapist Patricia Merkley on September 22, 2010, she said children and others in that population have benefited from the changes Shurtleff put in place. Merkley herself offers counseling services to fundamentalist Mormon families. Now that there is less fear of being arrested for practicing plural marriage, Merkley says more fundamentalist Mormons are asking her to help them deal with stressful problems that particularly affect large, polygamous households, including child abuse.

"It's become fully more of a dialogue, and the isolation of some communities has opened up," says Merkley. One positive change is that more child abuse is being reported. Although she has had to do the reporting in some cases, which sometimes "sets the trust back," Merkley says that most of the time, "the relationship rebounds and the work goes on."

WHAT PARENTS CAN DO

As has been already noted, children are at most risk for religious child maltreatment in religious authoritarian cultures. These cultures are characterized by a strict hierarchical social structure, the promotion of theological or cultural fears, and separatism. Religious authoritarianism harms children by usurping parental autonomy and weakening the parent-child bond. Therefore, it is critical that parents learn to recognize this phenomenon and find more tolerant, compassionate religious communities and places of worship in which to raise their children.

How does a person know if he or she is living in a religious authoritarian community? Often this can be difficult to figure out, especially if parents have themselves grown up in the same culture and know little about how others worship or live. However, there are questions that parents can ask themselves about the norms and behaviors of the community around them. For example:

- Is my faith community theologically exclusive? That is, do religious leaders and other worshippers claim to be the only people who know religious "truth"?
- Does my community fear or hold in contempt those who are not part of our faith?
- Do I feel at ease asking questions, voicing complaints, or expressing feelings of religious doubt to those in authority or others?
- Do I raise my child according to strict guidelines or beliefs held by my faith community?

- Would I be rebuked or treated coldly if I did not follow those norms, including enforcing strict discipline in the home and using physical punishment in ways that make me feel uneasy?
- Do my faith leaders tell us God wants us to spank our kids?
- Are children in my place of worship treated respectfully, even when they misbehave, or are they made to feel shameful?
- If parents or children need help managing their lives, does my place of worship offer suggestions for mental health services or simply tell them to talk to a member of the clergy, pray harder, or undergo an exorcism?

Some questions pertaining to child abuse can be especially revealing. For instance, parents should ask:

- If I were to find out that my child was abused by a member of my faith community, or if I had strong suspicions that such abuse had taken place, would I feel comfortable reporting that abuse to outside authorities, or would I feel obligated to first contact faith leaders and follow their instruction?
- If I did speak to faith leaders first, would they likely advise me to report the allegations to law enforcement or child protective services or to keep the problem within the church?

It is also important to question the power of leadership and the potential abuse of that power. As Keith Wright states in *Religious Abuse*, "No pastor or religious group has the right to speak for God, threatening divine wrath if we fail to answer a call to service. Only we know what burdens we already carry."[20]

So parents should ask:

- How much power does my religious leader hold?
- Do worshippers believe he or she has some sort of God hotline and thus can tell us how God wants us to live our lives?
- Does a religious leader try to scare people into faith?

Sometimes mothers and fathers might find the prospect of leaving their religious community daunting because it often means cutting ties with one's whole social network. In certain communities, moving out can mean giving up one's own powerful status. Episcopal priest and pastoral psychotherapist Sarah Rieth says it's important for adults in these situations to question their own relationship to power and to assess whether that power is being used in ways that benefit or harm others. For example, she says, adults must ask, "How have I abused power? What do I need to do to get that under control? Do I even believe abusing power is wrong?"

Finally, the very theology of one's place of worship is worth scrutinizing: Are we taught that God is a deity to be feared, rather than one who is there to love and protect us? Are we taught that we will suffer terribly if we do not follow certain religious rules or doctrines? Keith Wright, who spoke to me on September 29, 2010, believes the theology that the traditional Christian church teaches is "the root" of religious abuse:

> I think the major thing that needs to change is our understanding of God, that God is not this holy, fearsome, awful being who is constantly checking to see if we're playing by the rules, if we're doing what is pleasing to him. And, of course, the whole idea of God as "him," as a male deity, has to change. That's been destructive not only to children but [also] to women.

Wright, instead, sees God as something more ephemeral, referring to John 4:23, in which Jesus says, "God is Spirit."

He and others feel that believers' perceptions of God greatly affect how they raise their children, as those adults often relate to their children similarly to how they perceive that God relates to them. Therefore, when God is viewed as authoritarian and punitive, parents, too, will rule their households in such a fashion.

"Parents punishing their children for their misdeeds fits comfortably into a view of a god who is also perceived as a parental figure ready to punish sinful adults," writes John Shelby Spong in *The Sins of Scripture*. "It sounds very much as if god has a heavenly woodshed reserved for the physical punishment of god's 'wayward children,' or their designated surrogate."[21]

Boiling this down, critics of religious authoritarianism say that faith communities would be best served if they spent more time emphasizing love rather than fear, since, they feel, it is only through love that people can be truly close to God. An example would be believing in a metaphoric, real-world hell rather than a literal place where apostates are sent in the afterlife. 1 John 4:16 reflects a more compassionate view: "God is love, and he who abides in love abides in God, and God in him."

FAITH COMMUNITIES MAKING A DIFFERENCE

It is not only secular American organizations that are helping to reduce cases of religious child maltreatment and other forms of abuse. Much change is also under way in faith communities, as religious leaders are taking bold steps to raise awareness of child maltreatment issues and much more. For example, in May 2004, the United Methodist Church General Conference issued two resolutions concerning the physical punishment of children. Bucking the teachings of its founder, John Wesley, who believed in the physical punishment of children, the church now encourages members to adopt child disciplinary methods that do not include corporal punishment and calls upon all states to enact laws that prohibit physical punishment in schools and in day and residential childcare facilities.[22]

Another proactive stance was taken by the executive committee of the General Assembly Council of the Presbyterian Church (USA) in 2000 after the church faced allegations that large numbers of children had been abused in one of its missionary camps in the Democratic Republic of the Congo. In response, the church created an independent committee to investigate charges of physical and sexual abuse of children at a boarding school and a hostel in the Congo between 1945 and 1978. Following the release of the hair-raising 173-page report detailing abuses at the Congo facilities, the church complied with the report's recommendations of apologizing to victims and paying for counseling and retreats. The church also set up another independent panel that continues to investigate allegations of abuses in its missionary schools in the Congo and other countries.[23]

Religious leaders in Muslim communities are doing a great deal to learn about domestic violence and educate the people of their faith about such problems. Imams attend training sessions to learn how to help Muslim families struggling with those problems.[24] Therapist and domestic violence educator Salma Abugideiri says her organization, the Peaceful Families Project, talks to Muslim communities about domestic violence and trains social workers, mental health providers, public school administrators, and "anybody who's interested in improving their services to Muslims in their area" toward ending domestic violence.

In 2009, religious leaders in an Orthodox Jewish community in Brooklyn saw a young man's suicide as an opportunity to discuss a topic that had long been kept under wraps: child sexual abuse by rabbis. On November 5, 2009, twenty-four-year-old Motty Borger jumped from a hotel room balcony to his death two days after his wedding ceremony. The day before Borger killed himself, he had revealed to his new bride that he had been molested as a student at a yeshiva. Borger had also discussed the molestation with a friend's father, who told the press that Borger's alleged abuser was a prominent rabbi. That rabbi later went on trial and was charged with seventy-five counts of sexual assault involving three boys.[25]

Rather than keeping quiet about Borger's suicide, prominent Jewish leaders spoke out about how it illustrated an overall failure of Orthodox Jewish communities to meet the psychological needs of child abuse victims. One of those leaders was psychologist and rabbi Asher Lipner. In an article Lipner wrote for the blog the *Un-Orthodox Jew*, he points out that numerous victims of child sexual abuse, unable to cope with the long-term damaging psychological effects, have, like Borger, committed suicide. Lipner adds that the Jewish community needs to do a better job of attending to victims' subtle or obvious cries for help:

> There are simply not enough outlets for survivors to be heard and validated in our community. One survivor became suicidal after his letter to the editor of a frum [Orthodox Jewish] paper describing the anguish of sexual abuse was rejected. A patient of mine who unsuccessfully attempted suicide told me that he felt killing himself was the only way to get heard in our community. I wonder if Motty Borger may have felt the same way.[26]

To further the discussion, Lipner and other Jewish leaders declared the week of October 17, 2010, to be the National Jewish Week for the Prevention of Child Abuse. During that time, synagogues, yeshivas, and Jewish communities from across the country joined Jewish child advocacy and faith organizations to raise awareness of the physical, sexual, and emotional abuse of Jewish children.

Yet the devout can do a great deal more.

Kathryn Goering Reid, who runs a domestic violence shelter in Waco, Texas, explained to me that it's critical to reach out to victims of maltreatment to "break down the denial" of abuse, regardless of how long ago violations took place. To illustrate this point, Reid told me how she once gave a sermon in which she mentioned child abuse. Afterward, an elderly woman came up to her, and, for the first time in the woman's life, divulged that she and many other girls in her small town had been molested by a doctor who gave gynecological exams. "That may be the only time she says anything," says Reid, "but my openness to hear [her story] and then say, 'If you want to talk more about it, I'm strong enough to listen,' is huge."

Sarah Rieth agrees that talking about abuse is paramount. As she pointed out in our interview, abuse victims commonly scope out those who seem safe to talk to about their abuse and who will take them seriously. "If they don't ever hear about the need to protect children from abuse, these people are not going to come forward," says Rieth.

It is time for religious organizations to stop running away from the issue of child maltreatment and confront problems that sit on their doorstep. In my research, I have come up against this aversion to facing the subject time and time again. For example, I asked the publicity department of Joel Braverman High School, a Jewish yeshiva in Flatbush, New York, about a blog that collects stories of former students who describe having been physically abused by the school's former principal, Joel Braverman.[27] I wanted to know if the school would be willing to make a statement about the alleged physical abuse children received from the school's namesake. But my inquiry only was met with an e-mail that said, "We have no pertinent information regarding your topic,"[28] and a follow-up voicemail message was not returned.

Another example concerns Grace Communion International (GCI), a Christian denomination that claims to have forty-seven thousand members worldwide.[29] In 2009, the church changed its name—from the Worldwide Church of God to its current name—as part of a makeover that began by reforming its theology. Around 1995, the church decided that it would abandon what its website calls its "legalistic doctrines, exclusivist teaching, and prophetic speculation" and instead adopt a more tolerant, compassionate belief system centered on the teachings of Jesus Christ. Denominational president Joseph Tkach is quoted on the church's website saying, "We are a church that God radically transformed."[30]

Curious about how this "radical transformation" might be affecting children, I asked a communications officer if the church had an opinion on the matter. I also pointed to one of several websites that collects stories from former members who discuss their abusive childhoods growing up in the church. In response, GCI's communications department forwarded to me an e-mail from a church official who turned down my request for an interview. The official's e-mail stated that his knowledge of the church's earlier years was limited and urged me to be cautious in believing stories told by those who claimed to have been abused as children.[31]

I also asked the communications department of the Church of Jesus Christ of Latter-day Saints if an official would speak to me about possible ways the church could reach out to children who left or were excommunicated from the Fundamentalist Church of Jesus Christ of Latter-day Saints. Former FLDS children who leave the flock as teens or adults have a hard time making it on their own, since they often lack a proper education, have had little or no exposure to the outside world, and need help finding housing and employment. Given how the church frequently proclaims itself to be pro-family, I asked if an official might discuss the possibility of helping these kids, such as by setting up a fund to pay for social services. As in the other scenarios, I received an e-mail saying that church officials declined to participate in an interview.[32]

"We have to ask people of faith to do a lot of things," concludes Kathryn Goering Reid, and that includes spelling out what defines nurturing and caring parenting. "How can we use our knowledge and our research in what we know about children to provide an even better context for children so that they grow into healthy adults?" she asks. While religious leaders must step forward to make their places of worship more child victim–friendly, Reid says, "It's also going to require grassroots work on the part of laypeople who are concerned and have the courage to speak about this. The safety of children is everyone's responsibility."

It is not only victims who will benefit from such efforts. If more religious institutions and congregants engage in discussions about abuse and reach out to victims, faith organizations stand a chance of winning back the public's trust that has been so damaged due to well-publicized child sexual abuse scandals and a failure on the part of religious institutions and places of worship to help victims of abuse. As Keith Wright notes in *Religious Abuse*,

> There are millions of people who long for a relationship with God, but who cannot find that relationship in a church that will not own up to its limitations, its mistakes, its failure to put peace and justice and love ahead of self-interest and success and doctrinal correctness. There are millions of thinking, caring people in the church right now who find it hard to remain in an institution that will not take seriously its own faults and flaws and the abuse that it heaps upon its members.[33]

As of 2008, more than 16 percent of Americans did not affiliate themselves with any religion, and that population is growing faster than any religious group.[34] It's worth questioning whether one of the motivations people have for abandoning their faith is having suffered some degree of religious child maltreatment.

Retired Princeton Theological Seminary pastoral psychology professor Donald Capps warns about this exodus in *The Child's Song*:

> This is not a pleasant subject, especially for those of us who have deep personal attachments to the Christian faith. But we dare not avoid the subject, for the abuse of children in the name of religion may well be the most significant reason for why they leave the faith when they are old enough to do so. We must ask ourselves: Who can blame them? Why should they not abandon the scene of their silent torment?[35]

Chapter 23
ACKNOWLEDGING CHILDREN'S RIGHTS

Research for this book has entailed reading case after case of abuse and neglect, perusing dozens of studies, and talking to experts. Amid all this, two themes have continually run through the background: First, children are incredibly vulnerable to crimes of abuse and neglect; and, second, to better protect them, we must acknowledge that they have human rights. Karel Kurst-Swanger sums up the first message in *Worship and Sin: An Exploration of Religion-Related Crime in the United States*: Children are "particularly vulnerable to theologically based crimes, since their overall well-being is dependent upon their parents or caregivers."[1]

This vulnerability underscores the necessity that we grant children rights—rights that require us to meet children's psychological and emotional needs and respect them as individuals. Wisconsin legislator Terese Berceau raised the issue of children's rights when I spoke with her about faith healing–related child medical neglect. Berceau indicated that there is nothing wrong with parents relying on faith healing instead of doctors where their *own* health is concerned, but it's a different matter when it comes to the health of children: "Every adult has the choice, but children don't have a choice. And should children be subject to suffering and death for the religious choice of their parents?"

The Supreme Court spoke to this injustice some time ago, in 1944, when it concluded in *Prince v. Massachusetts* that children can be harmed due to their parents' religiosity: "Parents may be free to become martyrs themselves. But it does not follow they are free, in identical circumstances, to make martyrs of

316

their children before they have reached the age of full and legal discretion when they can make that choice for themselves."[2]

"We have a constitutional right to die for our religious convictions," said Oregon state senator Peter Courtney when he carried a bill to repeal his state's faith healing–related religious exemption. "We don't have a constitutional right to make our children do so."[3]

According to Sarah Rieth, "Maltreatment is an abuse of power because children depend on adults. They need us to care for them and not use them as objects for our own needs for control, for domination, for a hug, for anything. They're happy to please, and they're taught to respect authority, and all of that and more participates in facilitating the abuse of power." Rieth believes that the Christian church historically has not taken children seriously. Children have no voice, says Rieth, and no credibility with adults: "'They're little.' 'They're not mature.' 'Children make up stories.'" Viewing children as objects and harping on theological ideas about male supremacy and "honor your father and your mother," says Rieth, contribute to churches' failures to uphold children's rights.

Early on, this book discussed the most likely scenario for children to be at risk for religious maltreatment: when they live in religious authoritarian environments. Because these cultures are collectivist and do not highly value individualism, they typically do not support the idea that adults, much less children, are deserving of rights. It is the survival of the community that is most important; children's needs, therefore, take a backseat.

Survivors of religious child maltreatment commonly express how their pious families and communities failed to recognize their rights as individuals and even saw them as property. It is a sentiment that former Jehovah's Witness Nicolas Jacquette expressed when he testified before the French Parliament in 2006: "I . . . have lived the life of a child who was indoctrinated and never asked to be; who had no critical thinking whatsoever on what was transmitted to him or imposed onto him; and who was brought up as a person conditioned to serve the interests of the movement with a language, an education, and a codification system transmitted to me by my parents."[4]

While we typically hear religious organizations make glowing statements about children, such as being "gifts from God," these words ring hollow based on how children are truly viewed and treated.

"I personally rankle when people say, 'Children are the future of the church,'" says Rieth. "No, they're also the present of the church."

It's not that many religious communities dislike children. However, certain religious agendas, such as the need to proselytize, secure religious freedoms, and protect a religion's or faith group's image, can run roughshod over children's rights.

SPREADING THE FAITH

The first motivation stems from the need to strengthen or grow a religious organization or group. This book has mentioned numerous examples of children being unjustly used for this purpose. It has also explained how requiring parents to put in time for a religious organization can leave them insufficient time to properly care for their children's needs. Yet another example is the operation of missionary boarding schools, which are set up in foreign countries so that parents of the students are free to travel about, do charity work for impoverished people, and, simultaneously, convert them. As has been described, there has been widespread abuse in these schools where children are separated from their parents for long periods of time.

A report that details abuses at a New Tribes Mission (NTM) missionary school during the 1980s and 1990s in the West African nation Senegal highlights the way children's rights were trampled by the NTM's own religious agenda. The report concludes that the reason children were housed in the boarding schools was not for their own benefit but because they "were viewed as a hindrance to the work of God."[5]

Similarly, another report on abuses at a missionary school in the Democratic Republic of the Congo operated by the Presbyterian Church (USA), also points to a disregard of children's rights. For instance, the report shows that for about a decade, church officials repeatedly ignored "credible reports" of one missionary's repeated sexual abuses of numerous victims. The report notes that church officials, "rather than pointing to a judgment of intentional or reckless disregard of the interests of children . . . were *ad hoc*, naïve, or insufficiently focused on the welfare of children." Even in cases where officials did conduct investigations, "children did not seem to have been a high priority," the report says.[6]

Evidently, the "work of God" superseded all else, even children's safety.

FEARING A LOSS OF RELIGIOUS FREEDOM

Time and time again, when an issue that pertains to children's rights arises, someone of faith commonly declares that granting children more autonomy poses a threat to religious liberty. This battle cry is often heard in cases of religious child medical neglect, as governmental authorities try to prosecute faith healing–believing parents or remove children from their custody. For example, when Dale and Leilani Neumann, the parents of Kara Neumann, stood trial, they indignantly brandished their presumed right to religious freedom. "I do not regret trusting truly in the Lord for my daughter's health," Leilani Neumann testified.[7] Meanwhile, Dale Neumann held himself up as some sort of religious martyr: "I am guilty of trusting my Lord's wisdom completely. . . . Guilty of asking for heavenly intervention. Guilty of following Jesus Christ when the whole world does not understand. Guilty of obeying my God."[8]

Public officials often repeat the "religious freedom" mantra when children's rights are at stake. One particularly shocking example occurred in 1989, when an unconventional religious group called End Time Ministry decided to settle in Lake City, Florida. The town was wary of this faith healing–zealous sect after hearing that a baby had recently died from an untreated nosebleed. Lake City mayor T. Gerald Witt, however, was incensed that his constituents would not warmly welcome the newcomers. "It may be necessary for some babies to die to maintain our religious freedoms. It may be the price we have to pay. Everything has a price," Witt was quoted saying.[9]

While child advocates frequently laud the Supreme Court's 1944 *Prince v. Massachusetts* decision that prevented a Jehovah's Witness from having a child hand out church pamphlets, not everyone on the court went along with the idea. In his dissention, Justice Frank Murphy holds up Jehovah's Witnesses as controversial and persecuted:

> To them, along with other present-day religious minorities, befalls the burden of testing our devotion to the ideals and constitutional guarantees of religious freedom. We should therefore hesitate before approving the application of a statute that might be used as another instrument of oppression. Religious freedom is too sacred a right to be restricted or prohibited in any degree without convincing proof that a legitimate interest of the state is in grave danger.[10]

Sometimes the call for religious freedom is explained as a need to preserve the integrity of a religious culture. We again can look to the Supreme Court for an example, although it is one in which the court ruled *against* children's rights. In deciding the 1972 case of *Wisconsin v. Yoder*, the justices unanimously ruled that the Old Order Amish and the Conservative Amish Mennonite Church could take teenagers out of school after they had completed the eighth grade. The decision came after those faith groups stated that high school attendance was contrary to the Amish religion and way of life and that they would endanger their own salvation and that of their children by complying with the law pertaining to compulsory education.

In retrospect, it is clear that *Wisconsin* proved helpful to the Amish in keeping many young people in the religious fold. But while failing to receive a high school education may not necessarily harm those who remain living within Amish communities, what does it mean for those who seek a life on the outside? In deciding *Wisconsin*, Justice William O. Douglas ruled with the majority but offered these prescient words in his partial dissent:

> It is the future of the student, not the future of the parents, that is imperiled by today's decision. If a parent keeps his child out of school beyond the grade school, then the child will be forever barred from entry into the new and amazing world of diversity that we have today. The child may decide that that is the preferred course, or he may rebel. It is the student's judgment, not his parents', that is essential if we are to give full meaning to what we have said about the Bill of Rights and of the right of students to be masters of their own destiny. If he is harnessed to the Amish way of life by those in authority over him and if his education is truncated, his entire life may be stunted and deformed. The child, therefore, should be given an opportunity to be heard before the State gives the exemption which we honor today.[11]

Most frustrating is the media's persistent portrayal of these cases as a debate over two opposing values—the rights of parents to practice their faith and the rights of government to determine what is best for children. For instance, as Wisconsin struggled to decide whether to repeal its faith healing–related religious exemption, an Associated Press reporter described the measure as one that "opened a thicket of questions about when government can trump religion."[12]

Must these cases always be about religious rights versus the rights of the state? When is someone going to ask where *children's* rights fit in? Frank Schaeffer, a critic of America's conservative religious movement, rebukes those who claim First Amendment privileges in situations that involve the welfare of children. Writing for the *Huffington Post*, Schaeffer asserts, "Religious freedom means freedom to worship in the church of your choosing and—after you're eighteen—to believe anything you want. Before you're eighteen, society should protect you. Freedom in the hands of fools is becoming a dirty word. It is time to reconnect with reality and real family values, free from abusive religion."[13]

PUTTING ON A GOOD FACE

The need to preserve a religious entity's image often quashes children's rights. This book has detailed numerous instances in which religious institutions, groups, and individuals have hidden abuses for fear of tarnishing the reputation of their religion or sect. Of course, a driving force behind the need to appear blemish-free is often financial, as religious institutions try to avoid expensive lawsuits and keep up membership rolls.

A chorus of critics has castigated religious institutions for their failure to properly address child sexual abuses while those organizations prioritize their own earthly needs.

"Historically, 'spin control' and sealed records have been used to protect the faith community's reputation and to safeguard offenders rather than victims," writes Kibbie Ruth in *Child Maltreatment*.[14]

Understandably, the Catholic Church has been the biggest target of such vitriol.

"It's embarrassingly clear that the [Catholic] Church is less concerned with saving [children's] bodies from rapists than with saving priestly souls from hell and most concerned with saving the long-term reputation of the church itself," said British biologist and renowned atheist Richard Dawkins at a recent protest march against the pope.[15]

In *Abraham on Trial*, Carol Delaney remarks that the church's "glacially slow reaction" in cracking down on clergy-perpetrated child sexual abuse shows that the church's "primary objective was to protect the priests . . . identified with the institution, not the children who were hurt and abused."[16]

Law professor Marci Hamilton expresses a similar sentiment in *God vs. the Gavel*, noting that religious institutions' efforts to keep child sexual abuses secret says a great deal about the priorities of those organizations: "There is no question that they place the good of the organization above the needs of the child or the legitimate demands of society."[17]

THE UNITED NATIONS CONVENTION ON THE RIGHTS OF THE CHILD

For more than twenty years, child advocates have sought to have the United States ratify an international treaty, one that aims to establish rights for children and protect them from harm throughout the world. Ratifying this treaty is important, because it would put front and center the subject of child maltreatment, including that which is of a religious nature. However, this has not taken place, largely due to opposition from conservative groups, including religious organizations and churches.

The United Nations adopted the Convention on the Rights of the Child (CRC) on November 20, 1989, which promised to give minors a full range of human rights. The treaty contains fifty-four articles that adhere to four core principles: nondiscrimination; the best interests of the child; the right to life, survival, and development; and considering the views of the child in decisions which affect them, according to age and maturity.[18] Countries that ratify the treaty commit to protecting and ensuring children's rights. While there is no penalty for countries that fail to meet prescribed goals, they are monitored by an independent body of experts who review member states' self-reports and make recommendations.[19]

Most look upon the CRC as a vehicle to help keep alive the important international discussion on the subject of children's rights while providing the incentive for states to do well, given that their actions are being watched by the international community. The Campaign for US Ratification of the Convention on the Rights of the Child asserts that the CRC has improved children's well-being in countries that have ratified the treaty. For example, the United Kingdom has enacted laws specifying that both parents are jointly responsible for the upbringing of their children, and Romania has amended its penal code to provide more compassionate penalties for juveniles, such as requiring them to perform community service instead of serving prison time.[20]

Remarkably, however, the United States is one of only two UN countries that has not ratified the CRC.* (The other is Somalia, which has no functioning government. However, the Somali Cabinet of Ministers has said it intends to ratify the CRC.)[21] This fact is even more amazing considering that the United States was instrumental in drawing up the document. Under the Reagan administration, officials borrowed concepts from the US Constitution to be included in the CRC. The United States signed the CRC under President Bill Clinton in 1995, expressing the intention that the country would ratify the treaty at a later date, a move that must be approved by Congress.

And that is where things came to a halt. Conservative groups strongly opposed ratification, as did President George W. Bush, based on concerns that ratification would jeopardize America's sovereignty and parental rights. Some of the most vocal opponents have been religious conservatives, such as Senator Jesse Helms of South Carolina, who, in 1995, stated,

> The American people do not need yet another body determining what is in the best interest of US families. And the Senate should not inflict one on them. The UN Convention is incompatible with God-given rights and responsibilities of parents to raise their children. It is grotesque even to imagine handing this important privilege over to UN bureaucrats.[22]

Overall, America's religious community is divided over the issue of ratifying the CRC, with liberal-leaning institutions being in favor of ratification and conservative institutions being against it. Specifically, the United Methodist Church, the Evangelical Lutheran Church in America, the Presbyterian Church (USA), and the African Methodist Episcopal Church support ratification.[23]

On the other hand, in 2000, the Southern Baptist Convention (SBC) formed a resolution on the "threat of New Age globalism," in which the SBC urged the United States not to ratify the CRC, referring to it as one of many UN efforts that represent "assaults on the family."[24] Senator Jim DeMint of South Carolina initiated a resolution to prevent the Senate from voting on ratification. As of August 2010, the resolution had collected thirty cosponsors. DeMint has said that the treaty jeopardizes parental rights and puts in place provisions to protect children that are already contained in US laws. "We don't need an international law that was developed for a third world country," DeMint told the media, although the senator acknowledged that America's social services system has flaws.[25]

Intense opposition has come from the Home School Legal Defense Association (HSLDA), which is run by Michael Farris. A constitutional lawyer and an ordained Baptist minister, Farris has called the CRC "the most dangerous attack on parental rights in the history of the United States." One of the HSLDA's chief concerns is that the treaty will outlaw the spanking of children in the United States, due to provisions that speak to the need for school discipline to be "administered in a manner consistent with the child's human dignity" and the call for children to be protected from "all forms of physical or mental violence." The HSLDA also opposes the treaty's guaranteeing children "freedom of thought, conscience, and religion" for fear that it will "give children the right to object to their parents' religious training and participate in religious services of other cults."[26]

Meg Gardinier, chair of the US Campaign to Ratify the CRC, points out how the United States "led the charge" to create the treaty. She believes opponents are misconstruing what the document aims to do. "We've had people turn the really wonderful intent of the US around and have it mean something that it was never intended to suggest," says Gardinier, who spoke to me on October 26, 2010.

Child advocates rebuke religious conservatives for opposing ratification. In *The Hidden Shame of the Church*, Ron O'Grady states that the CRC "represents a quantum leap from the traditional Jewish and Christian values that we have been teaching for years and which were the basis on which we built Western society." He adds, "Even to speak of children possessing rights is a foreign language for many Christians. The ideal child for many is still 'the one who is seen and not heard.'"[27]

In our interview, Austin Presbyterian Theological Seminary interim dean David Jensen called the US failure to ratify the CRC "an utter blemish" in the eyes of the international community. He asks, "Do we really want to be seen as a place that doesn't believe that children have rights and a voice?"

If the Convention on the Rights of the Child is ever ratified, most likely it will happen when those who are children today are full-grown adults. While President Barack Obama has described America's failure to ratify the CRC as "embarrassing,"[28] as of February 2011, he had not publicly voiced support for the United States to ratify the agreement.

VIEWING CHILDREN IN A DIFFERENT WAY

Society has shown great improvement in how it perceives and treats children. Long ago, it was acceptable to sacrifice children to gods. And yet, we continue to witness another kind of sacrifice in pious households, communities, and institutions: the sacrifice of children's rights. It is high time to turn that mindset around and acknowledge that children are important individuals in our society and deserving of rights.

Supreme Court Justice William Douglas reflected this view in his partial dissent in *Wisconsin v. Yoder*. "Children themselves have constitutionally protectible interests. These children are 'persons' within the meaning of the Bill of Rights."[29]

Some Christian parenting books hold a similar view. For example, in *Grace-Based Parenting*, Tim Kimmel writes,

> I defend the right of children to be different if for no other reason than the fact that they are *children*. They are young. Their hearts stir with an almost miraculous sense of wonder. Their young minds run wild and sometimes perform crazy gauntlets within their imaginations. God made them this way. He chose to put these characteristics on the front side of their life. Obviously, He calls on parents to help them develop the maturity and skills to take on adulthood, but not at the expense of their unique nuances. This is an amazing time of their lives. When we get done leading them through it, the sense of amazement is still supposed to be in place—only more sophisticated.[30]

Another example is *Let the Children Come*, in which pastoral theology professor Bonnie J. Miller-McLemore states that children must be "fully respected as persons, valued as gifts, and viewed as [spiritual] agents." Miller-McLemore believes we will best meet children's needs "when these ideals are boldly proclaimed. This will happen only when religious communities help by upholding these visions."[31]

This respectful understanding of children, taken from a Christian perspective, is eloquently spelled out in the report that calls attention to abuses in the African missionary boarding school run by the Presbyterian Church (USA):

As Christians, we must understand children as inherently valuable members of Christ's community. Jesus highlighted not only their faith and openness, but [also] their vulnerability. This vulnerability puts children at risk, but it also places them close to God; their dependence on God may be what Jesus was trying to get his disciples to see as a model for their own faith. This vulnerability and dependence makes the protection and support of the community of faith even more important.[32]

Islamic leaders have also taken up this cause. In 2006, religious leaders drafted the covenant on the Rights of the Child for the 32nd Islamic Conference of Foreign Ministers in Yemen. Out of this effort emerged a ten-year plan outlining how the conference's fifty-seven Islamic states can better protect children's rights. The covenant speaks to the need to allow children certain freedoms. For example, it says, "Every child capable of forming his/her own personal views . . . shall have the right to express them freely in all matters affecting him/her." In addition, the covenant states that a child "shall not be subject to any restrictions" other than those imposed by law or that are necessary for the protection of public order and health.[33]

Many others advocate for children to be given autonomy in expressions of need and justice. As stated by Robin Grille in *Parenting for a Peaceful World,* "History bears out the prime importance of raising individuals who think for themselves and stand up to authority when it deserves to be challenged. . . . Children need to learn to obey their own instincts for considerate and caring behaviour, and for self-preservation. . . . What we need from our children is not their obedience. We need their *trust.*"[34]

These same lessons are being affirmed by those who choose not to raise their children with faith. In *Parenting beyond Belief,* atheist and educator Dale McGowan stresses the need to raise children so that they think independently, and he states that if his children are encouraged to do so and then "end up coming to conclusions different from my own—well, I'd have to consider the possibility that *I've* gotten it all wrong." Writes McGowan, "Part of our wonderfully complex job as parents is to facilitate that process without controlling it."[35]

"We assume we know all about children. But the ground under foot is constantly shifting. Assumed visions inherited from bygone Christianity and modern science no longer fit," writes Miller-McLemore in *Let the Children Come.* "Reimagining children, I am convinced, will lead to a renewed conception of the care of children as a religious practice."[36] And that practice, Miller-McLemore asserts, is not just the job of parents or mothers but of all Christians.[37] (I don't think Professor Miller-McLemore would mind if I extended that dictum so that it applies to all people.)

It is critical that people of faith recognize children's rights or at least show a willingness to engage in discussion about the concept. If they do not, children will continue to be vulnerable to all kinds of maltreatment. Americans must understand that religious doctrines that cause children to suffer physically or emotionally are of no value to society and that adhering to such interpretations is immoral and irresponsible. In addition to the moral imperative, acknowledging children's rights makes for a progressive and stronger society.

In opposing authoritarian parenting, Carol Delaney notes in *Abraham on Trial* that "breaking the will" of children "seems hardly the foundation for an emergent democracy."[38]

According to Maria Montessori, "Mankind can hope for a solution to its problems, among which the most urgent are those of peace and unity, only by turning its attention and energies to the discovery of the child and the development of the great potentialities of the human personality in the course of its construction."[39]

And, as African leader Nelson Mandela said, "There can be no keener revelation of a society's soul than the way in which it treats its children."[40]

As Kathryn Goering Reid noted in our discussion, no faith community condones child abuse, yet she believes there are still many important questions that the faithful should be asking: "Why do we tolerate it? Why aren't we more proactive about saying it's wrong, even though it's our biblical mandate to do that?" Reid points to numerous passages in the Old Testament and the Qur'an that instruct people to protect society's most vulnerable. She notes that these teachings are deeply embedded in Christianity, Judaism, and Islam, and they represent ideas that "all of us who descended from Abraham share. This is common ground."

People of all faiths, and of none at all, bear responsibility for the welfare of society's youngest members. That responsibility begins with fulfilling children's physical and emotional needs so that they can fully develop into compassionate and loving adults. Through the acknowledgement of children's rights, we can take a big step toward eradicating child maltreatment, including that which is perpetrated in the name of faith.

NOTES

AUTHOR'S NOTES

1. Bette L. Bottoms et al., "Religion-Related Child Physical Abuse: Characteristics and Psychological Outcomes," *Journal of Aggression, Maltreatment, and Trauma* 8, nos. 1–2 (June 2004): 89.

INTRODUCTION

1. Bette L. Bottoms et al., "Religion-Related Child Physical Abuse: Characteristics and Psychological Outcomes," *Journal of Aggression, Maltreatment, and Trauma* 8, nos. 1–2 (June 2004): 110.

CHAPTER 1: WHAT IS RELIGIOUS CHILD MALTREATMENT?

* The study was unable to determine whether these disorders were caused by actual abuse, were already present in patients prior to their alleged abuses, or, perhaps, contributed to patients fabricating false accusations. However, the study also reveals that psychologists reporting their patients' stories overwhelmingly believed the patients (page 101).

1. Stephen Frosh, "Religious Influences on Parenting," in *Handbook of Parenting: Theory and Research for Practice*, ed. Masud Hoghughi and Nicholas Long, 98–109 (Thousand Oaks, CA: Sage, 2004), 105.

2. Linda L. Barnes et al., "Spirituality, Religion, and Pediatrics: Intersecting Worlds of Healing," *Pediatrics* 104, no. 6 (October 2000): 900, http://pediatrics.aap publications.org/cgi/reprint/106/4/S1/899.

3. Ibid., 901.

4. William Shepard Walsh, *Curiosities of Popular Customs and of Rites, Ceremonies, Observances,* . . . (Philadelphia: J. B. Lippincott, 1898), 554.

5. Marcia J. Bunge, ed., *The Child in Christian Thought* (Grand Rapids, MI: William B. Eerdmans, 2001), 3.

6. Bonnie J. Miller-McLemore, *Let the Children Come: Reimagining Childhood from a Christian Perspective* (San Francisco: Jossey-Bass, 2003), xxi.

7. Barnes et al., "Spirituality, Religion, and Pediatrics," 901.

8. Michael D. Langone and Gary Eisenberg, "Children and Cults," in *Recovery from Cults: Help for Victims of Psychological and Spiritual Abuse*, ed. Michael D. Langone (New York: W. W. Norton, 1993), 330.

9. A. Markowitz and D. A. Halperin, "Cults and Children: The Abuse of the Young," *Cultic Studies Journal* 1 (1984): 145.

10. Judith L. Brutz and Bron B. Ingoldsby, "Conflict Resolution in Quaker Families," *Journal of Marriage and Family* 46, no. 1 (February 1984): 21, www.jstor.org/ stable/351859 (accessed October 24, 2010).

11. Bette L. Bottoms et al., "In the Name of God: A Profile of Religion-Related Child Abuse," *Journal of Social Issues* 51, no. 2 (1995): 91–92.

12. Seth M. Asser and Rita Swan, "Child Fatalities from Religion-Motivated Medical Neglect," *Pediatrics* 101, no. 4 (April 1998): 625, http://pediatrics.aap publications.org/cgi/content/full/101/4/625 (accessed December 29, 2008).

13. Darren E. Sherkat and Alfred Darnell, "The Effect of Parents' Fundamentalism on Children's Educational Attainment," *Journal for the Scientific Study of Religion* 38, no. 1 (1999): 28, http://www.wcfia.harvard.edu/sites/default/files/511__sherkat %202.pdf.

14. Shelly Jackson et al., "Predicting Abuse-Prone Parental Attitudes and Discipline Practices in a Nationally Representative Sample," *Child Abuse & Neglect* 23, no. 1 (1999): 16–17, http://www.sciencedirect.com/ (accessed October 24, 2010).

15. Geoffrey Stearns et al., *Final Report of the Independent Committee of Inquiry Presbyterian Church (U.S.A.)* (Louisville, KY: Presbyterian Church USA, September 2002), iv, http://www.pcusa.org/media/uploads/ici/pdfs/ici-report.pdf.

16. Bette L. Bottoms et al., "Religion-Related Child Physical Abuse: Characteristics and Psychological Outcomes," *Journal of Aggression, Maltreatment, and Trauma* 8, nos. 1–2 (June 2004): 106.

17. Rebecca Socolar, Elaine Cabinum-Foeller, and Sara Sinal, "Is Religiosity Associated with Corporal Punishment or Child Abuse?" *Southern Medical Journal* 101 no. 7 (July 2008): 707, http://journals.lww.com/smajournalonline/Fulltext/2008/07000/Is _Religiosity_Associated_with_Corporal_Punishment.22.aspx (accessed October 11, 2010).

18. Center for Effective Discipline, "U.S.: Corporal Punishment and Paddling Statistics by State and Race," Center for Effective Discipline, http://www.stophitting .com/index.php?page=statesbanning (accessed December 4, 2009).

19. US Department of Health & Human Services, *Child Maltreatment 2009* (Washington, DC: Administration for Children and Families, Children's Bureau, 2010), xii, http://www.acf.hhs.gov/programs/cb/pubs/cm09/cm09.pdf.

20. Ibid., xiii.

21. Ibid., 45.

22. Ibid., x.

23. "Childhood Trauma May Increase Risk of Psychotic Experiences—Royal College of Psychiatrists," *Medical News Today*, October 31, 2008, http://www.medical newstoday.com/articles/127673.php (accessed February 27, 2009).

24. Rick Nauert, "Victims of Child Abuse May Have PTSD," *Psych Central*, October 28, 2010, http://psychcentral.com/news/2010/10/28/victims-of-child -abuse-may-have-ptsd/20278.html (accessed October 29, 2010).

25. "Child Abuse—The Hidden Bruises," American Academy of Child & Adolescent Psychiatry, May 2008, http://www.aacap.org/cs/root/facts_for_families/ child_abuse_the_hidden_bruises (accessed October 31, 2009).

26. Phil E. Quinn, *Spare the Rod: Breaking the Cycle of Child Abuse* (Nashville: Abingdon Press, 1988), 59.

27. Cathy Spatz Widom, "Child Abuse, Neglect, and Violent Criminal Behavior," *Criminology* 27, no. 2 (May 1989): 251, http://www.proquest.com/en-US/ (accessed March 17, 2009).

28. Ching-Tung Wang and John Holton, "Total Estimated Cost of Child Abuse and Neglect in the United States," Prevent Child Abuse America, September 2007, http://www.preventchildabuse.org/about_us/media_releases/pcaa_pew_economic _impact_study_final.pdf (accessed March 17, 2009).

29. Quinn, *Spare the Rod*, 156.

30. Christopher G. Ellison and Matt Bradshaw, "Religious Beliefs, Sociopolitical Ideology, and Attitudes toward Corporal Punishment," *Journal of Family Issues* 30, no. 3 (2009): 334, http://online.sagepub.com/ (accessed February 16, 2009).

31. Barnes et al., "Spirituality, Religion, and Pediatrics," 901.

32. Karel Kurst-Swanger, *Worship and Sin: An Exploration of Religion-Related Crime in the United States* (New York: Peter Lang Publishing, 2008), 51–52.

33. Christopher Hitchens, *God Is Not Great: How Religion Poisons Everything* (New York: Twelve Books, 2007), 217–19.

34. Bottoms et al., "Religion-Related Child Physical Abuse,"106.

35. Ibid., 107.

36. Ibid.

37. Bishops' Committees on Women in Society and in the Church and Marriage and Family, "Walk in the Light: A Pastoral Response to Child Sexual Abuse" (statement, NCCB/USCC Administrative Board, 1995), at United States Conference of Catholic Bishops, http://usccb.org/laity/walk.shtml (accessed March 10, 2010).

38. Bottoms et al., "In the Name of God," 98.

39. Donald Capps, *The Child's Song: The Religious Abuse of Children* (Louisville: Westminster John Knox Press, 1995), 37.

40. *The Sewing Circle* (Fort Wayne, IN: Sewing Circle, 2009), 16.

41. Bottoms et al., "Religion-Related Child Physical Abuse,"106.

42. Marci A. Hamilton, *God vs. the Gavel: Religion and the Rule of Law* (New York: Cambridge University Press, 2005), 12.

43. Donald Capps, "Religion and Child Abuse: Perfect Together," *Journal for the Scientific Study of Religion* 31, no. 1 (March 1992): 2, http://www.jstor.org/stable/1386828 (accessed March 17, 2009).

44. Frank Schaeffer, "When Freedom Is a Dirty Word," *Huffington Post*, September 22, 2009, http://www.huffingtonpost.com/frank-schaeffer/when-freedom-is-a-dirty-w_b_294891.html (accessed March 28, 2010).

45. International Humanist and Ethical Union Board, "Religious Abuse of Children" (resolution, IHEU, London, June 20, 1997), http://www.iheu.org/node/2144 (accessed January 24, 2009).

46. Keith Wright, *Religious Abuse: A Pastor Explores the Many Ways Religion Can Hurt as Well as Heal* (Kelowna, BC: Northstone Publishing, 2001), 24.

47. Stephen Fry, "The Catholic Church's Prejudice Is Hypocritical and Arrogant" (Intelligence Squared debate, London, October 9, 2009), video at Intelligence², http://www.intelligencesquared.com/events/catholic-church (accessed October 25, 2010).

48. Prince v. Massachusetts, 321 U.S. 158 (1944), at FindLaw, http://caselaw.lp.findlaw.com/scripts/getcase.pl?court=US&vol=321&invol=158 (accessed March 17, 2009).

CHAPTER 2: A COUNTRY IN DENIAL

1. Keith Wright, *Religious Abuse: A Pastor Explores the Many Ways Religion Can Hurt as Well as Heal* (Kelowna, BC: Northstone Publishing, 2001), 99.

2. Kibbie S. Ruth, "Risk of Abuse in Faith Communities," in *Child Maltreatment: A Clinical Guide and Reference*, 3rd ed., ed. James A. Monteleone and Armand E. Brodeur, 539–55 (St. Louis: G. W. Medical, 2005), 541.

3. Message of Islam Team, "The Prophet's Mercy towards Children," Message of Islam, March 3, 2009, http://english.islammessage.com/articledetails.aspx?articleId=500 (accessed October 11, 2010).

4. Pew Forum on Religion and Public Life, *U.S. Religion Landscape Survey Report* (Washington, DC: Pew Forum Web Publishing and Communications, February 2008), 10, http://religions.pewforum.org/pdf/report-religious-landscape-study-full.pdf.

5. Albert L. Winseman, "Religion 'Very Important' to Most Americans," Gallup, December 20, 2005, http://www.gallup.com/poll/20539/Religion-Very-Important-Most-Americans.aspx (accessed March 17, 2009).

6. Harris Poll, "The Religious and Other Beliefs of Americans," Harris Interactive, November 29, 2007, http://www.harrisinteractive.com/vault/Harris-Interactive-Poll-Research-Religious-Beliefs-2007-11.pdf (accessed March 17, 2009).

7. Frank Newport, "Americans More Likely to Believe in God than Devil," Gallup, June 14, 2007, http://www.gallup.com/poll/27877/Americans-More-Likely-Believe-God-Than-Devil-Heaven-More-Than-Hell.aspx (accessed November 1, 2009).

8. Harris Poll, "Religious and Other Beliefs of Americans."

9. John D. Miller, Eugenie C. Scott, and Shinji Okamoto, "Public Acceptance of Evolution," *Science* 313, no. 8 (August 11, 2006): 765, at *The Richard Dawkins Foundation*, http://richarddawkins.net/articles/706 (accessed October 26, 2010).

10. Linda L. Barnes et al., "Spirituality, Religion, and Pediatrics: Intersecting Worlds of Healing," *Pediatrics* 104, no. 6 (October 2000): 899, http://pediatrics.aap publications.org/cgi/reprint/106/4/S1/899 (accessed October 5, 2010).

11. "Jesus Will Return by 2050, Say 40 Percent of Americans," *Telegraph*, June 22, 2010, http://www.telegraph.co.uk/news/newstopics/religion/7847625/Jesus -will-return-by-2050-say-40pc-of-Americans.html (accessed October 28, 2010).

12. Harris Poll, "Religious and Other Beliefs of Americans."

13. Ruth, "Risk of Abuse in Faith Communities," 544.

14. Carol Christian and Lisa Teachey, "Yates Believed Children Doomed/ Psychiatrist Says Mom Delusional, Fixated on Satan," *Houston Chronicle*, February 23, 2002, http://www.chron.com/CDA/archives/archive.mpl/2002_3520463/yates -believed-children-doomed-psychiatrist-says-m.html (accessed February 23, 2011).

15. Anne Berryman et al., "The Yates Odyssey," *Time*, July 26, 2006, http:// www.time.com/time/magazine/article/0,9171,1001706-1,00.html (accessed October 26, 2010).

16. Ad Hoc Committee for Sexual Abuse of the United States Conference of Catholic Bishops (USCCB), "Charter for the Protection of Children and Young People" (revised charter approved at General Meeting of the United States Conference of Catholic Bishops, Washington, DC, June 2005), in USCCB, *Promise to Protect, Pledge to Heal*, 1–20 (Washington, DC: United States Conference of Catholic Bishops, 2006), 3, http://www.usccb.org/ocyp/charter.pdf.

17. Marci A. Hamilton, *God vs. the Gavel: Religion and the Rule of Law* (New York: Cambridge University Press, 2005), 46–47.

18. Donald Capps, "Religion and Child Abuse: Perfect Together," *Journal for the Scientific Study of Religion* 31, no. 1 (March 1992): 7–8, http://www.jstor.org/ stable/1386828 (accessed March 17, 2009).

19. Etta Angell Wheeler, "The Story of Mary Ellen," American Humane Association, http://www.americanhumane.org/about-us/who-we-are/history/etta-wheeler -account.html (accessed October 9, 2010).

20. S. A. Watkins, "The Mary Ellen Myth: Correcting Child Welfare History," *Social Work* 35, no. 6 (1990): 500–503, at American Humane Association, http:// www.americanhumane.org/about-us/who-we-are/history/mary-ellen.html (accessed October 9, 2010).

21. Phil E. Quinn, *Cry Out! Inside the Terrifying World of an Abused Child* (Nashville: Abingdon Press, 1984), 199.

22. Wright, *Religious Abuse*, 62.

23. Peggy Halsey, *Abuse in the Family: Breaking the Church's Silence*, rev. ed. (New York: General Board of Global Ministries—United Methodist Church, 1990), 8.

24. Ann W. Annis and Rodger R. Rice, "A Survey of Abuse Prevalence in the Christian Reformed Church," *Journal of Religion and Abuse* 3, nos. 3–4 (June 2002): 7, http://search.ebscohost.com/ (accessed October 27, 2010).

25. Karen Terry and Margaret Leland Smith, *The Nature and Scope of the Problem of Sexual Abuse of Minors by Priests and Deacons in the United States, 1950–2002: 2006 Supplementary Report*, report for the United States Conference of Catholic Bishops, March 2006, 1, http://www.usccb.org/ocyp/JohnJayReport.pdf.

26. Rachel Yehuda et al., "History of Past Sexual Abuse in Married Observant Jewish Women," *American Journal of Psychiatry* 164 (November 2007): 1700, http://ajp.psychiatryonline.org/cgi/reprint/164/11/1700 (accessed November 1, 2009).

27. Robert D. McFadden, "Murder Case in Community of Families," *New York Times*, November 13, 1990, http://www.nytimes.com/1990/11/13/nyregion/murder-case-in-community-of-families.html?scp=3&sq=A+mother+was+charged+with+killing+her+8-year-old+son+in+a+case+that+has+highlighted+a+little-known+problem:+child+abuse+in+the+Orthodox+Jewish+community.&st=nyt (accessed September 27, 2010).

28. Sheryl Kornman, "Judge: Autistic's Mom to Serve 10 Years for 'Torture of Her Vulnerable Child,'" *Tucson Citizen*, September 19, 2008, http://tucsoncitizen.com/morgue/2008/09/19/97101-judge-autistic-s-mom-to-serve-10-years-for-torture-of-her-vulnerable-child/ (accessed October 22, 2010).

29. Hamilton, *God vs. the Gavel*, 3.

30. Associated Press, "Elizabeth Smart Tells of Close Call with Detective," CTV News, November 9, 2010, http://www.ctv.ca/CTVNews/World/20101109/elizabeth-smart-kidnapping-trial-101109/ (accessed November 9, 2010).

31. Ruth, "Risk of Abuse in Faith Communities," 540.

32. "Charges Dropped in Gwinnett Exorcism," WSBCTV (Atlanta), June 25, 2009, http://www.wsbtv.com/news/19856729/detail.html (accessed September 21, 2010).

33. Louise Anne Owens, *Train Up the Child: How Children Get Hurt in Churches* (Philadelphia: Xlibris, 2000), 20.

34. Ibid., 29.

CHAPTER 3: WHEN RELIGION BECOMES HARMFUL

* Altemeyer's definition of *fundamentalism* does not refer to its original meaning, going back to the conservative Protestant movement in the early part of the twentieth century. Rather, Altemeyer's psychological tests, which placed subjects on his Religious Fundamentalism Scale, measured people's *attitudes* toward their beliefs rather than the content. Altemeyer defines religious fundamentalism as "the belief that there is one set of religious teachings that clearly contains the fundamental, basic, intrinsic, essential, inerrant truth about humanity and deity; that this essential truth is fundamentally opposed by forces of evil which must be vigorously fought; that this truth must be followed today according to the fundamental, unchangeable practices of the past; and that those who believe and follow these fundamental teachings have a special relationship with the deity" (p. 379).

1. Andrew S. Wilson et al., "Stable Isotope and DNA Evidence for Ritual Sequences in Inca Child Sacrifice," *Proceedings of the National Academy of Sciences in the United States* 104, no. 42 (October 16, 2007): 16458–60, http://www.pnas.org/content/104/42/16456.full.pdf+html.

2. Ibid., 16459.

3. Ibid., 16450.

4. Gordon F. McEwan, *The Incas: New Perspectives* (New York: W. W. Norton, 2008), 107–108.

5. Nori J. Muster, "Authoritarian Culture and Child Abuse in ISKCON," *Cultic Studies Review* 3, no. 1 (2004), at *Surrealist.org*, http://www.surrealist.org/gurukula/articles/affpaper.html (accessed May 19, 2009).

6. Bob Altemeyer, *The Authoritarians* (Winnipeg: University of Manitoba, 2006), 8, http://members.shaw.ca/jeanaltemeyer/drbob/TheAuthoritarians.pdf.

7. Keith Wright, *Religious Abuse: A Pastor Explores the Many Ways Religion Can Hurt as Well as Heal* (Kelowna, BC: Northstone Publishing, 2001), 134.

8. Sarah Vowell, *The Wordy Shipmates* (New York: Penguin, 2008), 77.

9. William J. Bouwsma, *John Calvin: A Sixteenth-Century Portrait* (New York: Oxford University, 1988), 30.

10. Austin Cline, "Disobedience and the Bible," About.com, http://atheism.about.com/od/bibleoldtestament/a/disobedience.htm?nl=1 (accessed March 31, 2010).

11. Jonathan Edwards, "Sinners in the Hands of an Angry God" (sermon, Enfield, CT, July 8, 1741), at Writings of Jonathan Edwards, http://www.jonathan-edwards.org/Sinners.html (accessed December 27, 2009).

12. Got Questions Ministries, "What Does It Mean to Have the Fear of God?" GotQuestions.org, http://www.gotquestions.org/fear-God.html (accessed March 4, 2011).

13. Stephen Frosh, "Religious Influences on Parenting," in *Handbook of Parenting: Theory and Research for Practice*, ed. Masud Hoghughi and Nicholas Long, 98–109 (Thousand Oaks, CA: Sage, 2004), 100–101.

14. Margaret Thaler Singer, *Cults in Our Midst: The Continuing Fight against Their Hidden Menace*, rev. ed. (San Francisco: Jossey-Bass, 2003), 245.

15. Simone A. De Roos, Jurjen Iedema, and Diebren Miedema, "Influence of Maternal Denomination, God Concepts, and Child-Rearing Practices on Young Children's God Concepts," *Journal for the Scientific Study of Religion* 43, no. 4 (December 2004): 520, http://search.ebscohost.com/ (accessed May 19, 2009).

16. Christiane Brusselmans, *A Parents' Guide: Religion for Little Children* (1970; repr., Huntington, IN: Our Sunday Visitor Press, 1977), 15.

17. Benzion Sorotzkin, "The Role of Parents in the Current Crisis of Rebellious Adolescents: Dare We Discuss It? Can We Afford Not To?" Dr. Benzion Sorotzkin, PsyD, May 2005, http://drsorotzkin.com/role_of_parents.html (accessed April 12, 2010).

18. Mike Celizic, "Woman Describes 'Escape' from Polygamy," *Today*, April 8, 2008, http://today.msnbc.msn.com/id/24009286/ (accessed January 16, 2009).

19. Brusselmans, *Parents' Guide*, 15.

20. Robert Altemeyer, *Right-Wing Authoritarianism* (Winnipeg: University of Manitoba, 1981), 9.

21. Robert Altemeyer and Bruce Hunsberger, "Fundamentalism and Authoritarianism," in *Handbook of the Psychology of Religion and Spirituality* (New York: Guilford Press, 2005), 389.

22. Altemeyer, *Right-Wing Authoritarianism*, 21.

23. Tim Reiterman, *Raven: The Untold Story of the Rev. Jim Jones and His People* (New York: Penguin, 1982), 559.

24. Kenneth Wooden, *The Children of Jonestown* (Burr Ridge, IL: McGraw-Hill, 1980), 6.

25. "Jonestown: The Life and Death of People's Temple," *American Experience*, PBS, 2006, program transcript, 21–22, http://www-tc.pbs.org/wgbh/americanexperience/media/uploads/special_features/download_files/jonestown_transcript .pdf.

26. Singer, *Cults in Our Midst*, 243.

27. Ibid., 245.

28. Wooden, *Children of Jonestown*, 11–12.

29. Reiterman, *Raven*, 561.

30. Ibid., 559.

31. Ibid., 561.

32. Jack Hyles, *How to Rear Children* (Hammond, IN: Hyles-Anderson Publications, 1976), 136.

33. Joyce Meyer, "Helping Your Kids Win the Battle in Their Mind," Joyce Meyer Ministries, http://www.joycemeyer.org/NR/rdonlyres/7C7619AD-59DC-4E5D-B9EE-575A84784879/0/HelpingKidsWinBattle.pdf.

34. Jamie Dean, "Fear at Fanda," *World* 25, no. 19 (September 25, 2010), http://www.worldmag.com/articles/17134 (accessed October 14, 2010).

35. Kathryn Joyce, *Quiverfull: Inside the Christian Patriarchy Movement* (Boston: Beacon Press, 2009), 206.

36. Doni Whitsett and Stephen A. Kent, "Cults and Families," *Families in Society* 84, no. 4 (October–December 2003): 495, http://www.cifs.org.au/Families.pdf.

37. Daphne Bramham, "Bountiful Men Implicated in Human Smuggling Scheme to Send Child Brides to United States," *Vancouver Sun*, March 28, 2011, http://www.vancouversun.com/life/Bountiful+implicated+human+smuggling+scheme+send+child+brides+United/4513704/story.html (accessed March 29, 2011).

38. Robin Grille, *Parenting for a Peaceful World* (Sydney, Australia: Longueville Media, 2005), 115.

39. Morrow C. Graham, *They Call Me Mother Graham* (Old Tappan, NJ: Fleming H. Revell, 1977), 27–28.

40. Sarah Braasch, "The Scars of a Religious Upbringing," *Freethought Today* 27, no. 1 (January 2010): 6, at Freedom from Religion Foundation, http://www.ffrf.org/publications/freethought-today/articles/the-scars-of-a-religious-upbringing/ (accessed September 1, 2010).

41. Thaeda Franz, "Power, Patriarchy, and Sexual Abuse in the Christian

Church," *Traumatology* 8, no. 1 (March 2002): 8, PDF at Florida State University, 4, http://www.fsu.edu/~trauma/v8/Church.pdf.

42. *Damned to Heaven*, directed by Thomas Elliot (Los Angeles: Seventh Art Releasing, 2008), at Fresh Produce Media, http://www.freshfilm.com/damnedto heaven/ (accessed October 30, 2010).

43. Hillary McFarland, *Quivering Daughters: Hope and Healing for the Daughters of Patriarchy* (Dallas: Darklight Press, 2010), 19.

44. *Damned to Heaven.*

45. Kelli Kennedy, "Eating Disorders a Problem among Orthodox Jews," *Huffington Post*, December 10, 2010, http://www.huffingtonpost.com/2010/12/10/eating -disorders-a-proble_n_795224.html (accessed December 17, 2010).

46. Daisy, "Steadfast Daughters in a Quivering World; Part 5: Confessions of a Quiverfull Hero," *No Longer Quivering*, December 14, 2010, http://nolongerquivering .com/2010/12/14/quivering-daughters-in-a-steadfast-world-part-5-confessions-of-a -quiverfull-hero/ (accessed February 25, 2011).

47. Deena Guzder, "When Parents Call God Instead of the Doctor," *Time*, February 5, 2009, http://www.time.com/time/nation/article/0,8599,1877352,00.html. (accessed October 1, 2010).

48. David Wedge, "Cult Tied to Cases of Racist Violence, Kid Abuse," *Boston Herald*, October 29, 2005, at Ross Institute Internet Archives for the Study of Destructive Cults, Controversial Groups, and Movements, http://www.rickross.com/ reference/black_israelites/black_israelites1.html (accessed July 4, 2010).

49. Dave Wedge, "More Kids Will Die: Cult Mom Breaks Her Silence," *Boston Herald*, March 4, 2004, at *Religious News Blog*, http://www.religionnewsblog.com/ 6304 (accessed January 16, 2010).

CHAPTER 4: CHILD MALTREATMENT AND THE BIBLE

1. Proclamation No. 5014, "Year of the Bible—1983," February 3, 1983, at First Church of the Internet, http://www.firstchurchoftheinternet.org/studies/reagan.htm (accessed June 19, 2010).

2. Exec. Order No. 6100, "International Year of Bible Reading—1990," February 22, 1990, at First Church of the Internet, http://www.firstchurchoftheinternet.org/ studies/reagan.htm (accessed June 19, 2010).

3. Harris Poll, "The Religious and Other Beliefs of Americans," Harris Interactive, November 29, 2007, http://www.harrisinteractive.com/vault/Harris-Interactive -Poll-Research-Religious-Beliefs-2007-11.pdf (accessed March 17, 2009).

4. Pew Forum on Religion and Public Life, *U.S. Religion Landscape Survey Report* (Washington, DC: Pew Forum Web Publishing and Communications, February 2008), 5, http://religions.pewforum.org/pdf/report-religious-landscape-study-full.pdf.

5. John Shelby Spong, *The Sins of Scripture: Exposing the Bible's Texts of Hate to Reveal the God of Love* (San Francisco: HarperOne, 2005), 4.

6. Ted Hildebrandt, "Proverbs 22:6a: Train Up a Child?" *Grace Theological Journal*

9, no. 1 (1988): 15, at Grace Theological Seminary, http://gts.grace.edu/documents/Hildebrandt-Prov22-6Train-GTJ.pdf.

7. Ron O'Grady, *The Hidden Shame of the Church: Sexual Abuse of Children and the Church* (Geneva, Switzerland: WCC Publications, 2001), 25.

8. Adrian Thatcher, "Theology and Children: Towards a Theology of Child-hood," *Transformation* 23, no. 4 (October, 2006): 195, http://trn.sagepub.com/ (accessed October 31, 2010).

9. Sam Shamoun, "The Holy Bible on the Age of Marriage," Answering Islam: A Christian-Muslim Dialog, http://www.answering-islam.org/Shamoun/marriage_age.htm (accessed October 19, 2009).

10. Got Questions Ministries, "Why Did God Command Abraham to Sacrifice Isaac?" GotQuestions.org, http://www.gotquestions.org/Abraham-Isaac.html (accessed October 19, 2009).

11. Bob Deffinbaugh, "Abraham's Finest Hour," Bible.org, http://bible.org/seriespage/abrahams-finest-hour (assessed October 19, 2009).

12. Carol Delaney, *Abraham on Trial: The Social Legacy of Biblical Myth* (Princeton, NJ: Princeton University Press, 1998), 55–56.

13. Ibid., 66.

14. Ibid., 233.

15. Ibid., 5.

16. Ibid., 39.

PART 1: THE PAIN OF CHASTISEMENT—RELIGIOUS CHILD PHYSICAL ABUSE

* A more detailed definition of corporal punishment is offered by University of Michigan at Ann Arbor professor Elizabeth Gershoff, who defines child corporal punishment as "the use of physical force with the intention of causing the child to experience bodily pain or discomfort so as to correct or punish the child's behavior. This definition includes light physical force, such as a slap on a child's hand, as well as heavier physical force, including hitting children with hard objects such as a wooden spoon or paddle. However, physical punishment does not refer only to hitting children as a form of discipline; it also includes other practices that involve purposefully causing children to experience physical discomfort in order to punish them. Physical punishment thus also includes washing a child's mouth with soap, making a child kneel on sharp or painful objects (e.g., rice, a floor grate), placing hot sauce on a child's tongue, forcing a child to stand or sit in painful positions for long periods of time, and compelling a child to engage in excessive exercise or physical exertion." (*Report on Physical Punishment in the United States: What Research Tells Us about Its Effects on Children* [Columbus, OH: Center for Effective Discipline, 2008], 9, http://www.phoenixchildrens.com/PDFs/principles_and_practices-of_effective_discipline.pdf.)

1. Elizabeth T. Gershoff, *Report on Physical Punishment in the United States: What Research Tells Us about Its Effects on Children* (Columbus, OH: Center for Effective

Discipline, 2008), 17, http://www.phoenixchildrens.com/PDFs/principles_and
_practices-of_effective_discipline.pdf.

2. Ibid.

3. "UNC Study Shows Link between Spanking and Physical Abuse," University of North Carolina School of Medicine, August 9, 2008, http://www.med.unc.edu/www/news/2008-news-archives/august/unc-study-shows-link-between-spanking-and-physical-abuse/ (accessed November 24, 2009).

4. US Department of Health & Human Services, *Child Maltreatment 2009* (Washington, DC: Administration for Children and Families, Children's Bureau, 2010), 126, http://www.acf.hhs.gov/programs/cb/pubs/cm09/cm09.pdf.

5. Child Welfare Information Gateway (CWIG), "What Is Child Abuse and Neglect?" Child Welfare Information Gateway, 2008, http://www.childwelfare.gov/pubs/fact sheets/whatiscan.cfm (accessed October 19, 2009).

6. J. Goldman et al. (Office on Child Abuse and Neglect), "A Coordinated Response to Child Abuse and Neglect: The Foundation for Practice," Child Welfare Information Gateway, 2003, http://www.childwelfare.gov/pubs/usermanuals/foundation/foundationc.cfm (accessed December 3, 2009).

7. CWIG, "What Is Child Abuse and Neglect?"

8. US Department of Health & Human Services, *Child Maltreatment 2009*, 46.

9. Ibid., 66.

10. Gershoff, *Report on Physical Punishment in the United States*, 9.

11. Amber Smith, "One in Five Parents Would Spank in Certain Settings," *HealthDay News*, April 22, 2010, at *U.S. News and World Report Health*, http://health.usnews.com/health-news/family-health/childrens-health/articles/2010/04/22/one-in-five-parents-would-spank-in-certain-settings (accessed March 10, 2010).

12. "US: Corporal Punishment and Paddling Statistics by State and Race," Center for Effective Discipline, 2008, http://www.stophitting.com/index.php?page=states banning (accessed December 4, 2009).

13. Rick Lyman, "In Many Public Schools, the Paddle Is No Relic," *New York Times*, September 30, 2006, http://www.nytimes.com/2006/09/30/education/30punish.html (accessed April 16, 2010).

14. Patricia McBroom, "UC Berkeley Study Finds No Lasting Harm among Adolescents from Moderate Spanking Earlier in Childhood," University of California Berkeley, August 24, 2001, http://www.berkeley.edu/news/media/releases/2001/08/24_spank.html (accessed November 3, 2009).

15. Christopher G. Ellison and Matt Bradshaw, "Religious Beliefs, Sociopolitical Ideology, and Attitudes toward Corporal Punishment," *Journal of Family Issues* 30, no. 3 (2009): 336–37, http://online.sagepub.com/ (accessed February 16, 2009).

16. "Discipline and the Law," Center for Effective Discipline, http://www.stophitting.com/index.php?page=laws-main (accessed April 11, 2011).

17. Gershoff, *Report on Physical Punishment in the United States*, 7.

18. Ibid., 14.

19. Ibid., 15.

20. Ibid., 16.

21. University of New Hampshire Media Relations, "Spanking Kids Increases Risk of Sexual Problems as Adults, New Research Shows," University of New Hampshire, February 28, 2008, http://www.unh.edu/news/cj_nr/2008/feb/lw28spanking.cfm (accessed February 16, 2010).

22. Salynn Boyles, "Kids Who Get Spanked May Have Lower IQs," WebMD, September 24, 2009, http://www.webmd.com/parenting/news/20090924/kids-who-get-spanked-may-have-lower-iqs (accessed February 16, 2010).

23. Joshua Waxman, "Spare the Rod," *Beliefnet*, March 5, 2007, http://blog.beliefnet.com/virtualtalmud/2007/03/spare-rod.html (accessed January 5, 2010).

24. Alice Miller, *For Your Own Good: Hidden Cruelty in Child-Rearing and the Roots of Violence*, 3rd ed. (1980; repr., New York: Farrar, Strauss, and Giroux, 1990), 17.

CHAPTER 5: "THE ROD OF CORRECTION"

1. *Conservapedia*, s.v. "Corporal Punishment," http://www.conservapedia.com/Corporal_punishment (accessed February 16, 2010).

2. Roy Lessin, *Spanking: A Loving Discipline: Helpful and Practical Answers for Today's Parents* (Bloomington, MN: Bethany House, 2002), 23.

3. James G. Dwyer, *Religious Schools v. Children's Rights* (Ithaca, NY: Cornell University Press, 1998), 21.

4. Philip Greven, *Spare the Child: The Religious Roots of Punishment and the Psychological Impact of Physical Abuse* (New York: Vintage, 1992), 6.

5. Larry Kaplan, "Wisdom from the Talmud," in "Materials for the Christian Faith Community," at Center for Effective Discipline, http://www.stophitting.com/pdf/faithMaterial.pdf.

6. Samuel Martin, *Thy Rod and Thy Staff They Comfort Me: Christians and the Spanking Controversy* (Pasadena, CA: Sorensic, 2006), 49.

7. Ibid., 45.

8. Got Questions Ministries, "How Should Christians Discipline Their Children? What Does the Bible Say?" GotQuestions.org, http://www.gotquestions.org/disciplining-children.html (accessed February 17, 2010).

9. J. Richard Fugate, *What the Bible Says about . . . Child Training* (Citrus Heights, CA: Foundation for Biblical Research, 1996), 167.

10. Writing Committee, Governing Body of Jehovah's Witnesses, "The Bible's Viewpoint: The Rod of Discipline—Is It Out-of-Date?" *Awake!*, September 8, 1992, 26–27, from "Watchtower Library 2005" CD, http://www.watchtower.cc/files.html (accessed March 7, 2010).

11. Watchtower Bible and Tract Society of Jehovah's Witnesses, *The Secret of Family Happiness* (New York: Watchtower Bible and Tract Society of New York, 1996), 60, from "Watchtower Library 2005" CD, http://www.watchtower.cc/files.html (accessed March 7, 2010).

12. Lisa Whelchel, *Creative Correction: Extraordinary Ideas for Everyday Discipline* (Carol Stream, IL: Tyndale House, 2005), 179–80.

13. Fugate, *What the Bible Says about . . . Child Training*, 167.

14. Lessin, *Spanking*, 65–66.

15. Child Training Resources, "Our Chastening Instrument," advertisement at *I Speak of Dreams*, March 27, 2006, http://lizditz.typepad.com/i_speak_of_dreams/2006/03/buy_your_child_.html (accessed November 3, 2010).

16. Merrill F. Unger, *Unger's Bible Dictionary*, 19th ed. (Chicago: Moody Publishers, 1973), 931.

17. Randall J. Heskett, "Proverbs 23:13–14," *Interpretation* 55, no. 2 (2001): 181, http://www.questia.com (accessed November 3, 2010).

18. *Conservapedia*, s.v. "Solomon," http://www.conservapedia.com/Solomon (accessed October 15, 2010).

19. Barbara Rogers, "King Solomon: No Expert on Raising a Child," *Screams from Childhood*, January 2006, http://www.screamsfromchildhood.com/solomon.html (accessed March 7, 2010).

20. Mark Twain, *The Adventures of Huckleberry Finn* (1884; repr., Raleigh, NC: Hayes Barton, 2005), 44.

21. Joshua Waxman, "Spare the Rod," *Beliefnet*, March 5, 2007, http://blog.beliefnet.com/virtualtalmud/2007/03/spare-rod.html (accessed January 5, 2010).

22. Greven, *Spare the Child*, 51.

23. Ron Shor, "The Significance of Religion in Advancing a Culturally Sensitive Approach toward Child Maltreatment," *Families in Society* 79, no. 4 (1998): 402.

24. Kibbie S. Ruth, "Risk of Abuse in Faith Communities," in *Child Maltreatment: A Clinical Guide and Reference*, 3rd ed., ed. James A. Monteleone and Armand E. Brodeur, 539–55 (St. Louis: G. W. Medical, 2005), 545.

25. John Shelby Spong, *The Sins of Scripture: Exposing the Bible's Texts of Hate to Reveal the God of Love* (San Francisco: HarperOne, 2005), 146.

26. Lisa Holewa, "Wisconsin Church Members Charged with Abusing Infants," AOL News, March 26, 2011, http://www.aol.com/2011/03/26/members-of-aleitheia-bible-church-in-wisconsin-charged-with-abus/?icid=maing/main5/d12/sec1_lnk1/51942 (accessed March 28, 2011).

CHAPTER 6: AN OBSESSION WITH CHILD OBEDIENCE

1. Craig H. Hart, "Three Essential Parenting Principles," *BYU Magazine*, Spring 2003, http://magazine.byu.edu/?act=view&a=1236 (accessed March 28, 2010).

2. Ibid.

3. Benzion Sorotzkin, "The Role of Parents in the Current Crisis of Rebellious Adolescents," Dr. Benzion Sorotzkin, PsyD, May 2005, http://drsorotzkin.com/role_of_parents.html (accessed March 3, 2010).

4. Robin Grille, *Parenting for a Peaceful World* (Sydney, Australia: Longueville Media, 2005), 52.

5. Philip Greven, *Spare the Child: The Religious Roots of Punishment and the Psychological Impact of Physical Abuse* (New York: Vintage, 1992), 19–20.

6. Roy Lessin, *Spanking: A Loving Discipline: Helpful and Practical Answers for Today's Parents* (Bloomington, MN: Bethany House, 2002), 50.

7. Watchtower Bible and Tract Society of Jehovah's Witnesses, *The Secret of Family Happiness* (New York: Watchtower Bible and Tract Society of New York, 1996), 60, from "Watchtower Library 2005" CD, http://www.watchtower.cc/files.html (accessed March 7, 2010).

8. Writing Committee, Governing Body of Jehovah's Witnesses, "Train Your Child in the Right Way—and Do It from Infancy!" *Awake!*, May 22, 1987, 7–11, from "Watchtower Library 2005" CD, http://www.watchtower.cc/files.html (accessed March 7, 2010).

9. J. Richard Fugate, *What the Bible Says about . . . Child Training* (Citrus Heights, CA: Foundation for Biblical Research, 1996), 39.

10. Ibid., 43.

11. Vanessa L. Malcarne and John D. Burchard, "Investigations of Child Abuse/Neglect Allegations in Religious Cults: A Case Study in Vermont," *Behavioral Sciences & the Law* 10, no. 1 (Winter 1992): 75, http://ebscohost.com/ (accessed February 19, 2010).

12. Twelve Tribes, "Family FAQs: Do You Spank Your Children?" Twelve Tribes: The Commonwealth of Israel, http://www.twelvetribes.com/faq/family.html (accessed November 18, 2009).

13. "Our History," Remnant Fellowship Churches, http://www.remnant fellowship.org/1ABOUTOURCHURCH/OurHistory.aspx (accessed January 9, 2010).

14. "Firm Beliefs: Religious Movement at Center of Child Death Investigation," NewsChannel 5 (Nashville), February 4, 2004, http://www.newschannel5.com/Global/story.asp?S=5412250 (accessed April 1, 2010).

15. Randy Richmond and Jonathan Sher, "'There Has to Be Pain,' Church Says," *Toronto Sun*, July 7, 2001, at Project NoSpank, http://www.nospank.net/n-i11.htm (accessed October 12, 2009).

16. Irwin A. Hyman, *Reading, Writing, and the Hickory Stick: The Appalling Story of Physical and Psychological Abuse in American Schools* (Lanham, MD: Lexington Books, 1990), 40.

17. Robert J. Avrech, "Seraphic School Days or the Sadist of Yeshiva Flatbush," *Seraphic Secret*, June 8, 2005, http://www.seraphicpress.com/archives/2005/06/seraphic_school.php (accessed March 27, 2010).

18. William Coburn, *The Spanking Room* (Enumclaw, WA: WinePress Publishing, 2008), 6.

19. Ibid., 27.

20. Ibid., 2–3.

21. Clifford Ward, "Pastor Gets Supervision in Spanking Case," *Chicago Breaking News Center*, March 18, 2009, http://www.chicagobreakingnews.com/2009/03/pastor-found-guilty-in-spanking-case.html (accessed November 7, 2009).

22. Clifford Ward and John Keilman, "Minister in Spanking Case: Alleged Victim Testifies about Beatings," *Chicago Tribune*, March 18, 2009, http://articles

.chicagotribune.com/2009-03-18/news/0903170566_1_beatings-testifies-alleged (accessed June 20, 2010).

23. Billy Graham, *Just as I Am* (San Francisco: HarperCollins, 1997), 19.

24. Greven, *Spare the Child*, x.

25. Larry Christenson, *The Christian Family* (Minneapolis: Bethany House, 1970), 100.

26. "Firm Beliefs."

27. Maureen O'Donnell, Ana Mendieta, and Annie Sweeney, "Biblical Beating Kills Girl: Cops," *Chicago Sun Times*, November 13, 2001, at Project NoSpank, http://www.nospank.net/n-i65.htm (accessed November 13, 2000).

28. Jeff Coen, "Girl's Brother Testifies Father Fatally Beat Her," *Chicago Tribune*, April 26, 2006, http://pqasb.pqarchiver.com/chicagotribune/advancedsearch.html (accessed March 1, 2010).

29. Associated Press, "50 Years for Head of Maryland Cult Convicted in Child's Starving Death," *Washington Post*, May 18, 2010, http://voices.washingtonpost.com/crime-scene/baltimore/sentencing-for-md-cult-members.html (accessed May 19, 2010).

30. Al-Skudsi bin Hookah, "Maintaining Family Honor," *Gaza Gajeera*, January 20, 2003, at Homepage for Lewis Loflin, http://www.sullivan-county.com/id4/honor_killings.htm (accessed October 19, 2009).

31. Bud Gillett, "Friends: Murdered Teens Were Afraid of Their Dad," CBS 11 (Dallas/Fort Worth), January 2, 2008, http://cbs11tv.com/local/Yaser.Abbdel.Said .2.622026.html (accessed November 25, 2009).

32. Tanya Eiserer, "Slain Lewisville Sisters Mourned at Christian, Muslim Services," *Dallas Morning News*, January 6, 2008, http://www.dallasnews.com/shared content/dws/dn/latestnews/stories/010608dnmetfunerals.216ceab.html (accessed October 18, 2010).

33. Carol Delaney, *Abraham on Trial: The Social Legacy of Biblical Myth* (Princeton, NJ: Princeton University Press, 1998), 237–38.

34. Kevin Hoffmann, "KCK Church Voices Support for Pastors Accused of Killing Son," *Kansas City Star*, January 2, 2003, at Project NoSpank, http://www .nospank.net/n-j78.htm (November 24, 2009).

35. Ibid.

36. Associated Press, "Church Member Sentenced: Case Involved Restraining Kids with Belts, Cords," February 6, 2004, at Ross Institute Internet Archives for the Study of Destructive Cults, Controversial Groups, and Movements, http://www.rick ross.com/reference/gods_creation/gods_creation34.html (accessed November 24, 2009).

37. Tony Rizzo, "'You Must Love Discipline,' Edgar Children Were Taught," *Kansas City Star*, September 27, 2003, at Ross Institute Internet Archives for the Study of Destructive Cults, Controversial Groups, and Movements, http://www.rick ross.com/reference/gods_creation/gods_creation30.html (accessed November 24, 2009).

38. Horace Bushnell, *Christian Nurture* (New York: Scribner, Armstrong, 1876),

56–57, http://quod.lib.umich.edu/cgi/t/text/pageviewer-idx?c=moa;cc=moa;rgn =full%20 text;idno=AFZ0908.0001.001;didno=AFZ0908.0001.001;view=image;seq =0058 (accessed March 4, 2010).

39. Alice Miller, *The Body Never Lies: The Lingering Effects of Cruel Parenting* (New York: W. W. Norton, 2005), 24.

CHAPTER 7: CHILD SINFULNESS—A CHRISTIAN PROBLEM

1. Pew Forum on Religion and Public Life, *U.S. Religion Landscape Survey Report* (Washington, DC: Pew Forum Web Publishing and Communications, February 2008), 5, http://religions.pewforum.org/pdf/report-religious-landscape-study-full.pdf.

2. Robin Grille, *Parenting for a Peaceful World* (Sydney, Australia: Longueville Media, 2005), 52.

3. Jonathan Edwards, "Conversions and Revival in New England (1740)," quoted in *Children and Youth in America: A Documentary History*, vol. 1, *1600–1865*, ed. Robert H. Bremner (Cambridge, MA: Harvard University, 1970), 139.

4. Michael Lienesch, *Redeeming America: Piety and Politics in the New Christian Right* (Chapel Hill: University of North Carolina Press, 1993), 77.

5. J. Richard Fugate, *What the Bible Says about . . . Child Training* (Citrus Heights, CA: Foundation for Biblical Research, 1996), 63.

6. John Rosemond, *Parenting by the Book: Biblical Wisdom for Raising Your Child* (New York: Howard Books, 2007), 37.

7. Ibid., 37–38.

8. Ibid., 36.

9. Beverly LaHaye, *Understanding Your Child's Temperament* (Eugene, OR: Harvest House, 1999), 9.

10. James Dobson, *The New Strong-Willed Child: Birth through Adolescence* (Carol Stream, IL: Tyndale House, 2004), 46.

11. Bill Maier, "When Kids Run You Over," Focus on the Family, http://www.focusonthefamily.com/parenting/effective_biblical_discipline/approaches_to _discipline/when_kids_run_you_over.aspx (accessed November 21, 2009).

12. Ginger Plowman, *"Don't Make Me Count to Three!": A Mom's Look at Heart-Oriented Discipline* (Wapwallopen, PA: Shepherd Press, 2003), 29.

13. Fugate, *What the Bible Says about . . . Child Training*, 43.

14. James G. Dwyer, *Religious Schools v. Children's Rights* (Ithaca, NY: Cornell University, 1998), 21.

15. David J. Kolko, "Child Physical Abuse," in *The APSAC Handbook on Child Maltreatment*, 2nd ed., ed. John E. B. Myers et al., 21–54 (Thousand Oaks, CA: Sage, 2002), 26–27.

16. Carol Delaney, *Abraham on Trial: The Social Legacy of Biblical Myth* (Princeton, NJ: Princeton University, 1998), 237–38.

17. Patrick M. Sullivan and John F. Knutson, "Maltreatment and Disabilities: A Population-Based Epidemiological Study," *Child Abuse and Neglect* 24, no. 10 (2000): 1257.

18. N. E. Groce, *Violence against Disabled Children: UN Secretary General's Report on Violence against Children* (New York: UNICEF, 2005), 6, at *UNICEF*, http://www .unicef.org/videoaudio/PDFs/UNICEF_Violence_Against_Disabled_Children _Report_Distributed_Version.pdf.

19. Janet Pais, *Suffer the Children: A Theology of Liberation by a Victim of Child Abuse* (New York: Paulist Press, 1991), 30.

20. Christopher G. Ellison and Matt Bradshaw, "Religious Beliefs, Sociopolitical Ideology, and Attitudes toward Corporal Punishment," *Journal of Family Issues* 30, no. 3 (2009): 324, http://online.sagepub.com/ (accessed February 16, 2009).

21. Grille, *Parenting for a Peaceful World*, 6.

22. Ibid., 52.

23. Jack Hyles, *How to Rear Children* (Hammond, IN: Hyles-Anderson Publications, 1976), 93.

24. Ibid., 97.

25. Roy Lessin, *Spanking: Why, When, How?* (Bloomington, MN: Bethany House, 1979), 69.

26. James Dobson, *Dare to Discipline: A Psychologist Offers Urgent Advice to Parents and Teachers* (Wheaton, IL: Tyndale House Publishers, 1970), 26.

27. Bette L. Bottoms et al., "In the Name of God: A Profile of Religion-Related Child Abuse," *Journal of Social Issues* 51, no. 2 (1995): 85.

28. William Coburn, *The Spanking Room* (Enumclaw, WA: WinePress Publishing, 2008), 20–21.

29. Irwin A. Hyman, *Reading, Writing, and the Hickory Stick: The Appalling Story of Physical and Psychological Abuse in American Schools* (Lanham, MD: Lexington Books, 1990), 40.

30. George Ramos, "Judge Gives Mother 15 Years to Life in Daughter's Fatal Beating," *LA Times*, November 25, 1997, http://articles.latimes.com/1997/nov/25/ local/me-57634 (accessed October 20, 2009).

31. Bottoms et al., "In the Name of God," 87.

32. Ibid.

33. Ellison and Bradshaw, "Religious Beliefs, Sociopolitical Ideology, and Attitudes toward Corporal Punishment," 324.

34. Samuel Martin, *Thy Rod and Thy Staff They Comfort Me: Christians and the Spanking Controversy* (Pasadena, CA: Sorensic, 2006), 100.

35. Hyles, *How to Rear Children*, 95–96.

36. Writing Committee, Governing Body of Jehovah's Witnesses, "What Can We Do with Our Children?" *Awake!*, April 22, 1974, 15, from "Watchtower Library 2005" CD, http://www.watchtower.cc/files.html (accessed March 7, 2010).

37. Plowman, *"Don't Make Me Count to Three!"* 108.

38. Rosemond, *Parenting by the Book*, 195.

39. Vanessa L. Malcarne and John D. Burchard, "Investigations of Child Abuse/Neglect Allegations in Religious Cults: A Case Study in Vermont," *Behavioral Sciences & the Law* 10, no. 1 (Winter 1992): 79, http://ebscohost.com/ (accessed February 19, 2010).

40. Philip Greven, *Spare the Child: The Religious Roots of Punishment and the Psychological Impact of Physical Abuse* (New York: Vintage, 1992), 36–38.

41. Francis Wayland, "A Case of Conviction," *American Baptist Magazine*, October 1831, at "Nineteenth-Century Works about Children," Merrycoz.org, http://www.merrycoz.org/articles/WAYLAND.HTM (accessed April 18, 2010).

42. Ibid.

43. Martha Mitchell, *Encyclopedia Brunoniana*, s.v. "Wayland, Francis," http://www.brown.edu/Administration/News_Bureau/Databases/Encyclopedia/search.php?serial=W0110 (accessed March 12, 2011).

44. Greven, *Spare the Child*, 65.

45. Philip Greven, *The Protestant Temperament: Patterns of Child-Rearing, Religious Experience, and the Self in Early America* (Chicago: University of Chicago Press, 1998), 35.

46. Hyles, *How to Rear Children*, 99.

47. Daphne Branham, "Babies Often Tortured by Fundamentalist Polygamists: Witness," *Postmedia News*, January 12, 2011, at *Leader-Post*, http://www.allvoices.com/s/event-8318020/aHR0cDovL3d3dy5sZWFk ZXJwb3N0LmNvbS9saWZl L0JhYmllcytvZnRlbit0b3J0dXJlZCtmdW5kYW1lbnRhbGlzdCtwb2x5Z2FtaXN0 cytXaXRuZXNzLzQwwOTk5NzIvc3RvcnkuaHRtbA== (accessed March 6, 2011).

48. Matthew Chapman, "Breaking Their Will and Gaining Their Heart," Kindling Publications, http://www.kindlingpublications.com/articles/matthew/breaking_their_will_and_gaining_their_heart.php (accessed January 7, 2011).

49. Michael Pearl, "The Will to Dominate," *No Greater Joy*, September 2000, http://www.nogreaterjoy.org/index.php?id=20&tx_ttnews%5Btt_news%5D=98&tx_ttnews%5BbackPid%5D=22&cHash=ac6e7bf821 (accessed October 11, 2009).

50. Michael Pearl, "Childhood Training Marathon: Revised and Updated," *No Greater Joy*, November–December 2009, 4–5, http://www.nogreaterjoy.org/file admin/template/PDFs/2009_Nov-Dec_01.pdf

51. Greven, *Spare the Child*, 38–39.

52. Associated Press, "Spanking Victim's Mom Guilty," *Spokesman-Review*, July 15, 1983, 10, at Google News, http://news.google.com/newspapers?nid=1314&dat=19830715&id=6usRAAAAIBAJ&sjid=re4DAAAAIBAJ&pg=7132,7532129 (accessed March 7, 2010).

53. Greven, "Spare the Child," 39–40.

54. Keith Wright, *Religious Abuse: A Pastor Explores the Many Ways Religion Can Hurt as Well as Heal* (Kelowna, BC: Northstone Publishing, 2001), 71.

CHAPTER 8: THE PERILS OF MIXING FAITH AND CORPORAL PUNISHMENT

* The study considered fundamentalists to include Mormons, Pentecostals, Seventh-Day Adventists, Faith Assembly World Wide Church of Christ, Jehovah's Witnesses, and Christian Scientists. Protestants included Episcopalians, Baptists, Lutherans, Methodists, Presbyterians, and Quakers.

** In the 1979 study, the researcher used a subjective methodology in categorizing different religiosities of subjects rather than relying on scientific questionnaires. Furthermore, the author did not treat the different religious affiliations the same. For example, she had only one category of "Jewish," rather than breaking out a religiosity of, for instance, "Orthodox," while separating out different religiosities of Christians, including "fundamentalist." While the 1995 study looked at "abuse related to attempts to rid a child of the devil or evil spirits," it did not specify whether the perpetrators were performing rituals, such as exorcisms, or administering corporal punishment. The subjects of the 2005 study were college students, most of whom were not parents.

1. Christopher G. Ellison and Matt Bradshaw, "Religious Beliefs, Sociopolitical Ideology, and Attitudes toward Corporal Punishment," *Journal of Family Issues* 30, no. 3 (2009): 335–37, http://online.sagepub.com/ (accessed February 16, 2009).

2. Kathryn Neufeld, "Child-Rearing, Religion, and Abusive Parents," *Religious Education* 74, no. 3 (May/June 1979): 240, http://www.ebscohost.com/ (accessed March 3, 2010).

3. Bette L. Bottoms et al., "In the Name of God: A Profile of Religion-Related Child Abuse," *Journal of Social Issues* 51, no. 2 (1995): 98.

4. Christopher W. Dyslin and Cynthia J. Thomsen, "Religiosity and Risk of Perpetrating Child Physical Abuse: An Empirical Investigation," *Journal of Psychology and Theology* 33, no. 4 (2005): 291, http://centauro.cmq.edu.mx/dav/libela/pdfS/religios/080106078.pdf.

5. Ellison and Bradshaw, "Religious Beliefs, Sociopolitical Ideology, and Attitudes toward Corporal Punishment," 335.

6. Ibid., 336.

7. Phil E. Quinn, *Spare the Rod: Breaking the Cycle of Child Abuse* (Nashville: Abingdon Press, 1988), 168.

8. Elizabeth T. Gershoff, Pamela C. Miller, and George W. Holden, "Parenting Influences from the Pulpit: Religious Affiliation as a Determinant of Parental Corporal Punishment," *Journal of Family Psychology* 13, no. 3 (1999): 318, http://cat.inist.fr/?aModele=afficheN&cpsidt=1949017 (accessed September 19, 2009).

9. "Dr. James Dobson," Focus on the Family, http://www.focusonthefamily.com/about_us/profiles/dr_james_dobson.aspx (accessed December 3, 2009).

10. Roy Lessin, *Spanking: A Loving Discipline: Helpful and Practical Answers for Today's Parents* (Bloomington, MN: Bethany House, 2002), 23.

11. Larry Christenson, *The Christian Family* (Minneapolis: Bethany House, 1970), 91.

12. Michael Pearl, "In Defense of Biblical Chastisement, Part 2," *No Greater Joy*, October 2001, http://www.nogreaterjoy.org/index.php?id=84&cHash=0c46541c13&tx_ttnews[tt_news]=89&tx_ttnews[backPid]=12 (accessed November 30, 2009).

13. Michael Pearl and Debi Pearl, *To Train Up a Child*, rev. ed. (Pleasantville, TN: No Greater Joy Ministries, 2004), 38.

14. Lisa Whelchel, *Creative Correction: Extraordinary Ideas for Everyday Discipline* (Carol Stream, IL: Tyndale House, 2005), 184.

15. James Dobson, *Dare to Discipline: A Psychologist Offers Urgent Advice to Parents and Teachers* (Wheaton, IL: Tyndale House Publishers, 1970), 60.

16. Pearl, "In Defense of Biblical Chastisement, Part 2."

17. Beth Fenimore, "An Open Letter to Roy Lessin: Author of *Spanking: Why, When, How?*" Chris's Anti Spanking Web Site, September 7, 2005, http://cdugan 0.tripod.com/RoyLessinOpenLetter.html (accessed March 3, 2010).

18. Ibid.

19. Ibid.

20. Roy Lessin, *Spanking: Why, When, How?* (Bloomington, MN: Bethany House, 1979), 35.

21. Ibid., 75–76.

22. Roy Lessin, e-mail message to author, December 13, 2009.

23. Fenimore, "Open Letter to Roy Lessin."

24. Amanda Lamb, "Boy's Aunt: 'I Hope His Death Is Not in Vain,'" WRAL.com, June 12, 2008, http://www.wral.com/news/local/story/3036253/ (accessed November 30, 2009).

25. Pearl, "In Defense of Biblical Chastisement, Part 2."

26. Lamb, "Boy's Aunt."

27. Mandy Locke, "Dead Child's Mom Sought Discipline Tips," *News Observer*, April 18, 2010, http://www.newsobserver.com/2006/03/16/68172/dead-childs -mom-sought-discipline.html (accessed March 28, 2011).

28. Mandy Locke, "Paddock Will Pay for Son's Murder," *News Observer*, June 13, 2008, http://www.newsobserver.com/news/crime_safety/story/79604.html (accessed November 30, 2009).

29. "Schatz Couple in Court Today," *Paradise Post*, May 25, 2010, at Ross Institute Internet Archives for the Study of Destructive Cults, Controversial Groups, and Movements, http://www.rickross.com/reference/general/general1250.html (accessed February 26, 2011).

30. "Alleged 'Chastisement' Trial Delayed," *Oroville Mercury-Register*, February 18, 2011, http://www.orovillemr.com/news/ci_17428951 (accessed February 26, 2011).

31. Lynn Harris, "Godly Discipline Turned Deadly," *Salon.com*, February 22, 2010, http://www.salon.com/life/feature/2010/02/22/no_greater_joy (accessed October 22, 2010).

32. Terry Vau Dell, "Plea Delayed in Fatal Beating of Ridge Girl," *Chico Enterprise Record*, February 26, 2010, http://www.chicoer.com/news/ci_14475598.

33. Michael Pearl, "Response to Schatz Case," *No Greater Joy*, http://www .nogreaterjoy.org/answers/response-to-schatz-case (accessed September 21, 2010).

34. Mandy Locke, "Parenting Guru Is Revered, Reviled," *News Observer*, April 30, 2006, http://www.newsobserver.com/news/crime_safety/story/73811.html (accessed November 30, 2009).

35. Ibid.

36. Jon Shirek, "12 Jurors, 2 Parents, 1 Dead Child," 11Alive (Atlanta, GA), February 16, 2007, http://www.11alive.com/news/article_news.aspx?storyid=92234 &provider=top (accessed November 29, 2009).

37. Associated Press, "Parents Get Life Plus 30 Years in Child's Death," *USA Today*, March 27, 2007, http://www.usatoday.com/news/nation/2007-03-27-church -child-death_N.htm# (accessed November 29, 2009).

38. "Firm Beliefs: Religious Movement at Center of Child Death Investigation," NewsChannel 5 (Nashville), February 4, 2004, http://www.newschannel5.com/ story/5412250/religious-movement-at-center-of-child-death-investigation.

39. Daniel Yee and Anita Wadhwani, "Defense, Judge Argue in Georgia Child-Murder Trial, as Dead Boy's Brother Testifies," *Tennessean*, February 8, 2007, at Project NoSpank, http://www.nospank.net/n-q60r.htm (accessed November 29, 2009).

40. "Firm Beliefs."

41. Rose French, "Church Supporting Parents Sentenced in Child's Death," *Chattanooga Times Free Press*, April 1, 2007, http://www.allbusiness.com/crime-law -enforcement-corrections/criminal-offenses-crimes/14786053-1.html.

42. Marie M. Fortune, "'Christian' Child Abuse," *Working Together* (Fall 1983 newsletter, FaithTrust Institute), at Project NoSpank, http://www.nospank.net/ fortune.htm (accessed November 5, 2009).

43. Philip Greven, *Spare the Child: The Religious Roots of Punishment and the Psychological Impact of Physical Abuse* (New York: Vintage, 1992), 218.

PART 2: HARM WITHOUT HITTING—RELIGIOUS CHILD EMOTIONAL ABUSE

1. J. Goldman et al. (Office on Child Abuse and Neglect), "A Coordinated Response to Child Abuse and Neglect: The Foundation for Practice," Child Welfare Information Gateway, 2003, http://www.childwelfare.gov/pubs/usermanuals/ foundation/foundationc.cfm (accessed December 3, 2009).

2. Stuart N. Hart et al., "Psychological Maltreatment," in *The APSAC Handbook on Child Maltreatment*, 2nd ed., ed. John E. B. Myers et al., 79–103 (Thousand Oaks, CA: Sage, 2002), 84.

3. Ibid., 82.

4. Ibid., 84.

5. Ibid.

6. Gregory L. Jantz, *Healing the Scars of Emotional Abuse*, 3rd. ed. (Grand Rapids, MI: Revell, 2009), 12–13.

7. Martha Farrell Erickson and Byron Egeland, "Child Neglect," in *The APSAC Handbook on Child Maltreatment*, 2nd ed., ed. John E. B. Myers et al., 3–20 (Thousand Oaks, CA: Sage, 2002), 3.

8. Goldman et al., "Coordinated Response to Child Abuse and Neglect."

9. National Center on Child Abuse Prevention Research, "Fact Sheet: Emotional Child Abuse," Prevent Child Abuse America, http://member.preventchildabuse.org/ site/DocServer/emotional_child_abuse.pdf?docID=122 (accessed December 10, 2009).

10. Louise Anne Owens, *Train Up the Child: How Children Get Hurt in Churches* (Philadelphia: Xlibris, 2000), 67.

11. National Center on Child Abuse Prevention Research, "Fact Sheet."

12. Hart et al., "Psychological Maltreatment," 86.

13. Jantz, *Healing the Scars of Emotional Abuse*, 149.

14. Julia De Jonge, "On Breaking Wills: The Theological Roots of Violence in Families," *Journal of Psychology and Christianity* 14, no. 1 (1996): 30.

15. Hart et al., "Psychological Maltreatment," 80.

16. Richard Dawkins, *The God Delusion* (New York: Houghton Mifflin-Harcourt, 2006), 356–57.

17. Owens, *Train Up the Child*, 20.

18. Nate Phelps, "The Uncomfortable Grayness of Life" (speech, American Atheists Convention, Atlanta, GA, April 11, 2009), at Atheist Nexus, http://www.atheist nexus.org/page/nate-phelps-2009-aa-speech (accessed December 7, 2009).

CHAPTER 9: IS RELIGION GOOD OR BAD FOR A CHILD'S PSYCHE?

1. Ann Marie Sorenson, Carl F. Grindstaff, and R. Jay Turner, "Religious Involvement among Unmarried Adolescent Mothers: A Source of Emotional Support?" *Sociology of Religion* 56, no. 1 (1995): 72, http://socrel.oxfordjournals.org/cgi/reprint/56/1/71.pdf.

2. Ralph W. Wood Jr., Peter C. Hill, and Bernard Spilka, *The Psychology of Religion*, 4th ed., *An Empirical Approach* (New York: Guilford Press, 2009), 438.

3. Ibid., 441.

4. Ibid., 442.

5. Ibid., 455.

6. Sheena Sethi and Martin E.Seligman, "Optimism and Fundamentalism," *Psychological Science* 4, no. 4 (July 1993): 259, http://www.jstor.org/stable/40062552 (accessed February 22, 2010).

7. Harold G. Koenig, Michael E. McCullough, and David B. Larson, *The Handbook of Religion and Health* (New York: Oxford University, 2001), 71.

8. Ibid., 59.

9. Clay Routledge, "Is Religion Bad for Your Health?" *Psychology Today*, September 15, 2009, http://www.psychologytoday.com/blog/death-love-sex-magic/200909/is-religion-bad-your-health (accessed March 3, 2010).

10. Eli S. Chesen, *Religion May Be Hazardous to Your Health* (New York: Peter H. Wyden, 1972), 92.

11. Wood Jr., Hill, and Spilka, *Psychology of Religion*, 445.

12. Ibid., 457.

13. Ibid., 70.

14. Virginia Culver, "Emotional Upset Linked to Strictness in Religion," *Denver Post*, January 17, 1988, 8B.

15. Albert Ellis, "Psychotherapy and Atheistic Values: A Response to A. E. Bergin's Psychotherapy and Religious Values," *Journal of Consulting and Clinical Psychology* 48 (1980): 637, quoted in Koenig, McCullough, and Larson, *Handbook of Religion and Health*, 71 (see note 7).

16. Kelley McCabe et al., "A Workshop for People Born or Raised in Cultic Groups," *International Cultic Studies Association* 6, no. 1 (2007), http://www.icsahome.com/infoserv_articles/mccabe_kelley_sgaworkshop_en06.01.htm (accessed December 25, 2009).

17. Koenig, McCullough, and Larson, *Handbook of Religion and Health*, 71.

18. Ben Sorotzkin, "Understanding and Treating Perfectionism in Religious Adolescents," *Psychotherapy* 35, no. 1 (Spring 1998): 89–90.

19. Wood Jr., Hill, and Spilka, *Psychology of Religion*, 446.

20. Koenig, McCullough, and Larson, *Handbook of Religion and Health*, 69.

21. Wood Jr., Hill, and Spilka, *Psychology of Religion*, 457.

22. Culver, "Emotional Upset Linked to Strictness in Religion," 1B.

23. Wood Jr., Hill, and Spilka, *Psychology of Religion*, 454.

24. E. Mansell Pattison, Nikolajs A. Lapins, and Hans A. Doerr, "Faith Healing: A Study of Personality and Function," *Transcultural Psychiatry* 7, no. 1 (1970): 75, http://tps.sagepub.com/ (accessed July 8, 2010).

25. Jerry Bergman, "Paradise Postponed . . . and Postponed: Why Jehovah's Witnesses Have a High Mental Illness Level," *Christian Research Journal* (Summer 1996), PDF at Christian Research Institute, 1–6, http://www.equip.org/PDF/DJ601.pdf.

26. Wood Jr., Hill, and Spilka, *Psychology of Religion*, 454.

27. Sorotzkin, "Understanding and Treating Perfectionism in Religious Adolescents," 89–90.

28. Mental Health America and Thomson Healthcare, "Ranking America's Mental Health: An Analysis of Depression across the States," Mental Health America, http://www.mentalhealthamerica.net/go/state-ranking (accessed December 30, 2009).

29. Koenig, McCullough, and Larson, *Handbook of Religion and Health*, 77.

30. Ibid., 69.

31. Ibid., 70.

32. Routledge, "Is Religion Bad for Your Health?"

33. Stephen Frosh, "Religious Influences on Parenting," in *Handbook of Parenting: Theory and Research for Practice*, ed. Masud Hoghughi and Nicholas Long, 98–109 (Thousand Oaks, CA: Sage, 2004), 105.

34. Christian Smith and Phillip Kim, "Family Religious Involvement and the Quality of Parental Relationships for Families with Early Adolescents," *National Study of Youth and Religion Report* 5 (2003): 5, http://www.youthandreligion.org/publications/docs/family2.pdf (accessed May 18, 2009).

35. Stephen Vaisey and Christian Smith, "Catholic Guilt among U.S. Adolescents: A Research Note," *Review of Religious Research* 49, no. 4 (2008): 424.

36. Frosh, "Religious Influences on Parenting," 105.

37. Leona Furnari, "Born or Raised in High-Demand Groups: Developmental Considerations," *International Cultic Studies Association* 4, no. 3 (September 2005), http://www.icsahome.com/infoserv_articles/furnari_leona_bornraised_en0403.htm (accessed May 19, 2009).

38. McCabe et al., "Workshop for People Born or Raised in Cultic Groups."

39. Susan Landas, "Children and Cults: A Practical Guide," *Journal of Family Law* 29, no. 3 (1991), at International Cultic Studies Association, http://www.icsahome .com/infoserv_articles/landa_susan_childrenandcults.htm (accessed December 17, 2009).

40. Lois Kendall, "A Psychological Exploration into the Effects of Former Membership of 'Extremist Authoritarian Sects'" (PhD dissertation, Buckinghamshire Chilterns University College, UK, 2006), quoted in McCabe et al., "Workshop for People Born or Raised in Cultic Groups."

41. Martin H. Katchen, "Dissociative Disorders in Former Cult Members: Implications for the Sociocultural Model of the Etiology of Dissociative Identity Disorder," International Society of Political Psychology, 24, http://www.allacademic.com// meta/p_mla_apa_research_citation/2/0/4/7/7/pages204771/p204771-1.php.

42. BBC News, "Sect Leavers 'Have Mental Problems,'" *BBC News*, May 20, 2000, http://news.bbc.co.uk/2/hi/health/755588.stm (accessed July 9, 2010).

43. Sorotzkin, "Understanding and Treating Perfectionism in Religious Adolescents," 89–90.

44. Bergman, "Paradise Postponed . . . and Postponed," 4.

45. Wendell W. Watters, *Deadly Doctrine: Health, Illness, and Christian God-Talk* (Amherst, NY: Prometheus Books, 1992), 51.

46. Frosh, "Religious Influences on Parenting," 105.

47. Jason C. Bivins, *Religion of Fear: The Politics of Horror in Conservative Evangelicalism* (New York: Oxford University Press, 2008), 10.

48. Donald Capps, *The Child's Song: The Religious Abuse of Children* (Louisville: Westminster John Knox Press, 1995), 51.

49. Louise Anne Owens, *Train Up the Child: How Children Get Hurt in Churches* (Philadelphia: Xlibris Corporation, 2000), 68.

CHAPTER 10: SINFUL, DISOBEDIENT, EVIL, AND DEPRAVED— RELIGIOUS SPURNING

1. Stuart N. Hart et al., "Psychological Maltreatment," in *The APSAC Handbook on Child Maltreatment*, 2nd ed., ed. John E. B. Myers et al., 79–103 (Thousand Oaks, CA: Sage, 2002), 82.

2. Louise Anne Owens, *Train Up the Child: How Children Get Hurt in Churches* (Philadelphia: Xlibris, 2000), 20–21.

3. Ernest Hamlin Abbot, "On the Training of Parents: The Beginning of Wisdom," *Outlook* 88 (March 7, 1908): 547.

4. Terriergal, "A Four-Year-Old Who Knows She Needs a Savior," *Free Republic*, October 30, 2008, http://www.freerepublic.com/focus/news/2192104/posts (accessed November 8, 2010).

5. Becky Fischer, *Jesus Camp*, directed by Heidi Ewing and Rachael Grady (2006; New York: Magnolia Pictures, 2007 DVD release).

6. Melenie, "Long, Hard Road to Disbelief," ExChristian.net, March 21, 2008, http://exchristian.net/testimonies/2008/03/long-hard-road-to-disbelief.html (accessed December 9, 2009).

7. Wendell W. Watters, *Deadly Doctrine: Health, Illness, and Christian God-Talk* (Amherst, NY: Prometheus Books, 1992), 51–54.

CHAPTER 11: SCARING THEM INTO FAITH—RELIGIOUS TERRORIZING

1. Philip Greven, *Spare the Child: The Religious Roots of Punishment and the Psychological Impact of Physical Abuse* (New York: Vintage, 1992), 218.

2. Jason C. Bivins, *Religion of Fear: The Politics of Horror in Conservative Evangelicalism* (New York: Oxford University Press, 2008), 25.

3. Stuart N. Hart et al., "Psychological Maltreatment," in *The APSAC Handbook on Child Maltreatment*, 2nd ed., ed. John E. B. Myers et al., 79–103 (Thousand Oaks, CA: Sage, 2002), 82.

4. "The New England Primer," Internet Sacred Text Archive, http://www.sacred-texts.com/chr/nep/ (accessed July 11, 2010).

5. *New England Primer* (Boston, n.d., ca. 1687; repr., Boston, 1843), 31, at Internet Sacred Text Archive, http://www.sacred-texts.com/chr/nep/nep23.htm (accessed August 8, 2010).

6. Ibid., 30.

7. Ibid., 14.

8. John J. Furniss, "The Dungeons of Hell," chap. 24 in *Tracts for Spiritual Reading, Designed for First Communions, Retreats, Missions, &c* (Baltimore: Kelly & Piet, 1867).

9. Xavier Deneux, Sabrina Bus, and Leslie Matthews, *Hail Mary* (Grand Rapids, MI: William B. Eerdmans, 2006).

10. John Bradshaw, *Reclaiming Virtue: How We Can Develop the Moral Intelligence to Do the Right Thing at the Right Time for the Right Reason* (New York: Bantam Dell, 2009), 337–38.

11. Eli S. Chesen, *Religion May Be Hazardous to Your Health* (New York: Peter H. Wyden, 1972), 125–26.

12. E. Burke Rochford Jr. and Jennifer Heinlein, "Child Abuse in the Hare Krishna Movement: 1971–1986," *Cults and Society* 1, no.1 (2001), at International Cultic Studies Association, http://www.icsahome.com/infoserv_articles/rochford_burke_heinlein_childabuseiskcon.htm (accessed January 18, 2010).

13. Carolyn Jessop, *Escape* (New York: Broadway Books, 2007), 17–18.

14. Keith Wright, *Religious Abuse: A Pastor Explores the Many Ways Religion Can Hurt as Well as Heal* (Kelowna, BC: Northstone Publishing, 2001), 39.

15. Hella Winston, *Unchosen: The Hidden Lives of Hasidic Rebels* (Boston: Beacon Press, 2005), 134–35.

16. Sarah Braasch, "The Scars of a Religious Upbringing," *Freethought Today* 27, no. 1 (January–February 2010), http://www.ffrf.org/publications/freethought-today/articles/the-scars-of-a-religious-upbringing/ (accessed July 13, 2010).

17. Jack Hyles, *How to Rear Children* (Hammond, IN: Hyles-Anderson Publications, 1976), 145.

18. Kathy Jo Nicholson, interview by Gary Tuchmann, "Inside Warren Jeffs' World," CNN, July 31, 2007, http://www.cnn.com/2007/US/07/31/fleeing .polygamy/index.html?iref=newssearch#cnnSTCText (accessed July 13, 2010).

19. Hart M. Nelsen and Alice Kroliczak, "Parental Use of the Threat 'God Will Punish': Replication and Extension," *Journal for the Scientific Study of Religion* 23, no. 3 (1984): 267, http://ebscohost.com/ (accessed July 13, 2010).

CHAPTER 12: IN THE WORLD, NOT OF THE WORLD— RELIGIOUS ISOLATING AND EXPLOITING

1. Jack Kenny, "Court to Rule in Religion, Home-School Battle," *New American*, February 1, 2011, http://www.thenewamerican.com/index.php/culture/education/ 6130-court-to-rule-in-religion-home-school-battle (accessed February 2, 2011).

2. Julia Duin, "Home-Schooler Ordered to Attend Public School," *Washington Times*, September 4, 2009, http://www.washingtontimes.com/news/2009/sep/04/ home-schooled-christian-girl-ordered-to-join-publi/ (accessed January 18, 2010).

3. Kenny, "Court to Rule in Religion, Home-School Battle."

4. Stuart N. Hart et al., "Psychological Maltreatment," in *The APSAC Handbook on Child Maltreatment*, 2nd ed., ed. John E. B. Myers et al., 79–103 (Thousand Oaks, CA: Sage, 2002), 82.

5. Benzion Sorotzkin, "The Role of Parents in the Current Crisis of Rebellious Adolescents: Dare We Discuss It? Can We Afford Not To?" Dr. Benzion Sorotzkin, PsyD, May 2005, http://drsorotzkin.com/role_of_parents.html (accessed March 3, 2010).

6. Nicolas Jacquette, testimony given to the Enquiry Commission on the Influence of Cult Movements and the Consequences of Their Practices on the Physical and Mental Health of Minors, a commission of the French Parliament, September 26, 2006, http://www.silentlambs.org/frenchtestimony.htm (accessed December 13, 2009).

7. Ibid.

8. Prince v. Massachusetts, 321 U.S. 158 (1944), at FindLaw, http://caselaw.lp .findlaw.com/scripts/getcase.pl?court=US&vol=321&invol=158 (accessed September 17, 2010).

9. Becky Fischer, *Jesus Camp*, DVD, directed by Heidi Ewing and Rachel Grady (2006; New York: Magnolia Pictures, 2007 DVD release).

10. Barbara Grizzuti Harrison, "Children and the Cult," *New England Monthly*, December 1984, at Ross Institute Internet Archives for the Study of Destructive Cults, Controversial Groups, and Movements, http://www.rickross.com/reference/tribes/ tribes1.html (accessed November 17, 2009).

11. Ibid.

12. Jeane Macintosh, "Sect Children Are Used to Abuse," *New York Post*, April 8, 2001, at Ross Institute Internet Archives for the Study of Destructive Cults, Contro-

versial Groups, and Movements, http://www.rickross.com/reference/tribes/tribes19.html (accessed November 17, 2009).

13. "Suffer the Children," *Daily Mail* (Brisbane, Australia), August 22, 1999, at Ross Institute Internet Archives for the Study of Destructive Cults, Controversial Groups, and Movements, http://www.rickross.com/reference/tribes/tribes47.html (December 17, 2009).

14. Dave Wedge, "The Cult Next Door: Teen Shares Chilling Tale of Alleged Abuse inside the Twelve Tribes Sect," *Boston Herald*, September 4, 2001, at Ross Institute Internet Archives for the Study of Destructive Cults, Controversial Groups, and Movements, http://www.rickross.com/reference/tribes/tribes24.html (accessed November 17, 2009).

15. Caroline Fraser, *God's Perfect Child: Living and Dying in the Christian Science Church* (New York: Holt Paperbacks, 2000), 6.

16. Ibid., 6–7.

17. Ibid.

18. Kelley McCabe et al., "A Workshop for People Born or Raised in Cultic Groups," *International Cultic Studies Association* 6, no. 1 (2007), http://www.icsahome.com/infoserv_articles/mccabe_kelley_sgaworkshop_en06.01.htm (accessed December 25, 2009).

PART 3: VIOLATING A SACRED TRUST—RELIGIOUS CHILD SEXUAL ABUSE

1. James A. Monteleone and Armand E. Brodeur, eds. *Child Maltreatment: A Clinical Guide and Reference*, 3rd ed. (St. Louis: G. W. Medical, 2005), 209.

2. Child Welfare Information Gateway (CWIG), "What Is Child Abuse and Neglect?" Child Welfare Information Gateway, 2008, http://www.childwelfare.gov/pubs/factsheets/whatiscan.cfm (accessed February 15, 2010).

3. Ibid.

4. US Department of Health & Human Services, *Child Maltreatment 2009* (Washington: Administration for Children and Families, Children's Bureau, 2010), 47, http://www.acf.hhs.gov/programs/cb/pubs/cm09/cm09.pdf.

5. John Briere and Catherine Scott, *Principles of Trauma Therapy: A Guide to Symptoms, Evaluation, and Treatment* (Thousand Oaks, CA: Sage, 2006), 9.

6. "Who Are the Victims?" Rape, Abuse & Incest National Network (RAINN), http://www.rainn.org/get-information/statistics/sexual-assault-victims (accessed October 4, 2010).

7. Barbara E. Bogorad, "Sexual Abuse: Surviving the Pain," American Academy of Experts in Traumatic Stress, 1998, http://www.aaets.org/article31.htm (accessed May 9, 2010).

8. Subcommittee on Crime, Committee on the Judiciary, House of Representatives, *Cycle of Sexual Abuse: Research Inconclusive about Whether Child Victims Become Adult Abusers* (Washington, DC: US General Accounting Office, September 1996), 5.

9. Patricia Cohen, Jeffrey G. Johnson, and Suzanne Salzinger, "A Longitudinal

Analysis of Risk Factors for Child Maltreatment," *Child Abuse and Neglect* 22, no. 11 (1998): 1074.

10. Monteleone and Brodeur, *Child Maltreatment*, 210.

11. Cohen, Johnson, and Salzinger, "Longitudinal Analysis of Risk Factors for Child Maltreatment," 1074.

12. Thomas Brundage, "Update: Milwaukee Church Judge Clarifies Case of Abusive Priest Father Murphy," *Catholic Anchor*, March 29, 2010, http://catholicanchor .org/wordpress/?p=601 (accessed April 30, 2010).

13. "Incest," Rape, Abuse & Incest National Network (RAINN), http://www .rainn.org/get-information/types-of-sexual-assault/incest (accessed March 5, 2010).

14. Bogorad, "Sexual Abuse."

15. Ibid.

16. "Incest."

17. James F. Anderson, Nancie J. Mangels, and Adam Langsam, "Child Sexual Abuse: A Public Health Issue," *Criminal Justice Studies* 17, no. 1 (March 2004): 107.

18. Florence Rush, *The Best Kept Secret: Sexual Abuse of Children* (Englewood Cliffs, NJ: Prentice Hall, 1980), 6.

19. "Effects of Sexual Assault," Rape, Abuse & Incest National Network (RAINN), http://www.rainn.org/get-information/effects-of-sexual-assault (accessed March 5, 2010).

20. Thaeda Franz, "Power, Patriarchy, and Sexual Abuse in the Christian Church," *Traumatology* 8, no. 1 (March 2002): 5, PDF at Florida State University, 2, http://www.fsu.edu/~trauma/v8/Church.pdf.

21. Bernard Spilka et al., *The Psychology of Religion: An Empirical Approach*, 3rd ed. (New York: Guilford Press, 2003), 402.

22. Brundage, "Update."

23. Brent W. Jeffs, *Lost Boy* (New York: Broadway Books, 2009), 67.

24. National Review Board for the Protection of Children and Young People, "Scandals in the Church; Excerpts from Report on Abuse by Members of the Catholic Clergy," *New York Times*, February 28, 2004, http://www.nytimes.com/2004/02/ 28/us/scandals-church-excerpts-report-abuse-members-catholic-clergy.html?scp =8&sq=essential%20norms&st=cse (accessed June 24, 2010).

25. "Public Issues: Child Abuse," Church of Jesus Christ of Latter-day Saints Newsroom, http://www.newsroom.lds.org/ldsnewsroom/eng/public-issues/child -abuse (accessed May 24, 2010).

26. Writing Committee, Governing Body of Jehovah's Witnesses, "Comfort for Those with a 'Stricken Spirit,'" Watchtower, November 1, 1995, http://www .watchtower.org/e/19951101a/article_01.htm (accessed May 22, 2010).

CHAPTER 13: MURDERED SOULS

* One theory as to why Jewish authorities settled on that age is that it was believed that once a girl reached the age of three, her hymen would no longer grow back after sexual

intercourse. She would, therefore, no longer technically be a virgin and, therefore, be able to be betrothed.

1. Kibbie S. Ruth, "Risk of Abuse in Faith Communities," in *Child Maltreatment: A Clinical Guide and Reference*, 3rd ed., ed. James A. Monteleone and Armand E. Brodeur, 539–55 (St. Louis: G. W. Medical, 2005), 539.

2. Ibid., 539–40.

3. Karen Terry and Margaret Leland Smith, *The Nature and Scope of the Problem of Sexual Abuse of Minors by Priests and Deacons in the United States, 1950–2002* (Washington, DC: United States Conference of Catholic Bishops, 2004), 6, at Bishop Accountability.org, http://www.bishop-accountability.org/reports/2004_02_27_John Jay/index.html#exec (accessed April 29, 2010).

4. Ibid., 25.

5. Ruth, "Risk of Abuse in Faith Communities," 545.

6. Bette L. Bottoms et al., "In the Name of God: A Profile of Religion-Related Child Abuse," *Journal of Social Issues* 51, no. 2 (1995): 94.

7. Ibid., 90.

8. Thaeda Franz, "Power, Patriarchy, and Sexual Abuse in the Christian Church," *Traumatology* 8, no. 1 (March, 2002): 5, PDF at Florida State University, http://www.fsu.edu/~trauma/v8/Church.pdf.

9. Flora Jessop and Paul Brown, *Church of Lies* (San Francisco: Jossey-Bass, 2009), 13.

10. Ibid., 11.

11. Mike Echols, *Brother Tony's Boys: The Largest Case of Child Prostitution in U.S. History: The True Story* (Amherst, NY: Prometheus Books, 1996), 38–39.

12. Ibid., 126.

13. Ibid., 232.

14. Ibid., 269.

15. Nicholas Ledden, "Sex Abuse Case: Trial Set to Start Monday," *Daily Inter Lake*, March 2, 2008, http://www.dailyinterlake.com/news/local_montana/article _72eda278-ac33-5e4d-9ad7-f2e6c258eb6f.html (accessed May 8, 2010).

16. Ibid.

17. Vince Devlin, "Montana Supreme Court Rejects Heron Man's Appeal of Incest Conviction," *Missoulian*, April 28, 2010, http://missoulian.com/news/local/article_3172eb90-527f-11df-8b41-001cc4c03286.html (accessed May 8, 2010).

18. Florence Rush, *The Best Kept Secret: Sexual Abuse of Children* (Englewood Cliffs, NJ: Prentice Hall, 1980), 17.

19. Mark E. Pietrzyk, "Homosexuality and Child Sexual Abuse: Science, Religion, and the Slippery Slope," InternationalOrder.org, October 2006, http://www.internationalorder.org/scandal_response.html (accessed May 3, 2010).

20. Ibid.

21. Ibid.

22. Ibid.

23. Marshall Burns, "The U.S. Federal Age of Sexual Consent," SOL

Research.org, January 28, 2009, http://www.solresearch.org/~SOLR/rprt/USnatl AoC.asp (accessed May 12, 2010).

24. "Family International," Wapedia, http://wapedia.mobi/en/Children_of _God_(New_Religious_Movement) (accessed February 28, 2011).

25. Celeste Jones, Kristina Jones, and Juliana Buhring, *Not without My Sister: The True Story of Three Girls Violated and Betrayed* (London: HarperCollins, 2007), xiii–xiv.

26. ABC News, "Tale of the Tape: Former Children of God Member Seeks Revenge," *ABC Primetime Live*, January 27, 2005, at XFamily.org, http://www .xfamily.org/index.php/ABC_News:_Tale_of_the_Tape (accessed May 26, 2010).

27. "Family International."

28. "Our History," Family International, http://www.thefamily.org/en/ about/our-history/ (accessed June 5, 2010).

29. "Children: The Hope of the Future," Family International, http:// www.thefamily.org/en/children-hope-future/ (accessed June 5, 2010).

30. "Cults: Sordid Sex and Secrets," *Larry King Live*, CNN, July 31, 2008, at XFamily.org, http://www.xfamily.org/index.php/CNN_Larry_King_Live:_Cults: _Sordid_Sex_%26_Secrets%3F (accessed February 28, 2011).

31. Daphne Bramham, "Opinion: Mormon Prophet's Diaries Reveal Depraved Face of Polygamy," *Vancouver Sun*, February 26, 2011, http://www.vancouversun .com/life/Opinion+Mormon+prophet+diaries+reveal+depraved+face+polygamy /4350891/story.html#ixzz1FwKkiLdy (accessed February 28, 2011).

32. *Damned to Heaven*, directed by Thomas Elliot (Los Angeles: Seventh Art Releasing, 2008), at Fresh Produce Media, http://www.freshfilm.com/damnedto heaven/ (accessed October 30, 2010).

33. Texas Department of Health and Family Services, "Eldorado Investigation," Texas Department of Health and Family Services, December 22, 2008, 6, http:// www.dfps.state.tx.us/documents/about/pdf/2008-12-22_Eldorado.pdf.

34. Ibid., 5.

35. Ibid., 4.

36. Ibid., 14.

37. Carolyn Jessop, *Triumph: Life after the Cult—A Survivor's Lessons* (New York: Broadway Books, 2010), 84.

38. Hilary Hylton and Jeanette Moses, "The Polygamist Prophet: One Step Closer to a Texas Court," *Time*, September 8, 2010, http://www.time.com/time/nation/ article/0,8599,2016785,00.html (accessed September 11, 2010).

39. Ibid.

40. Daphne Bramham, "Bountiful Men Implicated in Human Smuggling Scheme to Send Child Brides to United States," *Vancouver Sun*, March 28, 2011, http:// vancouversun.com/life/Bountiful+implicated+human+smuggling+scheme+send +child+brides+United/4513704/story.html (accessed March 29, 2011).

41. Texas Department of Health and Family Services, "Eldorado Investigation," 15.

CHAPTER 14: RELIGIOUS POWER AND CHILD SEXUAL ABUSE

1. Kibbie S. Ruth, "Risk of Abuse in Faith Communities," in *Child Maltreatment: A Clinical Guide and Reference*, 3rd ed., ed. James A. Monteleone and Armand E. Brodeur, 539–55 (St. Louis: G. W. Medical, 2005), 548–49.

2. Karen Terry, "Child Sexual Abuse: A Review of the Literature," in *The Nature and Scope of the Problem of Sexual Abuse of Minors by Priests and Deacons in the United States, 1950–2002*, by Karen Terry et al. (Washington, DC: US Conference of Catholic Bishops, 2004), PDF at United States Conference of Catholic Bishops, 19, http://www.usccb.org/nrb/johnjaystudy/litreview.pdf.

3. Child Welfare Information Gateway (CWIG), "What Is Child Abuse and Neglect? Child Welfare Information Gateway, 2008, http://www.childwelfare.gov/pubs/fact sheets/whatiscan.cfm (accessed October 19, 2009).

4. Judith Lewis Herman, *Father-Daughter Incest* (Cambridge, MA: Harvard University, 2000), 27.

5. Ruth, "Risk of Abuse in Faith Communities," 541.

6. Carol Delaney, *Abraham on Trial: The Social Legacy of Biblical Myth* (Princeton, NJ: Princeton University Press, 1998), 240.

7. Ron O'Grady, *The Hidden Shame of the Church: Sexual Abuse of Children and the Church* (Geneva, Switzerland: WCC Publications, 2001), 39.

8. *Inside a Cult*, directed by Ben Anthony (National Geographic Channel, 2008), at National Geographic, http://channel.nationalgeographic.com/episode/inside-a-cult-3401/Overview#tab-Videos/05168_00 (accessed May 21, 2009).

9. Flora Jessop and Paul Brown, *Church of Lies* (San Francisco: Jossey-Bass, 2009), 11.

10. Carolyn Holderread Heggen, *Sexual Abuse in Christian Homes and Churches* (Eugene, OR: Wipf & Stock, 2006), 45.

11. Ruth, "Risk of Abuse in Faith Communities," 545.

12. Dinesh Ramde and Todd Richmond, "Deaf School Students Say Wisconsin Priest Abused Them," Associated Press, March 26, 2010, at ABC News, http://abcnews.go.com/US/wireStory?id=10206871 (accessed September 5, 2010).

13. Brent W. Jeffs, *Lost Boy* (New York: Broadway Books, 2009), 67.

14. "Cults: Sordid Sex and Secrets," *Larry King Live*, CNN, July 31, 2008, at XFamily.org, http://www.xfamily.org/index.php/CNN_Larry_King_Live:_Cults:_Sordid_Sex_%26_Secrets%3F (accessed March 6, 2011).

15. Bette L. Bottoms et al., "In the Name of God: A Profile of Religion-Related Child Abuse," *Journal of Social Issues* 51, no. 2 (1995): 94.

16. Ruth, "Risk of Abuse in Faith Communities," 542.

17. Jeffs, *Lost Boy*, 68.

18. Ruth, "Risk of Abuse in Faith Communities," 542.

19. Ibid.

20. Mike Echols, *Brother Tony's Boys: The Largest Case of Child Prostitution in U.S. History: The True Story* (Amherst, NY: Prometheus Books, 1996), 67.

21. Ibid., 234.

CHAPTER 15: FAILING VICTIMS

1. Ben Leubsdorf, "Pastor Finds '97 Response Regrettable: Congregant Allegedly Raped Girl, 15," *Concord Monitor*, June 16, 2010, http://www.concordmonitor.com/article/pastor-finds-97-response-regrettable?page=0,0 (accessed June 22, 2010).

2. Susan Donaldson James, "15-Year-Old Allegedly Raped, Then Forced to Confess to Church," ABC News, June 3, 2010, http://abcnews.go.com/Health/Mind MoodNews/alleged-rape-victim-accuses-trinity-baptist-church-deacon/story?id =10806348 (accessed June 3, 2010).

3. Trent Spiner, "Man Accused in Rape Admitted Paternity," *Concord Monitor*, June 19, 2010, http://www.concordmonitor.rste013lmp01.blackmesh.com/article/man-accused-in-rape-admitted-paternity (accessed June 22, 2010).

4. Leubsdorf, "Pastor Finds '97 Response Regrettable."

5. Ibid.

6. CBS News and Associated Press, "Woman: Church Covered Up My Rape as Teen," CBS News, May 29, 2010, http://www.cbsnews.com/stories/2010/05/29/earlyshow/saturday/main6530160.shtml (accessed May 29, 2010).

7. James, "15-Year-Old Allegedly Raped, Then Forced to Confess to Church."

8. Leubsdorf, "Pastor Finds '97 Response Regrettable."

9. James, "15-Year-Old Allegedly Raped, Then Forced to Confess to Church."

10. Lynne Tuohy, "Church in New Hampshire at Center of 1997 Rape Case," Associated Press, May 28, 2010, at *Arizona Republic*, http://www.azcentral.com/arizonarepublic/news/articles/2010/05/28/20100528Church-RapeCase0528.html (accessed September 10, 2010).

11. Bruce D. Perry et al., "Childhood Trauma, the Neurobiology of Adaptation, and Use-Dependent Development of the Brain: How States Become Traits," *Infant Mental Health Journal* 16, no. 4 (Winter 1995): 285, http://www.childtrauma.org/images/stories/Articles/state_trait_95.pdf (accessed July 16, 2010).

12. Steve Spaccarelli and Soni Kim, "Resilience Criteria and Factors Associated with Resilience in Sexually Abused Girls," *Child Abuse & Neglect* 19, no. 9 (September 1995): 1171, http://www.sciencedirect.com/ (accessed November 17, 2010).

13. Kibbie S. Ruth, "Risk of Abuse in Faith Communities," in *Child Maltreatment: A Clinical Guide and Reference*, 3rd ed., ed. James A. Monteleone and Armand E. Brodeur, 539–55 (St. Louis: G. W. Medical, 2005), 539.

14. Keith Wright, *Religious Abuse: A Pastor Explores the Many Ways Religion Can Hurt as Well as Heal* (Kelowna, BC: Northstone Publishing, 2001), 67.

15. Brent W. Jeffs, *Lost Boy* (New York: Broadway Books, 2009), 68.

16. Hella Winston, *Unchosen: The Hidden Lives of Hassidic Rebels* (Boston: Beacon Press, 2005), 134.

17. Asher Lipner, "A Chanukah Lesson about Sexual Abuse in Our Community," *Un-Orthodox Jew*, December 10, 2009, http://theunorthodoxjew.blogspot.com/2009/12/chanukah-lesson-about-sexual-abuse-in.html (accessed September 26, 2010).

18. Mark Clayton, "Sex Abuse Spans Spectrum of Churches," *Christian Science*

Monitor, April 5, 2002, http://www.csmonitor.com/2002/0405/p01s01-ussc.html (accessed April 30, 2010).

19. Bette L. Bottoms et al., "In the Name of God: A Profile of Religion-Related Child Abuse," *Journal of Social Issues* 51, no. 2 (1995): 94.

20. Ben Hirsch, "Opinion: The Next Step in Preventing Sexual Abuse," *Jewish Star*, April 23, 2010, http://thejewishstar.wordpress.com/2010/04/21/opinion-the -next-step-in-preventing-sexual-abuse/ (accessed June 1, 2010).

21. Asher Lipner, e-mail message to author, September 16, 2010.

22. *Twist of Faith*, directed by Kirby Dick (New York: HBO, 2005).

23. Nadya Labi, "The Gentle People," *Legal Affairs*, January/February 2005, http://www.legalaffairs.org/issues/January-February-2005/feature_labi_janfeb05 .msp (accessed June 10, 2010).

24. "Sexual Abuse in the Amish Community," ABC News *20/20*, December 10, 2004, program transcript, http://abcnews.go.com/2020/story?id=316371&page=1 (accessed May 22, 2010).

CHAPTER 16: SECRECY AND SILENCE AT THE TOP

1. Writing Committee, Governing Body of Jehovah's Witnesses, "Our Families: Jehovah's Witnesses and Child Protection," Jehovah's Witnesses Official Media Web Site, http://www.jw-media.org/aboutjw/article23.htm (accessed May 17, 2010).

2. "The Evil of Child Abuse," Church of Jesus Christ of Latter-day Saints News-room, November 21, 2005, http://beta-newsroom.lds.org/article/the-evil-of-child -abuse (accessed October 24, 2010).

3. Rabbinical Council of America, "2010 Convention Resolution: Condemning and Combating Child Abuse," Rabbinical Council of America, April 27, 2010, http:// www.rabbis.org/news/article.cfm?id=105544 (accessed November 13, 2010).

4. Ad Hoc Committee for Sexual Abuse of the United States Conference of Catholic Bishops (USCCB), "Charter for the Protection of Children and Young People" (revised charter approved at General Meeting of the United States Conference of Catholic Bishops, Washington DC, June 2005), in USCCB, *Promise to Protect, Pledge to Heal*, 1–20 (Washington, DC: United States Conference of Catholic Bishops, 2006), 9–18, http:// www.usccb.org/ocyp/charter.pdf.

5. Thomas Brundage, "Update: Milwaukee Church Judge Clarifies Case of Abu-sive Priest Father Murphy," *Catholic Anchor*, March 29, 2010, http://catholicanchor .org/wordpress/?p=601 (accessed April 30, 2010).

6. Episcopal Diocese of Western New York, *Policy and Procedures: Sexual Miscon-duct in the Church*, rev. ed. (Buffalo: Episcopal Diocese of Western New York, 2005), 3, http://www.episcopalwny.org/ (accessed November 13, 2010).

7. Jennifer Thomas, "Phoenix Dad Accused of Molesting Daughters: 2 Pastors Arrested for Not Reporting Abuse," AZfamily.com, July 28, 2010, http://www .azfamily.com/news/local/Phoenix-dad-accused-of-molesting-daughters-2-pastors -arrested-for-not-reporting-abuse-99483409.html (accessed October 12, 2010).

8. US Department of Health & Human Services, *Child Maltreatment 2009* (Washington, DC: Administration for Children and Families, Children's Bureau, 2010), 6, http://www.acf.hhs.gov/programs/cb/pubs/cm09/cm09.pdf.

9. Kibbie S. Ruth, "Risk of Abuse in Faith Communities," in *Child Maltreatment: A Clinical Guide and Reference*, 3rd ed., ed. James A. Monteleone and Armand E. Brodeur, 539–55 (St. Louis: G. W. Medical, 2005), 549.

10. Daniel H. Grossoehme, "Child Abuse Reporting: Clergy Perceptions," *Child Abuse & Neglect* 22, no. 7 (1998): 744–45, http://www.sciencedirect.com/ (accessed October 21, 2010).

11. Child Welfare Information Gateway (CWIG), "Clergy as Mandatory Reporters of Child Abuse and Neglect: Summary of State Laws," Child Welfare Information Gateway, April 2010, http://www.childwelfare.gov/systemwide/laws _policies/statutes/clergymandated.cfm (accessed September 12, 2010).

12. Marie M. Fortune, "Confidentiality and Mandatory Reporting: A Clergy Dilemna?" *Working Together* 6, no. 1 (Fall 1985), PDF at Faith Trust Institute, 1–3, http://www.faithtrustinstitute.org/resources/articles/Confidentiality-and-Mandatory -Reporting.pdf/?searchterm=clergy%20reporting.

13. Ibid., 3.

14. William Glaberson, "In Many Investigations, the Church Is Often the Sole Authority," *New York Times*, March 15, 2002, http://www.nytimes.com/2002/03/ 15/nyregion/in-many-investigations-the-church-is-often-the-sole-authority.html?scp =2&sq=william+glaberson&st=nyt (accessed September 14, 2010).

15. Fortune, "Confidentiality and Mandatory Reporting," 3.

16. Marci A. Hamilton, "The Rules against Scandal and What They Mean for the First Amendment's Religion Clauses," *Maryland Law Review* 69, no. 115 (2009): 115–31, http://www.law.umaryland.edu/academics/journals/mdlr/print/articles/69_1-115.pdf.

17. Marci A. Hamilton, "How Other Religious Organizations Echo the Roman Catholic Church's Rule against Scandal," at FindLaw, April 15, 2010, http://writ .news.findlaw.com/hamilton/20100415.html (accessed June 1, 2010).

18. Congregation for the Doctrine of the Faith to Bishops of the Entire Catholic Church, "Letter Sent from the Congregation for the Doctrine of the Faith to Bishops of the Entire Catholic Church and Other Ordinaries and Hierarchs Having an Interest regarding the Most Serious Offenses Reserved to the Congregation for the Doctrine of the Faith," May 18, 2001, at BishopAccountability.org, http://www.bishop-accountability .org/resources/resource-files/churchdocs/EpistulaEnglish.htm (accessed June 24, 2010).

19. John L. Allen Jr., *All the Pope's Men: The Inside Story of How the Vatican Really Thinks* (New York: Doubleday, 2004), 24.

20. John Thavis, "Vatican Official Urges Confidentiality by Confessors on Sex Abuse Sins," *Catholic News Service*, March 18, 2010, http://www.catholicnews .com/data/stories/cns/1001141.htm (accessed October 14, 2010).

21. Thomas, "Phoenix Dad Accused of Molesting Daughters."

22. Marie M. Fortune, "Pastors Who Don't Report," *Marie's Blog*, FaithTrust Institute, August 13, 2010, http://www.faithtrustinstitute.org/blog/marie-fortune/ 81/?searchterm =clergy%20report (accessed October 12, 2010).

23. Rachel Donadio, "Pope Lashes Out at Belgium after Raid on Church," *New York Times*, June 27, 2010, http://www.nytimes.com/2010/06/28/world/europe/28vatican.html (accessed June 29, 2010).

24. Associated Press, "Vatican Issuing Guidelines on Sex Abuse to Bishops," *USA Today*, November 19, 2010, http://www.usatoday.com/news/religion/2010-11-19-popemeeting19_ST_N.htm (accessed November 22, 2010).

25. National Review Board for the Protection of Children and Young People, "Scandals in the Church; Excerpts from Report on Abuse by Members of the Catholic Clergy," *New York Times*, February 28, 2004, http://www.nytimes.com/2004/02/28/us/scandals-church-excerpts-report-abuse-members-catholic-clergy.html?scp=8&sq=essential%20norms&st=cse (accessed June 24, 2010).

26. Cathy Lee Grossman, "Keating Blasts Bishops as He Departs from Post," *USA Today*, June 16, 2003, http://www.usatoday.com/news/nation/2003-06-16-keating_x.htm (accessed July 1, 2010).

27. Laurie Goodstein, "Ousted Members Contend Jehovah's Witnesses' Abuse Policy Hides Offenses," *New York Times*, August 11, 2002, http://www.nytimes.com/2002/08/11/national/11WITN.html (accessed November 13, 2010).

28. Marci A. Hamilton, "'Licentiousness' in Religious Organizations and Why It Is Not Protected under Religious Liberty Constitutional Provisions," *William and Mary Bill of Rights Journal* 18 (2010): 983, http://scholarship.law.wm.edu/cgi/viewcontent.cgi?article=1159&context=wmborj.

29. Thomas P. Doyle, "Crimen Sollicitationis: Observations," *In the Vineyard* 5, no. 17 (October 5, 2006), http://www.votf.org/vineyard/Oct5_2006/bbc.html (accessed May 15, 2010).

30. Ruth, "Risk of Abuse in Faith Communities,"540.

31. "Documents Sought in Priest Sex Abuse Lawsuit," *NBC Connecticut*, May 18, 2010, http://www.nbcconnecticut.com/news/local-beat/Documents-Sought-in-Priest-Sex-Abuse-Lawsuit-94105374.html (accessed September 12, 2010).

32. Gillian Flaccus, "Unsealed California Church Documents Show Abuse Allegations," Associated Press, October 24, 2010, at Yahoo! News, http://news.yahoo.com/s/ap/20101024/ap_on_re_us/us_california_church_abuse (accessed October 26, 2010).

33. Ruth, "Risk of Abuse in Faith Communities,"540.

34. Carol Delaney, *Abraham on Trial: The Social Legacy of Biblical Myth* (Princeton, NJ: Princeton University Press, 1998), 240–41.

35. Supreme and Holy Congregation of the Holy Office, *Instruction on the Manner of Proceeding in Cases of Solicitation* (Vatican Press, 1962), 23, at CBS News, http://www.cbsnews.com/htdocs/pdf/Criminales.pdf.

36. Ibid., 6–7.

37. Ibid., 6.

38. Ibid., 15.

39. Ibid., 7.

40. Ibid., 27.

41. John L. Allen Jr., "1962 Document Orders Secrecy in Sex Cases: Many

Bishops Unaware Obscure Missive Was in Their Archives," *National Catholic Reporter*, August 7, 2003, http://www.nationalcatholicreporter.org/update/bn080703.htm (accessed June 27, 2010).

42. Supreme and Holy Congregation of the Holy Office, *Instruction on the Manner of Proceeding in Cases of Solicitation*, 4.

43. Allen Jr., "1962 Document Orders Secrecy in Sex Cases."

44. Catholic News Service and *America*, "Vatican Official Says 1962 Norms on Solicitation No Longer Apply," *America*, September 1, 2003, http://www.america magazine.org/content/article.cfm?article_id=3127 (accessed May 25, 2010).

45. Supreme and Holy Congregation of the Holy Office, *Instruction on the Manner of Proceeding in Cases of Solicitation*, 20.

46. Congregation for the Doctrine of the Faith to Bishops of the Entire Catholic Church, "Letter."

47. Nicole Winfield, "Vatican: 1997 Abuse Letter 'Misunderstood,'" Associated Press, at *Daily News*, January 19, 2011, http://www.dailynews.com/news/ci _17141528 (accessed March 7, 2011).

48. Doyle, "Crimen Sollicitationis."

49. Writing Committee, Governing Body of Jehovah's Witnesses, "Jehovah's Witnesses Care for Victims of Child Abuse," Jehovah's Witnesses Official Media Web Site, November 21, 2007, http://www.jw-media.org/gbl/20071121.htm (accessed May 30, 2010).

50. Goodstein, "Ousted Members Contend Jehovah's Witnesses' Abuse Policy Hides Offenses."

51. Writing Committee, Governing Body of Jehovah's Witnesses, "Jehovah's Witnesses Care for Victims of Child Abuse."

52. Writing Committee, Governing Body of Jehovah's Witnesses, "Child Molesting: You Can Protect Your Child," *Awake!*, January 22, 1985, at *Watchtower*, http://www.watchtower.org/e/19850122/article_01.htm (accessed May 30, 2010).

53. Writing Committee, Governing Body of Jehovah's Witnesses, "Protect Your Children! If Your Child Is Abused" *Awake!*, October 8, 1993, at Watchtower, http://www.watchtower.org/e/19931008a/diagram_02.htm (accessed August 30, 2010).

54. Writing Committee, Governing Body of Jehovah's Witnesses, "Our Families."

55. Goodstein, "Ousted Members Say Jehovah's Witnesses' Policy on Abuse Hides Offenses."

56. Ibid.

57. Writing Committee, Governing Body of Jehovah's Witnesses, "Jehovah's Witnesses Care for Victims of Child Abuse."

58. Michal Lando, "NY Yeshiva Sued over 'Sexual Abuse,'" *Jerusalem Post*, April 2, 2008, at Truth Will Set You Free, http://wakeupfromyourslumber.com/ node/6301 (accessed May 30, 2010).

59. Hella Winston and Larry Cohler-Esses, "No Sex Charge for Kolko: Boys' Parents Foiled by DA," *New York Jewish Week*, April 8, 2008, http://www.thejewish week.com/news/national/no_sex_charge_kolko_boys'_parents_foiled_da_0 (accessed May 19, 2010).

60. Robert Kolker, "On the Rabbi's Knee: Do the Orthodox Jews Have a Catholic-Priest Problem?" *New York*, May 14, 2006, http://nymag.com/news/features/17010/ (accessed May 17, 2010).

61. Paul Vitello, "Orthodox Jews Rely More on Sex Abuse Prosecution," *New York Times*, October 13, 2009, http://www.nytimes.com/2009/10/14/nyregion/14abuse.html?_r=1&scp=1&sq="Orthodox%20Jews%20Rely%20More%20on%20Sex%20Abuse%20Prosecution"&st=cse (accessed June 2, 2010).

62. Carolyn Holderread Heggen, *Sexual Abuse in Christian Homes and Churches* (Eugene, OR: Wipf & Stock, 2006), 108–109.

63. CBS News and Associated Press, "Woman: Church Covered Up My Rape as Teen," CBS News, May 29, 2010, http://www.cbsnews.com/ stories/2010/05/29/earlyshow/saturday/main6530160.shtml (accessed May 29, 2010).

64. Ian Fisher and Laurie Goodstein, "Pope, in U.S., Is 'Ashamed' of Pedophile Priests," *New York Times*, April 16, 2008, http://www.nytimes.com/2008/04/16/us/nationalspecial2/16pope.html (accessed June 8, 2010).

65. Barbara Bradley Haggerty, "Vatican: Bishops Must Report Alleged Abuse to Police," NPR, April 12, 2010, http://www.npr.org/templates/story/story.php?storyId=125866557 (accessed October 26, 2010).

66. Nicole Winfield, "Thousands Flock to Vatican to Back Pope on Abuse Scandal," Associated Press, May 18, 2010, at *USA Today*, http://www.usatoday.com/news/religion/2010-05-16-pope-supporters-vatican_N.htm (accessed September 17, 2010).

PART 4: SIN OF DENIAL—RELIGIOUS CHILD MEDICAL NEGLECT

* Christian Science practitioners and nurses are trained through church-approved, nonmedical programs. Practitioners give spiritual "healings," while nurses help patients with everyday activities, such as feeding and hygiene.

1. David Margolick, "In Child Deaths, a Test for Christian Science," *New York Times*, August 6, 1990, http://www.nytimes.com/1990/08/06/us/in-child-deaths-a-test-for-christian-science.html (accessed July 4, 2010).

2. Ibid.

3. Caroline Fraser, *God's Perfect Child: Living and Dying in the Christian Science Church* (New York: Holt Paperbacks, 2000), 304.

4. Dorris Sue Wong, "Accused Father Tells of Son's Death: Twitchell Breaks Down Describing Final Hours," *Boston Globe*, May 31, 1990.

5. Fraser, *God's Perfect Child*, 304.

6. Child Welfare Information Gateway (CWIG), "What Is Child Abuse and Neglect?" Child Welfare Information Gateway, 2008, http://www.childwelfare.gov/pubs/factsheets/whatiscan.cfm (accessed July 4, 2010).

7. US Department of Health & Human Services, *Child Maltreatment 2009* (Washington, DC: Administration for Children and Families, Children's Bureau, 2010), 46, http://www.acf.hhs.gov/programs/cb/pubs/cm09/cm09.pdf.

8. Ibid., 65.

9. Martha Farrell Erickson and Byron Egeland, "Child Neglect," in *The APSAC Handbook on Child Maltreatment*, 2nd ed., ed. John E. B. Myers et al., 3–20 (Thousand Oaks, CA: Sage, 2002), 3.

10. Amy Siskind, "Child-Rearing Issues in Totalistic Groups," in *Misunderstanding Cults: Searching for Objectivity in a Controversial Field*, ed. Benjamin Zablocki and Thomas Robbins, 415–51 (Toronto: University of Toronto, 2001), 420.

11. Kibbie S. Ruth, "Risk of Abuse in Faith Communities," in *Child Maltreatment: A Clinical Guide and Reference*, 3rd ed., ed. James A. Monteleone and Armand E. Brodeur, 539–55 (St. Louis: G. W. Medical, 2005), 544–45.

12. Thaeda Franz, "Power, Patriarchy, and Sexual Abuse in the Christian Church," *Traumatology* 8, no. 1 (March 2002): 8, PDF at Florida State University, http://www.fsu.edu/~trauma/v8/Church.pdf.

13. Sarah M. Rieth, "Ignorance Is Not a Victimless Crime: The Case of the Caring Teacher, Part I," *Pastoral Psychology* 41, no. 3 (1993): 171, http://ebscohost.com/ (accessed November 16, 2010).

14. Harold G. Koenig, Michael E. McCullough, and David B. Larson, *Handbook of Religion and Health* (New York: Oxford University, 2001), 69.

15. "Starving Family Refused to Buy Food, Police Say," *New York Times*, January 7, 1989, http://www.nytimes.com/1989/01/07/us/starving-family-refused-to-buy-food-police-say.html (accessed July 4, 2010).

16. David Wedge, "Cult Tied to Cases of Racist Violence, Kid Abuse," *Boston Herald*, October 29, 2005, at Ross Institute Internet Archives for the Study of Destructive Cults, Controversial Groups, and Movements, http://www.rickross.com/reference/black_israelites/black_israelites1.html (accessed July 4, 2010).

17. Brian Handwerk, "Snake Handlers Hang on in Appalachian Churches," *National Geographic News*, April 7, 2003, "http://news.nationalgeographic.com/news/2003/04/0407_030407_snakehandlers.html (accessed July 4, 2010).

18. Brian Cabell, "Custody of 'Snake-Bite Orphans' Split Between Grandparents," CNN, February 12, 1999, http://www.cnn.com/US/9902/12/snake.bite.family/index.html (accessed July 4, 2010).

19. Keith Wright, *Religious Abuse: A Pastor Explores the Many Ways Religion Can Hurt as Well as Heal* (Kelowna, BC: Northstone Publishing, 2001), 18.

CHAPTER 17: WHY NO ONE CALLS IT *NEGLECT*

1. Linda L. Barnes et al., "Spirituality, Religion, and Pediatrics: Intersecting Worlds of Healing," *Pediatrics* 104, no. 6 (October 2000): 901, http://pediatrics.aappublications.org/cgi/reprint/106/4/S1/899 (accessed October 5, 2010).

2. Dónal O'Mathúna and Kellie Lang, "Medicine vs. Prayer: The Case of Kara Neumann," *Pediatric Nursing* 34, no. 5 (September–October 2008): 413, at BNET, http://findarticles.com/p/articles/mi_m0FSZ/is_5_34/ai_n31024432/ (accessed November 16, 2010).

3. "Faith Healing," American Cancer Society, http://www.cancer.org/Treatment/TreatmentsandSideEffects/ComplementaryandAlternativeMedicine/HerbsVitaminsandMinerals/faith-healing (accessed August 9, 2010).

4. Harold G. Koenig, Michael E. McCullough, and David B. Larson, *Handbook of Religion and Health* (New York: Oxford University, 2001), 64.

5. Committee on Bioethics, American Academy of Pediatrics (AAP), "Religious Objections to Medical Care," *Pediatrics* 99, no. 2 (February 1997): 279, at Circumcision Information and Reference Pages, http://www.cirp.org/library/ethics/AAP3/ (accessed June 19, 2010).

6. "Some Outbreaks of Vaccine-Preventable Disease in Groups with Religious or Philosophical Exemptions to Vaccination," Children's Healthcare Is a Legal Duty (CHILD), http://www.childrenshealthcare.org/immunizations.htm (accessed October 12, 2010).

7. Jack Kelley, "How Could Parents Let a Child Die? TV's 'Promised a Miracle' Explores a Tragic Case of Misguided Faith," *People*, May 16, 1988, http://www.people.com/people/archive/article/0,,20098967,00.html (accessed April 11, 2010).

8. Seth M. Asser and Rita Swan, "Child Fatalities from Religion-Motivated Medical Neglect," *Pediatrics* 101, no. 4 (April 1998), http://search.ebscohost.com/ (accessed December 29, 2008).

9. Deena Guzder, "When Parents Call God Instead of the Doctor," *Time*, February 5, 2009, http://www.time.com/time/nation/article/0,8599,1877352,00.html. (accessed October 1, 2010).

10. Daily Mail Reporter, "Christian Parents Who Refused 'Sinful' Medicine and Prayed as Their Toddler Son Died Are Spared Prison," *Daily Mail*, February 3, 2011, http://www.dailymail.co.uk/news/article-1353071/Christian-parents-shunned-medicine-prayer-son-died-spared-prison.html.

11. Rita Swan, "When Faith Fails Children," *Humanist*, November 2000, at BNET, http://findarticles.com/p/articles/mi_m1374/is_6_60/ai_78889718/ (accessed September 7, 2010).

12. David Margolick, "In Child Deaths, a Test for Christian Science," *New York Times*, August 6, 1990, http://www.nytimes.com/1990/08/06/us/in-child-deaths-a-test-for-christian-science.html?pagewanted=print (accessed July 4, 2010).

13. Howard Davidson, "Summary of Some Key Changes to the Federal Child Abuse Prevention & Treatment Act (CAPTA)," American Bar Association, 1996, http:// www.abanet.org/child/capta.shtml (accessed July 22, 2010).

14. Diane DePanfilis and Children's Bureau, Office on Child Abuse and Neglect, "Child Neglect: A Guide for Prevention, Assessment and Intervention," Administration for Children & Families, at Child Welfare Information Gateway, 2006, http://www.childwelfare.gov/pubs/usermanuals/neglect/chaptertwo.cfm (accessed October 1, 2010).

15. US Department of Health & Human Services, *Child Maltreatment 2009* (Washington, DC: Administration for Children and Families, Children's Bureau, 2010), 46, http://www.acf.hhs.gov/programs/cb/pubs/cm09/cm09.pdf.

16. Carole Jenny and Committee on Child Abuse and Neglect, "Recognizing and

Responding to Medical Neglect," *Pediatrics* 120, no. 6 (December 2007): 1385, http://aappolicy.aappublications.org/cgi/reprint/pediatrics;120/6/1385.pdf.

17. Asser and Swan, "Child Fatalities from Religion-Motivated Medical Neglect," 628.

18. Commonwealth v. David R. Twitchell, 416 Mass. 114, 617 N.E.2d 609 (1993), http://wings.buffalo.edu/law/bclc/web/matwitchell.htm (accessed September 21, 2010).

19. William McCall, "Child Deaths Test Faith-Healing Exemption," Associated Press, at *KATU.com* (Portland, OR), November 22, 2008, http://www.katu.com/news/34932419.html (accessed October 2, 2010).

20. Asser and Swan, "Child Fatalities from Religion-Motivated Medical Neglect," 625.

21. Howard Dubowitz, "Neglect of Children's Health Care," in *The APSAC Handbook on Child Maltreatment*, 3rd ed., ed. John E. B. Myers, 145–65 (Thousand Oaks, CA: Sage, 2011), 157.

22. Robert W. Tuttle, interview by Jesse Meriam, Pew Forum on Religion and Public Life, August 31, 2009, http://pewforum.org/Church-State-Law/Faith-Healing-and -the-Law.aspx (accessed August 9, 2010).

23. Seth Asser, "Legalized Child Abuse: Faith Healers and Child Deaths," in *Proceedings of the Amazing Meeting 3* (James Randi Educational Foundation, 2005) (paper presented at the Amazing Meeting 3, Las Vegas, NV, January 16, 2005), 23, http://www.csufresno.edu/physics/rhall/jref/tam3p/05_SA_tam3.pdf.

24. Committee on Bioethics, AAP, "Religious Objections to Medical Care."

25. Ibid.

26. "Questions," Christian Science, http://christianscience.com/questions/questions-christian-science-faq/ (accessed July 26, 2010).

27. 2009 Wisconsin Act 282, Senate Bill 667, sec. 17, 448.03, http://www.loislaw .com/livepublish8923/doclink.htp?dockey=6132028@WICODE&alias=WICODE &cite=448.03 (accessed September 8, 2010).

28. Davidson, "Summary of Some Key Changes to the Federal Child Abuse Prevention & Treatment Act (CAPTA)."

29. Martha Farrell Erickson and Byron Egeland, "Child Neglect," in *The APSAC Handbook on Child Maltreatment*, 2nd ed., ed. John E. B. Myers et al., 3–20 (Thousand Oaks, CA: Sage, 2002), 6.

30. Ibid.

31. Dubowitz, "Neglect of Children's Health Care," 145.

32. R. Albert Mohler Jr., "When Medicine and Faith Collide—What about the Child?" AlbertMohler.com, May 26, 2009, http://www.albertmohler.com/2009/05/26/when-medicine-and-faith-collide-what-about-the-child/ (accessed August 19, 2010).

33. Associated Press, "Faith-Healing Parents Given Jail Sentence," CBS News, October 7, 2009, http://www.cbsnews.com/stories/2009/10/06/national/main5367 848.shtml (accessed August 12, 2010).

CHAPTER 18: THE HAZARDS OF BLIND FAITH

1. Linda L. Barnes et al., "Spirituality, Religion, and Pediatrics: Intersecting Worlds of Healing," *Pediatrics* 104, no. 6 (October 2000): 901, http://pediatrics.aap publications.org/cgi/reprint/106/4/S1/899 (accessed October 5, 2010).

2. Jonathan Turley, "When a Child Dies, Faith Is No Defense," *Washington Post*, November 15, 2009, http://www.washingtonpost.com/wp-dyn/content/article/2009/11/13/AR2009111302220.html (accessed July 24, 2010).

3. Caroline Fraser, "Suffering Children and the Christian Science Church," *Atlantic Monthly*, April 2005, http://www.theatlantic.com/past/docs/unbound/flashbks/xsci/suffer.htm (accessed August 30, 2010).

4. Brigham Young, "The Holy Ghost Necessary in Preaching—Faith—Healing the Sick . . . ," *Journal of Discourses*, vol. 4 (London: S. W. Richards, 1857), 24, http://jod.mrm.org/4/20.

5. Mary Baker Eddy, *Manual of the Mother Church: The First Church of Christ Scientist*, 88th ed. (Boston: Allison V. Stewart, 1910), 15, at Mary Baker Eddy Science Institute, http://www.mbeinstitute.org/CManual/ChurchManual.pdf.

6. Mary Baker Eddy, "Science and Health with Key to the Scriptures," (1875; repr., Boston: Christian Scientist Publishing, 1910), http://www.mbeinstitute.org/SAH/SAH.htm (accessed November 12, 2010).

7. Turley, "When a Child Dies, Faith Is No Defense."

8. Mark Larabee, "The Battle over Faith Healing," *Oregonian*, November 28, 1998, http://blog.oregonlive.com/clackamascounty/2009/06/faithhealing_deaths_previous_s.html#a (accessed July 3, 2010).

9. Ibid.

10. "Questions," Christian Science, http://christianscience.com/questions/questions-christian-science-faq/ (accessed July 26, 2010).

11. Stephen Gottschalk, "Spiritual Healing on Trial: A Christian Scientist Reports," *Christian Century* 105 (June 22–29, 1988): 603, at Religion-Online.org, http://www.religion-online.org/showarticle.asp?title=953 (accessed July 6, 2010).

12. Shawn Francis Peters, *When Prayer Fails: Faith Healing, Children, and the Law* (New York: Oxford University Press, 2007), 13.

13. Caroline Fraser, *God's Perfect Child: Living and Dying in the Christian Science Church* (New York: Holt Paperbacks, 2000), 428.

14. Jack Kelley, "How Could Parents Let a Child Die? TV's 'Promised a Miracle' Explores a Tragic Case of Misguided Faith," *People*, May 16, 1988, http://www.people.com/people/archive/article/0,,20098967,00.html (accessed April 11, 2010).

15. Ibid.

16. Associated Press, "Police: Girl Dies after Parents Pray for Healing Instead of Seeking Medical Help," *FoxNews.com*, March 26, 2008, http://www.foxnews.com/story/0,2933,341574,00.html (accessed August 23, 2010).

17. Associated Press, "Charges against Parents in Diabetes Death," Today's TMJ4 (Milwaukee), May 21, 2009, http://www.todaystmj4.com/news/local/45626632.html (accessed August 23, 2010).

18. Worldwide Great Commission Fellowship on Christian Living, "Voice of Healing Revival," inJesus, September 15, 2009, http://injesus.com/message -archives/christian-living/wgcf/what-was-the-voice-of-healing-revival-1 (accessed March 6, 2011).

19. Cindy Jacobs, "Who's Afraid of Virginia?" *Rachel Maddow Show*, MSNBC, April 12, 2010, http://www.msnbc.msn.com/id/36460299 (accessed May 14, 2010).

20. Harold G. Koenig, Michael E. McCullough, and David B. Larson, *Handbook of Religion and Health* (New York: Oxford University, 2001), 69.

21. Fraser, *God's Perfect Child*, 422–23.

22. E. Mansell Pattison, Nikolajs A. Lapins, and Hans A. Doerr, "Faith Healing: A Study of Personality and Function," *Transcultural Psychiatry* 7, no. 1 (1970): 75–76, http://tps.sagepub.com/ (accessed July 8, 2010).

23. David Schoetz, "Parents' Faith Fails to Save Diabetic Girl," ABC News, March 27, 2008, http://abcnews.go.com/Health/DiabetesResource/story?id=453 6593&page=1 (accessed July 5, 2010).

24. Erik Gunn, "Death by Prayer," *Isthmus*, August 8, 2008, http://www .isthmus.com/isthmus/article.php?article=23430 (accessed July 27, 2010).

25. Associated Press, "Charges against Parents in Diabetes Death."

26. Gottschalk, "Spiritual Healing on Trial."

27. Larabee, "Battle over Faith Healing."

28. Fraser, "Suffering Children and the Christian Science Church."

29. Jamie Satterfield, "Debate over Faith as Health Care Begins in Loudon Courtroom," *Knoxville News Sentinel*, January 13, 2009, http://www.knoxnews.com/news/ 2009/jan/13/faith-as-health-care-debate-begins-in-loudon/ (accessed July 29, 2010).

30. Deena Guzder, "When Parents Call God Instead of the Doctor," *Time*, February 5, 2009, http://www.time.com/time/nation/article/0,8599,1877352,00.html. (accessed July 11, 2010).

31. Brenda McEvoy DeVellis, Robert F. DeVellis, and James C. Spilsbury, "Parental Actions When Children Are Sick: The Role of Belief in Divine Influence," *Basic and Applied Social Psychology* 9, no. 3 (September 1988): 185, http://ebscohost .com/ (accessed October 4, 2010).

32. Larabee, "Battle over Faith Healing."

33. Ibid.

34. William A. Wisdom, "The Skeptic as Expert Witness in the Case against the Faith Healers," *William A. Wisdom*, 2003, http://www.unconventional-wisdom.com/ WAW/FAITH-HEALERS.html (accessed July 14, 2010).

35. Larabee, "Battle over Faith Healing."

36. Barnes et al., "Spirituality, Religion, and Pediatrics," 901.

37. Elaine Welsome, "Born to Believe," *Denver Westword*, October 12, 2000, http:// www.westword.com/2000-10-12/news/born-to-believe/ (accessed July 25, 2010).

38. Shantell M. Kirkendoll and Ken Palmer, "Chemo Begins for Amish Girl," *Flint Journal*, April 22, 1999, at Ross Institute Internet Archives for the Study of Destructive Cults, Controversial Groups, and Movements, http://www.rickross .com/reference/amish/amish1.html (accessed March 29, 2010).

39. Mary Jayne McKay, "Genetic Disorders Hit Amish Hard," CBS News, June 8, 2005, http://www.cbsnews.com/stories/2005/06/08/60II/main700519_page2 .shtml?tag=contentMain;contentBody (accessed September 16, 2010).

40. Ibid.

41. Welsome, "Born to Believe."

42. Gunn, "Death by Prayer."

43. Kelley, "How Could Parents Let a Child Die?"

44. "Questions."

45. Fraser, *God's Perfect Child*, 408.

46. Eddy, "Science and Health with Key to the Scriptures."

47. Larabee, "Battle over Faith Healing."

48. A. M. Kaunitz et al., "Perinatal and Maternal Mortality in a Religious Group Avoiding Obstetric Care," *American Journal of Obstetrics and Gynecology* 150, no. 7 (December 1, 1984), abstract at National Center for Biotechnology Information, http://www.ncbi.nlm.nih.gov/pubmed/6507508 (accessed September 7, 2010).

49. Carol Balizet, *Born in Zion* (Euless, TX: ChristCenter Publications International, 1992), in Peters, *When Prayer Fails*, 155–56 (see note 11).

50. Peters, *When Prayer Fails*, 155–56.

51. Ibid.

52. Kristen Watts, "Cult Buster Warns Families," *West Australian*, May 12, 2001, at Ross Institute Internet Archives for the Study of Destructive Cults, Controversial Groups, and Movements, http://www.rickross.com/reference/zion/zion2.html (accessed July 11, 2010).

53. Ibid.

54. "'The Body of Christ': Descent from Benign Bible Study to Destructive Cult," *New England Institute of Religious Research*, http://www.neirr.org/AttleboroHistory New.htm (accessed June 15, 2010).

55. "Victims of Religion-Based Medical Neglect," Children's Healthcare Is a Legal Duty (CHILD), http://www.childrenshealthcare.org/victims.htm#Harrison (accessed July 12, 2010).

56. Joe Humphrey, "Witnesses: Stung Boy Seemed Fine," *St. Petersburg Times*, August 2, 2000, http://www.sptimes.com/News/080200/TampaBay/Witnesses _Stung_boy_.shtml (accessed July 16, 2010).

57. Sara H. Sinal, Elaine Cabinum-Foeller, and Rebecca Socolar, "Religion and Medical Neglect," *Southern Medical Journal* 101, no. 7 (2008): 703.

58. Virginia S. Harris, "Christian Science Spiritual Healing Practices," *Christian Science Journal* (excerpts from address, Spirituality and Healing in Medicine conference, Boston, MA, December 1997), at Christian Science, http://christianscience.com/ articles-journal/2007/10/11/christian-science-healing-practices/ (accessed August 12, 2010).

59. Charles Pinches, "Miracles: A Christian Theological Overview," *Southern Medical Journal* 100, no. 12 (December 2007), http://journals.lww.com/smajournal online/fulltext/2007/12000/miracles__a_christian_theological_overview.17.aspx (accessed March 6, 2011).

60. John Hooper, "Pope's Sainthood Setback after 'Miracle Cure' Nun Reported to Be Ill Again," *Guardian*, March 5, 2010, http://www.guardian.co.uk/world/2010/mar/05/nun-cured-pope-parkinsons-ill (accessed August 9, 2010).

61. "Laying on of Hands," Church of Jesus Christ of Latter-day Saints, http://lds.org/ldsorg/v/index.jsp?locale=0&sourceId=44219daac5d98010VgnVCM100000 4d82620a____&vgnextoid=bbd508f54922d010VgnVCM1000004d82620aRCRD (accessed March 6, 2011).

62. Steve Mayes, "Trial in Death of Infant Raises Questions of Parental Rights, Religious Freedom," *Oregonian*, June 21, 2009, at Ross Institute Internet Archives for the Study of Destructive Cults, Controversial Groups, and Movements, http://www.rickross.com/reference/foc/foc31.html (accessed August 9, 2010).

63. Schoetz, "Parents' Faith Fails to Save Diabetic Girl."

64. Gary B. Ferngren, *Medicine and Health Care in Early Christianity* (Baltimore: Johns Hopkins University, 2009), 5.

65. Ibid., 13.

66. Ibid., 3.

67. Dónal P. O'Mathúna and Kellie Lang, "Medicine vs. Prayer: The Case of Kara Neumann," *Pediatric Nursing* 34, no. 5 (September–October 2008): 415, at BNET, http://findarticles.com/p/articles/mi_m0FSZ/is_5_34/ai_n31024432/ (accessed November 16, 2010).

CHAPTER 19: FATAL PRAYERS

1. Leanne Roberts et al., "Intercessory Prayer for the Alleviation of Ill Health," *Cochrane Database of Systematic Reviews* 2 (2009): 2, http://c2.libsyn.com/media/22494/intercessory_prayer.pdf?nvb=20101117053838&nva=20101118054838&sid =cf61be9422cbe0ae4678d350d3ad1e44&l_sid=22494&l_eid=&l_mid=2057242&t =0d7fd67dc778752243b57 (accessed November 16, 2010).

2. Caroline Fraser, *God's Perfect Child: Living and Dying in the Christian Science Church* (New York: Holt Paperbacks, 2000), 424.

3. "Can Prayer Lower High Blood Pressure?" *Jet*, August 31, 1998, 15.

4. Claudia Wallis et al., "Faith & Healing," *Time*, June 24, 1996, http://www.time.com/time/printout/0,8816,984737,00.html (accessed October 3, 2010).

5. Seth M. Asser and Rita Swan, "Child Fatalities from Religion-Motivated Medical Neglect," *Pediatrics* 101, no. 4 (April 1998): 625, http://search.ebscohost.com/ (accessed December 29, 2008).

6. Ibid., 627.

7. Ibid., 625.

8. Ibid., 626.

9. Ibid.

10. Ibid.

11. Ibid., 626–27.

12. Ibid., 629.

13. Harold G. Koenig, Michael E. McCullough, and David B. Larson, *Handbook of Religion and Health* (New York: Oxford University, 2001), 68–69.

14. Asser and Swan, "Child Fatalities from Religion-Motivated Medical Neglect," 628.

15. Fraser, *God's Perfect Child*, 402.

16. Gale E. Wilson, "Christian Science and Longevity," *Journal of Forensic Sciences* 1, no. 4 (October 1956): 44.

17. "Science and Health with Key to the Scriptures by Mary Baker Eddy," Christian Science, http://christianscience.com/publications/science-and-health/ (accessed November 12, 2010).

18. David Margolick, "In Child Deaths, a Test for Christian Science," *New York Times*, August 6, 1990, http://www.nytimes.com/1990/08/06/us/in-child-deaths-a-test-for-christian-science.html?pagewanted=print (accessed September 10, 2010).

19. B. A. Robinson, "The Church of Christ, Scientist," Religious Tolerance, August 12, 2007, http://www.religioustolerance.org/cr_sci.htm (accessed September 4, 2010).

20. Wilson, "Christian Science and Longevity," 44.

21. US Centers for Disease Control and Prevention, "Comparative Mortality of Two College Groups, 1945–1983," *Morbidity and Mortality Weekly Report* 40, no. 33 (August 23, 1991), http://www.cdc.gov/mmwr/preview/mmwrhtml/00015022.htm (accessed August 30, 2010).

22. Wilson, "Christian Science and Longevity," 46.

23. James T. Richardson and John Dewitt, "Christian Science Spiritual Healing, the Law, and Public Opinion," *Journal of Church & State* 34, no. 3 (Summer 1992): 549, http:// search.ebscohost.com/ (accessed October 8, 2010).

24. Christian Science Board of Directors, "Christian Scientists and the Practice of Spiritual Healing," *Christian Science Sentinel* 93 (October 7, 1991), quoted in Richardson and Dewitt, "Christian Science Spiritual Healing, the Law, and Public Opinion," 557.

25. Fraser, *God's Perfect Child*, 402.

26. Thomas J. Wheeler, "A Scientific Look at Alternative Medicine," *Kentucky Council Against Health Fraud*, February 28, 2006, 3, http://kcahf.org/content/faith06.pdf.

27. Steve Mayes, "Oregon Lawmakers Appear Ready to End Legal Protections for Faith-Healing Parents," *Oregonian*, February 20, 2011, at OregonLive.com, http://www.oregonlive.com/oregon-city/index.ssf/2011/02/oregon_lawmakers_appear_ready_to_end_faith-healing_protections_for_parents_of_dying_children.html%203-2-11.

28. B. A. Robinson, "Jehovah's Witnesses Past Opposition to Vaccinations," Religious Tolerance, September 4, 2003, http://www.religioustolerance.org/witness6.htm (accessed July 16, 2010).

29. David Schoetz, "Parents' Faith Fails to Save Diabetic Girl," ABC News, March 27, 2008, http://abcnews.go.com/Health/DiabetesResource/story?id=4536593&page=1 (accessed July 5, 2010).

30. B.A. Robinson, "Jehovah's Witnesses (WTS) Opposition to Blood Transfusions," *Religious Tolerance*, July 27, 2008, http://www.religioustolerance.org/witness13.htm (accessed July 16, 2010).

31. Writing Committee, Governing Body of Jehovah's Witnesses, "The Real Value of Blood," *Awake!*, August 2006, at Watchtower, http://www.watchtower.org/e/200608/article_03.htm (accessed July 15, 2010).

32. Associated Jehovah's Witnesses for Reform on Blood (ATWRB), "Watchtower Blood Policy in 1961," *New Light on Blood*, http://www.ajwrb.org/index.shtml (accessed July 19, 2010).

33. Patrick Merida, "Cell Saver and Bloodless Surgery," University of Rhode Island, http://www.ele.uri.edu/courses/ele282/F08/Patrick_2.pdf (accessed July 16, 2010).

34. Associated Jehovah's Witnesses for Reform on Blood (ATWRB), "The Modern Historical Perspective," New Light on Blood, http://www.ajwrb.org/history/index.shtml#modern (accessed July 19, 2010).

35. Writing Committee, Governing Body of Jehovah's Witnesses, "Our View of Medical Care: Blood Transfusions," Jehovah's Witnesses Official Media Web Site, http://www.jw-media.org/aboutjw/article01.htm (accessed July 19, 2010).

36. Osamu Muramato, "Recent Developments in Medical Care of Jehovah's Witnesses," *Western Journal of Medicine* 170 (May 1999): 297, at National Center for Biotechnology Information, http://www.ncbi.nlm.nih.gov/pmc/articles/PMC1305593/pdf/westjmed00320-0051.pdf.

37. Associated Jehovah's Witnesses for Reform on Blood (ATWRB), "About AJWRB," New Light on Blood, http://www.ajwrb.org/about.shtml (accessed July 16, 2010).

38. Muramato, "Recent Developments in Medical Care of Jehovah's Witnesses," 299.

39. Ibid., 298–99.

40. AJWRB, "About AJWRB."

41. Associated Jehovah's Witnesses for Reform on Blood (AJWRB), "Welcome to the Watchtower Victims Memorial," New Light on Blood, http://www.ajwrb.org/victims/ index.shtml (accessed July 16, 2010).

42. Associated Jehovah's Witnesses for Reform on Blood (AJWRB), "Change from 1961 or No Change," New Light on Blood, http://www.ajwrb.org/index.shtml (accessed July 16, 2010).

43. Writing Committee, Governing Body of Jehovah's Witnesses, "Youths Who Have Power beyond What Is Normal," *Awake!*, May 22, 1994, 9–15, from "Watchtower Library 2005" CD, http://www.watchtower.cc/files.html (accessed July 16, 2010).

44. Jehovah's Witnesses, St., Washington v. King Cty. Hosp., 390 U.S. 598 (1968).

45. Cherie Black, "Boy Dies of Leukemia after Refusing Treatment for Religious Reasons," *Seattle Post-Intelligencer*, November 29, 2007, http://www.seattlepi.com/local/341458_leukemia29.html (accessed July 16, 2010).

46. Muramato, "Recent Developments in Medical Care of Jehovah's Witnesses," 300.

47. David van Biema and Dan Kray, "Faith or Healing?" *Time*, August 31, 1998, http://www.time.com/time/printout/0,8816,989006,00.html (accessed August 3, 2010).

48. Steve Mayes, "Oregon Faith-Healing Parents Fight to Get Baby Back, Face Criminal Charges," *Oregonian*, July 22, 2010, at OregonLive.com, http://www.oregonlive.com/oregon-city/index.ssf/2010/07/post_2.html (accessed July 29, 2010).

49. Steve Mayes, "Judge Sends Message with Prison Terms in Faith-Healing Case," *Oregonian*, March 8, 2010, at OregonLive.com, http://www.oregonlive.com/clackamascounty/index.ssf/2010/03/judge_sends_message_with_priso.html (accessed July 2, 2010).

50. Van Biema and Kray, "Faith or Healing?"

51. William McCall, "Faith-Healing Pair Acquitted of Manslaughter," Associated Press, at MSNBC, July 23, 2009. http://www.msnbc.msn.com/id/ 32112828/ (accessed October 9, 2010).

52. Tom Wolfe, "Worthington Gets Jail Time in Faith-Healing Death," *Oregonian*, July 31, 2009, at OregonLive.com, http://www.oregonlive.com/clackamascounty/index.ssf/2009/07/worthington_gets_jail_time_in.html (accessed August 9, 2010).

53. McCall, "Faith-Healing Pair Acquitted of Manslaughter."

54. Wolfe, "Worthington Gets Jail Time in Faith-Healing Death."

55. Mathew Graham, "Oregon City Boy Refused Medical Help before His Death," *Clackamas Review*, December 8, 2009, http://www.clackamasreview.com/news/print_story.php?story_id=126030316536283100 (accessed August 9, 2010).

56. Mathew Graham, "Doctor: Beagley's Condition Was 'Mind-Boggling,'" *Clackamas Review*, December 8, 2009, http://www.oregoncitynewsonline.com/news/story_2nd.php?story_id=126411526178046100 (accessed August 9, 2010).

57. Nicole Dungca, "Jeffrey and Marci Beagley Sentenced to 16 Months of Prison for Their Son's Faith-Healing Death," *Oregonian*, March 8, 2010, http://www.oregonlive.com/clackamascounty/index.ssf/2010/03/jeffrey_and_marci_beagley_sent.html (accesses August 9, 2010).

58. Steve Mayes, "Faith Healers Plead Not Guilty to Criminal Mistreatment of Their Infant Daughter," *Oregonian*, July 30, 2010, at OregonLive.com, http://www.oregonlive.com/oregon-city/index.ssf/2010/07/faith_healers_plead_not_guilty_to_criminal_mistreatment_of_their_infant_daughter.html (accessed July 30, 2010).

59. Mayes, "Oregon Faith-Healing Parents Fight to Get Baby Back, Face Criminal Charges."

60. Steve Mayes, "Oregon City Couple Plead Not Guilty in Faith-Healing Death of Their Infant Son," *Oregonian*, August 30, 2010, at OregonLive.com, http://www.oregonlive.com/oregon-city/index.ssf/2010/08/oregon_city_couple_plead_not_guilty_in_faith-healing_death_of_their_infant_son.html (accessed August 3, 2010).

61. Seth Asser, "Legalized Child Abuse: Faith Healers and Child Deaths" in *Pro-

ceedings of the Amazing Meeting 3 (James Randi Educational Foundation, 2005) (paper presented at the Amazing Meeting 3, Las Vegas, NV, January 16, 2005), 24, http://www.csufresno.edu/physics/rhall/jref/tam3p/05_SA_tam3.pdf.

62. Abby Haight, "Oregon Faith Healers Get 16 Months for Son's Death," Associated Press, at ABC News, March 8, 2010, http://abcnews.go.com/US/wire Story?id=10041941 (accessed October 9, 2010).

63. Philip Hager, "Court Power on Child Medical Tests Widened," *LA Times*, February 26, 1987, http://articles.latimes.com/1987-02-26/news/mn-6077_1 _juvenile-court (accessed April 15, 2011).

64. Lovesisthekey, "Controversial—Some Good Ideas but Please Use Caution!" customer review on Amazon.com, June 17, 2005, http://www.amazon.com/Born -Zion-Carol-Balizet/dp/B0006F77YQ/ref=sr_1_4?ie=UTF8&s=books&qid=128166 8260&sr=8-4 (accessed August 12, 2010).

65. Associated Press, "Couple Spared Prison in Sick Son's Death," *Boston Globe*, February 3, 2011, http://www.boston.com/news/nation/articles/2011/02/03/ couple_spared_prison_in_sick_sons_death/ (accessed February 21, 2011).

66. Jonathan Turley, "When a Child Dies, Faith Is No Defense," *Washington Post*, November 15, 2009, http://www.washingtonpost.com/wp-dyn/content/article/ 2009/11/13/AR2009111302220.html (accessed July 24, 2010).

67. Fraser, *God's Perfect Child*, 437.

CHAPTER 20: SORTING OUT THE DEMONS OF CHILD RITUAL ABUSE

* Like Davis, Dorris did not remember any of the abuse until she was forty-four. She says the memories were triggered when she caught a priest in her parish molesting kids and tried to get him fired, after which time the memories came flooding back, as if "someone turned on a movie reel." Some doubt the veracity of "recovered memories," claiming that they are fabricated with the help of therapists. However, Dorris was not in therapy when her memories began coming back to her. Also, experts say many children who suffer trauma, such as sexual abuse, forget the experiences only to recall them later in life.

1. John Earl, "The Dark Truth about the 'Dark Tunnels of McMartin': Judy Johnson's Increasingly Bizarre Behavior," *Issues in Child Abuse Accusations* 7, no. 2 (Spring 1995), at Institute for Psychological Therapies, http://www.ipt-forensics .com/journal/volume7/j7_2_1_12.htm. (accessed July 6, 2009).

2. Katherine Ramsland, "The McMartin Nightmare and the Hysteria Puppeteers," truTV, http://www.trutv.com/library/crime/criminal_mind/psychology/ mcmartin_daycare/5.html (accessed March 6, 2011).

3. "The Most Expensive Court Case in the U.S.A.," *Find the Lawyer*, August 14, 2010, http://find-the-lawyer.com/tag/mcmartin/ (accessed March 6, 2011).

4. Ibid.

5. Robert Reinhold, "2 Acquitted of Child Molestation in Nation's Longest Crim-

inal Trial," *New York Times*, January 19, 1990, http://www.nytimes.com/1990/01/19/us/2-acquitted-of-child-molestation-in-nation-s-longest-criminal-trial.html (accessed July 6, 2009).

6. Ibid.

7. Kyle Zirpolo, "I'm Sorry," as told to Debbie Nathan, *LA Times*, October 30, 2005, at Jesse Friedman's Web Site, http://www.freejesse.net/LATimes/Introduction.htm.

8. Reinhold, "2 Acquitted of Child Molestation in Nation's Longest Criminal Trial."

9. A. S. Ross, "Blame It on the Devil," *Redbook*, June 1994, 110.

10. James T. Richardson, Joel Best, and David G. Bromley, eds., *The Satanism Scare* (New York: Walter de Gruyter, 1991), 53.

11. Daniel Goleman, "Proof Lacking for Ritual Abuse by Satanists," *New York Times*, October 31, 1994, http://www.nytimes.com/1994/10/31/us/proof-lacking-for-ritual-abuse-by-satanists.html (accessed July 6, 2009).

12. Ross, "Blame It on the Devil," 88.

13. Nadine Brozan, "Witness Says She Fears 'Child Predator' Network," *New York Times*, September 18, 1984, http://www.nytimes.com/1984/09/18/us/witness-says-she-fears-child-predator-network.html (accessed July 6, 2009).

14. David Frankfurter, *Evil Incarnate: Rumors of Demonic Conspiracy and Satanic Abuse in History* (Princeton, NJ: Princeton University, 2006), 57.

15. Illinois Rev. Public Act, 90-0088, sec. 12-33 (1998), http://www.ilga.gov/legislation/publicacts/pubact90/acts/90-0088.html (accessed September 9, 2009).

16. Jeffrey S. Victor, *Satanic Panic: The Creation of a Contemporary Legend* (Chicago: Open Court Publishing, 1993), 302.

17. Ontario Consultants on Religious Tolerance, "Geraldo Rivera: Satanic Ritual Abuse & Recovered Memories," Religious Tolerance, November 7, 2007, http://www.religioustolerance.org/geraldo.htm (accessed March 6, 2011).

18. Peter Applebome, "Drugs, Death and the Occult Meet in Grisly Inquiry at Mexico Border," *New York Times*, April 13, 1989, http://www.nytimes.com/1989/04/13/us/drugs-death-and-the-occult-meet-in-grisly-inquiry-at-mexico-border.html (accessed July 6, 2009).

19. Mark Sauer, "Chasing Satan in Sacramento: Zealous Senator Pushes Law adding Ritual-Abuse Penalties," *San Diego Union-Tribune*, June 16, 1994, http://www.lexisnexis.com/ (accessed August 6, 2009).

20. Jeffrey S. Victor, "The Satanic Cult Scare and Allegations of Ritual Child Abuse," *Institute for Psychological Therapies* 3, no. 3 (Summer 1991), http://www.ipt-forensics.com/journal/volume3/j3_3_1.htm (accessed March 6, 2011).

21. Kenneth V. Lanning, "Satanic Ritual Abuse: A 1992 FBI Report," at Ross Institute Internet Archives for the Study of Destructive Cults, Controversial Groups, and Movements, http://www.rickross.com/reference/satanism/satanism1.html (accessed September 9, 2009).

22. Bob Passantino and Gretchen Passantino, "The Hard Facts about Satanic Ritual Abuse," Answers in Action, 1992, http://www.answers.org/satan/sra.html (accessed September 9, 2009).

23. Lady D, "Geraldo's Satanic Propaganda," *Oklahoma Pagan*, December 26, 2008, http://okpagan.blogspot.com/2008/12/geraldos-satanic-propaganda.html (accessed September 9, 2009).

24. Margaret Talbot, "The Devil in the Nursery," *New York Times Magazine*, January 7, 2001, 51–52, http://proquest.com/en-US/ (accessed July 6, 2009).

25. Martin J. Dorahy et al., "Religious Ritual and Dissociation in India and Australia," *Journal of Psychology* 131, no. 5 (September 1, 1997): 474.

26. Bernard Spilka et al., *The Psychology of Religion*, 3rd ed., *An Empirical Approach* (New York: Guilford Press, 2003), 236.

27. Marc Lacey, "After Sweat Lodge Deaths, Fewer Tourists with Spiritual Needs," *New York Times*, October 9, 2010, http://www.nytimes.com/2010/10/20/us/20sedona.html (accessed November 1, 2010).

28. Ontario Consultants on Religious Tolerance, "Ritual Abuse: An Introduction to All Points of View," ReligiousTolerance.org, 2005, http://www.religioustolerance.org/ra_intro.htm#def (accessed September 9, 2009).

29. Scherezade Faramarzi, "Mutilating for God: Some Children Are Forced into Bloody Rite," *Federal News Radio*, January 30, 2007, at Free Republic, http://www.freerepublic.com/focus/f-news/1777800/posts (accessed November 8, 2010).

30. Ariel Glucklich, *Sacred Pain: Hurting the Body for the Sake of the Soul* (New York: Oxford University Press, 2001), 129.

31. Anne A. Johnson Davis, *Hell Minus One: My Story of Deliverance from Satanic Ritual Abuse and My Journey to Freedom* (Tooele, UT: Transcript Bulletin, 2008), 131.

32. Ibid., 43–50.

33. Ibid., 83–84.

34. Ibid., 125–26.

35. Ibid., 2.

36. Jim Kouri, "Satanic or Ritualistic Crime and Murder," Examiner.com, April 14, 2009, http://www.examiner.com/law-enforcement-in-national/satanic-or-ritualistic-crime-and-murder (accessed October 30, 2010).

37. "Mother Set Girl, 6, on Fire in Voodoo Case, DA Says," *Queens Chronicle*, June 25, 2009, http://www.zwire.com/site/news.cfm?newsid=20336432&BRD=2731&PAG=461&dept_id=574905&rfi=6 (accessed July 9, 2009).

38. Jacob H. Fries, "Mother Drowned Daughter, 4, in Exorcism Rite, Police Say," *New York Times*, November 14, 2001, http://www.nytimes.com/2001/11/14/nyregion/mother-drowned-daughter-4-in-exorcism-rite-police-say.html (accessed July 20, 2009).

39. Laura Italiano, "'Exorcist Mom' Admits Drowning Girl," *New York Post*, June 26, 2003, http://www.lexisnexis.com (accessed September 9, 2009).

40. Joshua Thompson v. State of Texas, No. 03-04-00161-CR, 403d Dist. (TX 2005).

41. Marci A. Hamilton, *God vs. the Gavel: Religion and the Rule of Law* (Cambridge: Cambridge University, 2005), 40.

42. "Attempted Exorcism Ends in Man's Death: Police Use Stun Gun on Grandfather Seen Choking 3-Year-Old Girl," Associated Press, July 29, 2007, at MSNBC, http://www.msnbc.msn.com/id/20027027/ (accessed July 20, 2009).

43. Keith L. Alexander, "Judge Hears Jacks Trial Summations," *Washington Post*, July 28, 2009, http://www.washingtonpost.com/wp-dyn/content/article/2009/07/27/AR2009072702785.html (accessed July 29, 2009).

44. Keith L. Alexander, "Details of Jacks' Relationship with Eldest Daughter Emerge," *Washington Post*, July 15, 2009, http://www.washingtonpost.com/wp-dyn/content/article/2009/07/14/AR2009071402559.html (accessed July 29, 2009).

45. Paul Duggan, "D.C. Woman Who Killed 4 Daughters Is Given a 120-Year Sentence," *Washington Post*, December 19, 2009, http://www.washingtonpost.com/wp-dyn/content/article/2009/12/18/AR2009121803806_pf.html (accessed December 19, 2009).

46. David Schoetz, "Mom Fatally Slashes 'Demon' Daughter," ABC News, April 10, 2008, http://abcnews.go.com/us/Story?id=4626892&page=1 (accessed July 20, 2009).

47. Brenda Brown, "Baby Tortured to Death in Rusk County," *Kilgore News Herald*, December 4, 2008, http://www.kilgorenewsherald.com/news/2008/1204/front_page/001.html (accessed July 10, 2009).

48. "Judge Issues Gag Order in Case of 13-Month-Old Bludgeoned Child," *Tyler Morning Telegraph*, December 9, 2008, http://www.tylerpaper.com/article/200812 09/NEWS01/812090306/0/FEATURES0302 (accessed July 10, 2009).

49. Catherine Bell, *Ritual Perspectives and Dimensions* (New York: Oxford University Press, 1997), 115.

50. Kibbie S. Ruth, "Risk of Abuse in Faith Communities," in *Child Maltreatment: A Clinical Guide and Reference*, 3rd ed., ed. James A. Monteleone and Armand E. Brodeur, 539–55 (St. Louis: G. W. Medical, 2005), 544–45.

51. Frankfurter, *Evil Incarnate*, 223.

52. James Lewis, *Satanism Today: An Encyclopedia of Religion, Folklore, and Popular Culture* (Santa Barbara, CA: ABC-CLIO, 2001), 211.

53. Ibid., 209.

54. Ibid., 211.

55. Michael Cuneo, *American Exorcism: Expelling Demons in the Land of Plenty* (New York: Doubleday, 2001), xi.

56. Ibid., xii.

57. Gallup News Service, "Americans' Belief in Psychic and Paranormal Phenomena Is up over Last Decade," Gallup, June 8, 2001, http://www.gallup.com/poll/4483/americans-belief-psychic-paranormal-phenomena-over-last-decade.aspx (accessed November 1, 2010).

58. Pew Forum on Religion and Public Life, "68%—Goblins and Ghosts and Things That Go Bump in the Night," Pew Research Center, http://pewresearch.org/databank/dailynumber/?NumberID=885 (accessed November 1, 2010).

59. Caroline Fraser, "Ancient and Modern Exorcism, Alias Laying on of Hands, Denounced," *Children's Healthcare Is a Legal Duty* 2 (2009): 2–3, http://childrenshealth care.org/wp-content/uploads/2010/11/2009-02finallayout.pdf.

60. Cuneo, *American Exorcism*, xii.

61. Ibid., 203.

62. Ibid., 270–71.

63. Paul Burnell, "Exorcisms on the Rise," *Catholic Education Resource Center*, 2000, http://www.catholiceducation.org/articles/religion/re0418.html (accessed July 9, 2009).

64. Rachel Zoll, "Catholic Bishops: More Exorcisms Needed," Associated Press, November 12, 2010, at MSNBC, http://www.msnbc.msn.com/id/40151974/ns/us _news (accessed November 12, 2010).

65. Real Deliverance Ministries, "The War Manual," Real Deliverance Ministries, http://www.realdeliverance.com/purchase.shtml (accessed July 9, 2009).

66. "Bob Larson," Bob Larson—Spiritual Freedom Church, http://www .boblarson.org/aboutbob.html (accessed November 1, 2010).

67. Agnieszka Tennant, "Possessed or Obsessed?" *Christianity Today*, September 3, 2001, http://www.christianitytoday.com/ct/article_print.html?id=6626 (accessed November 1, 2010).

68. Bob Larson, "Demon Test," Bob Larson—Spiritual Freedom Church, http:// www.demontest.com/ (accessed October 29, 2010).

69. Tennant, "Possessed or Obsessed?"

70. Pleasant Glade Assembly of God v. Laura Schubert, No. 05-0916, Supreme Court of Texas, Brief on the Merits of Petitioner, June 8, 2006, http://www.supreme .courts.state.tx.us/ebriefs/05/05091608.pdf (accessed March 4, 2011).

71. Cuneo, *American Exorcism*, 280.

72. *Pleasant Glade Assembly of God v. Laura Schubert*.

73. Bette L. Bottoms et al., "In the Name of God: A Profile of Religion-Related Child Abuse," *Journal of Social Issues* 51, no. 2 (1995): 96.

74. "Manifested Glory Ministries Exorcism Video (FULL)—Manifested Glory Gay Exorcism," YouTube video, 9:22, posted by "mikeyblogs2," June 24, 2009, http:// www.youtube.com/watch?v=vhedHERfcXk&NR=1 (accessed October 30, 2010).

75. Kristen Hamill, "Video of Church's 'Casting Out' Gay 'Demon' in Teen Sparks Anger," CNN, June 25, 2009, http://edition.cnn.com/2009/US/06/25/ connecticut.gay.exorcism/index.html (accessed July 22, 2009).

76. "Firm Beliefs: Religious Movement at Center of Child Death Investigation," NewsChannel 5 (Nashville), February 4, 2004, http://www.newschannel5.com/ Global/story.asp?S=5412250 (accessed April 1, 2010).

77. Rita Swan, "Parents Get Life Plus Thirty Years in Fatal Beating," *Children's Healthcare Is a Legal Duty* 1 (2007), http://www.childrenshealthcare.org/PDF%20 Files\2007-01finallayout.pdf.

78. Bottoms et al., "In the Name of God," 109.

79. Cuneo, *American Exorcism*, 271.

80. Carl Sagan, *The Demon-Haunted World: Science as a Candle in the Dark* (New York: Random House, 1996), 159–60.

81. Deborah Hastings, "Louisiana Child Sex Case Revealed by Confession," Associated Press, August 7, 2009, at Free Library, http://www.thefreelibrary.com/ Louisiana+child+sex+case+revealed+by+confession-a01611960347 (accessed November 15, 2010).

CHAPTER 21: IS MALE OR FEMALE CIRCUMCISION RELIGIOUS CHILD MALTREATMENT?

* The mother made her case public by blogging about it. After the baby's death, she took down the posts giving details of how he died. Therefore, I do not feel it is appropriate to reveal those posts.

1. Dan Bollinger, "Lost Boys: An Estimate of U.S. Circumcision-Related Infant Deaths," *Thymos: Journal of Boyhood Studies* 4, no. 1 (Spring 2010): 205–19, at Faqs.org, http://www.faqs.org/periodicals/201004/2026622071.html (accessed November 5, 2010).

2. Chaya T. Merrill, Mika Nagamine, and Claudia Steiner, "Circumcisions Performed in U.S. Community Hospitals, 2005," Healthcare Cost and Utilization Project (HCUP) Statistical Brief #45, January 2008, 1, http://www.hcup-us.ahrq.gov/reports/statbriefs/sb45.pdf.

3. Council on Scientific Affairs (AMA), *Report 10: Neonatal Circumcision* (Chicago: American Medical Association, 1999), http://www.ama-assn.org/ama/no-index/about-ama/13585.shtml (accessed November 3, 2010).

4. "Statistics," Mgmbill.org, http://www.mgmbill.org/statistics.htm (accessed November 10, 2010).

5. Merrill, Nagamine, and Steiner, "Circumcisions Performed in U.S. Community Hospitals, 2005," 1.

6. "Rate of Circumcision in Adults and Newborns," Circinfo.net, http://www.circinfo.net/rates_of_circumcision.html (accessed November 21, 2010).

7. "Mohel FAQ," Traditional Circumcision by Rabbi Boruch Mozes, http://www.britpro.com/default.asp?p=mohel (accessed November 5, 2010).

8. "Circumcision Fact Sheet," *Info Circumcision*, http://www.infocirc.org/facts.htm (accessed November 19, 2010).

9. Brian J. Morris, "What Motivates Parents to Get Their Baby Boy Circumcised," Circinfo.net, http://www.circinfo.net/what_motivates_parents_to_get_their_baby_boy_circumcised.html (accessed March 5, 2010).

10. Council on Scientific Affairs (AMA), *Report 10*.

11. "Bris FAQ's," Rabbi Yehoshua Fromowitz, 2009, http://www.jewishmohel.com/brisquestions.html (accessed November 1, 2010).

12. Ibid.

13. James E. Peron, "Circumcision: Then and Now," *Many Blessings* 3 (Spring 2000): 41–42, at Circumcision Information and Resource Pages, http://www.cirp.org/library/history/peron2/ (accessed November 3, 2010).

14. "Jews Against Circumcision," Jews Against Circumcision, http://www.jewsagainstcircumcision.org/ (accessed November 5, 2010).

15. Sharon Lerner, "Maverick Mohel," *Village Voice*, February 1, 1998, 64, at NOHARMM, http://www.noharmm.org/maverick.htm.

16. World Health Organization and Joint United Nations Programme on

HIV/AIDS, *Male Circumcision: Global Trends and Determinants of Prevalence, Safety, and Acceptability* (Geneva, Switzerland: World Health Organization, 2007), 1, http://whqlibdoc.who.int/publications/2007/9789241596169_eng.pdf.

17. "Islam and Circumcision," Intactivism Pages, http://www.circumstitions.com/Islam.html (accessed November 3, 2010).

18. Laura Jesek, "What the Bible Really Says about Routine Infant Circumcision," Udonet.com, 2002, http://www.udonet.com/circumcision/christian.html (accessed November 3, 2010).

19. Pope Eugenius IV, *Bull of Union with the Copts (1442)*, trans. Norman P. Tanner, session 11, Ecunemical Council of Florence, Florence, Italy, February 4, 1442, at Circumcision Information and Resource Pages, http://www.cirp.org/library/cultural/councilflorence/ (accessed November 18, 2010).

20. Guy Pieters and Albert B. Lowenfels, "Infibulation in the Horn of Africa," *New York State Journal of Medicine* 77, no. 6 (April 1977), at Circumcision Information and Resource Pages, http://www.cirp.org/pages/female/pieters1/ (accessed November 19, 2010).

21. S. A. Aldeeb Abu-Sahlieh, "Muslims' Genitalia in the Hands of the Clergy," in *Male and Female Circumcision: Medical, Legal, and Ethical Considerations*, ed. George C. Denniston, Frederick Mansfield Hodges, and Marilyn Fayre, 131–72, proceedings of the Fifth International Symposium on Sexual Mutilations, Oxford, England, August 5–7, 1998 (New York: Kluwer Academic/Plenum Publishers, 1999), 148.

22. Committee on Bioethics, American Academy of Pediatrics (AAP), "Policy Statement: Ritual Genital Cutting of Female Minors," *Pediatrics* 125, no. 5 (May 2010): 1088–89, http://aappolicy.aappublications.org/cgi/reprint/pediatrics;125/5/1088.pdf.

23. World Health Organization, "Fact Sheet: Female Genital Mutilation," World Health Organization, February 2010, http://www.who.int/mediacentre/factsheets/fs241/en/index.html (accessed March 6, 2011).

24. Pieters and Lowenfels, "Infibulation in the Horn of Africa."

25. Nancy V. Yinger, "The Feminization of Migration: Obstacles to Good Health Care," Population Reference Bureau, January 2007, http://www.prb.org/Articles/2007/FeminizationofMigrationObstaclesHealthCare.aspx (accessed March 5, 2010).

26. Doriane Lambelet Coleman, "The Seattle Compromise: Multicultural Sensitivity and Americanization," *Duke Law Journal* 47, no. 717 (February 1998): 740, http://www.law.duke.edu/shell/cite.pl?47+Duke+L.+J.+717#F1 (accessed January 18, 2010).

27. Associated Press, "Georgia: Man Convicted in Daughter's Mutilation," *New York Times*, November 2, 2006, http://www.nytimes.com/2006/11/02/us/02brfs-001.html (accessed March 6, 2011).

28. Bob Gordon, "Mother in Georgia Charged with Female Genital Mutilation," *Digital Journal*, March 16, 2010, http://www.digitaljournal.com/article/289176 (accessed November 1, 2010).

29. Haseena Lockhat, *Female Genital Mutilation: Treating the Tears* (London: Middlesex University Press, 2004), 16.

30. Coleman, "Seattle Compromise," 732.

31. Thomas von der Osten-Sacken and Thomas Uwer, "Is Female Genital Mutilation an Islamic Problem?" *Middle East Quarterly* 14, no. 1 (Winter 2007), at Middle East Forum, http://www.meforum.org/1629/is-female-genital-mutilation-an-islamic -problem (accessed March 12, 2010).

32. "Islam and Circumcision."

33. Coleman, "Seattle Compromise," 731–33.

34. "Female Circumcision," Muslim Woman, http://www.themuslimwoman .com/hygiene/femalecircumcision.htm (accessed February 18, 2010).

35. Pieters and Lowenfels, "Infibulation in the Horn of Africa."

36. World Health Organization, "Fact Sheet."

37. Máire Ní Mhórdha, "Female Genital Cutting: Traditional Practice or Human Rights Violation? An Exploration of Interpretations of FGC and Its Implications for Development in Africa" (working paper, Australian National University, Master of Applied Anthropology and Participatory Development Program, January, 2007), 8, http://asiapacific.anu.edu.au/maapd/papers/wp-07-01.pdf.

38. "Female Genital Mutilation Causes Aggression," Radio Netherlands Worldwide, February 6, 2010, http://www.rnw.nl/english/article/female-genital-mutilation -causes-aggression (accessed November 7, 2010).

39. Brigitte Gabriel, *They Must Be Stopped: Why We Must Defeat Radical Islam and How We Can Do It* (New York: St. Martin's Press, 2008), 178.

40. Coleman, "Seattle Compromise," 737.

41. Committee on Bioethics, AAP, "Policy Statement," 1092.

42. "Female Circumcision."

43. Ros0818, "Have You Sunat Your Girls?" comment on MummySG, January 18, 2010, http://www.mummysg.com/forums/f40/have-you-sunat-your-girls-29826/ (accessed November 18, 2010).

44. John Duffy, "Masturbation and Clitoridectomy," *Journal of American Medical Association* 186, no. 3 (1963): 246, http://jama.ama-assn.org/cgi/content/summary/ 186/3/246 (accessed November 4, 2010).

45. John Duffy, "Clitoridectomy: A Nineteenth-Century Answer to Masturbation," Female Genital Cutting Education and Networking Project, 2003, http://www .fgmnetwork.org/articles/duffy.htm (accessed November 7, 2010).

46. James Whorton, "The Solitary Sin: The Superstition that Masturbation Could Cause Mental Illness," *Western Journal of Medicine* 175 (July 2001): 67, at National Center for Biotechnology Information, http://www.ncbi.nlm.nih.gov/pmc/articles/ PMC1071473/pdf/wjm17500066.pdf.

47. John Harvey Kellogg, *Plain Facts for Old and Young: Embracing the Natural History and Hygiene of Organic Life*, rev. ed. (1877; repr., Burlington, IA: I. F. Senger, 1891), 232–33, http://etext.lib.virginia.edu/etcbin/toccer-new2?id=KelPlai.sgm&images =images/modeng&data=/texts/english/modeng/parsed&tag=public&part=all (accessed November 5, 2010).

48. Ibid., 339.

49. Ibid.

50. Ibid., 282.

51. Ibid., 342.

52. Ibid., 285–87.

53. Duffy, "Clitoridectomy."

54. Kellogg, *Plain Facts for Old and Young*, 294–95.

55. Ann Dally, *Women under the Knife: A History of Surgery* (1991; repr., Edison, NJ: Castle Books, 2006), 159–60.

56. Ibid.

57. Duffy, "Clitoridectomy."

58. Ibid.

59. Dally, *Women under the Knife*, 180–81.

60. Ibid., 159–60.

61. Duffy, "Clitoridectomy."

62. Ibid.

63. Dally, *Women under the Knife*, 180–81.

64. Ibid.

65. Harold Shryock, *On Becoming a Woman: A Book for Teenage Girls* (n.p.: Review and Herald, 1951), 37–38.

66. Constance A. Bean, *Methods of Childbirth*, rev. ed. (North Yorkshire, UK: Quill, 1990), 227.

67. Peter Feibleman, "Natural Causes," *Doubletake* (Winter 1997), at Peter Feibleman, http://www.fictionwriter.com/double.htm (accessed November 3, 2010).

68. Ibid.

69. Ibid.

70. Ibid.

71. Patricia Robinett, *The Rape of Innocence: Female Genital Mutilation and Circumcision in the USA* (2006; repr., Eugene, OR: Nunzio Press, 2010), 115.

72. Council on Scientific Affairs (AMA), *Report 10*.

73. Edgar J. Schoen, "Should Newborns Be Circumcised? Yes," *Canadian Family Physician* 53, no. 12 (December 2007), at National Center for Biotechnology Information, http://www.ncbi.nlm.nih.gov/pmc/articles/PMC2231533/?tool=pubmed#b9-0532096 (accessed March 6, 2011).

74. "Bris FAQ's."

75. Council on Scientific Affairs (AMA), *Report 10*.

76. Douglas Gairdner, "The Fate of the Foreskin: A Study of Circumcision," *British Medical Journal* 2 (December 24, 1949): 1437, at National Center for Biotechnology Information, http://www.ncbi.nlm.nih.gov/pmc/articles/PMC2051968/pdf/brmedj03656-0009.pdf.

77. Council on Scientific Affairs (AMA), *Report 10*.

78. Fetus and Newborn Committee, Canadian Paediatric Society, "Neonatal Circumcision Revisited," *Canadian Medical Association Journal* 154, no. 6 (1996), at Canadian Paediatric Society, http://www.cps.ca/english/statements/FN/fn96-01.htm #COMPLICATIONS OF CIRCUMCISION (accessed November 7, 2010).

79. Council on Scientific Affairs (AMA), *Report 10*.